DAVID NICOLLE

MEDIEVAL WARFARE SOURCE BOOK

SOURCE BOOK

Warfare in Western Christendom

Statue of one of the founders or patrons of Naumberg Cathedral, mid-13th century, Germany.

DAVID NICOLLE
MEDIEVAL WARFARE
SOURCE BOOK
Warfare in Western Christendom

BROCKHAMPTON PRESS

Arms and Armour Press
An Imprint of the Cassell Group
Wellington House, 125 Strand,
London WC2R 0BB

This edition published 1999 by Brockhampton Press,
a member of Hodder Headline PLC Group

ISBN 1-86019-889-9

British Library Cataloguing-in-Publication
Data: a catalogue record for this book is
available from the British Library

Designed and edited by DAG Publications
Ltd. Designed by David Gibbons; layout by
Anthony A. Evans; edited by Michael Box-
all; Printed at Oriental Press, Dubai, U.A.E.

Jacket illustrations:

Front: 'Battle of Stamford Bridge; *L'Estoire de Seint Aedward le Rei* by the school of
Matthew Parris; English, c.1245. (MS. Ee359, folio 32v, Cambridge University Library).
Back, top: Wall painting by Altichiero, c.1375, in the chapel of St. James or St, Felix,
the Santo of St. Anthony, Padua. Back, bottom: The fortified port of Aigues-Mortes,
founded by Louis IX of France in 1240 as a base for his crusading expeditions
and completed by his son, Philip the Fair. (DAG)

Medieval Warfare Source Book,
Volume 2: Christian Europe and Its Neighbours
will follow the same pattern as this first volume, including Biographies,
Sources, Miscellanea, Glossary and Index. The main chapter headings
are planned as

Byzantines, Persians and Muslims (400–750)
Christian-Muslim Confrontation in Europe, Asia and Africa (750–1050)
Turks, Mongols, Timurids and the Rise of Russia (600–1400)
Crusade, Reconquista and Counter-Crusade (1050–1400)
China and the Far East (400–1400)

CONTENTS

INTRODUCTION

The Roman Empire had been a largely self-sufficient entity in both economic and cultural terms, with remarkably little interest in its neighbours, most of whom were regarded as barbarians from whom the Romans could learn little. The collapse of the western half of the Roman Empire, and the gradual evolution of its eastern part into the Byzantine Empire, was followed by several centuries during which western Europe remained backward. During this period the west was also a somewhat isolated and, from a global perspective, a rather unimportant corner of the huge Eurasian land-mass. Great events and richer, more powerful civilisations were to be found elsewhere – most obviously in the Middle East and Asia.

Nevertheless this Early Medieval period saw the foundations of a new medieval European civilisation being laid; foundations that are probably more important for modern Europe than were the distant though much admired classical civilisations of Greece and Rome. By the end of the Middle Ages western Europe had developed its own vigorous, prosperous, confident and distinctly aggressive

civilisation. This was, in fact, the basis of the Western Civilisation which would soon project its influence and its military power into every corner of the world.

Western Christendom had already regained some strength by the 8th century AD, though its wars remained largely internal. The first aggressive thrusts into a wider world came in the later 11th century, beginning with the Spanish *Reconquista* and the German drive eastwards into previously pagan Slav lands. These outward thrusts were soon followed by Crusades against the Muslim peoples of the Middle East and pagan Baltic peoples to the north-

Cantle or rear of a carved ivory saddle said to have belonged to Frederick I of Sicily, probably southern Italian, 1296–1337. The two horsemen wear arm and leg defences which first came into widespread use in Italy at about this time. The man on the left also has a dagger at his belt; a weapon that would again be accepted as suitable for a knight in the 14th century. (Musée du Louvre, Paris; photograph, Musées Nationaux)

east, as well as those perceived as heretics within Europe itself. Despite these dramatic events, most of Europe's military, economic and cultural efforts were still directed inwards throughout the rest of the medieval period. The real 'Triumph of the West' had to wait several more centuries and its success was largely built upon socio-military systems that had developed out of medieval Europe's seemingly endless internal conflicts rather than being a result of a series of unsuccessful Crusades.

This volume is intended as the first of a pair, though each, it is to be hoped, will be able to stand alone. It concentrates almost entirely on the internal warfare of medieval Europe, whereas the second volume will be concerned with western Europe's external wars such as the struggle against Islam. Eastern Europe and the epic struggles of the Byzantine Empire will also be placed in the second volume, together with the Muslim World itself, Central Asia, much of Africa, India and China.

Drawing such dividing lines is, of course, always arbitrary and potentially misleading. The most difficult decision was where to put the Spanish *Reconquista*, since this was clearly fought out on western European soil. But the modern concept of 'western Europe' as a political and cultural, as well as geographical, entity did not exist in the Middle Ages. Instead the inhabitants of most of what are now western and central Europe thought of themselves as part of *Christendom* – to which the Muslim inhabitants of Muslim-ruled

al-Andalus in the Iberian peninsula did not belong. As already stated, Iberian warfare was above all a struggle on Christendom's frontiers, not at its heart. The Middle Eastern Crusades were more obviously external campaigns. As the centuries passed, Orthodox Christian Byzantium was also increasingly seen as being different from western Catholic Christendom. Orthodox Christian Russia will be included in the second volume because its military and political priorities pointed south and east against the Turco-Mongol peoples of the vast Eurasian steppes. Less easily justified, perhaps, is the inclusion of the Orthodox Christian peoples of the Balkans in this first volume. They have, however, been included because, until the Muslim Ottoman Turks suddenly erupted into this area in the mid-14th century, the Balkan peoples were largely preoccupied with internal struggles and with the threat posed by Catholic neighbours to the north and west.

D. Nicolle; Woodhouse Eaves, 1995

An aerial view of Berkhampstead Castle, England; a late 11th century Norman motte and bailey timber castle to which stone walls were added in the 12th century. The almost conical motte or artificial hill can clearly be seen at the top of the picture. The broad moat, however, is still choked with weeds. (Photograph, English Heritage; A4175/1).

I
'BARBARIAN' INVASIONS
AND THE
'BARBARIAN' STATES
(400–650)

'BARBARIAN' INVASIONS AND THE 'BARBARIAN' STATES (400–650)

The tumultuous centuries that saw the collapse of the western half of the Roman Empire are sometimes known as the Age of Migrations. Entire peoples were on the move; not only those Germanic 'nations' that overran much of the Roman Empire itself but also Huns and other groups from Central Asia as well as African and Arabian tribes. The ancient world from the Roman Mediterranean, through the Sassanian Empire in Iran to the vast Chinese state was either turned upside down or severely shaken. Practically every cultural or political group from near barbaric tribes to sophisticated civilisations, from Ireland to the Chinese frontier, from Ethiopia to Scandinavia and Siberia, was involved in wars that reshaped the known world.

Even so, these conflicts did not destroy the ancient or classical cultures. Instead the barbarian conquerors who survived this Age of Migrations set up new states, most of which attempted to model themselves and their armies on the old empires that they had defeated. Meanwhile the old empires themselves still existed, though often in a weakened state, and their armies learned much from their 'barbarian' foes.

Major Campaigns

5th–8th centuries: Finnish emigrations from Estonia conquer and settle southern Finland.

407–10: Roman regular troops withdrawn from Britain, and Celtic Britons told to look to own defences.

Huge bronze statue of a Roman Emperor, either Valentian I, 364–75, or Theodosius I the Great, 379–95. It stands outside the church of San Sepolcro in Barletta, in southern Italy. By this time the great majority of Roman soldiers wore mail armour very much like that which would continue to be used throughout the early Middle Ages. Only senior figures such as emperors would still have worn this kind of traditional 'muscle-cuirass'; and then probably for parade purposes.

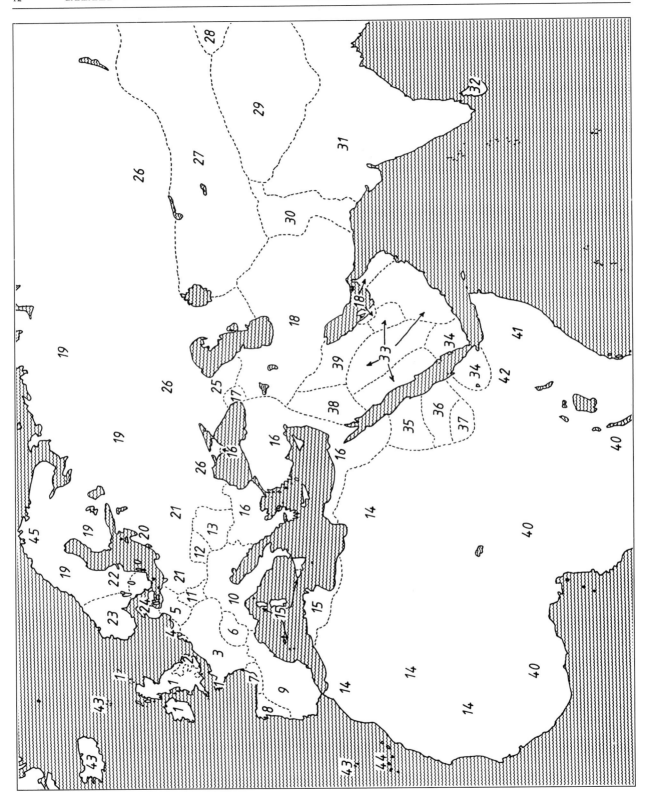

409–29: Iberian peninsula overrun by Germanic Vandals and Suevi plus Iranian Alans; Vandals and Alans conquer Roman North Africa.

410: Germanic Visigoths invade Italy, sack Rome.

414–56: Visigoth conquest of Iberian peninsula.

c.429: Celtic Britons defeat Germanic Anglo-Saxon and Celtic Pictish raiders at 'Alleluia' battle.

c.442–56: Rebellion by Anglo-Saxon *foederati* troops in Britain; start of the Anglo-Saxon conquest of Britain.

443–7: Turco-Mongol Black Huns invade Roman Balkans.

451: Romans and Germanic allies defeat Black Huns at battle of Catalaunian Fields.

453–5: Germans revolt against Hun rule; collapse of the Black Hun Empire.

455: Germanic Vandals sack Rome.

476: End of the Western Roman Empire (Eastern Roman Empire survives, henceforth referred to as the Byzantine Empire).

486: Germanic Franks defeat Syagrius, last 'Roman' governor of Gaul at Soissons; conquer all northern France except Brittany.

493: Germanic Ostrogoths take power in Italy.

507: Franks defeat Visigoths at Vouillé; conquer southwestern France.

c.516: Britons (traditionally led by Arthur) defeat Anglo-Saxons at 'Mount Badon'.

533–4: Vandal North Africa reconquered by Romano-Byzantines.

c.537: Traditional 'death of Arthur' at battle of Camlann.

536–54: Ostrogothic Italy reconquered by Romano-Byzantines.

554–624: Part of Visigothic southern Iberia reconquered by Romano-Byzantines.

558–70: Turco-Mongol Avars carve out a state in Central Europe.

568: Germanic Lombards conquer northern Italy.

c.577: Anglo-Saxon kingdom of Wessex defeats Britons, conquers southern Severn valley.

c.600: Slav tribes move south across Danube, begin gradual occupation of Balkans.

c.600–34: Anglo-Saxon kingdom of Northumbria defeats British kingdom of Strathclyde-Gododdin at Catterick, then a coalition of British kingdoms near Chester and Welsh kingdom of Gwynned at Hexham.

626–7: Unsuccessful Avar and Sassanian Persian siege of the Byzantine capital of Constantinople.

ARMY RECRUITMENT

During the early medieval Age of Migrations some peoples moved across great distances while others stayed in one place. Linguistic or cultural groups contributed soldiers over widely different regions. Some served the armies of rival empires while others fought in those of 'barbarian' successor kingdoms or carved out their own states. The Empires of Rome and Sassanian Iran had developed similar systems whereby peoples along their respective frontiers were listed and paid as auxiliary or 'allied' troops. This poses the problem of whether such imperial frontier forces should be considered as part of the empire to which they were attached or be seen as separate military groups. Any decision is likely to be arbitrary, though a dividing line may be drawn between those peoples whose fighting men were fully integrated into the Roman or Romano-Byzantine armies, and those who maintained a separate structure though often receiving imperial payment.

Then there is the question of quite what could be considered a distinctive group at this time. The medieval concept of a 'people' having a common ancestry, and thus forming a *gens* or 'race', was based on ancient Greek ideas of ethnic differences between such supposed 'races'. It also assumed that certain similarities within a *gens* were demonstrated by distinctive warlike capabilities. Apart from being unsound from an anthropological standpoint, and containing the seeds of later racist theories, this concept of distinct or separate early medieval ethnic groups is very misleading. The Age of Migrations, or *Völkerwanderung*, was a period of great cultural, tribal and broader ethnic mixing from which later medieval states and nations would ultimately emerge. Few if any of the larger barbarian 'nations' were drawn from a single ethnic background.

Romano-Byzantine Armies

By the end of the 4th century AD the great majority of Roman citizens no longer expected to serve in any real

Left: Europe and neighbouring lands, c.526

1. Celts
2. Anglo-Saxons
3. Franks
4. Frisians
5. Saxons
6. Burgundians
7. Cantabrians and Basques
8. Suevi
9. Visigoths
10. Ostrogoths
11. Thuringians
12. Lombards
13. Gepids
14. Berbers
15. Vandals
16. Romano-Byzantine Empire
17. Laz-Georgians
18. Sassanian Empire
19. Finno-Ugrians
20. Balts
21. Slavs
22. Swedes
23. Norwegians
24. Jutes and Danes
25. Alans
26. Turco-Mongols
27. Blue – 'Celestial' Turks
28. China
29. Tibet
30. Hephthalites, etc.
31. Fragmented Indian states
32. Lanka
33. Arab tribes and confederations
34. Axumite Empire
35. Nobatia
36. Makuria
37. Alwa
38. Ghassānids
39. Lakhmids
40. Bantu peoples
41. Somalis
42. Galla
43. Uninhabited
44. Guancho-Berbers
45. Saami-Lapps

military capacity. They had, in fact, been demilitarised for a very long time. An extraordinary variety of different crafts, trades and other groups of individuals were exempt by law from military conscription. So even when the need to conscript troops became acute, the Roman authorities had great difficulty in finding enough men, or of maintaining a pool of military reserves. Measures such as reducing the height requirement of potential recruits did little to help when military service was so unpopular that men would physically mutilate themselves just to avoid conscription. Similarly the efforts of the last Roman commanders in Gaul to incorporate low-quality garrison soldiers into the supposedly mobile field army merely reduced the quality of what should have been the Roman Empire's élite forces. At the end the only territory from which the western Roman Emperors could conscript soldiers was Italy itself, but this was so torn by social tensions that conscripts felt that there was very little justification for fighting. The last recorded conscriptions of 440 and 443 seem to have been only for local urban militias. Nevertheless, the last decades of the western Roman Empire did include cases where such locally conscripted forces coped well with local problems – if only at the level of bandit control.

When the end came in the mid-5th century there seem to have been no real 'Roman' troops left, only Germanic mercenaries or allied *foederati*. Of course Germanic soldiers had been recruited for many years but, until the catastrophic defeat at Edirne (Adrianopolis) in 378, these had largely been enlisted as individuals. After that defeat the desperate emperor enlisted entire tribal groups under their own existing tribal leaderships. The sack of Rome in 410 reduced the state's ability even to recruit German troops, as the western Empire was now too poor and its administration too damaged. The Emperor Honorius (394–423) managed to achieve a small military revival, enlisting Visigothic allies and even recruiting some native Romans, but it did not last. Under the ten emperors who ruled over the final quarter-century of the western Empire, Rome could neither conscript nor pay the army and fleet which alone would have enabled it to survive. In effect the last western Roman armies simply withered away. Meanwhile the eastern half of the Roman Empire survived, and eventually flourished. This was because it retained control of enough territory to provide a pool of military manpower and had enough trade to ensure that the emperor could pay these soldiers – at least occasionally.

The situation within Italy developed rather differently after it was reconquered from the Ostrogoths by the Romano-Byzantines in the mid-6th century. Here the known names of Byzantine regiments indicate local recruitment as well as the presence of troops from the eastern Mediterranean. Such locals included regular soldiers, auxiliaries and probably also urban militias, many of whom must surely have been Romano-Italians. By the late 6th century local government authorities and the nobility were both conscripting peasants for some kind of military duty within local Byzantine as well as in the newly emerging Papal forces of Rome.

Hun and Steppe Invaders

Inevitably much less is known about the armies of the various nomadic peoples who migrated across the Eurasian steppes from east to west during this period. Each conquered the one that had gone before, and each was pushed farther to the east by a succeeding wave. The Alans were Iranian-speaking nomads who dominated much of the western steppes until they were conquered by the Turco-Mongol Huns in the late 4th century. Some remained where they were, and were soon incorporated into Hun forces with whom they became virtually indistinguishable. Others found a refuge in the Caucasus mountains to the south where their descendants live to this day. Yet others fled west to join forces with the Germanic Vandals and Suevi while some moved into the Roman Empire where they were enlisted as skilled cavalry. Those Alans who settled in Roman Gaul played an important military role during Rome's struggle against the Huns in the mid-5th century, by which time they were, however, no longer a strictly nomadic people. By the mid-6th century these settled western Alans had also converted to Catholic Christianity.

The Huns remain something of an enigma. Not only are their origins still a mystery but the popular image of Turkic Central Asian nomads rampaging across Roman western Europe seems to be very inaccurate. By the early 5th century the Hun aristocracy had adopted many cultural characteristics from those Germanic peoples whom they had conquered, and from previous non-Turkish steppe nomads such as the Sarmatians and Alans. In fact the entire Hun people, if such a thing still existed, was a cultural and ethnic mixture.

Those Huns who continued to inhabit the western steppes of what are now southern Russia and the Ukraine remained largely nomadic, as their invasions of the Middle East and Iran show. But those Huns who crossed the Carpathian mountains into Central Europe soon lost almost all trace of nomadism – just as virtually all subsequent nomadic invaders of central Europe would do. These regions, even including the Great Plain of Hungary, simply could not support the vast horse herds needed to maintain a truly nomadic way of life. In fact it seems that the Hun war parties that ravaged Roman Europe included very few horsemen at all, but largely consisted of infantry warriors. Nor do the Hun forces seem to have been particularly Hun-Turkic in composition since they clearly included many so-called 'deserters' from other sources including various Germanic peoples and even from the Roman army itself. The Huns in the west simply do not fit any known stereotype and their empire was too temporary for many of its enigmas to be resolved.

Other early medieval nomadic conquerors from the steppes are easier to understand, though not necessarily better documented. For example the Avars of the 6th and 7th centuries, who had once been known as Juan-Juan when they inhabited the Mongol steppes north of China, are said to have forcibly recruited the rival Kutrigur Turks and used them as an advance screen of archers. The Avars themselves were probably the most sophisticated of all the early medieval invaders of Europe, and the one most influenced by Chinese civilisation, whereas the Kutrigurs were mere nomadic horse-archers, perhaps descended from the Huns. Nevertheless these Kutrigurs, with other Turkic tribes, evolved into the Bulgar people who went on to establish two quite separate states, one of which inherited much of the Avars' territory in south-eastern Europe after the latter had been defeated by Charlemagne. Before that, however, Bulgars had served as *foederati* on the Byzantine Empire's Balkan frontier. Another group of proto-Bulgars known as the Onagurs raided deep into Greece in the mid-7th century, subsequently settling in the Peloponnese under Byzantine rule and perhaps continuing to supply troops until they were assimilated into the rest of the population.

A further wave of less dramatic migrations was that of the Slavs who, though they as yet rarely posed a major political threat unless led by Turkic rulers, were not assimilated by the existing population. Instead they gradually changed a large part of the Balkans, as well as eastern Europe, into Slav-speaking lands.

Germanic Forces

The migrations of Germanic peoples were in some ways as dramatic as those of steppe conquerors from the east, and certainly more complex. During the earliest stages their military forces consisted of the freemen of the *volk*, tribe or people, led by its chief or king. All freemen were liable to serve in the army and in many cases this theoretically remained the case even after the *volk* in question had established a fixed state with a government administration and a recognisably structured army. Visigothic Spain provides a good example. Here, from the 6th to early 8th centuries, the army élite consisted of the nobility and their followers, with a lesser role going to provincial levies. The *comitatus* or élite force raised by the king himself may have retained some Germanic elements almost to the fall of the Visigothic state early in the 8th century, but by then the local levies and urban militias probably no longer had any discernible Germanic characteristics. Like several rulers of the period, King Wamba endeavoured to carry out military reforms but his efforts were unusual in proclaiming that one tenth of the slave population were also liable for military service.

'Theodosius I and his guards', depicted on a silver plate made in the late 4th century. The late Roman Emperor's guards are unarmoured, though they carry shields and spears. But both are wearing the heavy jewelled torques around their necks which indicated membership of the highest status units. (Biblioteca de la Real Academia de la Historia, Madrid)

Two sides of the carved base of the lost Column of the Emperor Arcadius, ruler of the eastern half of the Roman Empire 395–408, Istanbul. These drawings in the Freshfield Album were made by a visiting western artist, probably in the 16th century. One face of the column-base showed the guards of the Emperor with spears and large shields, two of the latter bearing early Christian symbols. Below them defeated enemies are dragged to a pagan-style victory ceremony, while the lowest panel illustrates a variety of military equipment including traditional 'muscle-cuirasses', three pairs of laminated arm or leg defences, and plenty of archery equipment. The lower panel on the other face of the column-base (opposite) also illustrates a great deal of arms and armour, including laminated limb protections and four helmets with integral face masks. Such military gear shows how far the late Roman army, above all its cavalry, had been influenced by its Middle Eastern and steppe-nomadic foes. (Trinity MS. O.17.2, Trinity College Library, Cambridge; photograph, Master and Fellows of Trinity College)

The Germanic Burgundians carved out their state in one of the richest regions of what had been Roman Gaul. This also appears to have been among the first 'barbarian' kingdoms to enlist ex-Roman garrison troops and to have taken over much of their military administration. In fact the main part of the Burgundian army soon seems to have consisted of paid professional soldiers rather then being a levy of Burgundian freemen. This force was then itself taken over by the Merovingian Franks when they conquered Burgundy in the early 6th century.

The Merovingian Frankish 'barbarian kingdom' was much larger than that of the Burgundians and it would eventually evolve into the Carolingian Empire. But even in its early days the Frankish kingdom included a wide variety of different military systems and methods of recruitment. All freemen, not merely those of Germanic

Two mosaics panels showing 'Abraham and Melkizadek' (left) and 'The Israelites attack Hai' (right); late Roman, early 5th century. This famous series of small mosaics provides a vital, though very stylised, source of information for the military equipment of the final decades of the western Roman Empire. Abraham's troops (left) are protected by mail hauberks of an almost medieval style, whereas their helmets still have tall horsehair or feathered crests in a more classical Roman style. The soldiers in the Israelite army attacking Hai (right) are equipped as late Roman or early Byzantine light infantry; their armour probably being of quilted material or leather in a style that apparently would not continue to be worn in early medieval western Europe. (Basilica of Santa Maria Maggiore, Rome)

origin, owed a duty of military service to the king; the Frankish war-bands of the 5th century even numbering Huns in their ranks. Clovis himself enrolled the troops of the last Roman governor in Gaul as well as the *laeti* military colonists of area. Nor is there any evidence to suggest that such soldiers felt that they were now serving a usurper or an illegitimate ruler. As the Frankish conquests continued, their armies came to include German-

ic Allemani from Romanised southern Germany, Germanic Visigoths from southern Gaul and the descendants of assorted ex-Roman troops from the same area. Yet the huge levies which resulted from this system declined in importance after the Franks suffered a series of defeats in Italy. Thereafter the Merovingian king tended to rely on an élite of warriors led by himself and his chief noblemen.

Stilicho, the German commander of the western Roman armies at the end of the 4th century, on a late Roman ivory panel, c.395. Stilicho's sword scabbard is suspended by a scabbard-slide from a relatively loose hip-belt;

itself almost certainly attached to the broader belt around the general's waist. His cloak is fastened by a highly decorated brooch, typical of this period, which can be seen on his right shoulder. (Tesoro del Duomo, Monza)

Roman soldier on an ivory plaque illustrating 'The Life of St Paul'; Italian, 5th century. This ordinary soldier wears almost exactly the same costume as General Stilicho, a generation or so earlier. He even has the same 'pudding-

basin' haircut, while the scabbard of his relatively short sword again has a narrow scabbard-slide on the outer face. (Museo Nazionale del Bargello, Florence)

'Battle between Greeks and Trojans', in the Virgilius Romanus manuscript, Italy, possibly made under the rule of Odoacer 476–93. This rather primitive manuscript illustration has much in common with the earlier mosaics in the Basilica of Santa Maria Maggiore, in Rome. The scale-like hauberks could be of scale, lamellar or mail construction, but archaeological evidence suggests that they are most likely to be the latter. The bow used by the Trojan on the left is clearly of a large composite form used by the Huns and various other Central Asian steppe peoples, as well as by the later Romans themselves. (MS. Lat. 3867, f.188v, Biblioteca Apostolica Vaticana, Rome; photograph Biblioteca Vaticana)

Not surprisingly the most obvious differences within Merovingian recruitment were those between very Romanised regions such as Aquitaine in the south-west, where the *hostis Vascanorum* of Gascon levies as well as local urban levies still existed, and the least Romanised, most Germanic region of Austrasia in the north-east. In fact urban militias played an increasingly important role in Merovingian Aquitaine and in Neustria in western Gaul, but were not recorded in Austrasia. By the second half of the 6th century it has even been suggested that southern soldiers descended from Gallo-Roman military families or from those most influenced by Roman military traditions now provided the best troops in the Frankish armies. Other evidence suggests that in Merovingian Gaul the old Gallo-Roman and the new Germanic-Frankish forces started to fuse together during the second half of the 6th cen-

Carved stone slab showing a cavalryman from Horn-hausen, German or western Slav c.700. This warrior has long hair but the front of his head appears to have been shaved, which suggests a Slav subject or Slav influence. Naturally he as yet uses no stirrups and may even be rid-ing bareback. The lug or flange behind the blade of his huge spear is of a type normally associated with infantry warfare, or at least with a two-handed almost 'fencing'-type spear technique. (Landesmuseum für Vorgeschichte, Halle)

tury. As such they became the foundation of a new military aristocracy.

From the mid-7th century the most important forces available to the Merovingian *Mayors of the Palace*, who had effectively taken control of the state from the now deca- dent Merovingian kings, were similar to those of other leading noblemen. Above all they consisted of the leader's own followers, often called *socii*, though the *Mayor of the Palace* would presumably also have had the ruler's own élite *centenae* at his command.

Celtic Forces

Whereas the history of the other early medieval ex-Roman regions of western Europe is relatively well documented, that of Britain during the years of the Anglo-Saxon con- quest is not. Archaeology has still to settle the question of whether the Germanic Anglo-Saxons became a political, military and culturally dominant minority over a Celtic .British population, or whether the indigenous British were largely exterminated or expelled. It is even unclear to what degree an Anglo-Saxon *ceorl* was necessarily a warrior as well as a settler-farmer. In the kingdom of Wessex he seems to have been a Germanic freeman warrior and farmer, but in the similarly Anglo-Saxon kingdom of Northumbria he was not necessarily both warrior and farmer. Such varia- tions between the tiny Germanic kingdoms of what was to become England may have resulted from differing degrees of residual Romano-Celtic influence in each, rather than in some unknown differences of military traditions brought from continental Europe by Anglo-Saxon settlers.

Paradoxically a little more seems to be known about the Celtic and Romano-Celtic military forces of these singu- larly undocumented early years. The Roman army in Britain had itself been far from homogeneous. For exam- ple Sarmatian armoured cavalry of ultimate Iranian steppe-nomad origin had been settled in the Fylde region of Lancashire in the 3rd century. This was apparently one of very few suitable grazing areas capable of maintaining substantial horse herds within Britain. How far any result- ing cavalry tradition survived in this part of the country by the time the Roman legions withdrew is unknown.

It is clear, however, that a great part of the static garri- son forces of Roman Britain had been assimilated into the local population. The bulk of such low-grade static or auxiliary troops would surely have remained behind when Constantine took the élite mobile field forces off on his quest to win the imperial crown of Rome. They were concentrated along the Saxon Shore in the east, and in the highly militarised north of Britain. Indeed north Britain was dominated by the army during the last decades of Roman rule whereas the richer south was dominated by large landowners, the poorer west by lesser landowners. Such a state of affairs must have influenced the military situation in the otherwise barely documented years of the 5th century after the Britons had been told to look after themselves by a Roman Empire tottering to its fall.

Whereas it seems that some Germanic troops had been settled in late Roman Britain, archaeological evidence sug- gests that they were closely linked to towns which they pre- sumably defended. It seems likely that the post-Roman Romano-British ruler or military dictator known as Vor- tigern, 'Great King' in the Celtic tongue of Britain, sum- moned further Germanic mercenaries in the mid-5th century. Maybe they were enlisted to help repel Pictish and Scottish raids from the north and west, or to take part in an internal Romano-British power struggle. It appears to have been a rebellion by these later Germanic Anglo-Saxon troops that triggered the Anglo-Saxon conquest of much of Britain. Evidence from the following century is extremely sparse, though surviving Celtic epic literature sheds some light on the powerful late 6th or early 7th century British kingdom of *Gododdin* which consisted of what had been the highly militarised zones on both sides of Hadrian's Wall. Its army is said to have been recruited from Pictland to the north, Celtic northern Wales and the remaining Celtic land of Elmet in the Pennine hills. When Celtic documen- tary evidence once again becomes available a century or so later, early Welsh laws show that unfree Welsh bondsmen were not themselves warriors, though they were expected to supply packhorses for a military élite of Welsh tribal gen- try. Celtic towns were now tiny, but nevertheless supplied labourers, horses and axes to construct strongholds. How far this reflected current military practice or that of an ear- lier period is, however, unclear.

Large numbers of the original Romano-British aristoc- racy had fled to Gaul during the catastrophic early years of the Anglo-Saxon conquest of Britain. Presumably they included part of the old military élite for they and their descendants formed a useful military force. This helped part of the Celtic region of Armorica in north-western Gaul to resist the Germanic Frankish conquest and then to continue flourishing as the distinct Celtic realm of Brit- tany. Not that British refugees were the only troops avail- able to what eventually became the Duchy of Brittany, for this area also provided a refuge for Gallo-Roman magnates with their own military followings as well as late Roman cavalrymen of Alan descent, and even Saxon settlers.

MILITARY ORGANISATION

The military organisation of early medieval armies reflect- ed the differing social organisations and sophistication of the societies they protected. While there were similarities between the armies of the two largest states of the period – the Romano-Byzantine and Sassanian Empires – these two super-powers were also influenced by, and had a military influence upon, their smaller neighbours. Rome similarly had a profound military influence upon its conquerors.

Romano-Byzantine Armies

The command and administrative structures of the Roman army were severely damaged by the 'barbarian' invasions of the late 4th century. In many areas these were never fully repaired. As a result the regional forces of the western Roman Empire differed from one another in the 5th century. The increasing military decentralisation of this century also led to a relaxation of the previously highly structured and centrally controlled system of *Magistri Militum*, with, for example, some provinces having their own separate 'Masters of Cavalry'. Meanwhile service conditions and payment for the ordinary Roman soldier, even in the eastern half of the Roman Empire which survived the 'barbarian' onslaught, became desperate.

Perhaps as a result of this process of fragmentation, there appear to have been an increasing number of different officer ranks within Romano-Byzantine armies. These now included the following: *Comes* or *Tribunus*, Commanding Officer; *Vicarius*, second in command; *Primicerius*, adjutant to a *Comes* or other commanding officer; *Senator*, *Ducenarius* and *Centenarius*, senior officer ranks; *Biarchus*, *Circitor* and *Semissalis*, junior officer ranks; *Campiductor*, regimental drill officer; *Draconarii* and *Signiferi*, standard-bearers; *Tubator*, trumpeter. The term *Primi* or *Primates* referred to officers in general while *Adorator* applied to a palace guardsman and *Lociservitor* to any form of deputy. At first an *Optio* was a quartermaster but later meant a commander of foreign mercenaries. *Auctenta* and *Bandiforus* were unclear ranks apparently only used in eastern parts of the Romano-Byzantine Empire.

The situation of the last Roman armies in Britain can be seen as a dramatic example of the fate of such forces and of their influence upon the immediate post-Roman situation. Roman Britannia had been divided into four provinces under three military commands. The *Dux Britanniarum* was responsible for the north, including Hadrian's Wall, and had his HQ at York, while the *Comes Litoris Saxonici* was in charge of coastal defences. Slightly later a *Comes Britanniarum* was placed in command of a mobile field army, most of which was again stationed in the north. Although the first two of these military commands was essentially static, the best of their troops probably left Britain early in the 5th century. The mobile field army of the *Comes Britanniarum* had already departed with the future Emperor Constantine in the 4th century. Any troops that remained would have been of low grade, perhaps comparable to the *limitanei* of other Roman frontier regions, and will be discussed below under Celtic forces.

The *limitanei* were, by definition, frontier troops, yet the *limes* or military frontiers of the late Roman Empire were rarely clearly defined. Instead they now seem to have been blurred and relatively easy to cross in either direction. In fact, many such *limes* became areas of cultural and ethnic mixing where 'barbarians' were Romanised and Romans often 'went native' to some degree. Despite the very reduced military quality of many early 5th century *limitanei* they generally remained proper garrison troops, perhaps often hereditary though not a mere peasant militia. As the western Roman Empire collapsed around them, there were massive desertions by these *limitanei* who often melted away in military terms and were absorbed by the local population. Equally clearly some units remained at their posts, hoping for support and pay from the Imperial government in Rome.

The military structure of reconquered Romano-Byzantine Italy was very different from that seen before the collapse of the western half of the old Roman Empire. From the start the new provincial army had, as was normal, been divided into two parts; a field army and the garrison troops. Both were under the overall command of *Exarchs* who had, in effect, inherited the duties of the late-Roman *Magister Militum*. Apart from the separate forces of the *Patrician* of Sicily, there were the three distinct military corps under the command of the *Exarchs* of Ravenna, Rome and Naples. They often acted separately, particularly after Byzantine Italy had been fragmented into virtually separate regions by the subsequent Lombard conquest. In addition there was, to the north-east, the *Magister Militum* of Istria whose very small forces also defended Venice.

Huns and Steppe Invaders

Warriors naturally had very high status in warlike societies such as those of the nomadic peoples of the Eurasian steppes. Nevertheless the Iranian Alans were unusual in taking this to such an extreme that they reputedly despised old men who had failed to die in battle. Turkic peoples, such as the Huns, respected age and experience in war, only those who had 'won a name' having the right to a carved monument after they died. Recognised heroes were distinguished by wearing special decorated belts and sometimes by joining together in warrior associations with distinctive enrolment ceremonies. For example, those of the White Huns who invaded the Sassanian Empire had a maximum of twenty 'hero' members.

The little that is known about the social and military organisation of the Black Huns indicates that established aristocratic families existed before they invaded eastern Europe. The early Bulgars, who may in fact have been partially descended from these Black Huns, first appear as a confederation of tribes plus Slav allies of considerably less prestige. Before the Bulgars of the Balkans converted to Christianity, and those of the Volga region became Muslim, the _Khāns_ or rulers of such areas delegated some military authority to various commanders, the most important being known as the _tarkhan_. The Avars, meanwhile, carved out a much more sophisticated and highly organised state than any other set up by nomad conquerors from the east. This was clearly seen in their military organisation and perhaps reflected a strong Chinese influence upon the Avars dating from their origins in Mongolia.

Germanic Forces

The Germanic 'barbarian' armies which invaded and overran so much of the Roman Empire in the 5th century were probably quite small compared to the total of Roman forces resisting them. But the bulk of the latter were in fixed garrisons and frontier defences rather than in mobile field armies. Despite their defeat of these Roman armies, many Germanic forces, and those of the Germanic successor states they established, continued to look upon the armies of the surviving Romano-Byzantine eastern half of the Empire as their military model. The main difference between such Germanic successor state armies and those of Byzantium was that, in general, the former had far less cavalry than the latter.

It seems likely that the remaining Roman forces in Gaul retained some elements of their old unit structure and administration even after being absorbed by the armies of the conquering Franks. In fact, the great Merovingian Frankish king Clovis seems to have attempted some kind of short-lived and unsuccessful revival of Roman military administration. Meanwhile the bulk of the freemen of the Frankish state served as an ill-organised massed levy under the leadership of their regional lords or *Counts*.

It was the failed operations of this type of early Frankish army in Italy that led Byzantine commentators, and later historians who relied solely on such sources, to describe the Merovingian army as an ill-organised, ill-equipped and ill-trained Germanic war-band. In reality there were also élite, essentially full-time professional, troops who formed the *comitati* military retinues of the king and his counts. Whether the majority of these were true cavalry or merely mounted infantry remains unclear. Bodyguard units of the Merovingian kings and their family were known as *armati*, 'armed men' or *pueri*, 'sons'. But after the most powerful counts at the Frankish court took over control of the state as the *Mayors of the Palace* in 638, it appears to have been rare for a Merovingian king to retain his own force of *pueri* armed followers.

Like all early Germanic rulers, the primary role of the Visigothic king was that of war-leader. Unlike the Merovingian Frankish kings, however, the Visigothic ruler never acquired a semi-divine status and a Visigothic king who failed in battle could easily be replaced by another member of the senior aristocracy. The Visigothic army also seems to have been under more immediate Byzantine influence than that of the Franks. Here the king's guards and closest followers were known as *gardingi* and *fideles;* the followers of the nobles being known as *bucellarii*. By the mid-7th century the king's *fideles* had already been guaranteed the permanent possession of lands given them by the king. A few years later one of the last Visigothic rulers, King Wamba, attempted to reform the army with the establishment of a noble bodyguard of Byzantine-inspired *spatharii* in addition to the existing *gardingi*, palace troops.

Compared to most other Germanic successor kingdoms, much less is known about the military organisation of the Anglo-Saxons during these early centuries. They are generally to be compared with the neighbouring Romano-British and other Celtic states. Nevertheless it does appear that whereas a Celtic ruler was always expected to command his own men in battle, an Anglo-Saxon king could delegate the leadership of an army to another member of the royal family.

Celtic Forces

Whatever its origins, there appears to have been an effective Romano-British army in existence following the 'departure of the legions' and the effective secession of Britain from the Roman Empire at the start of the 5th century. This army may in fact have remained intact until the real collapse of British resistance early in the 6th century. The little that is known of this so-called Dark Age of British history suggests that the first military leaders of a Romano-British resistance to the Anglo-Saxons came not from a revived Celtic tribal élite but from the existing Roman élite of *curiales*.

There was still plenty of urban life within what had been Roman Britannia during the second half of the 5th century and, to a lesser extent, also in Romano-British Strathclyde to the north of Hadrian's Wall. On the other hand the semi-nomadic society of this northern area largely depended on cattle raising. The main centre of Romano-British resistance appears to have been in the Severn valley and in the eastern foothills of Wales. The polemical Celtic chronicler Gildas wrote that post-Roman Britain was ruled by a *superbus tyranus* or 'proud tyrant' with several lesser *tyrani* beneath him. Such dominant figures would probably have been simply known as *regum* or kings at the time; these being referred to as *cyninges* in the equally obscure early Anglo-Saxon records. In reality such local rulers are likely to have evolved out of the late Roman *magistras* or urban governors.

The forces available to local Romano-British leaders, whether kings or 'magistrates', would probably have been based in the small hill forts of the period. These were no longer the great tribal Celtic centres of pre-Roman times, though many occupied the same sites. The epic *Gododdin*, a poem recalling the heroic defeat of a north British kingdom of the same name, described a 'great army' of three hundred heroes. This surely referred to its leaders alone since these came from many parts of the British Isles. Nevertheless three hundred was the traditional size of an early medieval Celtic ruler's *teula* or bodyguard.

At the same time there was also a clear residual Roman influence on these Romano-Celtic armies, even those from regions north of Hadrian's Wall. In fact several north British ruling dynasties claimed descent from a senior Roman officer of the Wall Command. This figure might be identified with Coel Hen (Old King Cole), traditionally the last Roman *Dux* of the North, whose army effectively made him an independent ruler though not as yet a king.

To the south and west a new Celtic identity was forged during the bitter resistance to Anglo-Saxon colonisation. This was the *Cymry* or *Cumbri*, a name which came from the Latino-Celtic term *combrogi* or 'companions' and originally appears to have applied to a military élite of largely cavalry warriors. To the Anglo-Saxons, of course, these

Cymry and *Cumbri* were merely Welsh, a term which in turn meant 'foreigners'. The oldest surviving Welsh laws dealing with military affairs are the *Laws of Hywel* and although they date from centuries later they may contain reflections of an earlier situation. These state that the chief of a king's bodyguard should be his son or nephew; such a bodyguard being in reality a private war band known as a *comitatus* in Latin, a *teula* in Welsh, or a *heod-geneatas* in Anglo-Saxon English. The members of this war band were also next in seniority beneath the ruling family itself.

The little that is known of Pictish northern Scotland during this period indicates that it consisted of a kingdom that included the western isles, and was unified under King Bridei who governed through a structured administration and led an effective army. As such, the early medieval Pictish north appears to have been a typical early medieval state having virtually nothing in common with the supposedly wild painted Pictish savages described by early Roman authors. A little more is known of Celtic Ireland at this time. Here society was divided into strict classes; the free and the unfree. The free were themselves subdivided into the *soernemen*, 'sacred free', who included the rulers, the *feni*, military leaders who were essentially the same as the *airig*, nobility, and the 'lower free' *soercheli* who owed both military service and tribute. The unfree majority were, in effect, serfs and slaves.

STRATEGY AND TACTICS

The widespread but now outdated idea that medieval armies lacked discipline is clearly incorrect, even in the Early Middle Ages. Equally it would be misleading to try to understand such early medieval discipline in modern terms. Much the same is true of early medieval strategy and battlefield tactics. Commanders merely did their best with what they had, while at the same time they used common sense, a will to win and a wish to keep the losses of their own side to a minimum. In other words they behaved just as any other normal military leader would be expected to behave.

Since rapid communication systems were virtually non-existent during these centuries, battlefield control was rudimentary even in the most sophisticated armies. Consequently tactics also tended to be simple with certain basic concepts being used over many centuries. The most obvious variable was the use made of differing terrain, and here the best medieval commanders showed themselves worthy of their calling. This was particularly true when the armies involved were small and largely consisted of only one type of troops. On the other hand, commanders of larger forces containing a variety of styles of cavalry and infantry were able to indulge in more ambitious tactics. Broader medieval strategy, however, was often remarkably ambitious and demonstrated a quite modern grasp of the essentials of geography, communications, transport, logistics, the role of fortifications and of morale.

Right: Tactics, 400–650
1. The distribution of Roman forces in the early 5th century, according to the Notitia Dignitatum.

2. The battle of Catalaunian Fields, 451. One Visigothic contingent seized control of high ground on the flank of the Hun camp. The battle itself began with a Hun charge which scattered the Alans before turning against the Visigoths under Theodoric. But the more heavily armoured Visigoths drove back the Huns who eventually abandoned the field. Throughout the battle the Roman infantry appear to have been largely static (after Bartholomew)
A. City of Châlons
B. River Marne
*   Roman and allied forces*

C. Theodoric and Visigoths
D. Aëtius and Romans
E. Sangiban and Alans
F. Torismund and Visigoths. Hun and vassal forces
G. Attila and Huns
H. Assorted contingents under Ardaric of the Gepids
I. Walamir, Theodemir and Widimir with Ostrogoths
J. Camp and baggage

3. Reconstruction of typical Hun tactics against a static enemy (after Von Pawlikowski-Cholewa)
A. Enemy
B. First position of horse-archers
C. Attack position of horse-archers
D. Munition supplies for horse-archers
E. Armoured support cavalry.
F. Infantry

Broad Strategy

The changes that were apparent in Romano-Byzantine strategy and tactics from the fall of the western Empire in the 5th century to the Muslim-Arab invasions of the early 7th century have been described as a shift from an old Roman reliance on iron discipline to a supposedly more Greek emphasis on clever generalship. The racist undertones of such a statement are very dubious, but there certainly was a growing concern for subtlety and for the misleading of an enemy on the part of late Roman and Romano-Byzantine military leaders.

Late Roman strategy has, inevitably, been seen in terms of its failure to save the western Empire rather than its success in keeping invaders at bay for so long and for preserving the eastern Empire virtually intact. During the 4th century it became clear that the Roman Empire could no longer maintain watertight borders. Frontier defence came to rely on a screen of garrisons backed up by several mobile field armies. This remained Roman strategy into the 5th century.

The role of largely static garrisons was to stop small incursions and to threaten the rear of larger invading forces. If an enemy were denied access to food supplies he was, theoretically, forced to disperse and forage; thus becoming vulnerable to attack by the nearest Roman field army. Such a Roman counter-attack could then be followed up by reprisal raids into enemy territory. This strategy worked well so long as the declining economic power of the Empire could maintain the necessary forces. Its

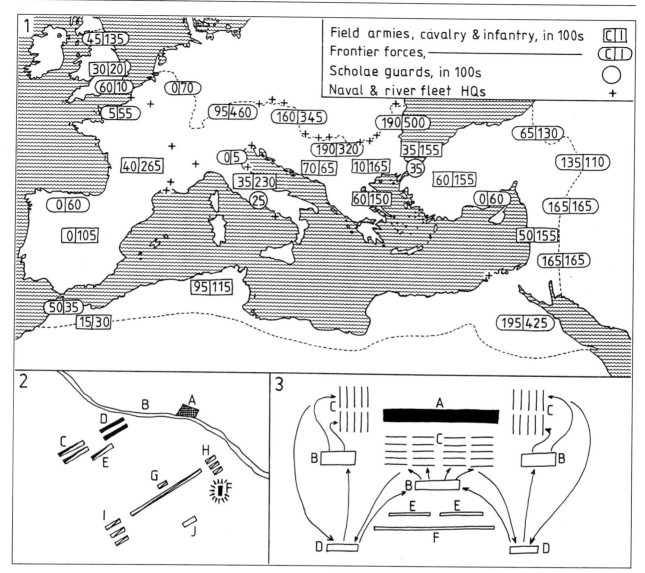

weakness lay in the fact that the field armies themselves had to be fragmented and regionalised or they would be unable to reach a raider before he left laden with booty. The Roman army also failed to achieve a decisive superiority in cavalry despite great efforts to improve this arm, while the quality of fixed frontier troops declined steadily as the Roman economy weakened.

The last century of the old Roman Empire saw mounting military pressure on various fronts; this being tackled in differing ways. Within Europe the Romans tried hard to retain control of a strategic corridor lying just north of the Alps. This not only provided the Empire's easiest east-west communication route, but also served as an advanced front to protect the Italian heartland. The region was, however, lost when the bulk of its defenders were withdrawn to face a Goth invasion of Italy itself. In the eastern

Empire, fixed garrisons were similarly backed up by field armies well into the 6th century, a system that clearly worked more successfully in the east than in the west.

There was a clear difference between the strategy and tactics used by Central Asian nomadic peoples within the steppe regions, and those used by peoples of Central Asian origin after they had left the Eurasian steppes to settle within Europe. For example, the Huns north of the Black Sea fought in a very different manner from the Huns in Central Europe. There are almost no references to Hun cavalry or fast-raiding nomadic Hun horsemen after the Hunnish people entered the Balkans in the late 4th century. Here it is important to point out that the great Hungarian Plain, the largest area of steppe or prairie grassland within Central Europe, was very small compared to the true Eurasian steppes to the east. It was also divided by rivers, marshes and forests which would make the assembling of a nomad-type of cavalry army very difficult. This fact influenced the evolution of Hun armies and of all those other nomadic Central Asian conquerors who followed in their footsteps, concluding with the Mongol invasions of the 13th century.

During the 5th century the Huns appeared more like raiders than conquerors. They could also be ambushed by almost static Roman forces and tended to get defeated if they faced regular Roman troops in battle. Similarly it is interesting to note that many major Hun raids were carried out at a time of year when there was very little available grass for their supposedly large number of horses. In addition Hun raids were often described as being slowed down by the great wagons in which they carried their booty. Heavy wagons had, of course, been used when the Huns lived on the steppes. But in the steppes such wagons were used to carry the tribes' women, children and tents – not normally being used in warfare. Altogether the European Huns seemed to live a predatory rather than nomadic way of life.

The strategic thinking of Germanic 'barbarian' leaders at the time of the Great Migrations is largely unknown, but the way in which some rulers of successor 'barbarian' kingdoms dealt with assorted military problems indicates that they were capable of broad strategic planning.

Frankish forces, for example, were noted for their high degree of strategic mobility and it was this that enabled the Merovingian kings to vary their strategy according to the situation. Basically, Merovingian warfare within the kingdom or during campaigns intended to extend its frontiers, aimed at the taking and keeping of cities and fortified *castrae*. Punitive or predatory warfare beyond the kingdom largely consisted of raiding for booty and extorting tribute from the Franks' neighbours. Much the same was true of other Germanic states, though the Visigoths of Spain did face a specific problem in the shape of continually rebellious Basques in the north of the country. The military problems posed by this situation were remarkably similar to those faced by the subsequent Muslim state of al-Andalus when facing the independent Christian statelets of northern Spain.

If it is difficult to be specific about Germanic post-Roman forces, this is even more the case with post-Roman Celtic forces within the British Isles. Generally speaking, it is assumed that there was no broad strategy in 5th to 7th century Britain and that warfare was merely an 'aristocratic way of life'. But this is to assume a lack of strategy merely because of a lack of clear evidence. It is probably true that, for the Romano-Celtic British, warfare was basically a matter of guerrilla-like cavalry raids intended to wipe out or evict creeping Anglo-Saxon colonisation. Nevertheless, the few available sources suggest a distinction between the short-range campaigns of the 6th century and the often much longer-range campaigns of the 7th century.

The *Gododdin* almost certainly recalled an ambitious Romano-Celtic attempt to split the Anglo-Saxon region of Bernicia (Northumberland) from that of Deira (Yorkshire) in a clear case of broad strategic thinking. Elsewhere, assaults on strongholds or prepared positions were rare, though there were sieges or at least battles outside fortified places. The purpose of the long dykes and ditches which were erected during this period remains a mystery. They could not have served as extensive fortifications, but the narrow gaps within these dykes and ditches could have served as ambush points against enemy raiders returning home with rustled cattle or other plunder.

Troop Types

Despite Roman efforts to develop a truly effective and élite cavalry arm, the evidence strongly suggests that late Roman infantry remained more reliable than late Roman cavalry. Nevertheless, of the sixty-seven units of archers listed in the *Notitia Dignitatum,* fifty-four were mounted. Spear-armed armoured cavalry were not a new idea but such *cataphracti* clearly increased in importance during this period. Most, though by no means all, were stationed in the eastern Empire. During the catastrophic 5th century the Romano-Byzantine armies evolved a composite spear- and bow-armed armoured cavalryman known as a *hippo-toxotai* who would prove very effective during the 6th century Romano-Byzantine reconquest of much of the west. A smaller élite of *clibanarii* cavalrymen rode armoured horses; a development closely associated with Sassanian Iran though probably invented in the settled Turco-Iranian areas of Transoxania.

In fact, the emergence of many different types of highly specialised troops seems to have been characteristic of the last century of the western Roman Empire. Again the *Notitia Dignitatum* provides interesting information. While there were horse-archers in all parts of the Empire, most were in the eastern field and garrison forces. Yet there were still more infantry archers in eastern field armies than there were horse-archers, while the latter predominated in eastern frontier forces. There was now only one unit of infantry slingers, this being in an eastern field army where all save one of the rather obscure *lanciarii*, spear-armed infantry, and *ballistarii*, perhaps 'field frame-mounted crossbow' troops, were also found. Specialist river-warfare troops were stationed on the Danube frontier, camel-riding *dromedarii*, mounted infantry not surprisingly being found in Egypt and Palestine, *exploratores* and *praeventores*, who are believed to have been 'scouts' mostly being stationed in the west, along with rather obscure *superventores* who have been tentatively identified as 'rearguard commandos'.

Even before the various waves of steppe nomad conquerors or refugees left the Eurasian steppes to enter a largely forested and agricultural Europe, their armies included several different types of troops. The Alans, for example, were described as having many well-armoured cavalrymen fighting with bow and spear, though they also had infantrymen to protect their few vital remaining horse pastures. The fearsome Huns are sometimes said to have 'dismounted' on entering Central Europe in the 4th century. They were, in fact, mostly described as fighting on foot during the 5th century and as using large shields of obvious infantry form. Many of these Hunnish infantry, however, remained very effective archers.

Unlike the Huns, the 6th century Avars seem to have retained a greater element of cavalry. Nevertheless, the Avar and allied Slav army which besieged Constantinople in 626 included many armoured foot soldiers. These are generally believed to have formed part of the dominant Avar élite, as did the armoured Avar horsemen, whereas unarmoured Slav infantry were clearly of lower military prestige.

Not surprisingly, Germanic armies, even those of the most successful successor states, did not include such a sophisticated variety of troop-types as did Romano-Byzantine armies. The Anglo-Saxons in Britain, for example, apparently only included infantrymen. The Ostrogoths, Visigoths and several other German 'nations' had archers but these fought on foot and did not generally use those powerful composite bows typical of both steppes peoples and Romano-Byzantine armies.

Meanwhile the Vandals, Alemanni and Visigoths included more horsemen than other Germanic forces, though the Ostrogoths also had cavalry armed with spear and sword. Much of the warfare between Visigoths and Franks in southern Gaul was carried out by cavalry. Even so, cavalry traditions appear to have survived more strongly within the Iberian peninsula than elsewhere in ex-Roman western Europe. It has even been suggested that the Visigothic period in Spain and Portugal saw a mixing of Romano-Celtic and Germanic Visigoth cavalry traditions to produce something new – something which may eventually have contributed to the distinctive Christian and Muslim Iberian styles of cavalry warfare seen in later centuries. Furthermore there is tantalising evidence to suggest that later 6th and 7th century Visigothic armies even included some horse-archers; presumably a tactic learned from the Romano-Byzantine-ruled regions of southern Spain.

Similarly there are plenty of references to Frankish cavalry in the 5th century, though by the middle of the following century the Frankish invasions of Italy appear to have been largely infantry affairs. In fact, there seem to be fewer references to Frankish horsemen in the later Merovingian period than in earlier years. On the other hand, the Lombards who invaded Italy in the 6th century did make notably greater use of cavalry than previous Germanic invaders. In total it might be safer to say that there was considerable variety within Germanic 'barbarian' armies. Meanwhile, the traditional view that there was a period during which Europe saw a revival in the importance of infantry and a decline in that of cavalry following the collapse of the western Roman Empire is, at best, an oversimplification.

Similar problems concern the types of troops found in Celtic armies. Surviving Romano-Celtic urban militias would have been almost entirely infantry. Outside the cities there may have been greater variation. The tribal peoples of Wales and the south-west would again have largely been foot soldiers whereas there may have been plenty of cavalry in the Pennines and West Midlands. The great majority, if not all of such horsemen would have ridden relatively small Celtic horses or large ponies since there is, as yet, no evidence of larger horses being bred within northern and western Britain. The cavalry themselves would seem to have been armed with javelins and spears, operating in the style of earlier Roman skirmishing cavalry rather than later Roman *cataphracti*.

Battle Tactics

In tactical rather than strategic terms, there were considerable changes during the 5th century. When this century began the remaining Roman armies appear to have fought in a rather static manner, leaving most manoeuvres to their 'barbarian' allies or auxiliaries. When fighting the Huns at the battle of Châlons in 451, for example, the Romans put themselves on the traditionally defensive left flank; the reputedly unreliable Alans being in the centre and the Visigoths on the traditionally offensive right flank.

Roman cavalry formations were still basically the same as those for the infantry, with separate centres and flank divisions consisting of a single extended line of horsemen eight rows deep, without reserves and relying on one great charge to decide the outcome of a battle. This system failed dismally against the Huns and Avars whose horse-archers could wear it down from a distance. So a new 'ideal' cavalry formation was developed during the late 5th and 6th centuries. At the same time Romano-Byzantine armies now evolved sophisticated battlefield manoeuvres using several different kinds of troops.

Whereas in the 4th and early 5th centuries Roman cavalry tactics had been based on those of the Iranian Sarmatian and Alan steppe nomads, most of these new tactics were learned by bitter experience from Rome's Turco-Mongol Central Asian foes. Since cavalry could rarely break disciplined infantry, at this or any other period of military history, the primary role of Romano-Byzantine armoured cavalry was to menace and render immobile an enemy's foot-soldiers while the light cavalry attempted to outflank, harass and even encircle the foe. This involved Romano-Byzantine cavalry operating in smaller but still closely packed units; the resulting *cuneos* formation having again been learned from steppe nomadic peoples. It was then passed on to the Romans' own Germanic and Middle Eastern enemies. The written sources of this period suggest that there were also changes in Romano-Byzantine infantry formations, though these seem to have been relatively minor.

The battlefield tactics of early medieval steppe nomadic forces and their descendants within Europe are less well documented than those of later centuries. The Alans, for example, were described as fighting in highly manoeuvrable, close-packed units, employing javelins and swords, feigned retreats and flank attacks. The little that is known of Attila the Hun's tactics within Europe seem much more Germanic than steppe nomadic. The sophisticated Avars, whose civil and military culture both betray strong Chinese influence, are similarly described as fighting in close-packed cavalry formations. The more primitive Slavs, by contrast, seem to have relied on ambush tactics in close country and forests, using javelins, poisoned arrows and large infantry shields followed up by a sudden massed infantry charge.

The invading Germanic peoples were equally varied in the sophistication, or otherwise, of their battlefield tactics. At one extreme the 5th and 6th century Anglo-Saxons hardly seem to have had tactics at all, at least in a meaningful sense. They may have fought as effective guerrilla raiders in forested areas, just as earlier Germans had fought against Roman invaders. But there is no evidence of Anglo-Saxon warriors using another early Germanic tactic of combined cavalry and light infantry assaults, which had also been used against the Romans. This latter tactic was based on a family or tribal formation described by their Roman opponents as resembling a *cuneus*. It was tactically similar to the harassment techniques of the steppe peoples, though the latter relied overwhelmingly on mounted troops.

Other aspects of Germanic tactics during the Age of Migrations suggests Sassanian influence from Iran, again via the nomadic peoples who invaded eastern and central Europe. The Visigoths, for example, clearly used the typically eastern tactic of the feigned retreat, perhaps having learned it during their long migrations across eastern Europe. Once settled within the Iberian peninsula, however, Visigoth cavalry largely seem to have relied on tactics of repeated attack and withdrawal almost certainly learned from their late Roman or Romano-Byzantine foes. In Italy, Ostrogothic infantry archers fought under the protection of their own cavalry, again reflecting Romano-Byzantine practice. It is also interesting to note that, according to a 6th century military manual, Romano-Byzantine troops should beware of an enemy – probably meaning the Ostrogoths – disguising themselves in Roman equipment so that they could get close to the Romans without being identified. In one relatively well recorded battle of 507, the Franks draw up their archers and javelin throwers behind other presumably spear-armed infantry when facing the Visigoths. Here Frankish cavalry were present, but served in an unspecified role.

There appear to have been few changes in Frankish tactics during the Merovingian period; the available cavalry largely being used for raiding and the pursuit of an already beaten foe, with no clear evidence of cavalry charges in battle. On the other hand the Thuringians attempted to catch Frankish horsemen in ditch-traps in 531; recalling a tactic used by Hephthalite White Huns against the Sassanian Persians in the previous century. During the 6th century, Burgundian troops, who were in reality perhaps Romano-Burgundians, trapped a force of Lombard cavalry in a forested mountainous area by blocking the road with felled trees. This was precisely the same tactic that would be used, though with less success, by Byzantine troops against Muslim-Arab invaders in the 8th century. Elsewhere it is clear that both Frankish and Lombardic horsemen would dismount to fight on foot if they got into difficulties.

The very inadequate written evidence concerning the military forces of the early medieval Romano-British and Celtic kingdoms might indicate a tactical preference for sudden dawn attacks on the part of Romano-British forces, perhaps after long night marches. Even the *Gododdin*, the best surviving source of information, does not clarify the tactical role of Celtic cavalry in battle. Some may have been mounted infantry who actually fought on foot; others merely the leaders of otherwise infantry troops. Those who remained on horseback appear to have fought with javelins, spears and swords while their *pedyt* or foot soldiers drew up in ranks or in a phalanx described as a 'battle square' or 'cattle pen'. The Romano-Celtic *dull* or battle array had a vanguard, centre and wings; the men fighting in close formation, each unit having a recognised leader.

Combat Styles

Late Roman, early Romano-Byzantine and other early medieval western European cavalry had not yet adopted stirrups. Yet a lack of stirrups did not limit the effectiveness of a horseman to anything like the extent that is popularly believed. This was particularly so when a framed saddle was used, this providing its rider with plenty of support. Most early Roman cavalry were armed with javelins rather than heavy thrusting spears, but longer spears were widely adopted under Sarmatian and Alan influence during the 4th century. Sarmatian influence did not, however, affect Roman archery whether on foot or on a horse.

At this time there were three basic ways of using a spear on horseback: either thrown as a javelin, thrust downwards with a raised arm, or thrust forward by swinging the arm. The *couched* spear or lance technique, in which the weapon was held tightly between the upper arm and chest while relying on the forward movement of the horse to drive the weapon at a foe, is popularly credited to the western European knights of the 11th or 12th centuries. In reality this *couched* technique was known at least to the 10th century Byzantines and appears to be shown in 7th or 8th century Central Asian art. In all cases, however, it appears to be closely associated with the adoption of stirrups and does not seem to have been used by Romano-Byzantine and early medieval European horsemen.

During this period the two-handed method of thrusting with a cavalry spear predominated and was clearly effective, even against an armoured foe. The weapon was, however, normally pointed along the right side of the horse's head; not to the left as with the later *couched* lance. Two-handed and single-handed thrusting techniques both enabled a cavalryman to retrieve his weapon with relative ease. This was not the case with the *couched* lance held along the left side of the horse's head – this latter style essentially being a once-only shock weapon. Unlike the later knight with his *couched* lance, the earlier spear-armed cavalryman rarely used a shield; this still generally being associated with close quarter weapons such as the sword. Occasional references to small shields being strapped to a spearman's upper arm to protect his neck and face may, however, indicate that such shields had widely spaced inner straps of the kind later called *enarmes*. Here the left arm was thrust through the *enarmes*, rather than the shield being grasped in the fist.

Since nothing comparable to the Romano-Byzantine training manuals exist for 'barbarian' western Europe, any understanding of how the Germanic warriors actually fought must rely on highly coloured epic myths and on archaeological evidence which is difficult to interpret. Earlier Roman sources indicated that the Germans used lighter parrying shields than the Romans' own heavy *scutum* shield. A subsequent development of this tradition is borne out by a recent highly detailed study of excavated Anglo-Saxon shield bosses. The earliest such bosses were rather flimsy, being attached to relatively thin shields held in the fist rather than on *enarmes* straps. It has also been suggested that these light shields and bosses could also have been used as a form of punching weapon. They continued in use until the 6th century. But from the 5th century onwards, more substantial shield bosses also appeared, though still on light shields. Their shape suggests an effort to parry or trap an enemy's sword-blade. During the 6th century thicker, heavier and perhaps larger shields came into use; their bosses again being relatively thin but more pronounced. These suggest an effort to deflect blows from straight ahead and imply a more static and passive use of the shield. This shape continued to develop throughout the 7th century, becoming larger, thicker and stronger.

One possible interpretation of such evidence, supported by the nature of battle damage suffered by some surviving shield bosses themselves, suggests an individual duelling type of warfare in the earliest phase without much use of javelins or other missile weapons. Subsequently, the men owning later types of shield-bosses appear to have fought in almost disciplined ranks or in mutually supportive formations, holding their shields more steadily and apparently now concerned only with threats from their immediate front. There has been insufficient study of the shield bosses of other regions to indicate that the same development was seen elsewhere in Europe. Clearly individual peoples did have their own combat styles; the 6th century Franks' use of characteristic *franciska* throwing axes being merely the most distinctive.

Field and Camp Fortifications

As already mentioned, most peoples of originally nomadic steppe origin made considerable use of large wagons for transport, though more rarely in battle. The Chinese even divided the early medieval Turkish tribes into those 'with wagons' and those 'without wagons'. Once inside Europe, however, the non-Turkish Alans were described as drawing such wagons into a defensive circle at night. For their part, the now largely dismounted Turco-Mongol Huns of Attila's army established a hilltop field-fortification of wagons at the battle of Châlons, to which they retreated when bested by the Romans and Visigoths. This would not normally be considered a steppe nomad tactic, though it is true that the Mongol armies of the later Middle Ages also used wagon encampments called *kuriyen*.

Even less is known about field fortification in Germanic 'barbarian' armies, though the Merovingians clearly did use some kind of wooden defences against mounted foes during a civil war early in the 6th century. Meanwhile the little evidence that survives concerning Romano-British warfare suggests a reliance on small, highly mobile mounted forces, and in such circumstances field fortifications are unlikely to have been used. If they did exist they would presumably have been a continuation of late Roman forms.

WEAPONRY AND HARNESS

Several different traditions of arms and armour, and the technologies which supported them, came into contact with one another during the early medieval period, and individual soldiers might obtain their kit from more than one source. The late Roman army, for example, in part equipped its Germanic *laeti*, military colonists, from Roman sources; the rest of what they needed apparently being provided by the men themselves. Rome's Germanic mercenaries also reportedly supplied their own armour in the late 4th century. Even regular troops only received their initial kit from the state; any replacements having to be purchased with cash supplied by the Roman government. The result is likely to have been far from uniform. Not surprisingly, archaeology does show that the decoration as well as the form of many pieces of late Roman military equipment were strongly influenced by steppe nomadic and Germanic fashions. Even the élite, originally Germanic, *optimates* cavalry of the 6th century Romano-Byzantine army kitted themselves out in their own distinctive style.

Similar variations could be found within some of the 'barbarian' successor states of western Europe. Merovingian Frankish forces of strongly Romanised Neustria and Aquitaine possessed much more armour than those from east of the river Rhine, while Alan fashions may have persisted within Brittany for several centuries.

Archery

Perhaps the most important technological developments in early medieval weaponry were those concerning archery. The composite bow had, of course, been known for centuries. Compared to the simple longbow made

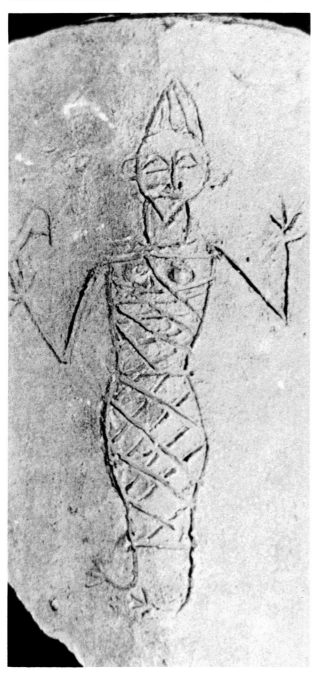

Inscribed clay tile from Madara in Bulgaria showing a warrior with a nomadic steppe type cuirass and a segmented helmet, probably early 7th century Bulgar. The brassiere-like chest protection is shown much more clearly in Central Asian wall-paintings of this and earlier centuries. (Archaeological Museum, Madara)

from a single stave of wood, the composite bow was constructed of wood, sinew, horn and often also bone. Unlike the simple longbow, it could be used on horseback though to regard the composite bow solely as the weapon of horse-archers would be very misleading. Different substances and slightly varying techniques were used in different areas, depending on the materials available and the local climate. The composite bow also gave greater power and velocity for the same weight, compared to a longbow. Perhaps as a result, more complex arrows would also develop, not only in terms of specialised shapes of arrowhead. Complex arrow-shafts wholly or partially of reed were made, these absorbing the shock of release more rapidly than a solid wooden arrow and thus straightening out more quickly. The much more acute angle of a composite bow's string, when fully drawn, also led to the evolution of the so-called 'Mongol' thumb-draw as opposed to various types of finger draw. However, it seems that only the Byzantines and those people of relatively recent steppe nomadic origin used this thumb-draw within central and southern Europe. It was not used in western Europe at all.

The Romans, like their predecessors in the Middle East, used an early form of composite bow generally known as the Scythian bow, and they clearly knew of the thumb-draw by the 3rd century. The invading Huns used another and generally larger form of composite bow which is believed to have developed from an eastern steppe form known as the Qum-Darya bow. It was almost certainly more powerful than the Scythian bow but, being larger, was not necessarily easier to use on horseback. This Hun bow was also larger than the Turkish bow which subsequently came to dominate horse-archery in most parts of Asia. The Roman version of the Hun bow was then adopted throughout the western Roman Empire and has even been found in southern Scotland. It continued to be used by several of the 'barbarian' successor states, including those of the Franks and Goths.

Recent tests have shown that Roman arrowheads were extremely effective when it came to penetrating single layers of mail armour, but were much less so against doubled layers and were relatively ineffective against scale or lamellar protections. While socketed arrowheads penetrated more effectively, the tanged type was less likely to break. In addition the tanged arrowhead was easier to range, thus enabling more rapid shooting, which may have contributed to its popularity among later medieval Middle Eastern archers with their highly developed tactics of rapid-fire shower-shooting. In the 6th century the Romano-Byzantines adopted yet another form of heavier composite bow from the invading Avars; a people with as strong a Chinese as Central Asian military heritage.

Bows of simple construction were, of course, used in many areas. Those of early medieval Scandinavia were basically longbows of yew. Others found farther north in Sweden were shorter 'flat bows' of a kind believed to be more suitable in very cold conditions. An Anglo-Saxon simple short bow has been found in the Isle of Wight, but this was almost certainly for hunting rather than war.

The question of early medieval hand-held as opposed to frame-mounted siege crossbows also remains to be resolved. These had been used by Chinese infantry since at least the 4th century BC. Small hunting crossbows are shown on Roman carvings from Gaul, but these are very different from those of China, perhaps having revolving *nuts* like those of medieval European and Middle Eastern crossbows. Such revolving crossbow *nuts* have been found in a presumed Roman or perhaps Romano-Celtic grave in

the west of England and in a 6th or 7th century site in south-western Scotland. Meanwhile a crossbow is clearly shown in an early medieval Pictish carving, again from Scotland. What can be said with reasonable certainty is that the hand-held crossbow never quite died out in western Europe; probably surviving as a hunting rather than war weapon until its revival in the 10th or 11th centuries.

Swords and Daggers

It is never easy to draw a precise dividing line between a long sword, a short sword and a dagger. Nevertheless

Decorations from a Hunnish dagger and its scabbard made from gold, silver and garnets, from Borovoge, eastern Kazakhstan, 5th century. The great majority of objects, including fragments of arms and armour that can be linked with the Huns have been found in the east, where the Huns spent the earlier part of their history; rather than in Europe where Attila carved out his brief empire. (State Hermitage Museum, St Petersburg)

these clearly existed as three distinct forms of weapon during the early medieval period. The long double-edged cavalry sword may have originated in China during the earlier Han period; then spreading to Central Asia, Iran, India and by the 6th century to Japan. Despite their fame as archers, those Huns who invaded both Sassanian Iran and the Roman Empire were also known for their long swords. Surviving examples have much in common with Sassanian weapons from Iran where several very large swords have, in fact, been found. The long cavalry *spatha* had, however, been increasing in popularity within the Roman armies since the late 4th century; the blades of such weapons ranging from 75 to 90 centimetres in length.

Two separate traditions of short sword met, and in some areas perhaps combined, during the early medieval period. These were the traditional Roman double-edged *gladius* or infantry stabbing-sword and the single-edged Germanic stabbing and cutting *seax* which may itself have been linked with the originally Central Asian <u>khanjar</u>. The very little written and archaeological evidence for Celtic and Romano-Celtic swords suggests that they were normally shorter than those of their Anglo-Saxon foes, lacking *quillons* and having tiny *pommels*. Evidence for a Romano-Celtic use of the Germanic *seax* is tenuous, and in any case Germanic weapons of the single-edged *seax*, *sax* or *scramasax* type could occasionally have blades up to 85 centimetres long, though the majority were much less. Meanwhile, knife-like daggers unlike the *seax* short-sword are amongst the most common weapons found in early medieval Irish excavations. The *seax* had been known for several centuries, but was particularly popular during the Age of Migrations. It might have reflected the influence of steppe nomadic peoples, though such a supposition is clouded by the fact that the western Black Huns in Europe appear to have made greater use of *seax*-like weapons than did the eastern White Huns in Iran, Afghanistan and Transoxania.

The adoption of a long cavalry sword inevitably affected the way swords were carried. A tight-fitting waist-belt suitable for a short *gladius* had already given way to a looser hip-belt and to a shoulder *baldric* in 3rd century Rome, both of these gradually declining during the 4th century in favour of a Germanic style of sword-belt which again rested on the hips. Most of these hip-belts probably stemmed from a loose Sassanian sword-belt in which the belt ran through an elongated scabbard-slide on the outer face of the weapon's scabbard. This system was fine on horseback but made the weapon difficult to draw when on foot. The next system, in which a scabbard hung from two slender buckled straps themselves attached to the sword-belt, meant that a weapon could not only be raised or lowered but the angle at which it hung could also be changed. This was a distinct advantage when on foot and was also useful on horseback. The two-strap system may first have been developed among the Hephthalite Huns of Transoxania or Afghanistan, and appears to have reached Europe via the Avars or perhaps the associated Bulgars.

Spears and Javelins

Highly developed archery tended to be characteristic of specific peoples, while swords remained the weapons of military or political élites almost everywhere. Spears, however, were the most common form of weapon in almost all areas. Nevertheless, they too could include very specialised forms in addition to the thrown javelin. Early Anglo-Saxon graves, for example, contained spears with distinctively narrow, almost square-sectioned, blades which could have been armour-piercing weapons. Their disappearance in the 7th century could, in turn, suggest a decline in the use of armour within the British Isles or point to the adoption of new, larger forms of shield. Written sources suggest that other spears may have been for cutting rather than thrusting, and as such might better be described as *staff weapons* rather than spears. These could include the 6th century Romano-Byzantine *dorodrepanon* and even some of the spears described in the 6th–7th century Romano-Celtic *Gododdin* poem. The earliest Scandinavian *sagas* also seem to include early versions of a single-edged 'hewing' weapon reminiscent of a later medieval *halbard*.

Javelins, of course, are basically small thrown spears and there was a general tendency for Roman javelins to get lighter from the 4th century onwards: each soldier carrying an increasing number of them. By the 5th century they included several specialised types; from the long *spiculum*, to the short *verutum* and lead-weighted *plumbata* which could also be fletched like a hand-thrown arrow. Again, the *Gododdin* makes abundant reference to javelins. Surviving Romano-Celtic examples include one with a long iron socket similar to the Germanic barbed *angon* which itself probably developed from the earlier Roman *pilum*. The purpose of the very long iron socket was, of course, to prevent an enemy from cutting off the blade if it lodged in his shield, without his having to lay down his shield. Any resulting flexibility in the socket was probably incidental.

Other Weapons

Naturally other weapons were also used during the early medieval period. The axe, for example, was known in late Roman armies and became widespread among the Germanic 'barbarian' peoples. The most characteristic axe of the period was the *franciska* throwing axe which generally weighed a little over 11 kilograms. Lassoes were always associated with Central Asian steppe warriors; both nomads and those from settled communities. Iranian nomad Alans and Turkic nomad Huns used this device; so apparently did the Goths during one period of their migrations across eastern Europe. Other weapons that are occasionally mentioned in the hands of ill-equipped general levies in 'barbarian' western Europe include wooden clubs and leather slings.

Above: War-axe head from Scandinavia, c.650. The small decorative cross suggests that this weapon was made in a Christian part of western Europe, probably Merovingian France or western Germany. (Private collection)

Right: Plain iron shield-boss and rivets, from Castel Trosino, probably Lombardic, 7th century. This came from a large wooden shield for use in war, rather than for parades. (Inv. 1650a, Museo dell'Alto Medio Evo, Rome)

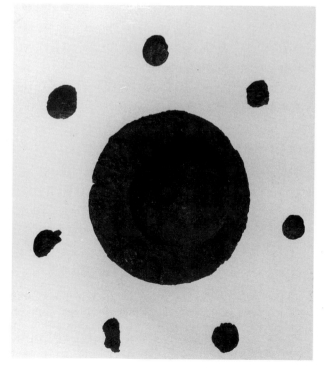

Shields

Of all forms of personal protection the simple shield was inevitably the most widespread. The limited available archaeological evidence indicates that Romano-Celtic Britain and Celtic Ireland continued a Roman tradition of using relatively thin shields with small bosses, whereas the shields of the Anglo-Saxons and other Germanic peoples were generally larger. The *Gododdin* describes the lime-washed white shields of its heroes; a motif also found in the earliest written Irish sources. The supposed 'punching' pointed bosses found in early Anglo-Saxon burials

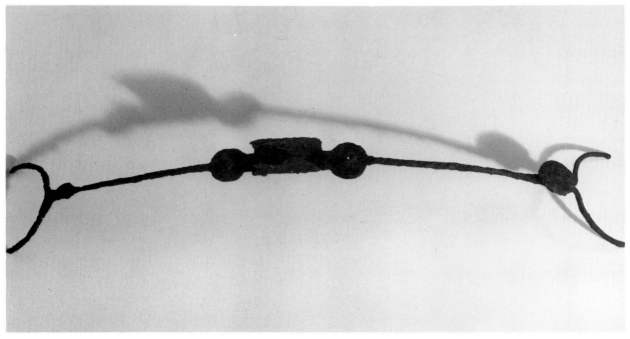

Opposite page, top: A: Shield-boss, probably from a parade shield or one for a guards unit, from Nocera Umbra, Byzantine southern Italy, 7th century. The basic bronze boss is decorated with cast-bronze elements, originally gilded, showing infantry or huntsmen in combat. (Inv. 35, Museum dell'Alto Medio Evo, Rome)

Opposite page, bottom: Iron internal strengthening element and grip from a shield, 61 centimetres long, probably Lombardic, 7th century. This long iron strip apparently came from the same shield as the boss shown alongside. The U-shaped ends would have stopped the iron rod from twisting, while the broad and almost folded iron at the centre would have gone around a sturdy wooden shield-grip. (Inv. 1650b, Museo dell'Alto Medio Evo, Rome)

Helmets

Armour provided more scope for variation in both shape and manner of construction. Following the abandonment of body-protecting plate armour by the later Romans, helmets were the largest pieces of metal plate protection seen until the reintroduction of plate armour into 14th century Europe. During the 4th century there had, in fact, been a significant change in the design and manufacture of helmets for the Roman army. Two new forms emerged: the segmented and framed *spangenhelm* which may have been based on those used by Rome's nomad foes on the Danube frontier, and a very simple two-piece helmet secured by a single band running front to back which was almost certainly of Middle Eastern Iranian origin. This latter form was particularly suited to the low-skill, mass production, arms manufacturing system of the final Roman century. Nevertheless, both types continued to be used during the early Middle Ages.

Beyond the Roman and Romano-Byzantine frontiers various surviving helmets seem to reflect a mixture of late Roman and local traditions. The most famous examples are the famous Vendel period helmets from Sweden and the magnificent Sutton Hoo helmet from Anglo-

also bring to mind a passage in a 6th century Romano-Byzantine military manual. This refers to the shields of the front rank of an infantry formation having spiked thrusting bosses. Wickerwork shields are normally associated with Middle Eastern peoples, but they were also used by Roman troops during training, being known as *scuta viminea* or *scuta talaris*.

Iron frame of a segmented spangenhelm from Benty Grange. It has a bronze boar as a crest and was originally covered with horn scales; Anglo-Saxon, late 7th century. A very similar helmet, with its scale-like covering and another animal crest, appears in an 8th century Anglo-Saxon manuscript now in St Petersburg. The boar, however, appears to have been a popular helmet decoration; another example having been found in Celtic Wales. (City Museum, Sheffield; photograph Arts and Museums Department, Sheffield)

Opposite page: The highly decorated 'Sutton Hoo helmet' of iron with abundant gilded bronze decoration, Anglo-Saxon or Germanic Saxon, c.500. This helmet was clearly very old when it was buried with an East Anglian ruler in the 7th century. Its partially gilded decorations include

small panels illustrating armoured warriors. (Department of Medieval and Later Antiquities, British Museum, London)

Saxon England. The presence of face-masks or visors on some of these helmets may also stem from late Roman cavalry fashions. Other simpler helmets may have consisted only of an iron frame filled or covered with leather or laminated horn segments. Even here, however, it should be pointed out that many low-grade late Roman frontier troops were described as having leather head protections.

Whereas late Roman equipment included an early form of the medieval mail *coif* covering the entire head, the Iranian and steppe tradition was to fasten a mail *aventail* to the edge of a helmet. During the Age of Migrations it was the Iranian *aventail* that seems to have had most influence among Germanic armourers, the 'barbarian' successor states and even in Scandinavia.

Body Armour

Two forms of body armour predominated during this period: mail and *lamellar*, both of which were flexible. Scale armour had declined in importance though having not entirely disappeared. Mail itself could vary both in the size of the rings used in their construction, and the way they were connected to one another. Roman mail was almost invariably all riveted, or had alternating riveted and soldered links, but not using punched links. These early mail links could also be remarkably small. A mail hauberk known as a *saba, zaba* or *lorikion* continued to be by far the most important form of body armour in 5th and 6th century Romano-Byzantine armies. Worn over a one-centimetre-thick padded garment, it was the ancestor of the medieval *gambeson* and of later *arming doublets*.

Mail armour seems to have been rare in Anglo-Saxon England but it is mentioned in early Celtic poetry, being called a *lluric*, from the Latin *lorikis*. Mail may have been more widespread in continental Europe and Scandinavia where it was known by variations of the Germanic terms *serk, seirch* and *sarwat*. This, perhaps surprisingly, seems to have stemmed from the Iranian word for mail, *zirh*, which in turn suggests military influence from the east rather than from Rome. Eastern military influence is confirmed by the fact that Migration Period mail from Scandinavia mostly uses alternating punched and riveted links in the Persian style.

Scale or lamellar armour was often worn over a mail hauberk, the only major exception to this being among nomadic steppe warriors, most of whom had no mail. This even seems to have been the case within some of the richer Germanic successor states of western Europe, though the use of ill-defined and often archaic Latin terminology can confuse the issue. In 575, for example, a Frankish Count was described as wearing a *toracibus*, cuirass, and *loricis*, coat of mail. A further term, *brunia*, has been variously interpreted as a scale coat, a mail *hauberk*, or as the Germanic word for a *toracibus*, cuirass. It may, in truth, have been a general term for various types of body protection.

During this period Romano-Byzantine sources indicate that heavy infantry wore some kind of cuirass over a mail hauberk. *Lamellar* armour, usually of bronze, had, of course, been used by troops of eastern Mediterranean origin in the Roman army. But it probably remained rare until the 6th century when there were Roman-Byzantine references to gilded *thorax* cuirasses being worn by senior military leaders.

Lamellar armour had long been especially characteristic of steppe nomadic warriors, and the Huns appear to have continued using it after entering Europe. One description of an early 5th century Hun mercenary in Roman service portrays him as wearing a cuirass that protected his body but not his shoulders; in other words a typical Asiatic form of limited *lamellar* armour. Surviving fragments of early medieval metal *lamellae* from the Crimea are believed to be Avar. These use basically the same lacing system that was used in Tibet almost until modern times, and which was very different from the lacing of Roman *lamellar* armour.

Limb Defences

Separate pieces of armour for the arms and legs were no longer fashioned from shaped pieces of bronze, but were built up of iron or bronze vertical *splints* or from horizontal *lames*. The slightly flexible *laminated* system seems to have been used for late Roman cavalry limb defences. It is also clearly illustrated in western Asian and Central Asian art up to, and well beyond, the 6th century. Some remarkable, though crudely made, fragments of *splinted* armour from the Vendel period were found in Scandinavia and are now believed to have been protections for the lower arms and shins. Leg armours mentioned in Merovingian Frankish sources were known as *ocreae* in Latin or *bagnbergae* in German; these probably being similar to the surviving examples from Scandinavia.

Horse Harness

Technological developments in horse harness were particularly dramatic from the 4th to 7th centuries. During this period the wood-framed saddle came into general use in most areas, though not in all. Whether the framed saddle used in the Romano-Byzantine Mediterranean region was based entirely on that previously developed by nomadic peoples of the steppes, or reflected the influence of Mid-

'Trojan Council', in the Virgilius Vaticanus manuscript; Italy, early 5th century. The illustrations in this manuscript are more damaged than in some other surviving books from the last years of the Roman Empire, but the standard of the pictures is actually very high. Here a group of Trojan soldiers wear short-sleeved hauberks, clearly of mail, with mail coifs – a form of protection normally associated with a period several centuries later in medieval western Europe. They are shown in a few other examples of late Roman art but are usually worn by 'easterners' such as the Trojans in this source. This suggests that the mail hauberk with an integral mail coif was, in fact, of eastern Mediterranean origin. (MS. Lat. 3225, f.73v, Biblioteca Apostolica Vaticana, Rome; photograph Biblioteca Vaticana)

dle Eastern wood-framed camel saddles, remains unclear. The slightly later medieval Middle Eastern wood-framed saddle, rather than the nomad saddle, is now believed to have been the prototype from which the subsequent medieval western European war-saddle developed.

Quite why the Roman and Sassanian 'four-horned saddle' was abandoned in the late 4th and 5th centuries also remains a mystery. Recent experiments have shown that this horned saddle provided excellent support to a rider wielding a sword or spear. On the other hand the nomad form of framed saddle, as used by Huns, Avars and other subsequent waves of invaders, was probably more suitable for a horse-archer. The Emperor Constantine reportedly introduced the new saddle to 'strengthen the solidity of the rider's seat'; the precise weight of such saddles then being enshrined in the Emperor Theodosius II's Legal Code of AD 438.

The curb bit, which enabled a rider to control his horse with much lighter pressure than was needed with a snaffle bit, is said to have been invented by the Celts many centuries earlier. It was certainly popular in Sassanian Iran but did not become more widespread until the early medieval period.

The most dramatic development in horse harness during these centuries was, however, the adoption of stirrups. Even so the importance of this development has been over-emphasised by most historians, particularly in the military context. All-rope or leather 'toe stirrups' had been known in India since the 1st century AD, and they continued to be used in Africa and other parts of the world until modern times. The true, fully developed or rigid stirrup was invented in eastern Asia; either in the eastern steppe regions, in Korea or northern China. Such stirrups are usually seen in terms of how they could help a cavalryman be more effective, either as a horse-archer or when using other weapons. What has not been so widely recognised is the fact that stirrups also gave support to the legs on long-distance rides. They also reduced the effects of cold by improving the circulation in a rider's legs. This was, in fact, probably why they were developed in one of the coldest horse-rearing parts of the world; one in which nomadic or semi-nomadic peoples spent an enormous part of their lives in the saddle.

The earliest known rigid stirrup came from 4th century north-eastern China and it had a wooden step. Wholly or partially wooden stirrups continued to be used in Central Asia, the Caucasus and Russia for many centuries, though few survive because they were made of perishable materials. Stirrups were first mentioned in written sources in 5th century China, where the first illustration was also found a century later. They were clearly used by the Juan-Juan nomads of China's northern frontier in the 5th century and the Avar descendants of these people who equally clearly brought stirrups to Europe. Avar stirrups were of cast bronze or iron and the Avars are generally credited with the sudden spread of rigid stirrups in the west; the

Romano-Byzantines having adopted them by the end of the 6th century.

Horse Armour
Before looking in detail at the question of horse armour, the interesting use of small bells as a form of cavalry decoration might be mentioned as evidence of another possible example of the spread of horse harness fashions from Central Asia to western Europe. Apparent pom-poms or bells are shown on the spear-shafts of Turkish armoured horsemen in the early medieval rock-carvings of Mongolia. They also appear more clearly in 6th century wall-paintings from eastern Turkestan. Small spherical bronze bells are common among the metalwork excavated in immediately pre-Islamic archaeological sites in Transoxania. In 9th–10th century Iran cavalrymen proudly proclaimed that they 'had bells'; the implication being that other cavalry of this period did not. Bells as a form of harness decoration were similarly found in the 6th century Frankish kingdom, particularly in northern France and the Champagne area.

Horse armour had long been characteristic of the élite cavalry of the steppes. Here most warriors are thought to have ridden relatively small horses or large ponies. But the main problem facing an armoured horse was heat exhaustion, not weight. Various types of scale, lamellar or felt horse armour are known to have been used in different parts of the world, but above all in Central Asia. The 6th century Avars, however, used a more limited fashion which covered only the front of the horse, its neck and perhaps its head. Such armour was of iron *lamellae* or felt and was the primary influence upon Romano-Byzantine horse armour of a similar period. Evidence is, however, lacking for the survival of horse armour anywhere else in Europe with the possible, but questionable, exception of Brittany.

FORTIFICATION

Until recent years there has been a widespread belief that only the Romano-Byzantine Empire was capable of building effective fortifications and of conducting real siege operations during the early medieval period, at least within Europe. Even the Sassanian Empire of Iran was regarded as a pale reflection of Rome and of Byzantium, while other peoples were assumed to have had neither interest nor capability in military architecture or the art of siege warfare. Such opinions were, in fact, largely based on those of the Romano-Byzantines themselves who scorned all their foes when it came to siege and counter-siege.

Romano-Byzantine Armies
The late Roman and Romano-Byzantine Empire put considerable effort and huge expense into fortification. The archaeological record also indicates that there were many

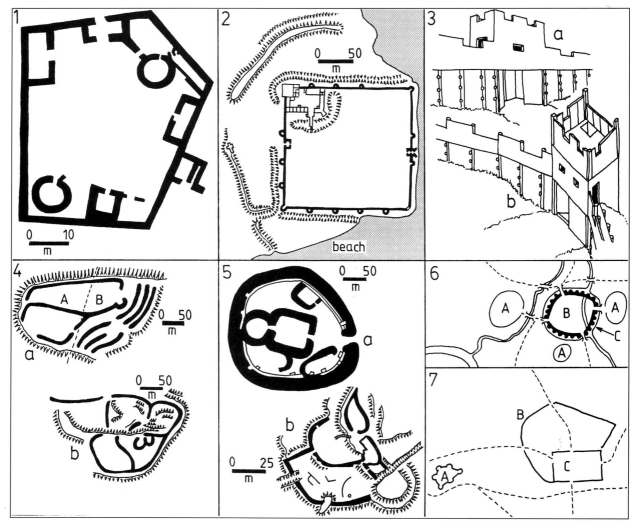

more fortified places than were listed in the *Notitia Digni-tatum.* At the beginning of the 5th century these ranged from great cities to small fortified towns; from defended bridgeheads and ferry-ports on both banks of the Rhine, through huge walls like Hadrian's Wall in northern Britain to the small fortified farmsteads of both frontier and central provinces.

During the 5th and 6th centuries, following the loss of the western Empire, the Romano-Byzantine Empire in the east strengthened existing Roman fortifications and built entirely new ones. Some of the resulting edifices remain astonishing works of military engineering; the most dramatic example being the land walls of Constantinople – now Istanbul. The strengthening of the fortifications of a number of ports also indicated the growing importance of sea communications to an empire whose main enemies were all land based.

Generally speaking, the larger fortifications primarily existed to provide a refuge for local populations and their

livestock from the ever-present threat of raids by 'barbarians' from beyond the Empire's now shrunken frontiers. Some of these refuges could be vast. For example, the whole eastern tip of Thrace was 'defended' by the Emperor Maurice's long rampart and ditch which stretched from the Sea of Marmara to the Black Sea.

At the other end of the scale were hundreds of local fortifications which again provided a refuge for local inhabitants. These sprang up near the river Rhine, in Gaul and even within Italy itself during the last decades of the western Roman Empire. Some were quite impressive; consisting of fortified villas with high walls and *portcullised* gates. The function of smaller forts was described in detail in a 6th century Romano-Byzantine military manual. This stated that they were to observe the enemy – actual or potential – receive enemy deserters, stop their own fugitives, and serve as assembly points against raiders. In Italy and present-day Turkey many large settlements may also already have been 'migrating' from the valleys to nearby more

Left: Fortifications, 400–650

1. A group of defended huts at Din Lligwy in Anglesey, Wales; 4th century, incorporating two rectangular iron-smelting workshops (after Houlder)

2. The late Roman Saxon Shore fortress at Portchester in Hampshire, England; showing earthworks added to the interior and exterior in Anglo-Saxon times (after HMSO)

3. Reconstructions of the fortifications at South Cadbury in Somerset, England; as they might have appeared in the 'Arthurian' 6th century (after Alcock and Whitton)

a Main gate of timber and stone

b South-west gate-tower with wickerwork 'battlements', a timber tower, a timber and stone wall backed by an earth rampart

4. Pictish fortifications

A North Pictish ramparts at Burghead, 4th–5th century (after Roy)

A: existing

B: destroyed in the 19th century

b Pictish fort at Dundurn, 7th century (after Christison and Peachem)

5. Irish and Scots fortifications

a Irish fortified farmstead at Leacanabuaile in County Kerry, early medieval

b Dal Riata fort at Dunadd, Argyll, early medieval (after Christison)

6. Dijon in the 6th century (after Rouche)

A Merovingian cemeteries

B Walls and ditch of the castrum.

C Moat filled from stream

7. Cambrai in the 6th century (after Rouche)

A Selle fortress

B Roman castrum.

C Walls of Dodilo

Above: The 'Porta Nigra' fortified gate of Trier in Germany; Roman, 4th century. The gate is a massive structure of blackened sand- stone which subsequently formed part of the city's defences for several centuries, until it was converted to a church in the mid-11th century. Even then it remained one of the strongest buildings in the medieval city of Trier.

Right: The 'Porta San Paolo' fortified gate in the southern walls of Rome. The basic gate was probably built by the Emperor Honorius in the late 4th or early 5th century. The towers may have been heightened, together with those of other fortified gates in Rome's ancient walls, by the Germanic Ostrogoths in about 500. The entire structure was further strengthened by the Romano-Byzantines in the 6th century and remained an essential and very strong part of the city's fortifications for many more centuries. (Photograph, Colette Nicolle)

defensible hilltops – a process which was to become common from the 7th century onwards.

Huns and Steppe Invaders
The Huns may not have erected any lasting fortifications during their brief occupation of central Europe, but there is no reason to assume that all other conquerors of Central Asian steppe origin lacked interest in military architecture. On the contrary, some evidence strongly indicates the reverse. Pliska, the first Bulgar capital in the Balkans, may have re-used the ruins of Roman buildings but the Bulgars added an earthen rampart, while the construction of a palace within these defences appears to have included several architectural features of Central Asian origin.

Germanic Forces
The Germanic successor states in western Europe do not appear to have added much to the existing late Roman fortification of those regions they conquered. But they did continue to use such walled cities, towns and smaller *castellae*, and to have maintained many of them in good repair. This was particularly true of the Romanised Burgundians, Ostrogoths and Visigoths, though even the Merovingian Franks also used existing Roman fortifications. A notable exception were the Anglo-Saxons in Britain where there is very little evidence for the use of any form of military architecture. Even the major Anglo-Saxon base and invasion bridgehead of Bamburgh on the Northumbrian coast

only appears to have been 'hedged' in the early centuries, though a wall was added later. An Anglo-Saxon fortified corral for livestock has also been found at Yeavering in Northumberland, but this may have been adapted from a previous Romano-Celtic structure.

Celtic Forces
The Celts clearly made much greater use of various types of old and newer fortifications than did their Anglo-Saxon foes. The Roman defences of Britain were still largely intact, as they were on the Continent of Europe. There is even archaeological evidence to suggest that the walls of some cities, particularly those in the west of the island, had been strengthened with additional bastions during the late 4th century. These were probably to support anti-personnel counter-siege weapons such as the *ballista*. The fortifications of Cirencester, which was a vital communications centre in the west of Romano-Celtic Britain, were also repaired in the mid-5th century. But from then on the archaeological evidence points to a gradual decline and, in effect, the slow fading away of fortified cities east of the river Severn.

Other cities farther west and in the north remained important Romano-British military bases, almost certainly with efforts being made to keep their fortifications in working order. Wroxeter, for example, was probably the main centre of the last decades of Romano-Celtic resistance and it still served a similar purpose for the Welsh

Left: The south-eastern walls of Thessaloniki; Roman, late 4th century. The large circular tower in the distance was added by the Ottoman Turks in the later Middle Ages. Such walls and rectangular towers are built of alternating rows of brick and stone. This was typical of Romano-Byzantine fortifications, though the reasons for this style of construction are not entirely understood. It may have made the walls less likely to collapse in the event of enemy mining operations.

Right: One of the so-called 'Visigothic Towers' in the inner walls of Carcassonne in southern France. This wall follows the line of the city's Roman fortifications, its towers and walls being maintained and strengthened during the 6th to 9th centuries. Part of the wall may actually have been of late-Roman construction, including the lower rows of much larger pieces of cut stone; the upper courses of smaller but still well-cut stone clearly being of later date.

The 'Devil's Ditch' in Cambridgeshire, England; one of several ramparts erected either by the Celts against the Anglo-Saxons or to mark the frontier between different Anglo-Saxon kingdoms, 6th–7th centuries. Despite the fact that both rampart and ditch have been eroded by well over a thousand years of wind and rain, the Ditch remains as witness to an astonishingly large engineering project.

principality of Powys until the beginning of the 6th century. Far to the north, Carlisle, one of the main centres of the Romano-Celtic kingdom of Strathclyde, still had its Roman aqueduct in working order in about 685. This being the case, it seems most unlikely that Carlisle's even more important defensive walls would have been allowed to collapse.

Carlisle was also the primary military base at the western end of Hadrian's Wall; at least part of which also appears to have been both garrisoned and repaired well into the 6th century. Unlike the Roman forts of the Yorkshire coast, which seem to have been destroyed in battle, those of Hadrian's Wall, the Pennine Hills and even of the Saxon Shore in south-eastern Britain, did not meet violent ends. One rare example of what is believed to be a newly

built Romano-Celtic fort has, in fact, been found on the eastern side of the Pennines. This indicates new construction in a late Roman style, in addition to the mere repairing of existing fortifications. Elsewhere most Romano-Celtic fortifications consisted of small hill forts, some on sites used before the Romans arrived, others in new locations. With the notable exception of Cadbury Hill in the south-west, these were much smaller than the ancient Celtic tribal hill-top fortresses.

Cadbury, however, was an extensive fortification of dry-stone walls plus timber palisades and a gate, with timber buildings inside. It may, in fact, have been the Camelot of Arthurian legend. Like many smaller Romano-Celtic fortifications, that on Cadbury Hill probably dates from the late 5th century which was, perhaps, the true 'Arthurian

centuries. Again, they were built in a distinctive way, massive timbers being used to lace their dry-stone walls together. Most of the ancient Pictish *broch* dry-stone towers of the far north seem to have been demolished during the 2nd century; their stones being re-used for peaceful houses. Stone 'ring-forts' comparable to the *cashels* of Ireland were similarly found in Scotland.

Within Ireland itself there were two separate forms of fortification; the dry-stone *cashel* which normally lacked a defensive ditch, and the round *rath* which consisted of a ditch and earth bank, probably surmounted by a timber palisade. Such *raths* came in a variety of sizes, some being mere refuges while others were probably tribal capitals. Perhaps most distinctive of all Celtic fortifications were the *crannogs* of Ireland and Scotland. These were basically artificial timber islands built near the edges of lakes or marshes. They had been common in ancient times, then seem to have died out until they re-appeared during the turbulent first millennium AD.

SIEGE WARFARE

Documentary evidence for the techniques of siege warfare in the early Middle Ages is extremely unevenly spread. A great deal may be known about Romano-Byzantine siege and counter-siege tactics and equipment, but very little specific information survives concerning the other peoples of Europe.

Romano-Byzantine Armies
There was clear continuity from the Roman late 4th century to the Romano-Byzantine 6th century, and indeed well beyond. The defenders of a late Roman fortification could protect their wall by hanging large shock-absorbent mats in front of it, while an attacking army could attempt to roll a wheeled wooden siege tower or a large ram close to such a wall. Some fortifications seem to have had additional earth ramparts erected ahead of the wall, perhaps as a barrier against such movable siege engines, or perhaps as a cover behind which the defenders could assemble before making a sortie.

Sources dating from the 6th century refer to much the same devices, including a variety of stone-throwing and large arrow-shooting machines. Yet there was, perhaps, also an increased emphasis on oil-based incendiary weapons such as fire-pots to be thrown by hand or shot from *ballistae*. Other experimental and peculiar ideas were similarly recorded. For example, there were said to be some sort of double-shot *ballistae* defending the Roman Empire's Rhine frontier during the final decades. This idea resurfaced in a late 12th century Egyptian work on weapons, both actual and experimental, and in 12th or 13th century Venice.

Romano-Byzantine stone-throwing or large arrow-shooting siege and counter-siege engines were essentially based on the torsion principle, mostly getting their power

Age' of British history. The importance of such sites seems to be recalled in 6th century Welsh poetry; one poem laments the death of the hero Uthyr Pendragon and celebrates his 'breaking of a hundred forts'. Romano-Celtic Britain was also characterised by a number of long ditches and dikes. Their function is less obvious than those of the Sassanian Empire in the Middle East. Although many came to be accepted as frontiers between the petty Anglo-Saxon and Celtic states of Britain, they were surely too costly to have been thrown up for that purpose alone.

Northern Scotland and Ireland had never been occupied by the Romans and here other forms of fortification were built. The large Pictish stone fortresses of north-eastern Scotland remained in use down to the 8th and 9th

from twisted ropes of animal sinew. The beam-sling stone-throwing *mangonel* had not yet reached Europe, though it had already been invented in China and may have been known in Central Asia. Perhaps the most important change in such Romano-Byzantine machines, and in those of the western European Germanic successor states, was an apparent shift from the highly accurate, easy to aim, two-armed Roman *ballista* to the single-armed *onager*. Whereas the former was a sophisticated, indeed elaborate machine which needed its two separately 'powered' arms to be finely tuned, the *onager* was a crude but rugged device which was much easier to construct. It was, however, much more difficult to change the aim of an *onager*. As a result such *onagers* would probably have been used in batteries covering an enemy's expected line of approach. Once again the knowledge of both these types of machine must have survived. The simple *onager* clearly continued in use without a break, while a machine comparable to the complicated *ballista* subsequently re-appeared in various parts of the Middle East and, rather later, in western Europe.

Hun and Steppe Invaders

The little that is known about siege warfare among the steppe nomadic peoples shows that they were a channel for Chinese ideas and new forms of siege engine spreading from the east into Europe. Once inside Europe, however, the most sophisticated of these Asian peoples, such as the Avars, seem to have combined such Far Eastern military technology with that of their Romano-Byzantine foes to became some of the most effective siege engineers in early medieval history.

Germanic Forces

The Germanic 'barbarians' seem to have learned all they knew of siege warfare from their late Roman foes. Since armies such as that of the Merovingian Frankish kingdom enlisted ex-Roman soldiers and their descendants, it is hardly surprising that they were described as using Roman-type devices during their siege of Avignon in about AD 501. Later in the 6th century these Franks were clearly also making use of wheeled battering rams beneath protective wooden roofs. Furthermore, the written evidence strongly suggests that the armies of the Mediterranean south of the Merovingian kingdom were more effective in siege warfare than were those of the less Romanised Merovingian north.

Celtic Forces

No clear information survives about the siege tactics of Celtic peoples during this period. Those who had been in closest contact with the Romans were now very much on the defensive. Yet they were not as isolated from what remained of the Romano-Byzantine Empire as is sometimes thought. For this reason, if for no other, the Celts of southern Britain and of Brittany can be assumed to have retained some knowledge of Romano-Byzantine

siege technology, though they may have had little reason to use it.

NAVAL WARFARE

Naval warfare was not highly developed during this period. In the previous Mediterranean world Rome had been the only naval power for centuries, while the collapse of the western Roman Empire led to a revival of piracy rather than posing a serious threat to what remained of the Empire in the East. Consequently a powerful Romano-Byzantine navy did not emerge at once. In fact such a fleet only developed in response to a subsequent threat; that of the Muslim-Arab Caliphate in the 7th century. Much the same was true along the Atlantic seaboard where naval warfare remained essentially a matter of small-scale coastal raiding.

The Mediterranean

The early medieval centuries saw the start of a process of technological revolution that would have a profound effect on medieval European naval warfare, as well as on maritime trade and the balance of power in the Mediterranean. The huge Roman grain ships of earlier centuries had disappeared by the 7th century. By then the most important of the changes in ship design may already have started, though its real impact was to be felt slightly later. This was a gradual shift from hull-first to frame-first construction. In the older system the outer watertight skin of a ship's hull was constructed first; its internal strengthening ribs and frame being added afterwards. In the later system the frame was constructed first, as in modern shipbuilding, with a layer of watertight planks then being attached to such a frame. Whereas the old hull-first construction was hugely expensive in both timber, time and skill, the subsequent frame-first hull required much less timber, appears to have been quicker, and demanded fewer highly skilled shipbuilders, though perhaps many less skilled labourers.

In Romano-Byzantine Egypt, meanwhile, other technological changes could be seen. These amounted to a break with the Pharaonic and Graeco-Roman past and the appearance of what would become the more advanced

Trojan ships in a gale', in the Virgilius Romanus manuscript; Italy, possibly made under the rule of Odoacer 476–93. These ships present a number of interesting details normally associated with medieval rather than Roman galleys. They may already have lateen or at least lug sails, though this is not entirely clear. What is certain is that their rams are lifted well clear of the waterline, and are thus much closer in character to the later calcar oar-breaking and boarding 'beak', than to the true ancient Graeco-Roman ship-sinking ram. (MS. Lat. 3867, f.77r, Biblioteca Apostolica Vaticana, Rome; photograph Biblioteca Vaticana)

medieval science of marine technology. Most if not all stemmed from the eastern seas, Red Sea and Indian Ocean, and included a basically triangular *lateen* sail or its probable lug sail predecessor as well as minor changes in hull design. In such a context it should be remembered that the two main Romano-Byzantine naval bases in Egypt, Alexandria on the Mediterranean and Clysma near Suez on the Red Sea, were then linked via the river Nile and a man-made canal. The single stern-rudder had been known in China since the 1st century BC. By the T'ang period such Chinese stern rudders were even being controlled by means of wheels, pulleys and ropes. Yet there is no evidence that this sophisticated technology was known in the Indian Ocean, let alone the Red Sea or Mediterranean, during the early medieval centuries.

The Germanic Goths who occupied much of what is now the Ukraine were not seamen. But they or their non-German subjects do seem to have taken over the trading connections of the previous Bosphoran kingdom and to have raided southwards across the Black Sea on several occasions. The German-speaking communities that continued to live in the Crimea until the 13th century are believed to have been descended from those Goths who refused to flee westward ahead of the Huns in the 4th and 5th centuries AD.

The Northern Seas

The identity of the Germanic 'pirates' who raided down the Roman Empire's Atlantic seaboard as far as Spain and even Morocco remain very unclear but they are unlikely to have been Franks. The latter only seem to have turned to the sea in the early 6th century. Even so, the Merovingian fleet which defeated the Danes in AD 515 was probably crewed largely by non-Franks. It may even have been built

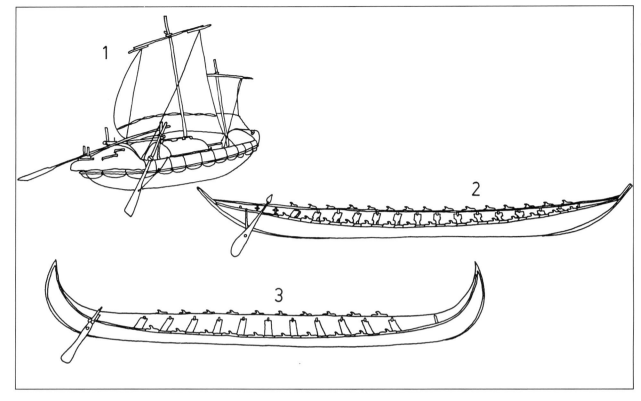

Shipping, 400–650
1. *Reconstruction of a sea-going early medieval Irish curragh, skin-covered boat. Vessels such as this maintained communications between the various Celtic parts of Ireland and western Britain (after Severin)*
2. *Sea-going boat from Nydam in Schleswig, Denmark; early 4th century. Such rowing*

boats could not mount sails but were essentially the same as those used by the Anglo-Saxons in their migration to Britain (after Landström)
3. *Ship from Kvalsund, Norway; 7th century. This again was powered by oars but could also mount a sail and was a much stronger vessel than the earlier Nydam boat (after Landström)*

upon what remained of the old Roman naval structure in Gaul. Much the same would seem to have been the case with the highly effective Merovingian river fleets. Clearly the Anglo-Saxons reached Britain by sea and they were recorded as being dangerous raiders as early as the 4th century. But thereafter there is remarkably little mention of Anglo-Saxons as seafarers during the 5th and 6th centuries.

In contrast, the Celtic Scots of Ireland and Picts of Scotland remained formidable at sea, though the Picts appear to have declined in relation to the Scots who had, for some time, been colonising western Scotland. Nevertheless their victims were generally fellow Celts, Romano-Britons rather than Germanic Anglo-Saxons. The vessels of these northern and western Celtic seamen appear to have been

skin-covered *curraghs*. Yet these were not the little coracles still seen on some Welsh rivers. They had much more in common with the ocean-going skin-covered vessels of western Irish fishermen during the late 19th and early 20th centuries. Pictish and Scottish *curraghs* could have eight oarsmen on each side, plus a steering oar and a substantial sail.

The most powerful Celtic fleet was that of the kingdom of Dal Riata in western Scotland. This was the area colonised by Irish 'Scots' who, of course, eventually gave Scotland its name. By the 8th century this 'Scottish' navy could fight fleet actions at sea and was so important to the kingdom of Dal Riata that the military organisation of the state was based on groups of houses, each of which had to supply 'twice seven rowing benches to each twenty houses'.

River Warfare
iver warfare, or at least river-borne military transport, had been brought to a high level of efficiency by the late Roman and Romano-Byzantine armies in Europe. Mention is even made of artillery being mounted on boats, and of rafts having raised towers manned by archers to clear the banks before other troops crossed a river. Nothing appears to be known about river navigation among the Huns and other steppe nomads of the early Middle Ages, though river transport would later play a very important role, particularly along the great rivers of the western steppes in what are now southern Russia and the Ukraine.

II
EARLY MEDIEVAL
EUROPE (650–1100)

EARLY MEDIEVAL EUROPE (650–1100)

The Early Middle Ages saw the creation of many new nations in Europe. Elsewhere the late Roman Empire, now more simply known as the Byzantine Empire, survived despite being ringed by predatory enemies. Meanwhile the powerful new civilisation of Iberian Islam, or al-Andalus, evolved in Spain and Portugal (Byzantine and Andalusian-Spanish warfare will be dealt with in Volume II). In northern and eastern Europe, as well as along the Celtic Atlantic fringe, centralised states with structured armies were much slower to develop. But even here both ancient and newly arrived peoples, civilised as in Ireland or near barbarian as in Scandinavia and eastern Europe, were slowly emerging from the mists of pre-history and legend to establish effective political and military structures.

The identification of these nations and their armies is relatively clear-cut in southern and western Europe, but is not always the case elsewhere. A lack of written records means that historians often have to rely on archaeology or the interpretation of myths. Fortunately such myths survive in sufficiently large numbers to shed at least a murky light on Scandinavia and the Baltic region. Comparable epics and traditional chronicles do the same for the British Isles, central and to a lesser extent eastern Europe. Nevertheless a great many questions remain to be answered. Many such questions were, unfortunately, further confused by the dubious, nationalistic – even racist – scholarship of some 19th and 20th century historians.

One perhaps extreme example illustrates the potential for confusion. The Black and White Onagurs were two of those tribes which migrated into Europe from the east during the early medieval period. They were probably the same people as the Huns who had been driven eastward, back into the steppes of southern Russia and the Ukraine in the 5th century. They also had close, but not entirely clear, links with the Bulgars; another essentially Turkic people from the east. The White Onagurs seem to have taken over the ex-Avar areas of Hungary, following the Avars' defeat by Charlemagne but before the Finno-Ugrian Magyar ancestors of the modern Hungarians arrived in this same area. By the time the Magyars did arrive, the plain of Hungary was probably already inhabited by a mixed Turco-Bulgar, Slav and Finno-Ugrian population which had arrived with the Onagurs, plus the remnants of earlier communities. The Magyars then conquered and absorbed them all.

Major Campaigns
655: Pagan Anglo-Saxon kingdom of Mercia defeated by Christian Anglo-Saxon kingdom of Northumbria.
658–720: Anglo-Saxon kingdom of Wessex conquers Celtic British–Welsh area of Somerset and Devon.
679–80: Bulgars invade the Byzantine Empire; establish a Bulgarian state south of the river Danube.
685: Celtic northern Picts defeat Anglo-Saxon Northumbrians at Dunnichen.

687: Carolingian family wins battle of Tertry to dominate the Frankish kingdom.
741: Celtic Picts defeat Celtic Scots (Irish) of Dal Riata.
751: Germanic Lombards capture Ravenna, completing their conquest of northern Italy.
774: Carolingian Franks defeat Lombards to conquer northern Italy.
793: First dated Scandinavian Norse-Viking raid on England.
803: Carolingian destruction of the Avar state in central Europe.
811: Bulgars defeat Byzantines at Edirne (Adrianopolis).
814 or 815: Celtic Welsh Cornwall conquered by Anglo-Saxon kingdom of Wessex.
834–45: Danish-Norse raids on the mouth of the river Rhine, northern France (Normandy) and northern Germany.
841: Establishment of Norse-Viking military and trading base at Dublin in Ireland.
c.843: Southern Pictish leadership assassinated, Picts accept Scottish (Irish) king and the establishment of the kingdom of Alban in most of northern Scotland.
865–7: Norse-Viking 'Great Army' raids across England.
870: Norse-Viking capture the capital of the Celtic North British kingdom of Strathclyde in south-western Scotland.
c.870: Beginning of Norse-Viking occupation and settlement of Iceland.
871–9: Anglo-Saxon kingdom of Wessex defeats Norse army at the battle of Ashdown.
c.895: Kingdom of Norway established following the battle of Hafrsfiord.
c.895–900: Finno-Ugrian Magyars (Hungarians) cross the Carpathian mountains; conquer the Hungarian Plain.
906: Destruction of the Slav kingdom of Moravia by the Magyars.
912–18: Anglo-Saxon Wessex conquers Norse-ruled East Anglia and Norse-ruled Mercia.
919–27: Anglo-Saxon Wessex conquers the Norse kingdom of York in northern England.
933: Large Magyar raid into Germany.
936: German invasion of Slav regions of (what is now) eastern Germany.
937: Anglo-Saxon Wessex defeats a Celtic and Norse-Viking alliance at the battle of Brunaburgh. Large-scale Magyar raid across Germany, eastern France and the complete length of Italy.
938–66: Campaigns by the German Emperor to assert imperial control over Germany and northern Italy.
946: German invasion of eastern France.
950: German invasion of Bohemia.
954–5: Large Magyar raids into Flanders and Bavaria.
955: Magyars defeated by the German Empire at the battle of the Lech; German invasion of Slav region of (what is now) eastern Germany.
959: Unification of Anglo-Saxon England under the kings of Wessex.

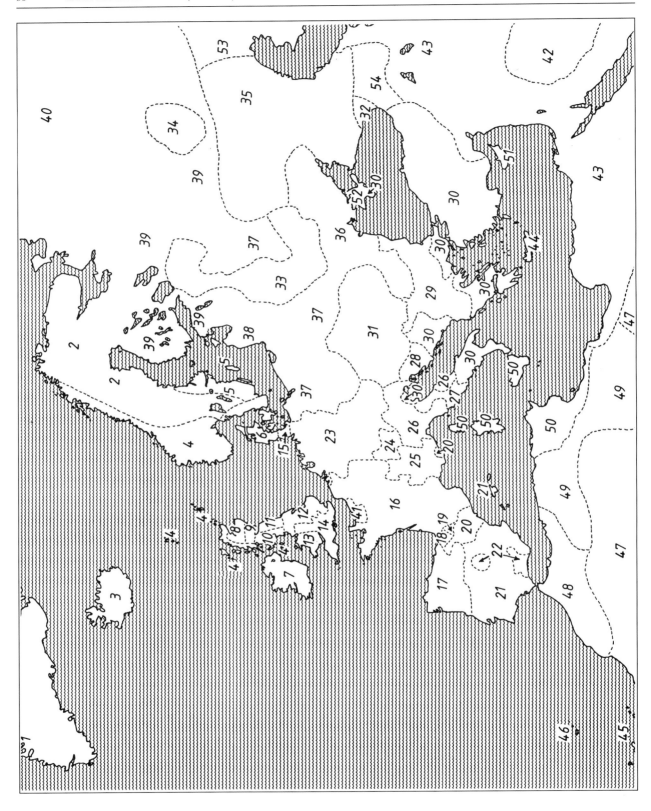

962: Anglo-Saxon kingdom of Northumbria loses the Edinburgh region to the Scottish kingdom of Alban.

983: Western Slav uprising against German rule in the river Elbe region.

987: Catalonia wins independence from the Carolingian French state.

990–1018: Polish conquests (some temporary) of Silesia, Little Poland (southern Poland), Moravia and Bohemia.

995: German conquest of Pomerania on the Baltic coast.

Late 10th century: Norse-Viking discovery and colonisation of Greenland; attempted settlement of parts of the north-eastern coast of North America.

1002–37: Imperial German control imposed on northern Italy.

1014: Celtic-Irish defeat Norse-Irish at the battle of Clontarf.

1018: Scottish kingdom of Alban defeats Anglo-Saxon kingdom of Northumbria at Carham; conquers Border region of modern Scotland; Byzantines destroy first Bulgarian kingdom in the Balkans.

1033: Pomerania wins independence from Germans and Poles.

1034–8: Celtic-Norse kingdom of Strathclyde and Galloway annexed by kingdom of Alban to create a united kingdom of Scotland.

Mid-11th century: Turkish Pechenegs occupy the lower Danubian plain (modern southern Romania and northern Bulgaria).

1066: Anglo-Saxon kingdom of England defeats Norwegian invasion at the battle of Stamford Bridge; Anglo-Saxons are defeated by Norman invasion at the battle of Hastings.

1068–9: Normans defeat Anglo-Saxon uprising.

1071: Italo-Normans complete their conquest of southern Italy.

1081: Italo-Normans defeat Byzantines at Durres.

1091: Balkan Pechenegs defeated by Byzantine Empire.

1096–9: First Crusade crosses Europe, Byzantine Empire and Muslim Syria to conquer Jerusalem.

ARMY RECRUITMENT

The Carolingian Empire and France

The leading western European military power of the early Middle Ages was the Carolingian Empire centred upon France and western Germany. Its standing army, or *scara*, was descended from that of the Merovingian Frankish kingdom but was now much larger. In fact the Carolingians were able to field greater forces than any of their enemies. The military burden still fell heaviest on the Franks themselves, or northern French as they were gradually coming to be known. But Carolingian armies also included Burgundians, Bavarians, Provençals, Occitans or southern French, as well as Lombards from Italy. Military service was increasingly tied to the possession or holding of land; the type of service and amount of equipment demanded of an individual being linked to the size of the latter's estate or *fief*.

Theoretically, all freemen still had an obligation of military service, but in reality this varied from one part of the Carolingian Empire to another. In some areas ordinary people, including priests, still fought in defence of castles and towns, but in the south the Emperor soon came to rely on non-Frankish professional *milites*, the forerunners of the medieval knight. Most of these were of Provençal, Aquitainian, Gascon or Visigothic origins. Of these the Gascons already had an excellent reputation as effective mercenary troops by the 8th century. There was even a reference to the enlistment of Muslim soldiers, though only during a rebellion against Carolingian authority.

Cavalry was now clearly of increasing importance in the Carolingian army, many of the first such horsemen apparently being Visigothic refugees from Muslim-ruled Spain. But by the 9th century the best cavalry were Lombards from northern Italy. Other light cavalry may have been recruited in fringe areas such as the Basque country, Brittany, Frisia and the newly conquered territories of eastern Germany.

Left: Europe, c. 911

1. Inuit-Eskimos
2. Saami-Lapps
3. Norwegian settlements
4. Norway
5. Sweden
6. Denmark
7. Irish kingdoms
8. Moray
9. Alba
10. Strathclyde
11. Northumberland
12. 'Danelaw'
13. Welsh principalities
14. Wessex
15. Hedeby
16. France
17. León
18. Navarre
19. Aragon
20. Minor Muslim states or enclaves
21. Amirate of Cordova
22. Rebel or autonomous areas within Amirate of Cordova
23. Kingdom of Germany
24. Upper Burgundy
25. Lower Burgundy
26. Kingdom of Italy
27. Papal States
28. Croatia
29. Bulgaria
30. Byzantine Empire
31. Hungary
32. Laz
33. Rus
34. Volga Bulgars
35. Khazars
36. Pechenegs
37. Slavs
38. Balts
39. Finns
40. Ugrians
41. Normans
42. Qarmatians
43. ʿAbbāsid Caliphate
44. Arab Amirate of Crete
45. Guanches
46. Uninhabited
47. Pagan Berbers
48. Idrīsids
49. Rustamids
50. Aghlabids
51. Joint ʿAbbāsid-Byzantine control
52. Goths
53. Ghuzz Turks
54. Armenia

Above: *A page from the Trierer Apokalypse; Carolingian manuscript, 8th–9th centuries. Despite the simplicity of the drawing, the similarity between the soldiers on the lower panel and those in 5th century late Roman carved ivory panels is obvious, even down to their haircuts. None of the riders yet uses stirrups; while the bare feet and long costumes of those on the left look remarkably Middle Eastern, perhaps reflecting Byzantine influence or that from Muslim-ruled Spain. (Cod. 31, f.63, Stadtbibliothek, Trier)*

Infantry still had a vital role to play and the *bannum*, general levy, or the *lantweri*, as it would be called in German-speaking areas, could be summoned from any part of the Carolingian state if an invasion were feared. Other lesser obligations included the provision of livestock or wagons for the army, and enforced labour on the building or repair of fortifications. Along the uneasy eastern frontier of the Carolingian Empire the defence of such fortifications usually relied upon local professional soldiers known as the *warda*.

During those generally peaceful years before the Viking invasions, a general infantry levy seems to have decayed and there was also a decline in the importance of unarmoured light cavalry. Warfare was, in fact, becoming dominated by the élite *milites* under the leadership of local or provincial feudal lords; a process strengthened by the fact that such troops alone seemed capable of dealing with Viking raiders. In France, by the 11th century, the virtually autonomous feudal aristocracy and their formidable retinues of armoured cavalry *milites* almost acted as military entrepreneurs. Sometimes they operated on their own; at other times they joined other lords in military 'joint ventures' in which their armed followers were almost like 'share-holders'. Warfare had, in fact, become a business as well as a way of life for the military élite.

Straightforward mercenaries, hiring themselves out on an individual basis, were also increasingly important in 11th century France, garrisoning castles and forming the core of the French ruler's army as he began the long hard struggle to restore the authority of the crown over his fragmented kingdom. During the 10th and 11th centuries southern France, or the Midi, was virtually independent with its own language of Occitan, as well as its own distinctive culture and military systems. This region was much less feudalised than northern France. Here a new class of professional *milites* served as local garrisons or in the retinues of great lords; often being paid in cash through local taxation, though many did have their own territorial estates as well.

The Empire: Germany

Following the fragmentation of the Carolingian Empire in the late 9th century, Germany emerged as the centre of what would eventually become known as the Holy Roman Empire. This huge rambling state would normally simply be called 'The Empire' by medieval western Europeans. Within a few decades Germany felt the full brunt of attack by Scandinavian Vikings from the north and by Magyars or Hungarians from the south-east. At the same time the German Empire consolidated and then expanded its own control over Slav peoples immediately to the east.

The raising of sufficient troops to meet these threats and ambitions was clearly a problem for the German Emperors, though the nobility, the Church and the peasantry all had clear military obligations. By the late 10th century the role of Church lands in furnishing armoured cavalry seems to have been particularly important, though the German imperial army also included horsemen from Swabia, Franconia, Bavaria, Saxony and Slav Bohemia. Saxony had, in fact, been the home territory of the new Ottonian ruling dynasty but it remained a relatively poor region with, at first, few armoured cavalry. Neighbouring, and even poorer, Thuringia continued to provide largely *inermes*, unarmoured horsemen, for many decades. Nevertheless the armoured *milites* had become the dominant

military élite by the 11th century, just as they had in France. The relative economic backwardness of Germany during this period, and its consequent lack of a money economy, also accounted for the rare appearance of mercenaries. Even so, allied Poles and Bohemians were quite often recorded. Another very distinctive sort of troops was, meanwhile, emerging in Germany; troops rarely seen elsewhere in western Europe. These were the *dienstleute* or *ministeriales*, non-noble 'serf cavalry'. They probably evolved out of the serf or even slave-origin guard units recruited by German magnates in the 11th century.

Generally speaking, the 'lower orders' were progressively being excluded from warfare in most parts of Germany, except in defence of the country's few fortified towns. Nevertheless infantry still had a part to play in certain special areas. This was the case in poorer provinces such as Saxony and Thuringia, and in isolated regions of marsh or mountain where military conditions still made foot soldiers valuable. Saxon peasant troops, the *agrarii milites* of the 10th century, were highly experienced and thus proved useful in warfare against Slav tribes to the east. They also demonstrated their worth against Norse-Viking and Magyar raiders. Nevertheless the last recorded general levy of peasants' militias was in AD 946. Thereafter such levies were only summoned locally in response to specific emergencies, and even these declined as the Viking and Magyar threats faded in the mid-11th century. Instead, urban militias started to appear in economically more developed areas within the Empire; notably in parts of the Duchy of Lotharingia in the west.

The Empire: Italy

The situation in Italy could hardly have been more different, despite the fact that a large part of the country was technically part of the Empire. Before Charlemagne's conquest of Lombard northern Italy, the originally Germanic Lombards formed an exceptionally well-equipped cavalry élite which long resisted giving equal military rights to indigenous Italian troops. In fact they did not do so until the mid-8th century. In central Italy, in what would become the Papal States, the ex-Carolingian *milites* merged with an existing landowning upper class who were largely of Latin-Roman origin to produce a new military aristocracy. During the 8th and 9th centuries there were probably still two separate 'Church' armies in central Italy; that of the Pope and that of the Archbishop of Ravenna, the latter having his own small cavalry bodyguard plus a levy of local cavalry enlisted by his bishops.

Military recruitment in northern Italy, before the fragmentation of the Carolingian Empire, was based upon an individual's wealth. For example, the poor were only expected to guard the coast against Muslim naval raids while the very poorest were exempt from military service altogether. From then on, however, the distinctively urban character of medieval northern Italian armies became steadily more apparent. Here cities had survived, and latterly even flourished, since the fall of the western Roman

Empire in a way not seen anywhere else except in Muslim-ruled al-Andalus in the Iberian peninsula. Most Italian cities actually belonged to the Church, rather than to the local nobility.

By the 10th century all free towns had their own professional *milites* backed up by citizen *cives* with clear military obligations. A century later the majority of Italian cities could field their own small but highly effective armies of *valvassores*, cavalry, of whom the *primi milites* or *milites majores* formed an élite and, in fact, an urban aristocracy. Less wealthy citizens formed what became the most effective infantry of 11th and 12th century western Christendom. Meanwhile, in the countryside the local aristocracy had their *mesnie* or *masnata*, military retinues of *gastaldii* or *milites*, most living off their own fiefs or estates, these being supported by rather less effective rural militias. Despite the fact that such Italian forces were among the militarily most potent in western Europe, the political and economic influence of the Italian cities ensured that the Emperor was rarely able to persuade them to serve north of the Alps.

Southern Italy

While northern Italy fell to the Carolingians, the now largely assimilated Italianised Lombards maintained their independence in southern Italy. Here they shared the region with a number of isolated Byzantine provinces and, at various times, with Muslim-occupied enclaves. There was no real feudal structure in early medieval southern Italy and military service depended upon a personal contract rather than being tied to the possession of land. Even the rural-based military aristocracy seems largely to have disappeared by the 10th century. Instead it was replaced by urban militias of both noble and bourgeois origin, plus local levies of serf origin who garrisoned the castles of their local lords.

A new Norman kingdom was, however, carved out in southern Italy and Sicily during the 11th century. Here the Normans were so few in number that they not only had to encourage other non-Norman northern knights to join them, but also had to rely on local troops. On the mainland of southern Italy such local troops consisted of Italian and Greek-Byzantine militias as well as rural non-military cavalry, often recruited from Church and monastic lands. In ex-Muslim Sicily the Normans almost immediately started recruiting their conquered Arab, Berber and indigenous converted Sicilian-Muslim foes; finding them not only the most loyal but also the most effective non-Norman troops available.

Anglo-Saxon England

Anglo-Saxon England, though in many ways strongly influenced by the Carolingian Empire, remained militarily distinct throughout the early Middle Ages. It was politically and militarily fragmented until almost the end of this period; yet the armies of various Anglo-Saxon kingdoms did have much in common. For example, there were almost always three separate forms of military obligation: first, service in an army itself; secondly, 'borough work' or the defending and building of fortifications; and thirdly, the maintenance of bridges.

By the 8th century each Anglo-Saxon king had his own élite of military followers, normally known as his *gesithas* or *comites*. Meanwhile the *folc* or people in general still had a military role, though it is hard to identify. *Thegns*, who themselves formed a local élite, were summoned and led by a king's representative or *earldorman*, or by the Church. That much was probably universal throughout almost all the Anglo-Saxon kingdoms; but Anglo-Saxon armies also differed from one another. Northumbria in the far north, for example, ruled over a large Celtic or 'North Welsh' subject population. From the late 7th century onwards, its army tended to be a largely static local defence force. Wessex, in the far south-west, included a large and prosperous but still potentially warlike landowning nobility. This enabled the rulers of Wessex to assemble an effective army for campaigns outside the borders of the kingdom itself. Meanwhile in Kent in the south-east, Frankish Carolingian influence was stronger than elsewhere. More is known about military recruitment in Mercia, in the Midlands of England. Here the army included a noble class of landowners known as *twelfhynde*, each equal in 'value' or status to six *coerls* who were themselves prosperous peasants rather than unfree serfs. It also seems likely that Mercia made greater military demands upon its population in order to maintain a large army with which it dominated much of Britain for many years. Even monks had to help build strategic bridges, and perhaps to garrison forts.

Information becomes more detailed in the 10th century, though the basic military systems remained much the same. In Wessex, for example, one man was theoretically levied from each *hide* or specified acreage of land for bridge and borough duties; one from each five *hides* for service in the army. The 'single *hide*' and 'five *hide*' units may have been a typical or at least theoretical basis for military recruitment in Anglo-Saxon England, but its real financial value clearly varied in different places and at different times.

Fundamental change only came about in the early 11th century, both as a result of the Norse-Viking invasions and during the period when Scandinavian kings actually ruled Anglo-Saxon England. Despite a ferocious struggle against the Vikings in the 9th and 10th centuries, the bulk of the Anglo-Saxon population had much fewer military obligations by the 11th century. From then on the heaviest burden fell on the south and west of England, in the heartlands of what had been the Kingdom of Wessex which, of course, had carried out the successful struggle against the Vikings.

A minor threat was still posed by Celtic Welsh raiders and so urban militias seem to have been more highly developed along the Welsh frontier. In most areas the general levy or *fyrd* still existed, though in slightly different forms in the overwhelmingly Anglo-Saxon south and in the strongly Scandinavian-influenced or settled north of the country. Yet the military scene was now dominated by professional soldiers in the service of both the king and of great provincial *earls*. The *thegns* now also formed a local aristocracy from which the military followers of kings and *earls* were largely recruited.

Richer men also often paid mercenaries to take their place if summoned for military service, but it remains unclear precisely how many of the king's own *housecarls*, *lithsmen* and *butescarls* should really be described as professional mercenaries. The *housecarls* were, in fact, an élite force first recruited by England's Danish king, Cnut, in 1018 to help him combat the growing power of the Anglo-Saxon *earls* or higher nobility. Some decades later the Anglo-Saxon dynasty of Wessex regained the English throne in the person of Edward the Confessor who had spent much of his life in Normandy. He, in turn, recruited Norman *milites* or knights as part of an effort to modernise the Anglo-Saxon army.

Celtic Regions
The Scandinavian Viking impact on the Celtic regions of the British Isles and on Ireland was just as dramatic as it was on Anglo-Saxon England – in some ways even more so. Prior to the Viking onslaughts the existing Celtic military traditions had, however, not been frozen and unchanging. In fact, they had continued to develop within their own rather limited horizons.

The Scots-Irish kingdom of Dal Riata in the western Highlands and Islands was, for example, above all a naval power. Its forces were summoned on a family or *cenéla* basis, there being three main *cenél* families or 'clans'. Every twenty households within such a *cenél* had to furnish twenty-eight oarsmen to man two warships. While the northern Picts of Orkney and the Hebrides were absorbed into the Norse 'Kingdom of the Isles', much of Scots-Irish Dal Riata was drawn into the steadily expanding Kingdom of Alba; itself the forerunner of the medieval Kingdom of Scotland. Scotland would, in fact, remain remarkably diverse in military terms throughout the Middle Ages. Its rulers drew upon the Northumbrian military heritage and English-speaking *thanes* of the south-east, the 'North Welsh' heritage and warriors of the south-west, the Scots-Irish of Dal Riata, the Celtic Picts of the north-east and eventually also the Norse of the 'Kingdom of the Isles'. In the mid-11th century the rival Scottish kings, Macbeth and Duncan, both enlisted a small number of Norman mercenaries; these men already being seen as the cavalry élite of their day.

Within Ireland the Viking raids and Norse settlement led to the emergence of a new group of warriors of mixed origin known as the Gall-gaidil, who were first mentioned in the mid-9th century. By then the Latin-based term *laích* or 'non-cleric' had largely come to mean a 'warrior'. On the other hand it appears almost certain that Celtic Irish clergymen continued to take part in warfare. This is strongly suggested by a number of 8th and 9th century laws which first exempted them from military service, and then attempted to bar them from fighting in the army.

The remaining British-Celtic or Welsh regions of Britain consisted of Wales itself and Cornwall, at least until the latter was conquered by Anglo-Saxon Wessex around 814. In both these British areas military recruitment was theoretically based upon the *cantref* or 'one hundred farmsteads'; each perhaps supplying one hundred warriors. This was clearly the case in Wales and is strongly suggested by the small amount of surviving evidence for Cornwall.

The Normans: Normandy and the British Isles
The Norse-Viking settlers or Normans of northern France soon lost most, though not all, of their Scandinavian military heritage. Their military aristocracy was very new compared to that of their French, and indeed of their Anglo-Saxon, neighbours. The Duke of Normandy was also relatively much more powerful within the Duchy of Normandy than was the King of France within his kingdom. As a result the duke could pick his own men and raise them to considerable power. And there were clearly plenty of highly skilled, indeed very warlike, individuals to choose from.

As a result Normandy soon became a significant exporter of armoured *miles* or knights in the early 11th century. By 1066, the year of Duke William's ambitious invasion of Anglo-Saxon England, Normandy seemed full of both landholding and landless cavalry. These included the *milites* or *mediae nobilitatis*, who were probably vassals of the duke and his leading followers, as well as *gregarii* or *stipendiarii* who served for wages and were bound to their leader by less formal oaths of allegiance. The Norman army similarly included significant numbers of spear-armed foot soldiers and infantry archers, making one of the most cohesive and effective fighting forces seen in the 11th century. In addition the duke could still summon the *arrière-ban* or general levy of all freemen. For the invasion of England, Duke William also enlisted the help of substantial allied forces from both Brittany and Flanders.

Once the Normans had completed their conquest of England they found themselves ruling a relatively prosperous and comparatively peaceful kingdom. A large part of the old Anglo-Saxon military élite had been wiped out during the Norman Conquest and in unsuccessful attempts at resistance. The Normans' subsequent attempt to convert several remaining Anglo-Saxon military groups into *miles* or knights failed, but the old local levy or *fyrd* remained. So did the obligation to erect castles and probably to maintain bridges. By the late 11th century the rank and file of the Anglo-Norman army was of varied origins. It already included Normans, French, Flemings, Bretons, noblemen hoping to regain a lost inheritance, adventurers, mercenaries including both knights and crossbowmen, assimilated English and Welsh. Indeed the latter seem to have been better able to fit into the new order than did the Anglo-Saxons themselves.

Scandinavia and the Baltic

Not surprisingly, the fringes of medieval Europe developed their own singular military characteristics, and this was as true of Scandinavia in the north as it was of Norman Sicily in the south. In Denmark, for example, the *liedang* levy of men, ships and military equipment emerged in its fully developed form in the 10th century. Nevertheless, the expectation that all freemen should help defend an area if it were attacked was fundamentally the same as that found in Germanic or Germanic-influenced parts of Europe. In Norway a complete levy was only summoned in defence, but a half-levy could also be called up for offensive operations.

Throughout most of this period Scandinavia was an exporter of military manpower, usually as predatory raiders but sometimes as professional mercenaries. After the mid-11th century, however, there was a small but interesting influx of foreigners. Among the most significant were Anglo-Saxon refugees from those once-élite families who had lost both status and a military role after the Norman Conquest of 1066. Others had been forced to flee after supporting an abortive Danish invasion of England in 1069. Some of these men joined the bodyguard of Norway's king; more went to Denmark from where they joined in several unsuccessful Danish invasions of England in the 1070s. Many also travelled on to Byzantium where they eventually came to dominate the Byzantine Emperor's famous *Varangian Guard*.

Eastern Europe

The military situation in eastern Europe and the Balkans was even more varied from the 8th to 11th centuries. There appear to be no significant references to foreign soldiers during the years when Poland emerged as an independent kingdom. This was, of course, still a poor, backward, fragmented and rather isolated region. In fact, one early 10th century Slav tribe near Meissen in what is now eastern Germany was recorded as being so poor following a famine that its fighting men hired themselves

out, apparently as a unit, to neighbouring tribes or states.

None of the emerging eastern European states had such a distinctive military system as did Hungary. The Avars, who were overthrown by Charlemagne, and the Magyars who took over the great Hungarian Plain two centuries later, both seem to have made greater use of cavalry than did their predecessors in this area, the Huns. Nevertheless, even this might be exaggerated since both Avar and Magyar armies included a large number of infantry.

The Magyars, or Hungarians as they became, themselves consisted of an aristocratic élite of horse-archers using Central Asian steppe, or more probably Sassanian-style, tactics. They were not strictly speaking nomads, but were a transhumant pastoral people who also depended upon farming and fishing. Even in the mid-10th century the emerging kingdom of Hungary included two distinct communities; a dominant Magyar military élite which clung to a horse-centred way of life, and a mass of settled peasantry of varied but largely non-Magyar origins. The latter included a great many Slavs who clearly played an important, though subsidiary, military role; particularly in defence of the northern frontiers in what is now Slovakia. By the late

Below: Bronze belt strap-end showing a horse-archer hunting; from Klarafalva, Avar, early 8th century. He is using a much more advanced and regularly recurved composite bow, almost of the later Turkish form. The keyhole-shaped object on his right hip is an arrow-quiver. It is clearly of the Central Asian nomadic form which incorporated a lid or flap fully to enclose the arrows and thus protect them from the elements. (Mora Ferenc Museum, Szeged)

Right: Rock-relief carving on a cliff-face near Madara, believed to show the Bulgarian Khān; Tervel, 701–18, hunting a lion with a greyhound. The dating of this rock-relief carving is still a matter of debate; some scholars believe that it is Thracian from many centuries BC. The similarity with Sassanian Persian rock-reliefs is striking, however, even down to some elements of the sadly very eroded horse harness.

10th century the rulers of Hungary were hiring Russian, Italian and German mercenaries as well as encouraging their own Magyar tribal followers to settle as a *jobbágy*, local military élite, around the castles which were now springing up in various parts of the kingdom. The Russian mercenaries soon disappeared, but during the 11th century Stephen, the first anointed King of Hungary, attracted a large numbers of *hospites*, foreigner troops and settlers of perhaps largely Bavarian and Italian origin, to his court. There they were joined by a small number of Anglo-Saxon refugee-soldiers.

Meanwhile a large part of the Magyar Hungarian élite remained true to their own basically tribal and horse-oriented military culture. The survival of this distinctive way of life in the very centre of Europe was helped by several subsequent waves of Turkic steppe peoples who arrived, not as conquerors like the Magyars themselves, but as refugees from more powerful peoples farther east.

This flow of Central Asian tribes westwards along the Eurasian steppe 'corridor' from Mongolia, through Turkestan to the Ukraine and, once over the Carpathian mountains, into Hungary, remained a constant feature of medieval eastern and central European history. The Huns were not the first, though the Mongols were perhaps the last. The Pechenegs were the most numerous of those who

entered Hungary during the late 10th and 11th centuries; fleeing the Kipchaqs behind them. They arrived first as raiders, then being permitted to settle after their defeat by the Hungarian king. Subsequently these Pechenegs could be found defending the western frontier of Hungary against German encroachment, in Slovakia as a precaution against the Poles, and in the north-east as a barrier against the Russians. Another smaller Turkish tribe which fled the Kipchaqs into Hungary in the 11th century were the Berends.

Some nomadic groups, moving westwards, chose to turn south into the steppes of Wallachia in what is now southern Romania, rather than cross the Carpathian mountains. Many pressed on into Byzantine territory, where their fate was similar to those of the nomads who penetrated Hungary. Large numbers of true nomads were never, in fact, a characteristic of the Balkans. This remained an area more suited to a transhumant seminomadic pastoral life, rather than to the true nomadism of the steppes.

Those powerful nomadic peoples who did penetrate the Balkans naturally had a considerable impact on military recruitment and military organisation in the newly emerging, largely Slav, states of this region. They would soon be better described as semi-nomads, and although they con-

'Psalter' from the School of Corbie; French, 9th century. Whether this foot soldier really is using an oval shield, or the artist was attempting an uncharacteristic piece of perspective drawing, remains unknown. The man's sword, with its large pommel but very short broad quillons, is, however, very early in design. (MS. 18, f.67, Bibliothèque Municipale, Amiens)

tinued to play a significant role for many centuries, the armies of states like Bulgaria were, in numerical terms at least, overwhelmingly Slav from the 8th to early 10th centuries. The same was even more true of Serbia and Croatia as they also emerged as separate entities. The main difference between Serbia and Croatia on the one hand, and Bulgaria on the other, was the latter's ability to recruit substantial numbers of ex-Byzantine prisoners of war. Such troops, not surprisingly, brought with them many advanced, and indeed sophisticated, military techniques or structures.

MILITARY ORGANISATION

The Carolingian Empire and France
Early Carolingian military organisation was basically the same as that of the preceding Merovingian Franks. The small army of Austrasia in what are now the Benelux countries, north-eastern France and western Germany formed its core. It also provided the ruler's most loyal followers, including most of those men placed in charge of conquered territories. *Benefices* of land were now given in return for military service; those who received such land forming a new force of *vassi dominici* troops. But such estates were not at first hereditary and it took many years for a hereditary system to become widely accepted.

Even so, early Carolingian rulers enjoyed greater effective power than most of their foes. As a result they were usually capable of fielding larger armies. The élite *scara* basically consisted of young warriors living near the ruler's palace; though they could also be sent to garrison other important places. Charlemagne's own *scara* appears to have been divided into three ranks or perhaps three guard units: the *scholares*, the *scola* and the *milites aulae regiae*, these clearly being inspired by Romano-Byzantine prototypes. The ancient Roman army was also held up as a model of discipline and for its supposed lack of superfluous finery.

The *scara* was clearly mounted, though it may still have included mounted infantry as well as true cavalrymen. Charlemagne certainly put great effort into maintaining the quality and training of his armoured cavalry. A new *lantweri* or militia system was also introduced to ensure that the *benefice* estates of the military élite were defended while their owners were on campaign. This was particularly necessary in exposed frontier regions where *benefice* holders might otherwise have been reluctant to march off on distant campaigns leaving their own land exposed to enemy raiding. Several of the frontier regions were themselves governed by almost autonomous *Counts*, some of whom had their own vassals to garrison the area. On other frontiers local professional *warda* soldiers lived in military colonies, again of apparent Romano-Byzantine inspiration. The newly conquered *Limes Saxonicus* in northern Germany were, in fact, organised remarkably like a Byzantine *akritai* frontier.

On campaign the Carolingian army was led by the ruler or by his *majordome*, deputy, while men of loyal Frankish origin commanded all the main units. The cavalry was theoretically divided into units of one hundred; each with its own banner. Latin terminology was used, though sometimes in an inappropriate way. Consequently, vernacular terminology of early Germanic origin not only gives a more reliable picture, but was absorbed by many later medieval languages. Thus the *scara* élite army became the *scharen*, *echielles* or *schieri*; the *bandwa* flag became the *banieren* or *banières*; while there may also have been a Germanic term behind the subsequent word for army divisions, *bataelgen*, *batailles* or *battaglie*.

By the late 10th century the term *miles* took over from *vassus* or *fidelis* to indicate a warrior, and would gradually take on the connotations of 'medieval knight'. It did not, however, indicate superior social status until the mid-11th century. But from then on the *miles* knight was inextricably bound up with a feudal system based on landholding, in which each social class, at least in theory, played its part. The peasantry fed the military class; the military defending the peasantry and offering military support to the ruler via a local lord, while the ruler himself offered land to the lord and by extension to the military knight. The fact that this 'pyramid of service and reward' almost nowhere worked in quite such a neat fashion cannot alter the fact that it was seen as an ideal. It was, in fact, regarded as such by both the military themselves, and by the Church which had long interpreted the world in terms of 'estates' or classes. Whether or not the idealised 'feudal system' was ever a reality, the castle had, by the 11th century, become the focus of rural life, local defence and local administration. This was particularly apparent in northern France and many other similar areas with, as yet, very few or small and insignificant towns.

The situation in southern France developed in a different way. Here a large class of small freehold-landowners continued to owe military service as *fideles* or followers of a local lord, rather than becoming his feudal vassals as in the north. Here service remained more personal. By the 11th century there were a great many *milites* or *caballarios* cavalrymen of free, but not quite knightly, status, garrisoning the many castles which had sprung up across the region. Many, if not most, of these *milites* still owned their own small amounts of land; but this was often a secondary consideration to men who now saw themselves as professional soldiers paid through local taxation. Other such professionals, both infantry and cavalry, were similarly recruited from a class of minor officials which had existed since Roman times. Others even came from the class of unfree serf peasants.

The Empire: Germany

The break-up of the Carolingian Empire in the late 9th century saw Germany and Italy each develop its own distinctive military system; despite the fact that much of Italy formed part of what might be called a 'German Empire'. Within Germany itself, however, the ancient pre-Christian tribal regions had survived in the form of Duchies. Now their Dukes re-emerged as a local political as well as merely military leadership. This was also reflected in 10th century German armies; particularly those from Saxony which reflected such tribal origins, with units from Westfalia, Engern, Eastfalia and Thuringia.

These regions had no real cavalry tradition of their own. Instead the new rulers of Germany, whose power was based in Saxony, created a new armoured cavalry 'tradition'. This proved itself capable of defeating the raiding Magyars – though only after many years of savage warfare. Next, the Emperors set about restructuring the German military system. Above all they created an essentially cavalry force of *milites* led by Dukes, Counts and frontier marcher lords known as *Margraves*. As in northern France, the local knights or *miles armatus* were supported by *benefice* estates, though in the newly conquered Slav areas of what is now eastern Germany they were more directly maintained by a subject population. The Church continued to play a greater or more obvious military and political role than in France. Perhaps as a result the term *miles* had more spiritual, less overtly sword and power-wielding connotations in Germany than in France or England.

The Empire: Italy

South of the Alps, Italy had long been both richer and economically more developed than either France or Germany. Yet it may also have been militarily less sophisticated than the Carolingian heartlands farther north. Nevertheless, the army of the 8th century Lombard kingdom was better armed and had a higher proportion of cavalry than did that of the early Carolingians; its troops being led by a Duke or Count, or by a *gastaldius* representing the ruler himself.

Book of Maccabees, from St. Gall; Ottonian Germany, c.924. Not one horseman in this battle-scene is using a couched lance; all brandish them aloft and thrust either forwards or downwards in the old style of combat. Each spear also has two pairs of lugs or flanges beneath its blade. The men have relatively small, short-sleeved mail hauberks. Most of their helmets, however, appear to be of rounded two-piece construction like late Roman helmets, though a few are pointed. Where it is visible, these helmets also have some form of pendant neck protection which is clearly not a mail coif. In fact it looks more like a type of aventail as was used in eastern lands for many more centuries. (MS. Periz. Fol. 17, Universiteits-bibliotheek, Rijks Universiteit, Leiden)

Following Charlemagne's conquest of northern and central Italy the personal military retinues of *gasindii* of the newly imposed Frankish Counts rose still further in importance. Here each Count was responsible for a city and diocese in this very urbanised part of Europe, while exposed frontier regions were placed under a *Marquis* – comparable to the *Margraves* of Germany.

At the start of the 11th century the bulk of the northern and central Italian military aristocracy still lived in rural castles defended by their own *mesnie* armed retinues, many of whom in turn had their own *fiefs*. But this basically feudal structure was not reflected in the towns and cities, most of which were now governed by bishops and defended by their own urban militias. The latter primarily consisted of *primi milites* under *vidame* lieutenants, who served as *capitani*, 'captains of the people' and 'captains of the gates', supported by *milites minores*, vassal *vavassores* and, at the lowest rank, the *vavassini*. Theoretically all such troops were available to the German Emperor north of the Alps. In reality they fought for their own local interests, particularly in the cities. On several occasions they also fought against Imperial German armies – often with considerable success. These cities were not, however, yet communes. The first recorded communal militia or *compagna* of all arms-bearing men led by elected consuls, was organised in Genoa in 1097. It emerged in response to the Preaching of the First Crusade, rather than as a direct result of local military need.

Once again the military situation evolved rather differently in central Italy where the militias of Rome and Ravenna appear to have become permanent organisations during the 8th and 9th centuries. That of Ravenna consisted of twelve sections; eleven being *bandi*, military formations of local *iuvenes*, young men, and *numeri*, garrison troops, the twelfth being reserved for non-combatant men of the Church. In Rome such units were led by aristocractic *patronii*, while the Pope could also call upon the landed military aristocracy of the surrounding areas. Further pressure from Muslim naval raids led to the evolution of a small but effective Papal Roman army as well as urban militias in most other central Italian cities by the 11th century.

Southern Italy

The Church also played a leading role in the military organisation of southern Italy; particularly in the remaining Lombard Duchies and Principalities of this part of the country, as well as in some coastal cities. In several areas bishops and abbots not only built castles and had their own cavalry retinues, but even personally led these men into battle. During this period, however, the only maritime city of southern Italy which is known to have had its own land forces or *milites* was Naples. This, of course, excludes the forces of the strictly Byzantine regions of Apulia and Calabria.

Anglo-Saxon England

Anglo-Saxon England was influenced by developments in the Carolingian Empire and its successor states, most obviously France. Yet England's military organisation remained very distinct. In the 7th and 8th centuries, for example, the warriors of the Kingdom of Northumbria were supposedly supported by *benefice* estates, much as in Charlemagne's Empire. Perhaps partially as a result of this pressure on available land, there soon appears to have been a troublesome surplus of landless young fighting men and of redundant soldiers in areas that had enjoyed a prolonged spell of peace, at least until the sudden arrival of the Vikings. A continuing threat of Welsh raids seems to have kept the Mercian army busy, while the kings of Wessex seem to have managed to maintain an effective, easily mobilised and remarkable mobile army without too many social strains. Here all land remained theoretically the king's, to be taken back if military obligations were neglected. In reality, however, the estates of the military élite of Wessex soon became hereditary. In the small Anglo-Saxon Kingdom of Kent, there was little evidence of a military aristocracy holding land from the king. Instead the *leorde* or royal army seems to have remained closer to the old concept of a personal retinue of loyal followers.

Throughout most of the Anglo-Saxon era the local *hundred*, or subdivision of a shire, remained the theoretical basis of military organisation and recruitment. It even survived in the Viking-ruled and Norse-settled north where it was known by the new Scandinavian name of *wapentake*. The *hundred* continued to be recorded during the early Anglo-Norman period, and in some respects even later. Before the unification of Anglo-Saxon England, the *fyrd* or local levy could be summoned without specific royal permission. Here it appeared that each section of the various Anglo-Saxon armies was normally led by an *earldorman*, while the élite of more disciplined *thegns* served in a king's own retinue under his direct command. Even after Anglo-Saxon England was finally united, it seems as if larger armies still fought in distinct regional or even ethnic units.

Several significant changes took place during the last century of Anglo-Saxon history. England was now united

Left: *Relief-carved cross-slab, probably illustrating a defeat of the Anglo-Saxon North-umbrians by the Kingdom of Alba; Pictish, 8th century. Several interesting feature are clear on this simple but lively carving. For example, one Pict has his large round shield – here shown almost in section from the side – hung from a giuge around his neck and resting upon his left arm. He has a man armed with a sword and small shield ahead of him, and another spearman to the rear. This is almost exactly the same system of men in ranks that would still be used by 12th century north Italian infantry, and by 14th century infantry from Flanders. The Anglo-Saxon horse-man charging from the right also wears a rounded helmet with a long nasal, very similar to the helmet found a few years ago in 8th century Anglo-Saxon York. (Aberlemno churchyard, Scotland)*

under the ruling dynasty of Wessex, except for a brief interlude when it formed part of a Danish Empire. Meanwhile most small campaigns consisted of frontier operations carried out by professional forces, whereas larger campaigns were usually defensive in nature. The military élite was clearly becoming more professional. For example, a new force of royal *housecarls* was set up, perhaps inspired by the *jomsvikings* of Denmark. They were not exactly mercenaries, but do seem to have had a corporate contract with the ruler. Under this they were maintained and paid by means of taxation. Some *housecarls* were used to garrison fortified boroughs, the rest being based at court where, with the household *thegns* and socially higher ranking *cnihtas*, they formed the king's personal retinue.

Left: *Egil the archer defending his home', carved whalebone panel on the famous Franks Casket; Northumbrian Anglo-Saxon, early 8th century. The same kind of rounded helmet with a long nasal is worn by one of the attackers. Surprisingly, perhaps, the helmeted man is not one of the two figures who have mail hauberks. Egil himself, within his walled or stockaded home, is clearly using a very crude form of simple bow; probably an early type of longbow. (Inv. 67.1-20.1, British Museum, London)*

Other *thegns* owed their immediate allegiance to the Church, or to one of the great *Earls* who now dominated large parts of the country. Some of these *Earls* eventually had their own units of *housecarls*. In battle, however, it seems that the *thegns* fought around a nucleus of élite royal *housecarls*. Another new force, the *butscarls*, were also mentioned during the last years of Anglo-Saxon England; perhaps being mercenary naval troops. The great *Earls* similarly now controlled the provincial *fyrd* or levies. On other occasions these are again recorded being led by bishops or by local royal representatives such as *high reeves* and *sherifs*. While there seems to have been no geographical limitation on the duties required of a *fyrd*, it never appears to have fought outside its own region except when forming part of a larger royal army.

Celtic Regions

If Anglo-Saxon England was different from most of the rest of Europe, then the Celtic lands of the far west and north-west were even more so. Nevertheless, they, like Anglo-Saxon England, were again strongly influenced by the Norse-Vikings.

Little is known of the military organisation of Pictish northern Scotland. This was a matrilineal society, though ruled by kings, and later evidence suggests that various regions were governed by hereditary *mormaers* who may also have had local military responsibilities. Meanwhile an army on campaign was commanded by a *toiseach*. There was probably a comparable commander for the fleet, since the Picts remained a considerable naval power. Much more is known about Scots-Irish Dal Riata in the west. Here a *Rí Ruirech* high-king ruled over several sub-kings, while the fighting men were both summoned and organised according to their *cenél* or clan. Sixty to one hundred households theoretically produced one *baile* or military unit; though this organisation was in fact more naval than land-based. The basic unit was a *davach*; being enough to crew one fighting ship. These could also be subdivided into *ceathramh:* perhaps to be identified as fighting 'squads'. Dal Riata was an exceptionally fragmented kingdom, consisting as it did of separate islands and peninsulas. As a result its essentially early Irish military structure did not evolve much further; unlike the military situation within Ireland itself. Nevertheless the *davach* survived the Norse-Viking occupation and colonisation of so much of the Scottish Highlands and Islands; though it was given a new name, becoming the *tír unga* naval-military unit of later years.

A new kingdom, that of Scotland itself, was meanwhile evolving on the mainland. Here the *thane*, modelled upon the *thegn* of the Anglo-Saxon kingdom of Northumbria, was the basis of military organisation. He was also responsible for summoning troops at a *shire* level, while the higher aristocracy of Scottish *Earls* did the same at a regional level. The Scottish *shire* also remained the basic military unit. By the 11th century, however, the Scottish kings had shifted the centre of their state southwards, away from the

Gilded bronze container of the Stowe Missal; Celtic Irish, 11th–12th centuries. The main difference between this little warrior on foot and those in most art from Britain, and indeed the rest of Europe, is the very small shield or buckler which he carries. Such small bucklers are typical of most early medieval Celtic Irish sources and suggest a skirmishing, light infantry form of tactics unlike the shield wall tactics of the Anglo-Saxons and the Scandinavian Vikings from the 9th century onwards. (National Museum of Ireland, Dublin)

eastern Highlands to the central Lowlands of Scotland. This more fertile and more easily governed region they then used as their military powerbase; almost after the fashion of an Anglo-Norman *marcher* or frontier lord.

Wales and Cornwall still had much in common; social and military classes in both areas still reflecting their shared Romano-British origins. The *plou* or people, from the Latin *plebes*, were divided into a number of *tref*, tribes or families. These in turn inhabited several *ker*, households which were, however, quite separate from a *caer* or fortified site. In Cornwall the *cantref* military division of one hundred households was also known as a *keverang*, meaning 'battle'. Even after Cornwall was conquered by Anglo-Saxon Wessex in 814 or 815, its military organisation remained much as it had been before, except for the division of the two easternmost *keverangs* into five smaller units.

Traditional Irish kings ruled men, not land, which gave them considerable military authority. Their *tuatha* tribal forces varied in size but were again theoretically based upon units of one hundred; each such *cet* being commanded by a noble *aire*. A *tricha cet* of three hundred constituted a large army and would be subdivided into *baile* units, each recruited from a specific territory. This military system survived basically unchanged until the end of Celtic Irish independence later in the Middle Ages.

The Normans: Normandy and the British Isles

The Duchy of Normandy in northern France was, of course, itself of Viking origin and by the 11th century its armies were among the most highly organised in western Europe. The typical, though far from universal, Norman knight held a *fief de haubert* which enabled him to maintain himself, his horse and his increasingly expensive military equipment. Such *fiefs* varied a great deal in size and value; yet the concept of the 'poor knight' was strictly relative. No truly poor man could be capable of maintaining his own effectiveness as a properly armoured cavalryman. On the other hand, there were plenty of lower-status but still land-holding military *vavasseurs*. These troops, situated between the knight and the peasantry, fitted rather untidily into the theoretical feudal structure.

The imposition of a centralised military and governmental system on the Duchy of Normandy was largely the work of Duke William – soon to become King William the Conqueror of England. In fact he achieved a remarkable degree of co-operation between the ruler and his military aristocracy; largely by adopting a warlike and aggressive policy, winning new lands and putting his own most loyal followers in charge of key castles as well as military forces.

At first the Norman élite of newly conquered England carried a much heavier military burden than they had done within Normandy itself. Their king was not really interested in how sufficient numbers of knights were raised; simply that they be available when he needed them. Nor did these Anglo-Norman knights really settle down into their new country until the conquest was sta-

bilised in the late 1070s. From then on, however, the remarkable stability and relative peace achieved by the Anglo-Norman monarchy led to a gradual demilitarisation of this new Anglo-Norman aristocracy when compared to their colleagues in France.

Only the Royal Household or *familia regis* remained as a really efficient military structure. It furnished guards and escorts, and formed the nucleus of a larger army in time of war. Within the *familia regis* the king's *master constable* was placed in charge of discipline at Court. It was he who provided guards and was also responsible for the horses and messengers, as well as for the Royal Hunt.

Princes and great barons also had their own smaller military *familia*. The household knights in such a *familia* would normally be young *bachelors*; not necessarily unmarried men but those still awaiting their inheritance or perhaps a reward from their lord which would enable them to maintain their own households. These *bachelors* were normally under the command of a *marshal* or *constable*. Even so the numbers of such household knights declined rapidly as Anglo-Norman England became one of the most peaceful countries in western Europe.

The only real exceptions to this bucolic state of affairs within England were found in frontier *Marches* and along the eastern coast which was still under a threat of Scandinavian invasion. In fact, by the late 11th century many so-called knight's *fees* or *fiefs* no longer supported real knights; particularly on monastic land. Here and elsewhere the Anglo-Norman knights so recently descended from William the Conqueror's fearsome followers had become a rather typically English rural gentry. *Castle guard*, the garrisoning of a lord's or a king's fortified places, had been a new form of military obligation introduced by the Normans; yet as the years passed even this tended to be done by paid professional substitutes.

Scandinavia and the Baltic

While the originally Viking Normans rapidly developed the most effective military system seen in western Europe, in Scandinavia itself the Norse-Vikings' own infantry-dominated military traditions were changing. This was largely, though not entirely, a result of German influence from the south. Early in the 9th century the king of Denmark raised the first recorded real cavalry forces in Scandinavia. Thereafter Viking armies included an ever increasing number of mounted men, with a proportionate decline in the significance of infantry, except, perhaps, in the Viking-ruled parts of the British Isles.

From the late 10th century large and extremely sophisticated military camps also appeared in Denmark. These probably contained permanent garrisons; indicating strong, effective discipline and a high degree of professionalism. Similarly the *jomsvikings* emerged as a sort of professional military 'commune' with their own rules of conduct and customs, and living on Danish royal estates. Progress was slower in Norway and Sweden with no clear

Carved deer antler in the form of a helmeted head; Scandinavian, 11th century. Despite its highly stylised, purely conical shape, this helmet is obviously a spangen-helm of riveted segment construction, with a long nasal. (Statens Historiska Museer, Stockholm; Antik-varisk-topografiska arkivet, photograph, Sóren Hallgren)

formal subdivision of the *here* or army until the second half of the 10th century.

During these centuries the other peoples of the Baltic emerge into the light of history. In 8th century Finland, for example, a Finno-Ugrian population previously dominated by Scandinavian culture now developed its own distinctive culture with its associated military systems. At this stage the Estonians south of the Gulf of Finland were still virtually identical with the Finns on the northern side; but farther south the Baltic peoples of what are now southern Latvia, Lithuania and coastal Poland already had fiercely effective tribal armies. Such tribal forces were known as a *karias* among the Lithuanians, and as a *karya* among the Prussians.

These pagan tribes became increasingly militarised during the 11th century. As a result more rigid social and military divisions emerged as the Balts' Christian neighbours sought to impose their own cultures upon what would remain the last bastions of paganism within Europe. But as yet they remained tribally organised. The Prussians never really achieved a national identity, while that of the Lithuanians had to await the 12th century when it was forged in exceptionally ferocious guerrilla warfare against invading Crusader forces from Scandinavia and Germany.

Eastern Europe

South of the Balts lay the lands of the western Slavs. Of these the Poles became Catholic, whereas the Slav tribes of what is now north-eastern Germany remained fiercely pagan for many decades. Among these pagan Slav tribes, the high priest of the idol Svantovit in the pagan shrine at Arkona is recorded as having his own war-band of three hundred dedicated horsemen.

By the 10th century the ruler of Poland also had a small élite force known as his *druzyna* which, like comparable royal forces to the west, could form the core of a larger army. But, well into the 12th century, the great majority of Polish warriors remained unarmoured infantry. Even among the cavalry, armoured troops remained rare until the 11th century. Like Poland, the slightly richer and more urbanised Czech state of Bohemia was under strong German military influence. In fact Bohemia would be absorbed into the German Empire. Although never losing its Slav identity, Bohemia became, in almost all other respects, virtually identical with its German neighbours.

The ethnic diversity of early medieval Hungary led to a singularly complex military structure. The original Finno-Ugrian Magyar tribes had each been led by a *hadnagy* or duke. These men then selected their prince from the Arpad ruling family; other major military decisions theoretically being made by the whole Magyar people in assembly. The army, during this early phase, traditionally consisted of seven sections made up of one hundred and eight clans, each divided into theoretical military units of a hundred men, in turn subdivided into groups of a dozen riders.

In reality, of course, the organisation, leadership and conduct of warfare was soon taken over by tribal leaders and their retinues of full-time warriors; at least after the Magyar people had conquered the Hungarian plain. Magyar raids westward across Germany and south into Italy may have been defeated during the 10th century, but the Magyars clung to their newly conquered homeland. There they built a powerful medieval state which not only successfully resisted German attempts at conquest, but gradually took control of a huge part of central and eastern Europe.

As a result, slightly different forms of military organisation, or at least varying military terminology, were found in various parts of the medieval Hungarian state. For example, the rank of *gyula* was second only to that of a royal prince and was found in Transylvania, while the rank of *ispán*, provincial governor, came from the Slav title of *zhupan*. Western Hungary was, like Bohemia and Poland, under stronger western European military and cultural influence; but in Transylvania, in the east of the medieval kingdom of Hungary, several earlier almost nomadic characteristics survived. Here, local military lords, many of whom seem to have been of Romanian or Vlach rather than Magyar origin, might live in rambling wooden houses surrounded by stables for their and their retinues' best horses. Meanwhile other semi-wild horse herds were tended by what can only be described as 'cowboys' in the surrounding countryside. Further differences were reflected in the fact that in Transylvania there might be a small Orthodox, rather than Catholic, monastery next to the local lord's dwelling hall. This part of Europe was, of course, geographically closer to Byzantine Constantinople than to Rome or Paris.

Byzantine Orthodox Christianity also came to dominate most of the Balkans to the south. Nevertheless, there were significant Catholic enclaves such as those of Slovenia, Croatia, the Dalmatian coast of the Adriatic, and parts of Albania. The military structures of these regions developed under strong Carolingian influence during the 8th and 9th centuries. This was followed by powerful German and Hungarian military influence, and even of direct rule over some areas, in the 11th century. Yet the social structures of many such areas remained largely tribal well into the 11th century.

Byzantine influence was also strong, though it only had a permanent military impact in areas that became Orthodox Christian. These included Serbia, Bulgaria and most of Albania, plus Wallachia and Moldavia in what is now Romania. A small number of élite Byzantine-style armoured cavalry may first have appeared in Serbian armies by the 10th century, and thereafter Serbia was fully within the Byzantine sphere of military traditions. Conditions were rather different to the east, in what would eventually emerge as the Romanian principalities of Wallachia and Moldavia. Here successive waves of Turkic nomadic peoples migrated into what was in effect the westernmost limits of the vast Eurasian steppe-lands. Most such tribes achieved a brief local dominance; forming a military aristocracy before they were either absorbed by the indigenous peoples or had to flee from the steppes altogether. Many such groups did, in fact, cross the Carpathian mountains to the west or the river Danube to the south as yet another wave of nomads came snapping at their heels.

South of the Danube, the originally Turkic or even Hunnic Bulgars were themselves no longer strictly steppe nomads by the time they conquered most of Thrace from the Romano-Byzantine Empire in the 7th century. Thereafter, they built a kingdom and a very effective army, with the same concern for fortifications as shown by their Byzantine rivals. The new army of this settled Bulgarian state was dominated by the *boyars* or great tribal nobles, who apparently retained a military role even after Bulgaria converted to Christianity in the 9th century. These years also saw significant military changes with the appearance of a smaller, more élite force under stricter royal control. The details of its military administration clearly reflected Byzantine inspiration. But earlier Turkic traditions remained; particularly in the Bulgarian army's continuing reputation for fierce discipline. The kingdom itself was also divided into military provinces; its frontiers being guarded by full-time professional troops. All of this contributed to early medieval Bulgaria becoming the most powerful state in the Balkans, often rivalling the Byzantine Empire itself.

STRATEGY AND TACTICS

Early medieval Western European strategy was based on raiding and ravaging. As such it reflected Vegatius' statement that 'famine is more terrible than the sword' – even if the military commanders in question had no actual knowledge of that late Roman military theorist. The common soldier fought either in defence of his home or in the hope of profit; in other words for booty. Meanwhile defending forces attempted to limit the damage caused by enemy ravaging. In more sophisticated armies this involved attacking an invader's supply lines and harassing his foragers, but only engaging him in battle as a last resort or if the conditions where clearly very favourable. The main problem facing both attackers and defenders was that of maintaining their armies in the field for as long as possible. This could clearly be very difficult at a time when, and in areas where, logistical support and the ability to feed or pay troops was rudimentary at best.

Broad Strategy

The Carolingian Empire proved itself very effective in dealing with its various strategic problems. In the 8th century Carolingian armies probably still included a large proportion of infantry; these making great use of river transport while campaigning over remarkably long distances. Charlemagne introduced few major changes, but the relative size and efficiency of his forces often enabled

Right: Tactics, 650–1100
1. The years during which Charlemagne and his immediate successors launched invasions against their neighbours; showing the system of multi-pronged invasions and of convergence by several armies in the heart of enemy territory favoured by the Carolingians (after Verbruggen)
2. Hypothetical reconstruction of the Carolingian cursores cavalry training exercise. This was based on late Roman, Byzantine and early Islamic tactics; involving several squadrons charging in sequence, probably throwing javelins, then returning to their positions (after Pawlikowski-Cholewa)
3. The battle of Hastings, 1066. An initial attack by Norman archers supported by infantry failed to break the Anglo-Saxon shield wall. Norman cavalry then made repeated uphill charges against the Anglo-Saxons.

The Bretons either retreated or made a feigned retreat, drawing the enemy's right wing of fyrd after them; the latter then being cut down by a counter-charge. This manoeuvre was repeated at least once until the enemy were sufficiently weakened for a final Norman charge to overrun the Anglo-Saxon position. During the subsequent pursuit Norman cavalry are said to have lost heavily when many were trapped in the Malfosse. (after Allen Brown)
A. Probable position of the Malfosse
B. Marshy ground Anglo-Saxon forces
C. King Harold and élite housecarls.
D. Lightly armed fyrd. Norman forces
E. Infantry and archers
F. Bretons
G. Duke William and Normans
H. French

his army to divide into several columns which then converged upon the heart of an enemy's territory. Even so, Carolingian conquests were carried out by much smaller armies than those that marched beneath the eagles of ancient Rome. Their speed of march also strongly suggests considerable use of large mounted infantry forces in addition to the cavalry. Careful preparation long in advance, the assembling of adequate supplies and transport, the use of secret night marches, as well as frequently appalling massacres of non-Christian foes in the name of religion, contributed to Charlemagne's ability to mount large and successful campaigns at least once a year. Not surprisingly, they also made his armies greatly feared.

The fate of different Carolingian military frontier provinces or *Marches* similarly reflected the different foes whom they faced. The Spanish March failed because it was up against a perhaps even more sophisticated, more highly organised and motivated Andalusian-Islamic frontier system. Meanwhile the Carolingian *Marches* in Germany, and to a lesser extent in Croatia, were successful as active base areas for mobile frontier forces who faced far more primitive enemies.

With the fragmentation of the Carolingian Empire, and the gradual emergence of the Kingdom of France in which most of the early rulers had extremely little real authority, warfare degenerated into a generally localised

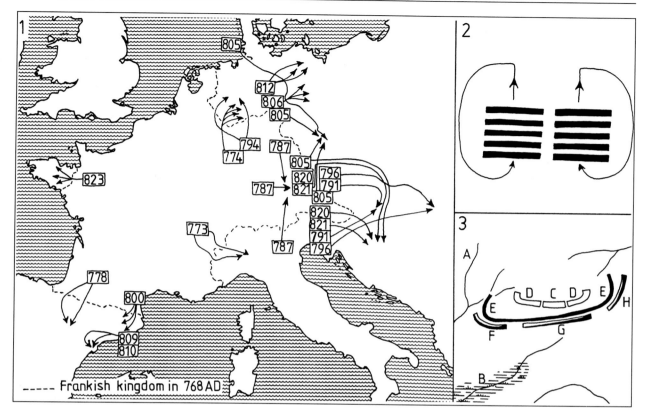

affair. These years were characterised by local lords feud-
ing with their neighbours and little effective interference
from the crown. Yet the 11th century also saw the start of
more than a hundred years of grim campaigning by the
French kings in a prolonged effort to control the various
turbulent regional power centres. Even so, the extremely
warlike career of a great regional lord such as Fulk Nera of
Anjou, during the first half of the 11th century, included
remarkably few full-scale battles. The provincial warfare of
this period was still largely a matter of raiding, ravaging,
besieging and defending fortified places.

Several of the new Ottonian Imperial German dynasty's
largest campaigns were south of the Alps. Again, these
were efforts to maintain imperial authority in an Italy
which was steadily slipping out of the Emperor's real control. Such expeditionary forces normally assembled in
Bavaria before crossing the Brenner Pass where they
would re-assemble in Lombardy. On other occasions German imperial armies from Swabia used the St Gothard
Pass; those from Burgundy crossing the Mont Cenis Pass.
Italy itself also faced the persistent threat of seaborne Muslim raids. Here, however, the local Italian forces gradually
showed themselves to be more effective than were those of
the north who faced the Vikings' threat. Despite their
domestic differences and rivalries, the seemingly fragmented local powers of Italy generally combined to defeat
such naval invaders.

Infantry clearly dominated warfare in Anglo-Saxon England to the very end of the Anglo-Saxon state. Even so the
strategy pursued against the Viking invaders, primarily by
the Kingdom of Wessex, eventually proved successful. The
Norse invaders came by sea and often penetrated far up
many of England's rivers. Consequently the Anglo-Saxons
put considerable effort into the securing of river-crossing
points by erecting fortifications nearby. Where possible
rivers were also blocked with fortified bridges; these soon
became vital defensive features. The same would also be
seen in parts of France. Meanwhile warfare on the Welsh
and Scottish borders largely remained a matter of raid and
counter-raid. Nevertheless, by the 11th century Anglo-
Saxon campaigns in these areas were mostly undertaken
by small forces of professional and, in some cases, apparently mounted troops.

Very little strategy, as such, seems discernible in the
internal warfare of the Celtic lands themselves. In all areas
it remained a case of minor skirmishing. Ireland was particularly noted for cattle rustling between rival chieftains;
each striving to win both wealth and prestige in what
sometimes seems to have been little more than a violent
sport.

The Normans could hardly have been more different in
their attitudes to warfare. By the 11th century Norman
armies were noted for their discipline, while their commanders were noted for their remarkable patience as well

as their caution. Norman warfare was, in fact, characterised by careful reconnaissance, prolonged sieges and blockades, occasional battles which were usually associated with such sieges, a preference for diplomacy whenever possible. Negotiation was clearly regarded as better than the unnecessary spilling of blood; particularly if that blood belonged to the military élite. A willingness to retreat when circumstances were unfavourable, and an ability to carry out winter campaigns were further characteristics of Norman warfare. Close attention to the security of supplies and supply lines, as well as considerable use of espionage and great effort to find traitors within an enemy's ranks were also typical of the Normans' realistic and unromantic attitude towards warfare.

The Normans were similarly careful when it came to offensive operations. For example, Duke William's invasion of England in 1066 was a classic case of the use of a well-balanced 'combined army' of infantry and cavalry, with adequate logistical and naval support. Even so, William's uncharacteristic decision to risk all at the battle of Hastings probably reflected the fact that the Anglo-Saxons had hemmed in the invading Norman army. This might even have felt itself to be in danger of being cut off by sea. Ferocious ravaging of Anglo-Saxon territory after the Normans' victory at Hastings was the normal sequel to such a victory on the battlefield; as were the Anglo-Saxons' attempt at guerrilla resistance. This itself was then countered by the Norman policy of castle-building, their controlling of the main towns and roads, and of Duke William's holding of senior Anglo-Saxon figures as hostages. In reality it was the Normans' ruthless policy of ravaging recalcitrant territories that eventually brought Anglo-Saxon England to its knees – not the battle of Hastings alone.

Similar, though perhaps less intensively ferocious, tactics were used by the Normans to control Wales. Unlike previous Anglo-Saxon campaigns in this area, the Normans followed up their raids with castle building and by the slow piecemeal conquest of much of the country. Meanwhile, on the Scottish borders there was no effort at Norman conquest; merely the traditional rapid small-scale raiding to keep the Scots quiet.

Scandinavian warfare on land, and that of the rest of the Baltic, was essentially the same as the warfare seen in Anglo-Saxon England. Both were still rooted in early medieval Germanic tribal infantry traditions. The Vikings were, however, far more innovative when fighting at sea and, paradoxically perhaps, when campaigning overseas. Those Norse-Viking forces which swept across so much of England from the mid-9th century onwards, for example, seized horses wherever they could. Partly as a result they often achieved greater strategic mobility than did the defending Anglo-Saxons.

Unlike many other invaders of 10th century Europe, the Magyars changed their military objectives after taking control of the huge Hungarian Plain. From then on they raided solely for booty, not for conquest. Furthermore, as soon as they themselves were threatened by imperial German and Kievan Russian armies in the late 10th century, these Magyar-Hungarians started to adopt western European defensive strategies. This was particularly apparent along the western and north-eastern frontiers of the Hungarian state. To the south Hungarian strategy remained more offensive. Here they faced Balkan Slav tribes whose own forces still largely consisted of infantry. These Balkan Slavs were also widely regarded as being militarily backward; relying on ambushes in densely forested country or rapid raiding in which their recognised skill in riverine warfare gave them some advantages.

Troop Types

Concern for the condition of pasture prior to a campaign clearly indicated the importance of horses to Carolingian armies. Yet this did not of itself prove that cavalry now dominated such Carolingian forces. In fact much of the evidence continues to suggest that mounted infantry were what gave early Carolingian armies their undeniable tactical superiority.

The idea that an Arab and Berber Muslim threat from the south prompted a sudden conversion to cavalry warfare among Carolingian Franks who had traditionally been famed as infantry warriors is highly dubious. For a start the Muslim armies of this period themselves still relied above all on mounted infantry rather than large numbers of cavalry. In fact it seems to have been the Carolingians' later loss of strategic mobility that lay behind their initially static tactics against Viking raids. Although such localised defence was often successful, it merely tended to push the Norse invaders somewhere else. If any external threats did, in fact, lie behind the undeniable rise of cavalry to military dominance during the Carolingian period, it was those posed by Vikings, Magyars and later Muslim seaborne raiders of the 9th and 10th centuries; not the early Muslim thrusts north from Spain in the 8th century.

Much the same pattern could be seen in Germany and Italy following the break-up of the Carolingian state. The only real difference was the continuing importance of infantry in German border warfare against the neighbouring pagan Slavs. But even here armoured cavalry increased in importance from the mid-10th century onwards.

By the 10th and 11th centuries it was only in such fringe areas that infantry continued to play a dominant military role. Elsewhere warfare came to be dominated by horsemen; either as mounted infantry or as true cavalry. Nevertheless it is often very difficult to distinguish between mounted infantry and cavalry during this period. The Carolingian Franks may have included a few mounted men even in the early 7th century, while the Celtic Bretons clearly maintained a strong cavalry tradition throughout the early Middle Ages. Charlemagne's often quoted early 9th century regulations concerning the equipment required of an armoured horseman sound, however, more like those of a mounted infantryman than of a cavalry-man. For example, they included archery equipment, and there is no clear evidence that Carolingian troops ever fought as horse-archers – a tactic totally at variance with their military heritage and traditions. Other evidence points, in fact, to a continued employment of men who fought on foot well into the 11th century, though by then they largely operated in support of the cavalry who had now achieved undoubted military predominance.

Even in Germany it seems that many of the best infantry archers came to battle on horseback; in other words they were mounted infantry. Nevertheless, the most effective German troops against enemies such as the Magyars were now cavalry. The first clear use of large numbers of real cavalry in what became the Carolingian Empire was probably in Lombard northern Italy. Here the mid-8th century military regulations of a Lombard king described both armoured and unarmoured horsemen; the latter perhaps being mounted infantry, while archery was left to men on foot. Plenty of cavalry were still available in 9th century central Italy though, for some as yet unknown reason, cavalry appear to have been in short supply in the south by the 10th and 11th centuries.

The early Anglo-Saxons again had no cavalry traditions. Even the development of mounted infantry seems to have had to await the late 10th and 11th centuries. By that time élite troops such as the *housecarls* and richer *thegns* clearly had horses; but there is virtually no evidence that they actually fought on horseback. The only probable exception may have been in the far north of England. Here much earlier Celtic British light cavalry traditions may have survived in small-scale border warfare. The Picts do appear to have fought on ponyback, at least judging by their art of the 7th to 9th centuries; yet there is little evidence for any further use of cavalry within Scotland during the 10th and 11th centuries. A similar early Celtic tradition of light cavalry warfare may have survived for rather longer in Ireland; perhaps throughout the entire Middle Ages.

Archery was also used to a perhaps limited extent by the Anglo-Saxons, though it seems to have remained a rather despised form of warfare. The Norwegians are said to have used it to a greater extent, particularly in the open stages of a battle and at sea. Archery was also apparent in the other Scandinavian and Baltic countries. Here there were several references to mounted men in the forces of richer rulers, though real cavalry did not appear to any great extent until the mid-12th century.

Farther south, in Poland, the archaeological record suggests that warfare was dominated by spear-armed infantry until the 10th century. Then there seems to have been a sudden rise in the importance of archery. Nevertheless relatively few men were mounted, as was also the case among the western Slavs along the German frontier. On the other hand a mid-10th century Muslim traveller specifically stated that the Obodrite tribe of what is now the German Baltic coast were rich in both armour and swords. A

change from offensive to defensive strategy in 11th century Hungary is widely assumed to have led to the virtual disappearance of traditional Magyar light cavalry, but while this may have been true in the west of the country it was probably not the case in the east. Nor would it have been entirely true among the still pastoral, if no longer semi-nomadic, peoples of the Great Plain of central Hungary.

Battle Tactics

Most military commanders of this period may have tried hard to avoid full-scale battles, but when these were fought the primary aim was still normally to kill or capture the enemy commander. A medieval army, like its ancient predecessors, would almost inevitably collapse once this was achieved. Most western European armies were, according to Byzantine sources, arrayed by tribe or kinship and tended to adopt defensive tactics. The Byzantine view that they were also disobedient, lacking in stamina and discipline, as well as being easily tricked by such tactics as feigned flight, may, however, have been out of date even by the 8th century.

The classic interpretation of Charles Martel's victory over a Muslim raiding force at Poitiers maintains that the Christian Franks allowed their enemy to dash themselves to pieces against a stern but static defensive array. Yet this is probably quite wrong; for the evidence could equally well be interpreted as the Franks charging and overrunning the Muslim–Arab camp in a sudden and unexpected assault. There were, in fact, few changes in Carolingian battle tactics over the next two centuries – at least when compared to the great development in broader strategy. By the 10th century those German armies that faced the Magyar Hungarians attempted to lure their more nimble foe into close combat. Their success in doing so perhaps says more about the Magyars than it does about the Germans themselves. At the decisive battle of the Lech in 955, for example, the Magyar archers were only able to loose one volley before being struck by a German cavalry counter-charge. Detailed descriptions of battles in 10th century Italy show that these post-Carolingian forces used ambush tactics and battlefield reserves.

Meanwhile battlefield tactics in Anglo-Saxon England remained much simpler; apparently almost always consisting of a solid array of dismounted troops defended by large shields held close together. Battle itself often started with archery in an attempt to weaken the opposition's 'shield wall'; this being followed by man-to-man close combat. Land battles in Scandinavia were virtually identical with those in Anglo-Saxon England, the only real tactics being infantry archery and the *skjaldborg* 'shield wall' around a leader.

The Normans similarly used archery to weaken an enemy at the start of a battle. As at Hastings in 1066, these archers were followed, or more probably defended by, armoured infantry who might themselves also attack the enemy line. But the main offensive role in Norman armies clearly fell to the cavalry. Norman commanders equally clearly made use of the feigned flight tactic. This may always have persisted in France since Roman times, or it might have been re-learned by Norman troops who fought against Byzantine and Muslim foes in southern Italy and who in turn taught it to their cousins back in Normandy.

Early Magyar tactics have generally been regarded as typical of Central Asian steppe peoples. But the Magyars themselves were not actually a steppe people. Rather they originated from the forest and steppe fringes. Their horse-archery tactics also seem to have had more in common with the 'shower-shooting' of the Sassanians and contemporary Muslim armies rather than the harassment tactics of truly nomadic Turco-Mongol peoples of the steppes. The Byzantines regarded these early Magyars as particularly dangerous when retreating, since they made considerable use of feigned flight tactics. They were also described as being capable of switching from the use of the bow to the use of the spear and back again at a moment's notice.

These Magyars clearly continued to use feigned flight tactics during their 10th century European campaigns, but tried to avoid close combat with heavily armoured western foes wherever possible. The fact they were only capable of loosing one volley of arrows at the battle of the Lech before being struck by a German counter-charge similarly suggests either that many of the Magyar archers were now on foot, or that they were drawn up in ranks rather like a Sassanian or Muslim cavalry force. As such they would have been less able to wheel aside; or at least not as rapidly as true nomadic horse-archers.

Byzantine sources similarly indicate that, by the 9th and 10th centuries, the Bulgarians also fought in ordered ranks rather than using steppe nomad dispersal or harassment tactics. Perhaps this was because Bulgarian armies now included so many Slav warriors. The Slavs themselves were described as having virtually no 'order of battle', of relying on a single noisy charge and of normally giving up if this one charge failed.

Combat Styles

The evolution of combat skills in western Europe from the 7th to 11th centuries saw one of the most significant changes in the history of cavalry warfare, though in fact it turned out to be a tactical dead-end. This was the evolution of the *couched* lance technique in which the weapon was held tight beneath a rider's upper arm. He then used the forward movement of his horse to give impetus to his weapon. The earlier European cavalry spear techniques were epitomised by the Bretons who, in the 9th century, still used javelins; charging and wheeling aside then charging once again. Other early European cavalry swung their spears underarm, or made overarm thrusts, or wielded the weapon with both hands.

Such techniques persisted well into the 11th century, and in some fringe areas they remained in use throughout the Middle Ages. They similarly remained standard practice among non-European cavalry. To regard them as somehow primitive could be very misleading. In fact several variations on these early techniques returned to western European 'lancer' warfare in the 19th century. A great deal of debate still surrounds the origin of the *couched* lance itself. It was probably brought to its full development in 10th century Byzantium and, judging by available pictorial evidence, may first have been adopted in western Europe in southern Italy, where it was almost certainly a result of Byzantine influence. The *couched* lance then became highly characteristic of French and Norman knightly cavalry; perhaps having been taken northwards by Normans who had campaigned in southern Italy.

Tactical formations of small but densely packed cavalry squadrons, suited to the *couched* lance technique, already existed in Carolingian armies. They had, however, originally been designed for repeated attack–withdraw–attack tactics inherited from Rome and still used by both Byzantine and Muslim armies. Such Carolingian *cunei* or *conrois* formations, like the *acie* or *liek* of 10th century Germany, normally seem to have included about fifty men. Norman knights, who were generally rated as the best of the 11th century, similarly used couched lances in *conrois* formations; usually in multiples of ten men. Meanwhile it is important to note that, unlike earlier rapid attack and withdrawal tactics, the knights' horses now walked into the charge. They avoided trotting, which was painful for an armoured rider and tiring for his cold-blooded mount, then went into a slow canter rather than a gallop for the final charge itself.

Infantry fighting skills would see many changes in the future but they remained remarkably consistent until the 11th century. They were perhaps epitomised in Anglo-Saxon England. Here the sword-armed, shield-carrying foot soldier remained an élite. To sling a shield on one's back was regarded as particularly brave and may have been the reality behind the otherwise poetic concept of the bare-chested *berserk* warrior. Such fighting seems to have consisted of short periods of close hewing, followed by a pause for breath. The power of blows rather than their speed or number was admired, and as a result enormous injuries could be inflicted, especially to the unshielded legs. The Vikings traditionally fought in the same manner; their heavier weapons and armour coming as a particular shock to the Irish where an old tradition of almost gentlemanly duels by champions was now gradually abandoned. It is also interesting to note that even when cavalry came to dominate warfare in Germany, the Germans, and above all the Saxons, retained a reputation as sword fighters while the French and Normans were famed as lancers.

Field and Camp Fortification

There is little evidence of change in the use of field fortifications or of fortified encampments in western Europe from the 8th to 11th centuries. Carolingian military regulations make it clear that large armies were expected to erect wooden field fortifications. Yet it also seems as though some of Europe's invaders made more effective use of such defences than did the Carolingians. In fact Viking encampments, protected by ditches and stockades, were formidable enough to repulse Anglo-Saxon infantry attacks. They could also force Carolingian armoured cavalry to dismount before attacking them on foot. Such fortified encampments similarly served as gathering points for marauding armies as they spread out to ravage and loot. During the 11th century, and probably also earlier, the Magyars were described as using wagons to protect their camps. This once again casts their armies in the same mould as that of the Huns and Sassanians.

WEAPONRY AND HARNESS

European arms and armour of the early medieval period are widely assumed to have been simple, rather uniform and far from abundant. This is a great oversimplification, though it would be true to say that armour was very expensive even in a relatively prosperous state like the Carolingian Empire. Similarly, it was largely reserved for a rich military élite. Some of the regulations issued by early medieval kings may also have projected an ideal

based upon Byzantine practice, rather than reflecting what was achievable in an economically stagnant western Europe. But it was not only 'ideals' that came from Byzantium. Byzantine styles of military equipment and probably a fair amount of actual weaponry also came westward, reaching as far afield as Scandinavia. At the same time there was strong military influence from the steppe peoples of the east. Islamic military influence was more localised, some reaching western Europe via the steppe nomads, some coming directly from the Middle East, North Africa, the Muslim parts of the Iberian peninsula and from Muslim-ruled Sicily. Archaeological finds in central European regions like Moravia not only illustrate the differing arms and armour traditions that met in such places, but can indicate what tradition was dominant at any particular time.

Archery

Perhaps no aspect of European military technology so obviously reflected these differing influences, both internal and external, as did archery. Bows of more than two metres in length have been found in 8th century German graves, while in Poland archaeologists have found a rela-

'Demon with a crossbow', carved capital; southern French, c.1096. This is one of the very earliest carvings to show a crossbow in medieval European art. The fact that it is being spanned by a devil probably indicates that the Church strongly disapproved of the crossbow at this time. The weapon is of an early form, spanned by hand and lacking a stirrup so that the crossbowman had to place his feet on the bow itself. (Cathedral of St Sernin, Toulouse)

tively sudden shift from unbarbed to barbed arrowheads in a period when archery changed from being merely a means of hunting to a war weapon in the 10th century. Such arrows would again have been shot from longbows. Longbows were certainly used by the Vikings and probably also by the Normans at the battle of Hastings in 1066.

Shorter, so-called flat-bows may, however, have been used in the Carolingian Empire after late Roman forms of composite bow fell out of use. Similarly they are said to have been used in Celtic Wales. Since flat-bows were less sensitive to extreme cold than were longbows, they were also used throughout the medieval period and indeed beyond in the sub-Arctic far north. The only regions where real composite bows appear to have remained in use were Byzantine- and Muslim-influenced Italy, and by the recently nomadic peoples of what is now Hungary. Here the Avars used supposedly more advanced, shorter, more curved and more 'Turkish' composite bows than did the Magyars who came later. Archaeological evidence, in fact, shows that Magyar bows were similar to those of the earlier Sassanian Persians, rather than Turks, and probably had much in common with the composite bows used in the Islamic but pre-Turkish, pre-11th century Middle East.

As far as western European warfare was concerned, the re-emergence of the crossbow was of greatest significance. It had almost certainly survived since Roman times as a hunting weapon in some areas. In fact the crossbow had probably been unsuited to the small-scale skirmishing warfare which characterised the early medieval period. But with an increase in siege warfare in the 10th century, the crossbow re-appeared in the hands of infantry soldiers. It was first reported in northern France and was soon mentioned in Scandinavia where it was known as the 'lock-bow'. The earliest known surviving weapon of this period dates from the 11th century. Its bowstring was released or shot by the upwards movement of a wooden plug. It did not incorporate the revolving release *nut* as had been used in Roman crossbows and would become normal with later medieval weapons. The later 11th century then saw the spread of several technical improvements to the crossbow; not least in a wider use of pole-lathes which enabled crossbow *nuts* to be made in large quantity. The Normans adopted this weapon with enthusiasm, possibly having some in 1066, and clearly astonishing the Byzantines with the power of their crossbows in 1096.

Swords and Daggers

The sword remained the most prestigious weapon throughout the early medieval period. Although the dagger-like *seax* or *scramasax* remained in use into the early Carolingian era, the western cavalry élite now largely abandoned their use. In parts of Scandinavia, meanwhile, the small single-edged *seax* evolved into a large, single-edged sword. At the same time Scandinavia's close economic and military links with Byzantium, Russia and even Central Asia may also have played a part in the unexpect-

ed appearance of such 'proto-sabres' in the far north of Europe.

The Viking invasion of Ireland had a particularly dramatic impact on the previously archaic weapons of this island. The small early medieval swords of both Ireland and Scotland had developed out of late Roman designs and, in the case of Ireland, the 7th century also saw the sudden appearance of a blade which widened rather than tapered towards its tip. The closest parallels with this distinctive weapon were in India, though similar swords may also have been used by the early Muslim-Arabs. As yet

Left: Seax short-sword; possibly 8th–11th centuries. Again, the dating of a simple seax blade is very difficult, though this weapon is also believed to have come from Scandinavia. (Private collection)

Right: Dagger with 'Odin's raven' shaped grip; Scandinavian, 9th–10th centuries. The use of Odin's Raven, the symbol of death in battle in Norse-Viking culture, almost ensures that this weapon dates from the pre-Christian period. (Private collection)

there is no clear evidence linking these distant weapons with Ireland, despite the known trading and religious connections between Christian Ireland and pre-Islamic Christian Spain.

The great majority of Viking swords were themselves fully within the steadily evolving tradition of western European swords. In fact, a great many of the best Scandinavian blades were probably imported from late Carolingian and Ottonian Germany. Like early Germanic peoples such as the Anglo-Saxons, the Norse-Vikings also gave names and attributed mythical origins to their finest sword-blades. Archaeological evidence from Poland and the Baltic, where swords were still buried with their owners well into the medieval period, indicates that wooden scabbards could have carved decorations. They were often covered with cloth or leather and might have had an oiled fur lining to prevent the blade from rusting.

Spears and Javelins

Spears, and to a lesser extent javelins, were much more common workaday weapons than the prestigious sword. Yet they too changed over the centuries. Javelins tended to be associated with militarily backward peoples such as the Slavs and Celts. Nevertheless the 11th century Anglo-Saxons still copied the light Welsh *gafluch* javelin; calling it a *gafeluc* or *gaveloc*. Up to three at a time would be carried, and they were in no way regarded as inferior or peasant weapons. Archaeological evidence from eastern Europe indicates that, at least in these regions, the ordinary infantry spear was only about two metres long. No complete Carolingian examples appear to exist, though surviving spearheads confirm pictorial evidence which shows that crossbars beneath the blade continued to be used well into the 11th century. This would have been completely unsuited to the *couched* lance technique and would, in fact, have been more effective in the hands of infantry or at least of horsemen who 'fenced' with their spears rather than using them solely as thrusting weapons.

Other Weapons

Other weapons played a minor role, with the possible exception of the war-axe. The Vikings were, of course, famous for their great infantry axes and such weapons were subsequently adopted by various peoples under Norse-Viking influence, most obviously in Scotland and in late Anglo-Saxon England. Much smaller, narrow-blad-

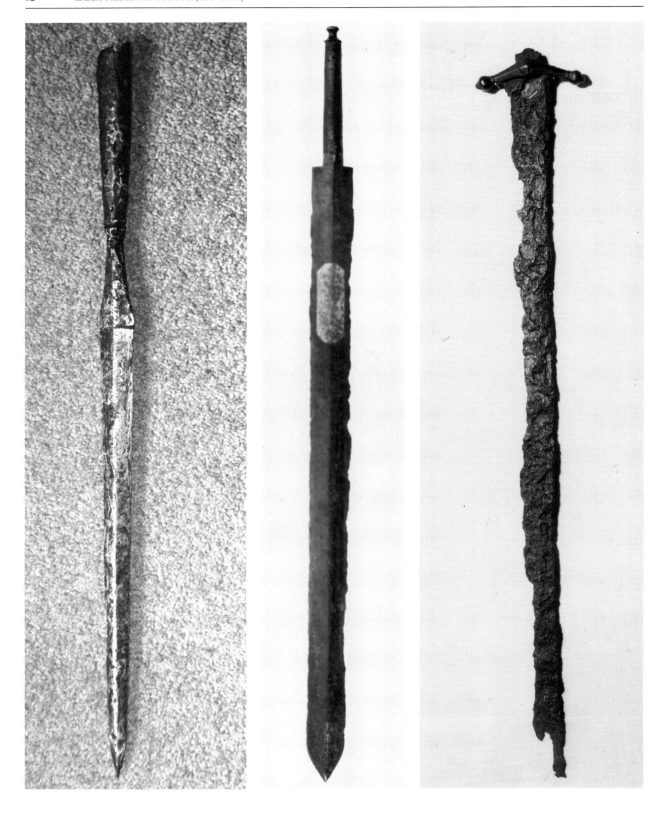

Opposite page, left: Spearhead; 8th–11th centuries. The dating of a relatively simple spearhead is extremely difficult. This example is, however, of particularly fine manufacture and is believed to have come from Scandinavia. The slit form of socket suggests that the weapon was primarily designed to be thrown as a javelin and not to have been wielded like a spear, as the point where it was attached to its haft would have had little lateral strength. (Private collection)

Opposite page, centre: Sword of sub-Roman spatha type; Celtic Irish, 5th–7th centuries. Before the sudden descent of the Vikings upon Ireland, Irish weapons remained remarkably old-fashioned. This sword is, in fact, a development of a much earlier Roman cavalry type. (National Museum of Ireland, Dublin)

Opposite page, right: Sabre with bronze quillons from Nemesócsa; Magyar, 10th century. Single-edged sabres entered central Europe from the east, being brought in by people of Turco-Mongol or Finno-Ugrian origin. They were essentially a light cavalry weapon, unlike the heavier armour-breaking swords of western Europe. The earlier Hungarian sabres, like this example, had very little curvature. (Hungarian National Museum, Budapest).

ed, axes were similarly used in several Slav areas; though this resulted from the influence of steppe peoples to the east.

Simple clubs were used by the poor in Ireland and possibly among Anglo-Saxon peasants; whereas the metallic mace again seems to have come from the eastern steppes or from Byzantium. A crude wooden club shown in the hands of both Duke William and Bishop Odo on the Bayeux Tapestry remains something of a mystery. It was almost certainly not a real weapon. Rather, it may have been a wooden *baculus* derived from the symbolic wooden 'club of power' of Norse Scandinavian origin.

Shields

Pictorial sources indicate that small round shields were used by Celtic horsemen at least into the 9th century. Meanwhile the great majority of western European shields were larger round types, primarily designed for use on foot. Those of the Anglo-Saxons were said to be made of lime wood with an iron boss and rim strengthening. Those of the Vikings, and probably most other peoples including the Anglo-Saxons, were also covered with leather. The origin of the pointed, kite-shaped, so-called Norman shield which appeared relatively suddenly in the 11th century remains a matter of debate. It was designed primarily for use on horseback but might, paradoxically, have developed from the tall but flat-based infantry shields used in some Mediterranean and Middle Eastern regions. The true kite-shaped shield is, however, normally regarded as a western European invention. Nevertheless there is clear evidence that it was being used by Byzantine heavily armoured cavalry as early as the 10th century.

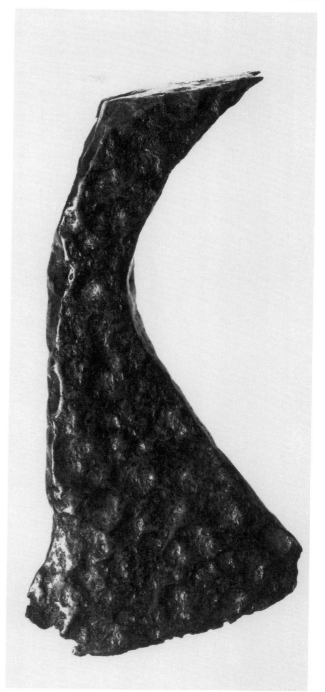

Above: Throwing axe; Scandinavian, 9th–10th centuries. This form of franciska had been widespread among the early medieval Germanic 'barbarian' warriors who overthrew the western Roman Empire. It then declined in popularity except, it seems, in pagan Scandinavia. (Private collection)

Helmets

Recent discoveries show that late Roman forms of helmet construction and design remained in use for several centuries after the fall of the western half of the Roman Empire, particularly in the British Isles and Scandinavia. The same was true of the Roman style of making mail, though this was perhaps more common in the southern parts of Europe. Nevertheless, apparently archaic features such as 10th century partial face-guards and 11th or 12th century pendant cheek-flaps seen on some Scandinavian helmets may reflect links with Byzantium rather than survivals of a now chronologically distant Roman influence.

But other forms of decoration, such as 'eyes' added to the brows of some helmets from the Danube region, have been attributed to residual late-Roman ideas.

The pointed helmet which came to dominate European military fashions by the 11th century clearly had eastern origins, yet it evolved in several different ways. In eastern and Magyar-ruled central Europe helmets built up of directly riveted segments were essentially the same as those seen in Russia, the Eurasian steppes and perhaps in Byzantium. Those constructed of segments attached to a cross-like iron frame, though also ultimately of eastern inspiration, came to be typical of early medieval western

Opposite page: Iron helmet with gilded bronze decorations from York. It originally had a mail aventail attached to the rim; Northumbrian Anglo-Saxon, mid-8th century. Apart from clearly being the reality between various pieces of 8th century art from England and neighbouring Scotland, this helmet is a development of a type that had been common during the last decades of the Roman Empire. It is of basically four-piece construction; though the brim-band and the two cross-bands which go over the top of the head are now so wide that they cover more of the head than do the four basic segments of the helmet bowl. Cheek-pieces were another early feature which would soon die out in subsequent medieval helmets. (York Archaeological Trust Picture Library, York)

Right: One-piece iron helmet with gilded decoration from Hungary. This far more advanced helmet was probably basically of Byzantine or perhaps central European origin, with Pecheneg Turkish decoration added later; 11th–12th centuries. The use of 'eyes' as decorations on the front of a helmet again dates back for many centuries to the late Roman period. (Inv. Nemiya no. 2, Déri Museum, Debrecen)

'Guards at the Holy Sepulchre', ivory situla from Milan; northern Italian, c.980. Each guard wears a short-sleeved mail hauberk which almost reaches his knees; though in most cases this is largely obscured by the men's cloaks. The most interesting feature, however, is the vertical elements on the front of their helmets, which either suggests a totally anachronistic sliding nasal, or a form of decoration attached to the front of a strengthening piece that joins the halves of a two-piece helmet. Such a decoration is found on a Persian helmet of five centuries earlier, and on manuscript illustrations from Spain almost five hundred years later. Here, however, it remains something of a mystery. (Inv. n.A.18-1933, Victoria and Albert Museum, London)

Europe. In some cases the segments or the covering of such framed helmets appear to have been of horn or hardened leather. Pictorial sources, and a tiny handful of surviving helmets, clearly indicate that this framed construction remained in use after the 11th century. By then, however, one-piece iron helmets of the so-called Norman type were widespread. The necessary technology to make such defences again came from the east, though in this instance almost certainly from the Muslim world. The face-protecting nasals on such helmets could also be remarkably broad; sufficient to obscure the wearer's identity. This happened to William the Conqueror at the battle of Hastings and nearly caused a panic in the ranks when a rumour spread that the Duke was dead.

The brimmed *chapel de fer* iron hat or 'war-hat' poses more of a problem. It seems to be shown, though far from clearly, in late Roman art. It then continued to appear in early medieval pictorial sources, but these may simply have been echoing late Roman art rather than illustrating current reality. On the other hand, the brimmed 'war-hat' was known in China, at least by the 11th century, and is believed to have been used in many parts of Central Asia. The fashion may indeed have reached the Byzantine Empire from that direction, while there is some documentary evidence for its use in late Viking Scandinavia. It is even possible that references to Viking raiders wearing 'winged helmets' actually referred to brimmed helmets, rather than the feathered or horned creations beloved of Hollywood film-makers.

Body Armour

Mail was almost universally the most common form of body armour during this period, though there was a clear distinction between long and short forms of mail *hauberk*.

'David beheads Goliath', carved capital; French, c.1120. Goliath is shown here as a very typical early 12th century French knight, with his mail hauberk and broad straight sword. But his helmet is less usual. It is of a fluted design, lacks a nasal – perhaps to allow David's sling-stone to be shown – and is held on his head by a chin-strap which seems to go through a small extension on the side of the helmet. (Basilica of Sainte Madeleine, Vezelay)

Left: 'Vision of Habukuk', in the Bible de St Vaast; northern French, early 11th century. Apart from the apparent king or bishop in the middle of this little group of cavalrymen, they are all equipped in an old-fashioned manner for this period. In fact, they probably reflect the horsemen of the 10th rather than 11th centuries. The stirrup is obviously now in use, though the couched lance clearly is not. The flexible protections seen beneath their helmets are also clearly of mail, and could be assumed to be mail coifs – except that the leading horseman does not wear a mail hauberk. (MS. 435, Bibliothèque Municipale, Arras)

felt protections, which would again suggest close contact with the Muslim Middle East. Meanwhile a dubious later copy of a supposedly 11th century Anglo-Saxon source stated that a light leather *corietum* cuirass was more suitable than heavy iron mail when pursuing the Welsh in their mountains.

Limb Defences

Mail *hauberks* with long sleeves were rare, though not unknown, and two *hauberks*, one with long sleeves and one with short, could be worn at once. *Bainbergae* leg protections were mentioned in 8th century Frankish military laws, but in general leg armour remained extremely rare until the 11th century. Mail leg protections then began to be adopted more frequently by some of the armoured cavalry élite.

Horse Harness

Several important developments took place in European horse harness, though their immediate significance has been greatly exaggerated by most modern scholars. Stirrups, for example, were known by the 8th century, but were not at once widely used. The only exceptions seem to be those peoples who recently came from the east, such as the Avars and Magyars. The earliest clear written and pictorial references to stirrups in France or Germany date from the mid and late 9th century, but at that time they may have been far from universal. Even the Slavs, who were immediate neighbours and subjects of the Turco-Mongol Avars, do not appear to have copied Avar stirrups. Similarly, the stirrups adopted by several western and central European peoples in the 9th and 10th centuries were of a completely different design from those used by both Avars and Magyars. In fact they look like iron versions of leather stirrups with wooden treads; sometimes even including non-functional lumps on the outside of the vertical elements, comparable to the ends of wooden stirrup-treads as they were threaded through leather supporting straps. This could indicate eastern European or Byzantine inspiration with, rather unexpectedly, the Norse-Vikings playing a significant role as disseminators of this new addition to horse harness in the 9th or even 10th centuries.

Not surprisingly, it was more common in richer areas than in poorer or isolated regions. By the late 11th century separate mail coifs to protect the head and neck had also been introduced; again almost certainly from the east, from Byzantium or Islam. The *ventail* or mail flap laced across the lower part of the wearer's face was also known by the 11th century. Its relative novelty may, in fact, have accounted for its appearance as otherwise unintelligible mailed rectangles on the chests of some riders in the Bayeux Tapestry.

Lamellar armour, in which many small plates were laced together with thongs, was clearly known in areas under Byzantine or eastern influence. This may have included 9th century Italy and certainly included 10th century Sweden. References to non-metallic armour are fewer and more obscure. Magyar horse-archers are said to have worn

*'Visions of SS Peter and Paul';
carved font of Tournai workmanship; northern France,
end of 11th–early 12th
centuries. Almost every aspect
of this fallen knight and his
horse are typical of the period,
but not all. The mail hauberk
is now full length and has
long sleeves, but the helmet is
still of a low-domed round
shape rather than the conical
form normally associated with
northern Europe. The stirrups
are also round, in a style in
reality probably restricted
to eastern Europe or the
Byzantine Empire. (Church
of Our Lady, Dendermonde,
Belgium)*

Manuscript decoration; French, mid–late 11th century. The artist who drew this little picture seems to have wanted to emphasise the close-packed nature of a French cavalry conrois formation, particularly when armed with couched lances. The horsemen's conical helmets with large nasals, and their kite-shaped shields, point to the future of western European cavalry warfare, whereas their apparent lack of mail hauberks and very bent leg riding position hark back to earlier traditions. (MS. 228, f.90r, Bibliothèque Municipale, Le Mans)

Other developments were a reintroduction of horse-shoes, probably from the Middle East where they had remained almost essential in dry and stony terrain, and a new form of more supportive wood-framed saddle, again of Middle Eastern Islamic derivation. This new saddle was also associated with breast and crupper straps around the front and rear of the horse. Significantly, perhaps, the breast-strap was even more important to the development of the *couched* lance than was the deep saddle itself, though the very raised pommel and cantle of the latter gave the rider with the *couched* lance much greater support than did earlier forms of saddle. This, however, only appeared in the 11th century as a result of, rather than as a contributory factor to, the development of *couched* lance tactics.

Horse Armour

Horse armour, though known in late Roman times and still used by Byzantine, Islamic and Central Asian cavalry, dropped out of use in western Europe with the possible exception of Celtic Brittany. Here it is apparently mentioned in the 9th century.

FORTIFICATION

A true castle was a fortification and a residence rather than a mere fortress, but within such a simplified definition many variations would appear by the end of the 11th century. This period also saw the development of very sophisticated timber fortifications, even in some areas where good stone was abundant. This may have reflected a lack of sufficient numbers of competent masons. But it is important to realise that wooden fortresses were not, by definition, weaker than those of stone. Nor were they necessarily very vulnerable to fire; particularly when made of new timber in often damp parts of the western world.

The Carolingian Empire and France

The aggressive and expanding Carolingian Empire was not particularly famous for its military architecture. In many if not most cases the defences of its royal palaces were more apparent than real. In this the Carolingians had much in common with the early Islamic Umayyad dynasty of Caliphs. Some more businesslike *curtes regiae* 'royal forts' were, however, built at strategic points. They seem to have been based upon the design of Roman forts; often being erected in precisely the same spots, with a ditch, earth rampart and plain stone, timber or interlaced brushwood wall, though lacking turrets. Such royal forts served as military bases and refuges, rather than being designed to withstand full-scale sieges. Only on the war-torn frontiers were more substantial fortifications erected. This was particularly apparent in Saxony where some quite large Carolingian fortresses continued to use the pagan Saxons' own architectural tradition of formidable round citadels with thick ramparts and deep moats.

The Viking, Saracen and then Magyar threats of the 9th and 10th centuries changed this comfortable situation and led to a considerable building of fortifications in many parts of western Europe. The royal veto on nobles erecting fortresses without specific royal permission may also have been dropped. As a result defensive bridges and bridgeheads appeared along many rivers, together with fortresses where they met the sea. Meanwhile, the decayed Roman curtain walls of many towns were hurriedly repaired. Despite the crumbling of royal authority, the king remained at least theoretically the 'owner' of many such urban fortifications.

An increasing number of often very small fortifications remained characteristic of the 10th and 11th centuries, with the *motte and bailey* castle being the most distinctive new form. By the 11th century formidable stone castles and keeps were appearing in northern areas where previous early medieval fortifications had been built entirely of wood. Farther south stone had always been the traditional material. Here there is evidence that some existing aristocratic stone halls were strengthened and heightened to become early forms of the *donjon* so typical of the 12th century. At the same time there was increasing concern to use naturally defensible sites, such as rocky outcrops. All of this points to the increasing military importance of these numerous fortifications, both old and new. Fortified churches became another feature of southern France, in an area where the Church itself took a leading role in encouraging fortification during a period of near anarchy.

Germany

A similar process occurred in Germany, following the break-up of the Carolingian Empire. The palaces of the new Ottonian ruling dynasty now had real fortifications, unlike the superficial defences of earlier Carolingian palaces. Meanwhile churches, abbeys and towns were given defensive walls in the face of Norse-Viking and Magyar raids. By the end of the 10th century there was, in addition, a planned system of provincial fortifications designed to control the conquered Slavs in the east of the German Empire.

Italy

One of the earliest large-scale efforts to strengthen the many defences inherited from the Roman Empire took place in Rome itself. Here almost twenty kilometres of city wall, with its many towers, and even some aqueducts were maintained or restored to a good state of repair throughout the 9th century. On the other hand some of the new, rather than restored ancient, fortifications in central Italy appear to have been remarkably simple structures. One notable surviving example lacks any towers, while its main defence consists of a plain, rather thin wall, to which a timber walkway could be added, the latter simply consisting of planks and scaffolding.

The Magyar and renewed Muslim raids of the 10th century, however, prompted a period of intensive defensive building known as the *incastellamento*, which was further

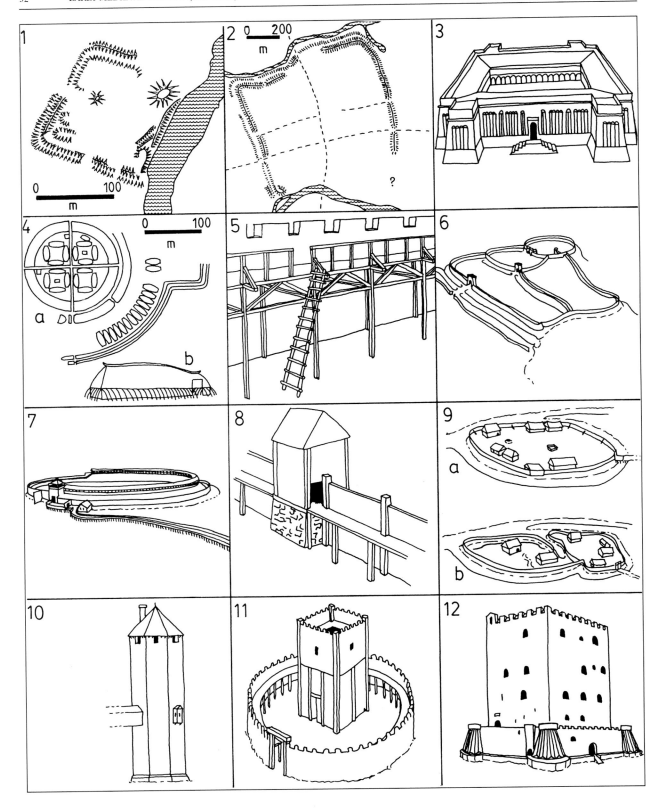

Left: Fortifications, 650–1100

1. *Mathrafal Castle, Powys, Wales; a Celtic rectangular fortified camp on the river Banwy which may have been the capital of the 9th–10th century Welsh principality of Powys. A conical Norman motte was added to one corner in the late 11th or 12th century (after Musson and Spurgeon)*
2. *Wareham, Dorset, England; the earthwork defences of the 9th century Anglo-Saxon burh between the rivers Piddle and Frome (after Hinton)*
3. *Reconstruction of the fortified palace in the Bulgarian capital of Pliska, Bulgaria; early 9th century. It is built in a remarkable mixture of Central Asian, Byzantine and Persian styles (after Esin)*
4. *a Plan of the fortified barracks at Trelleborg, Denmark, 10th–early 11th centuries. The circular earth ramparts enclose regularly arranged barracks and are protected by another ditch and rampart running between two areas of swampy ground (after Olsen)*
b One of several hypothetical reconstructions of a bar racks hall at Trelleborg (after Olsen)
5. *Interior of the wall at Castel Paterno showing a suggested reconstruction of the wooden walk-way; central Italy, 10th century (after Jamieson)*
6. *Simplified reconstruction of the fortress at Werla, Germany; late 10th century. The series of earth ramparts, walls and gates are indicated, but the interior buildings are omitted (after Anderson)*
7. *Reconstruction of the western Slav fortress at Behren-Lübchin, eastern Germany, 10th century. The*

fortress was built on a partly artificial island in a lake. Again the interior buildings are not shown (after Hensel)
8. *Reconstruction of the stone and timber tower at Mirville Castle, Normandy, 11th century. The base of this tower was the only stone structure in the castle (after Le Maho)*
9. *Reconstructions of the first two construction periods at Der Husterknupp, Germany, late 9th–11th centuries, before the addition of a conical motte in the late 11th or 12th century. The original settlement was weakly defended by a ditch and palisade, but was subsequently divided into two parts, one being given a raised mound near the centre (after Higham and Barker)*
10. *Reconstruction of the bergfried tower of Steinsberg castle, Germany, late 11th–12th centuries. A fully developed example of the tall isolated bergfried refuge tower concept, connected at second floor level to neighbouring dwelling houses by a draw-bridge (after Tuulse)*
11. *Reconstruction of the wooden tower and wall on top of the motte at Abinger Castle, England, late 11th century. The lower part of the tower has been enclosed in a hypothetical wattle and daub wall as a precaution against attack by fire*
12. *Adrano Castle, Norman Sicily, late 11th century. The tower was erected on the ruins of a previous Arab fortification but continued to use many aspects of Muslim defensive design. The outer wall and turrets are a later addition (after Caciagli and Tuulse)*

encouraged by a widespread collapse of authority and security. Once again the Church played a leading role in this process. But this time the military architecture involved was more advanced than that seen north of the Alps; probably being of partially Byzantine or Islamic inspiration.

Anglo-Saxon England

Anglo-Saxon England was not as backward in terms of military architecture as might have been expected. Many kings' and *thegns'* halls had long been protected by a hedge, stockade, ditch or rampart. Some even had a stout wooden gatehouse. The earlier tradition of erecting long frontier dikes also continued, with the largest of them all, Offa's Dike, marking a good proportion of the Anglo-Welsh border. The siting of this extraordinary piece of military engineering suggests that it was built in agreement with the neighbouring Welsh prince, in which case it may have been a joint effort against cattle rustlers. Smaller dykes in the same area included Wats Dyke, which tended to follow ravines where possible, and the Rowe Ditch which was a causeway across often flooded ground, probably to assist the rapid deployment of soldiers. Causeways across marshy land were used by King Alfred of Wessex during the darkest days of his resistance to the Norse-Vikings. Island sanctuaries in the Fens of eastern England also enabled Anglo-Saxon resistance to the Normans to survive for quite a long time.

Small fortified towns or *burghs* formed another essential element in the Anglo-Saxon struggle against the Norse-Vikings. To a lesser extent they also helped contain Welsh raiding. Most such *burghs* appear to have had a rectangular plan, reminiscent of Carolingian forts, but their defences were normally very simple. Most seem to have consisted of an earth rampart with a timber-fronted or turfed revetment and a mortared stone wall, perhaps with a wooden palisade on top.

Celtic Regions

Fortifications in the Celtic lands followed far older traditions which dated back either to the Romans in Wales and perhaps also in southern Scotland, and to ancient Celtic ring-forts in Ireland and northern Scotland. These Irish ring-forts often consisted of a *rath* defensive wall around a *liss* open space in which stood the *tech* or living quarters. The *crannog*, a fortified artificial island in a lake or marsh, was also seen in both Scotland and Ireland. During the 10th and 11th centuries a striking new form of defence against Viking invaders appeared, again in both Scotland and Ireland. This was a tall round, usually windowless, tower with a conical stone roof and a door three to five metres above ground level. It was perhaps the archetypal example of passive defence, since absolutely no provision for defensive fire was included.

The Normans: Normandy and the British Isles

The Normans were erecting fortified houses and even a stone *donjon* tower at Rouen as early as the 10th century;

yet they are most closely associated with the *motte and bailey* type of castle. The origins of this are unclear, but may have been in low-lying coastal areas of northern France and Flanders that remained particularly vulnerable to Norse-Viking attack. By the 11th century the Duke of Normandy had imposed his own authority over the building of fortifications, as he did over other military matters. As a consequence he sought, usually successfully, to limit the size of castles that were not his own, as well as the permitted depth of their ditches and the height of their banks. He could also ban more than a single palisade and refuse permission for the addition of battlements.

Scandinavia and the Baltic
In Scandinavia stone fortifications had been rare in the pre-Viking period. Those that did exist seem to have been almost entirely abandoned during the Viking era itself, but were often reoccupied from the 11th century onwards. Towns were also few and largely unfortified; several linear ditch defences were thrown up, largely to protect southern Denmark from Carolingian counter-attack in the 9th century.

But towards the end of the Viking period some remarkably ambitious and regularly planned circular fortresses suddenly appeared in Denmark. The fortress at Trelleborg, for example, is regarded as having been the most sci-

entifically planned in western Europe since Roman times; though this, of course, excludes those fortifications erected in Muslim al-Andalus far to the south. In fact, Trelleborg's extreme precision of design suggests Byzantine or Islamic influence, the late Vikings being in very close commercial and military contact with such areas at this time. Viking settlements overseas were also often fortified, particularly in England where the new settlers were on the defensive most of the time. On the other hand, the Viking-Danish urban fortifications in England appear to have been more advanced, at least in some respects, than those of the Anglo-Saxons themselves.

Eastern Europe
The Vikings were also close neighbours, and frequent foes, of the western Slavs. The latter had their own highly developed tradition of very strong earth and timber citadels, often with remarkably sophisticated gate structures. Farther south the Avar state was surrounded by a ring of strongholds which Charlemagne's armies had to overcome before conquering the Avars. These seem to have been known as the 'Nine Rings of the Avars' and they proved so formidable that they entered German folklore. Once the Magyars were forced on to the defensive by German imperial counter-attacks in the later 10th century, they too built fortifications, apparently in the style of their German and Slav neighbours.

Opposite page: Mathrafal Castle, Powys, Wales. This Celtic Welsh rectangular earthwork enclosure of the 9th–10th centuries, had a Norman motte added in the far corner, perhaps in the 12th century. The rectangular enclosure itself was almost certainly a continuation of small Roman-style fortifications; this technique probably never having died out among the Romano-Celtic peoples of what had been the Roman province of Britannia.

Right: The refuge tower at Abernethy which had been the capital of the southern Picts, Perthshire; Scottish, 11th– early 12th centuries. The tall cylindrical defensive towers which were built in Ireland, and to a lesser extent in Scotland, largely as a consequence of the Viking invasions, were a completely new concept which owed nothing to the Celts' distant Roman heritage.

Western side of the partially excavated palace-castle of Doué-la-Fontaine, built as one of the Count of Blois' stone halls, c.900. It was converted to a donjon or keep about fifty years later and is, therefore, one of the earliest donjons in France, or indeed anywhere in western Europe. When it was converted to a fortress its original ground-floor entrances were blocked up, and probably also buried, to be replaced by a door opening directly on to the upper floor. (Photograph, M. de Bouard)

Farther east, where the steppe nomads mingled with the Slav and Vlach tribes of southern Moldavia in what is now Romania, earth and wood fortresses were again erected during the 10th century. The still semi-nomadic Bulgars had built fortifications in this same area during the 7th century, even before they conquered what is now Bulgaria. Once they had carved out a kingdom in the latter area, however, these Bulgarians built many other forts. Most seem to have been of rather rough construction; being designed to seal the Rhodope mountains against Byzantine counter-attacks. Yet the Bulgars also restored the existing Romano–Byzantine defences of lowland cities in Thrace.

SIEGE WARFARE

Defence remained largely passive throughout the early medieval period, with little attempt being made to engage the besiegers in an effective manner. Only by making sorties and fighting against direct assault did the defenders normally come into physical contact with their attackers. On the other hand, sieges did play a paramount role in early Carolingian warfare; particularly in southern France, Italy, to a lesser extent Saxony and notably against the Avars.

Above: Citadel and bergfried tower at Eckartsberga, Thuringia; German, 10th–11th centuries. Eckartsberga is one of the best preserved of the early medieval imperial German fortifications in the east. When it was built it stood very close to the turbulent frontier with neighbouring largely pagan Slav tribes. The Slav-speaking Sorb minority still inhabit a region close to the eastern frontier of modern Germany, not far distant from the castle.

Opposite page, bottom:
1. Torsion-powered stone-throwing device of Romano-Greek origin; known to the Romano-Byzantines as an onager, to the Arabs as a ʿarrādah, and often called a ballista in western European sources (after Quennell)
2. A common form of man-powered stone-throwing mangonel, of Chinese origin and introduced to Europe by the Avars; often also called a perrièr (after Hill)

The Carolingian Empire and France

There are plenty of references to stone-throwing machines of presumably late Roman type being used in Carolingian siege warfare. These were generally aimed at gates rather than walls. Scaling ladders and rope ladders, the *testudo* movable wooden shed or perhaps infantry protection of interlocking shields, as well as battering rams were all employed. Small fortifications were clearly vul-

Right: 'Siege of Jerusalem', in the Commentaries of Hayman on Ezekiel, from Auxerre; French, c.1000. The text of Ezekiel stated that the siege was 'shown upon a tile', this being shown as a rectangular area at the top of the page. In addition to two very early representations of hand-held crossbows, the besiegers appear to be rolling forward two wheeled rams or bores. (MS. Lat. 12302, f.1, Bibliothèque Nationale, Paris)

nerable to such assault, but the siege of a large city like Pavia in northern Italy could take many months. During such a prolonged or difficult siege the Carolingians, like the Romans before them, piled up earth mounds from which their stone-throwing engines or perhaps large frame-mounted crossbows could operate. Both these forms of machine, of course, shot missiles along an essentially horizontal trajectory – unlike the later beam-sling *mangonel* which threw its missiles high, after the manner of a modern mortar. Mining operations were mentioned, though rarely, while Carolingian rulers also indulged in acts of extraordinary barbarity against defeated garrisons;

the clear purpose of such actions being to terrify other places into submission.

During the second half of the 9th century simple versions of the man-powered, beam-sling *mangonel* were introduced into Carolingian France. At first they might have been made and even operated by Byzantine military engineers. Such simple *mangonels* may then have become relatively common during the next hundred years. Nevertheless, sieges were now normally on a very limited scale. Larger targets such as fortified towns posed serious problems for the small armies of the 10th and 11th centuries. Perhaps as a result, increased efforts seem to have

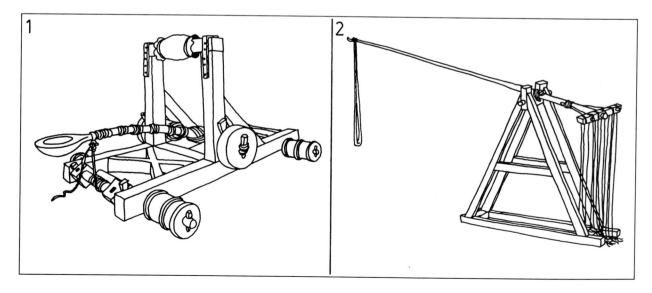

been made to get spies into such towns to find their weak spots. Otherwise an attacking force might have to rely on a sudden assault in the hope of seizing an unsecured gate.

More often than not, the attackers had to fall back on a prolonged blockade; operating from their own fortified camp erected nearby since they were rarely able to surround the entire fortifications of a town. Both sides now used small stone-throwing engines while the attackers might also dig trenches in order to reach the enemy wall in relative safety. Once there, they could erect various forms of wooden tower or sturdy shed from which to

Right: *The gateway of the Abbey of St. Nazarius at Lorsch in Germany was probably made around 774 AD. It is the most famous and best preserved example of symbolic rather than real fortification from the Carolingian period. Nevertheless the style of architecture showed what Charlemagne's military architects were capable of.*

attack the wall itself. Meanwhile the defenders would attempt to wrench their enemies out of such wooden structures using large hooks on wooden poles.

Other Regions

Elsewhere in Europe, other peoples had siege techniques of varied degrees of sophistication. Even the early 8th century pagan Saxons of northern Germany used some kinds of siege engines. In contrast, the Anglo-Saxons of England continued to rely on hand-to-hand fighting, with their few fortifications merely giving a height advantage to the defenders. Norse-Viking siege warfare was largely copied from that of their Carolingian foes. Nevertheless, it was typical that these Norsemen learned fast and soon had siege engines of their own.

The Magyars, unlike their Avar predecessors, reportedly had no real knowledge of siege warfare when they first reached central Europe in the late 9th century; but, like the Norse-Vikings, they soon learned from their western and perhaps Byzantine foes. The Bulgars may have been in a similar situation in the 9th century, having new forms of siege engines built for them by at least one Muslim Arab prisoner who had escaped from the Byzantines.

NAVAL WARFARE

Before the Norse-Vikings erupted out of Scandinavia in the far north of Europe, there appears to have been relatively little real naval warfare in northern waters. The situation in the Mediterranean was very different and river warfare also played a significant role.

The Mediterranean

Remarkably little detailed information survives about naval warfare in Italy during this period when the maritime cities of Amalfi, Pisa, Genoa and Venice began competing with the Muslim-Arabs and Berbers for domination of the western Mediterranean. The ships involved were clearly the same as those used by both Byzantine and Muslim fleets. The same was probably true of naval tactics. But plenty of skilled sailors and marines were available in the coastal towns of Italy. These would soon be recruited by the Normans as they carved out their new kingdoms in southern Italy and Sicily.

Farther east the Slav Croats emerged during the mid and late 11th century as sufficient of an Adriatic naval power to worry Venice – the state which would soon become the naval super-power of the entire region.

The Northern Seas

The first effective sea-going Carolingian fleet may have been that of Charlemagne which operated against the Frisians of what is now the North Sea coast of northern Holland and Germany. The Frisians were themselves regarded as perhaps the most daring sailors of the northern seas during the 7th and 8th centuries. A subsequent Carolingian fleet attempted to defend the huge Channel and Atlantic coastline of the Carolingian Empire. It was supported by some kind of coastguard system, but together they clearly failed against the Viking onslaughts of the 9th and 10th centuries .

King Alfred is credited with establishing an Anglo-Saxon navy structured along Norse-Viking lines. It seems to have been capable of meeting the Vikings on equal terms, and by the end of the 10th century was even able to carry out a pre-emptive raid against Viking bases in northern

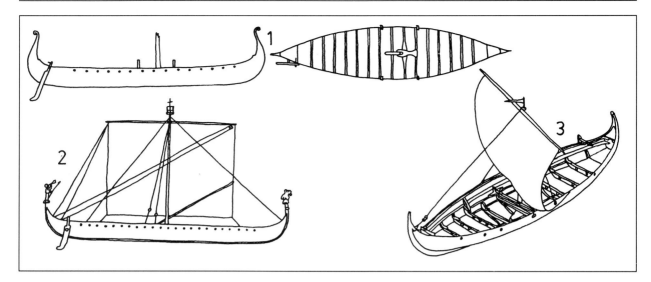

France. The 11th century Anglo-Saxon fleet was still organised, recruited and equipped according to much the same laws as applied to the army on land. Meanwhile the king himself soon seems to have had fourteen 'royal ships'; each with sixty *butscarls*, who were perhaps marines, in addition to *lithsmen* or sailors. Many other vessels were provided by the various south-eastern ports of Anglo-Saxon England in return for legal privileges. The fleet reportedly mustered for inspection each year at Sandwich.

Several Celtic areas also retained their own distinctive naval traditions. Although the ships involved still appear to have been large forms of light, shallow-draught, skin-covered coracles even as late as the 8th and 9th centuries, they could still prove effective as fighting vessels.

Not surprisingly, the Normans' naval traditions were a development of those of their Norse-Viking ancestors, though perhaps with some organisational aspects learned from the Carolingian French. King William II of England's own Royal Ship was, for example, commanded by a *sergeant*, a role which may have been hereditary. Meanwhile several of the main ports of Anglo-Norman England were expected to serve as 'guardians of the sea', even before the development of the famous system of *Cinque Ports*. The men involved were known as *piratae* which, at that time, meant sailors trained to fight at sea rather than pirates in the later sense.

In Scandinavia the various fleets were so important that the entire military system of a country like Denmark was essentially geared to naval warfare. It was based on a *leidang* or levy of ships, men and military equipment. Naval warfare, however, may still have differed in detail between the various Scandinavian lands. For example, archery seems to have been more important at sea in Sweden, whereas it appears to have been more important on land in Norway. Yet everywhere, it seems that the term *stafnbúi*, 'stem man', referred to one of those élite troops who stood at the prow of the ship in naval battles. Meanwhile

Shipping, 650–1100
1. Side-view and plan of the Oseberg ship; Norway, early 9th century. This vessel could be sailed or rowed and was a coastal pleasure craft rather than a fighting ship. It was also constructed in the ancient hull or skin-first technique rather than the newer frame-first system.

2. Reconstruction of William the Conqueror's flagship, the Mora; Norman, mid-11th century. It was essentially a large Viking-style warship, though now with a 'fighting-top' at its masthead (after Landström)
3. Reconstruction of the smaller Skuldelev merchant ship; Denmark, late 10th century (after Stenz)

sea-battles themselves largely consisted of boarding and then close fighting, as on land.

By the 11th century, several other peoples of the Baltic region had fighting ships comparable to those of the Scandinavian Vikings, though in general their ships are said to have been smaller. These Baltic rivals of the Norsemen included the Curonian and Prussian Balts as well as the Slavs of the southern Baltic coast.

River Warfare
The first Carolingian armies were supported by river boats when campaigning against Muslim raiders in southern France. They also launched a fleet on the river Inn in what is now Austria to cow the Bavarians into surrender. Farther east there is no apparent evidence to indicate that the Poles made much use of their great rivers in warfare. The Magyar Hungarians, however, certainly had river fleets on the Danube and Sava when attacking Byzantine-held Belgrade. Their ships were even able to defend themselves from the Byzantines' own greatly feared Greek Fire. Rather later, in 1052, the Emperor Henry III of Germany invaded Hungary, supported by a substantial fleet of boats sailing down the Danube. Nevertheless this operation was less successful than the Hungarians' own use of river warships.

III
THE HIGH MIDDLE
AGES (1100–1275)

THE HIGH MIDDLE AGES (1100–1275)

From the late 11th century great efforts were made, primarily by the Papacy, to divert the warlike energies of Christendom away from internal conflicts, great or small, into aggressive campaigns against the Muslim world and against the pagan peoples of north-eastern Europe. This certainly led to expansionist external wars, but was soon diverted into campaigns against Orthodox fellow Christians in the east, and against those perceived as heretics or who merely opposed Papal power within western Europe itself.

The newly powerful centralising monarchies of Europe meanwhile clashed with local feudal powers and with the increasingly independent cities which were now flexing their political as well as economic muscles in various regions. Warfare and armies changed considerably during the 12th and 13th centuries; with increasing professionalisation and a reliance on mercenary troops, the latter often being recruited from poorer or marginal regions of Europe.

Major Campaigns

1108: Italo-Normans under Bohemond of Taranto defeated by Byzantines.

1109: War between French and Anglo-Normans in France.

1111–19: Campaigns by the French king to impose royal authority within France; these defeated by the Anglo-Normans at Brémule.

1124: War between France and the German Empire.

1125: Renewal of German expansion eastwards into Slav lands.

1135: Kingdom of Scotland seizes western Highlands from Norway.

1135–54: Intermittent civil war in England.

1136: Full-scale baronial revolt in England.

1138: Scottish invasion of England defeated at the battle of the Standard.

1141–4: Count of Anjou (Angevins) conquers Normandy.

1147: German Crusade against the pagans of the southern Baltic coast.

1154–86: Six imperial German expeditions into Italy.

1171: English invasion of Ireland.

1173–4: Baronial revolt in England.

1176: 'Lombard League' of Italian cities defeats the German Emperor.

1186: Vlach-Bulgar revolt against Byzantium; foundation of the second Bulgarian kingdom in the southern Balkans.

1190–4: Imperial German invasions of southern Italy.

1191–7: Danes invade pagan Finland and Estonia.

1194: Imperial German overthrow of the Norman kingdom of Sicily.

1194–8: English recover French lands previously lost to the French king.

1199: Crusade against the pagan Livonians in the Baltic.

1204: French crown's reconquest of Normandy, Anjou and Poitou from the English Angevin king.

1206: Danish Crusade against Osel in the Baltic.

1209–13: Crusade against Albigensian Cathar 'heretics' in southern France; northern French Crusader victory at Muret.

1210: Danes attack pagan Prussians.

1214: English and German invasion of France defeated at the battle of Bouvines.

1216: Unsuccessful French invasion of England.

1219: Danes invade pagan Estonia.

1224: French conquer English-ruled territory in Saintonge and Poitou in central France.

1226–9: Crusade against Cathar 'heretics' in southern France.

1228–30: Papal invasion of German-ruled southern Italy.

1229–34: Crusader conquest of pagan Prussia.

1240: First Swedish Crusade to pagan Finland.

1242: Prussian revolt against the Crusader Teutonic Knights; Russian Novgorod defeats Teutonic Knights at battle of Lake Peipus.

1249: Swedes occupy Finland.

Mid-13th century: Civil wars in Iceland.

1251: Civil war in Sweden.

1254: Further Crusade against pagan Prussians.

1260: Pagan Lithuanians defeat Crusaders at Durben; further revolt of Prussians against Crusader occupation.

1264: Baronial revolt in France.

1266: Kingdom of Scotland occupies Hebrides and the Isle of Man.

1266–8: French Crusade against the Pope's enemies in southern Italy, winning victories at Benevento and Tagliacozzo.

ARMY RECRUITMENT

France

The French ruler could, in theory, summon very large feudal forces from all quarters of his kingdom; including both *knightly* cavalry and infantry. During this period foreign mercenary troops also rose in importance, though their significance may have been exaggerated since the army remained essentially French. None the less the commutation of military service for money payment and a fast-expanding money economy both enabled the King of France, as well as his great nobles, to hire mercenaries. In this way they freed themselves from having to rely solely on feudal forces. The most important impact of such a change lay in the fact that paid professional troops remained in service for as long as their wages or their contracts continued. In contrast, feudal forces normally went home at the end of their forty days of military obligation.

At the same time various factors led to a decline in the number of available French *knights* during the 13th century. As a result largely, though not entirely, mercenary armies came into existence. One such factor was the increasing cost of full *knightly* military equipment. This also lay behind a proportional increase in the numbers of less abundantly equipped *squires*.

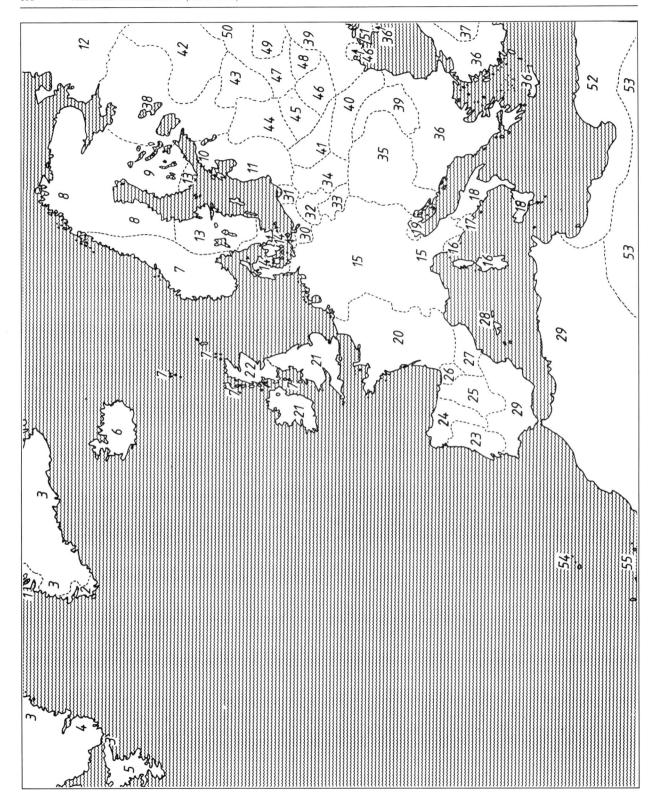

Nevertheless, it would be misleading to draw too sharp a distinction between the feudal and the mercenary *knight* or *squire*. By the late 12th century those French *knights* who clung to a military way of life had, in reality, already become full-time professional soldiers. Those from northern France were either 'self employed' in the sense of being members of a higher feudal aristocracy operating for their own and their families' benefit, or they were military vassals of such lords. Or they were *ministerial knights* serving in such a lord's court; such *ministerial knights* often apparently being promoted non-noble *sergeants*. Or they could simply be mercenaries who hired themselves out for the best pay available.

Within this quasi-feudal structure there were several complex levels of status; the precise meanings of each clearly varying in different parts of France as well as changing from the early 12th to the late 13th centuries. For example, the *juvens* in northern France may have been young members of the military aristocracy who had not yet come into their own inheritances. A *donzel* in 12th century southern France may similarly have been a young nobleman, but by the mid-13th century these *donzels* were also included among low-status *sirvens*, or perhaps they stood between a *sirvens* and a fully fledged *knight* in terms of status.

In addition there were several clear differences between the *knightly* hierarchies of northern and southern France. *Ministerial knights*, tied by their almost non-noble status to their lord, were virtually unknown in the south. Instead paid *stipendiary knights* were common. These southern French *stipendiary knights* were, however, not mercenaries in the true sense of the word, since they received their pay in return for feudal military obligation. As such the *stipendiary* payment rather was a feudal reward replacing the *fief* or grant of land assumed in what might be called classical or typical feudalism. At this point it should, perhaps, be clearly stated that in the opinions of most modern scholars there never really was a 'typical' feudal system; instead there being a whole series of variations upon a basic political or social theme.

Many southern French *stipendiary knights* were actually classed as *chevaliers de maisnade*, members of a lord's military household, who also tended to be related to him by blood. In fact most military vassals in the south lived in towns, rather than in rural areas as in the north. Whereas the 12th century northern French *squire* was either aspiring to the status of a *knight*, or was at least of roughly the same social if not military status, the southern French *escudier* was still a paid servant or a simple soldier of lowly origin. Nevertheless, by the 13th century the status of the southern *escudier* appears to have risen; at least in military terms.

Changes were similarly taking place among the feudal infantry forces of the kingdom of France. By the beginning of the 12th century rural levies may already have been refusing to operate outside their own immediate territory; yet they remained important for local defence well into the 13th century. Urban militias were, meanwhile, rising in importance and here even the town's women were sometimes involved. For example they were on a number of occasions described as pulling the ropes of 'man'-powered *mangonels*. Northern French urban militias seem, in fact, to have been the French king's main source of infantry during the 12th century. Towns which had won the status of communes generally had to accept quite significant military obligations in return for these privileges. For instance they supplied the king's army with a specified number of infantry *sergeants* as well as transport wagons. Despite the somewhat prejudiced picture presented in chronicles and literature, which were largely written for an aristocratic readership, such urban militias could be quite effective, particularly in defence against foreign invasion. On occasions they even defeated bands of marauding unemployed professional mercenaries; though in open battle militia infantry normally needed the help of *knightly* cavalry.

The available evidence suggests that urban bourgeois militias were even more important in the south. They defended fortified towns effectively and also enforced local law and order, even against professional knights who violated the various 'Peace' movements proclaimed by the

'David and Goliath', in the St Etienne Bible from Cîteaux; French, 1109. Goliath has been given fully knightly arms and armour of the early 12th century, including a mail coif which forms an integral part of his hauberk. This illustration also shows the internal holding straps or enarmes of his large shield, as well as the guide strap around his neck. (MS. 14, Bibliothèque Municipale, Dijon)

Church or the king. Within the cities, towns and even rural districts of the southern half of France, there was clearly a very strong sense of communal identity. Here each social class accepted its own specific military duties without apparent resentment. Military duties were, in fact, still widely seen as a privilege rather than an onerous burden. By the late 13th century such southern French militias were of sufficient military value to be summoned almost every year. They served either for the French crown against the English crown, which then held much of south-western France, or vice versa.

Mercenaries did, of course, play an important role. Mercenary cavalry were largely recruited from within France itself, though they also came from neighbouring poorer or overpopulated regions. Other high-ranking 'professionals' included the king's own military officials, the governors of towns and the commanders of royal castles. Many of these were recruited from the ranks of lesser *knights*, or from families who had traditionally provided the French crown with loyal servants. Soon they were also being drawn from the sons of a newly rich and influential merchant class.

The reputation of mercenary infantry was, in almost complete contrast, generally very bad at this time – at least among the ordinary people and the clerical chroniclers. A

'Heroes duelling', on a painted wedding chest; Breton, 12th century. The figures possibly represent Tristan and Morhaut from one of the Arthurian legends, which were very popular in Celtic Brittany. They are particularly interesting because they are fighting without any armour, other than helmets, and carry exceptionally large shields; perhaps of a kind known as a talevas. (Cathedral Treasury, Vannes; photograph, Archives Départementales du Morbihan)

great many came from Brabant in what is now Belgium and the Netherlands. In additional to these Brabançons there were Triaverdins, who perhaps came from the Trier region farther east, and the fearsome Cottereaux whose name is still not fully understood. All were highly effective though ruthless foot soldiers. Their reputed savagery may, however, have reflected the way they themselves were despised by the aristocratic military class who still dominated warfare.

The Empire: Germany

Throughout the 12th century and well into the 14th, Germany was an exporter rather than an employer of surplus military manpower. The German Emperor, who was also titular ruler of Switzerland, Austria, most of Italy, much of what is now eastern France, part of Poland, Bohemia, Moravia and Slovenia, was often seen as the senior monarch of western Christendom. But in reality his military power was often more apparent than real. That part of the imperial army recruited from north of the Alps was still very regional. Each duke or other great magnate recruited his own forces within his own territories; these territories themselves still reflecting the ancient tribal divi-

Left: 'Camilla and Turnus besiege Montalbanus', in the Eneide of Heinrich von Veldeke manuscript; German, late 12th–early 13th centuries. The early forms of great helm seen in German art often have elaborate crests, as worn by the defenders in this picture, or cloth or hat-like decorative coverings as worn by the attackers. One of the attackers also wears a mail coif which only appears to leave small holes for his eyes; an idea rarely seen outside the Germany Empire. (MS. germ. fol. 282, f.46v, Staatsbibliothek zu Berlin)

Right: 'The Betrayal', carved relief; Italian, mid-12th century. The soldiers in this carving use a variety of shields, some of them clearly of the very tall type associated with the successful militia infantry warfare of northern Italy. The forward tipped points of their helmets, and the slight extensions down the neck, are both typically Italian and were rarely seen north of the Alps. (Crypt of Pistoia Cathedral)

sions of Germans and, to a lesser extent, also of the westernmost Slav peoples.

Within this fragmented structure the system of recruitment was also somewhat old fashioned; at least when compared to the recruitment systems currently evolving in France, England and Italy. At the same time the German system showed certain characteristic features rarely seen elsewhere. Perhaps the most distinctive was the unfree 'serf cavalry' of the 12th century, known as *dienstleute* in German or *ministeriales* in Latin. These men had no estates or *fiefs* of their own and, as a result, they were completely dependent on their feudal lord. Nevertheless, they did receive wages if they served outside their own particular province. Such *dienstleute* or *ministeriales* were particularly numerous in the many large Church-ruled regions of Germany.

The Empire: Italy

The contrast between a rather backward Germany north of the Alps and a fast changing, almost modern northern Italy to the south of the mountains was very apparent during the 12th and 13th centuries. Although the Italian countryside was, with the exception of the most mountainous areas, feudally organised, it was increasingly dominated by wealthy towns. Much of the Italian nobility now lived in these towns, including aristocratic families who owned large estates elsewhere.

Here in the flourishing towns and cities of northern and central Italy, military obligations were based upon wealth as much as, if not more than, upon inherited social rank. The revolutionary potential of this situation was exacerbated by the fact that, whereas in most parts of Europe wealth and aristocratic status still normally went hand in hand, this was no longer the case in mercantile Italy.

Despite the increasingly obvious differences between Italy and her northern neighbours, military recruitment within Italy remained overwhelmingly feudal in the sense of being based upon duties and obligations rather than merely upon payment. During the 12th century military service was owed to the German Emperor, but such direct imperial feudal obligations declined steeply during the 13th century. Meanwhile the powerful and highly effective urban militias were recruited on a similar basis; though here an individual's military obligation was owed to the city and only indirectly to some distant imperial overlord. Local *patricians* or members of the aristocratic élite provided the *milites* or *knights*, and also usually the military leadership. Other *milites* were drawn from non-noble families who had long traditions of serving on horseback and which were wealthy enough to afford the increasingly high cost of full cavalry equipment as well as suitable war-horses. Foreign observers of such cities as 12th century Florence were shocked by the Florentine willingness to *knight* suitable merchants or even craftsmen. But at the same

time they grudgingly admitted the high military profi-
ciency of the Florentine cavalry.

Less is known about the situation in the Italian countryside where, however, rural *fideles* may have included cavalry as well as infantry levies. In many ways the role and
status of non-noble Italian feudal troops was similar to that
seen in southern France. The *scutiferi*, for example, may
have been prosperous peasants whose military obligations
were tied to their possession of land. As such they were on
the lowest rung of a ladder of feudal military service. The
rural *contado* around an autonomous city also provided
that city with pioneers and labourers to support the city's
own fighting militia.

Though strictly mercenary troops appeared later in Italy
than in France, they were recorded by the early 12th century. In addition to such real mercenaries, Italian cities
often hired out their own militia forces to neighbouring
rulers in the 12th century. This habit could be seen as the
first stirrings of what became the distinctive *condottieri*
'mercenary company' system of 14th century Italy. In
many cases, however, this was disguised as an alliance. The
complex interplay of such alliances, urban 'leagues' and
military-commercial arrangements even included Byzantine forces; these being recorded in Ancona in the 12th
century.

Southern Italy

The Byzantines had been finally forced out of southern
Italy in the late 11th century, to be replaced by a Norman
kingdom which also included ex-Muslim Sicily. Building
upon the very mixed military heritage of these areas, the
Italo-Normans created an exceptionally effective army and
navy. Here most of the population still had a theoretical
military obligation throughout the 12th century; in fact
men from feudal vassals, urban militias and rural levies
formed half the Italo-Norman army. The most effective
half of the army was, however, paid, but it was still not
'mercenary' in the true sense of the term. The most
important troops in question were those drawn from the
Muslim population of Sicily. Their military service was, in
fact, a form of feudal obligation; since they fought for
their Norman conquerors in return for protection and
religious toleration from these new rulers. The élite of
such Muslim troops also formed one of the king's two
guard units; the other being recruited from among the
Normans themselves.

The strictly feudal cavalry of this Italo-Norman state
came from both the new Norman and the longer established Lombardic *knightly* class. In addition there were the
milites urban *knights* of cities such as Naples and Bari. Generally speaking, however, the Normans tried to keep their
own military élite and that of the old Lombards separate;
in general apparently avoiding too much reliance on local
troops within the southern Italian mainland. In most areas
the local peasantry only supplied military labour and occasional local garrisons. The typical northern Norman system of the *arrière ban* or general levy existed in theory, but

*Relief carving of 'King Herod
with his guards'; southern
French, early 13th century.
The two most important
features where the arms and
armour of Herod's guards
are concerned, are the clearly
separate mail coifs which they
wear, these ending in a bib-like
shape on their chests, and two
different methods of attaching
sword-belts to their scabbard.
Meanwhile the belt of Herod's
own sword appears to be
wrapped around the scabbard
as it lies on his lap. (Façade of
the church of St Trophime,
Arles)*

was only used in emergencies. There was, however, no
avoiding a reliance on locals when it came to naval recruitment. Here the Italian coastal cities provided both ships
and men.

The most notable exception to the Italo-Normans'
unwillingness to give a prominent role to their indigenous
subjects concerned the Sicilian Muslims. Men of this community were recruited in large numbers from a very early
date and soon became the most reliable as well as most
effective element in the Italo-Norman army. They were, in
fact, especially renowned as military engineers. Sicilian
Muslims remained a vital element within the Italo-Norman army until the fall of the Norman kingdom, but they
were only used in Italy or the Balkans – not against their
fellow Muslims in North Africa.

The high military reputation of these Siculo-Muslim
troops, particularly as light infantry archers, was such that
they survived the fall of the Normans themselves by several generations and continued to serve the new rulers of

southern Italy almost until the mid-13th century. By that time, however, the remaining Muslim communities had been transferred from Sicily to the Italian mainland; their military element living in the city of Lucera where they formed a permanent garrison. By the time that these last remnants of Italian Islam were eventually forcibly converted to Christianity, they spoke Italian rather than Arabic and had lost virtually all contact with the heartlands of Islam.

Meanwhile the few real mercenaries in Norman Italy included some infantry from England and France, plus sailors and marines from northern Italy. German cavalry were also enlisted by Manfred, son of the Emperor Frederick II, who ruled the area during the mid-13th century. The later 13th century similarly saw large numbers of Spanish troops moving to southern Italy in search of employment. Some came originally as the feudal followers of various competing commanders; others simply as mercenaries.

England

Far to the north, the kingdom of England under its Anglo-Norman and then Angevin-Plantagenet ruling dynasties, was a relatively peaceful corner of Christendom. At least it became so after the end of the civil war between King Stephen and Empress Matilda in the mid-12th century. Household *knights* had, however, been characteristic of the early 12th century and seem largely to have consisted of *juvenes* or *bacheliers*; younger men who could, in fact, be married though they normally had neither children nor as yet *fiefs* of their own. As such these *juvenes* or *bacheliers* were not 'established' as members of the feudal aristocracy and, since they received pay, they had a certain amount in common with mercenaries. The *vavassors* of the Anglo-Norman state were mostly found in Normandy rather than England. They may have been non-noble holders of military *fiefs*, with lower status and less abundant military equipment than the *knights* themselves.

Left: Effigy of Count Raoul II de Beaumont; French, c.1220. The effigy of Raoul II is one of the earliest such funerary carvings in Europe. The count has a tall, almost flat-topped helmet with a nasal, a mail coif which covers the lower part of his face, a mail hauberk which includes mail mittens, and mail chausses on his legs. His shield is also of the later, short but broader, type, seen from the very late 12th century onwards. (Musée Archéologique, Le Mans; photograph, Musées du Mans)

As the threat of external invasion virtually disappeared during the 12th century, so real feudal military obligations declined within England. The duty to take part in small-scale raiding effectively disappeared; *castle guard* or garrison duty often only being done for payment, while service in the king's army was increasingly replaced by the payment of *scutage*, 'shield money'. This in turn enabled the ruler to hire better trained and more effective professional mercenary troops. Most of England's wars were now fought overseas, largely in France, where money for mercenaries was much more useful than a feudal host which would only serve for a relatively short period. Nevertheless, the Anglo-Norman feudal aristocracy of England continued to provide a small military élite as well as the military leadership.

The urban militias and rural *fyrd* declined throughout most of England, in both its importance and its standards of training. On the other hand the militia of London remained effective for longer than most others. Even so, a theoretical military obligation remained enshrined in law, if rarely used in practice.

Not surprisingly, the main exceptions were found in troubled frontier areas, such as the far north which faced the ever-present threat of Scottish raids or invasion. Here an apparently ancient form of non-*knightly* military obligation was again tied to the holding of land. It was known as *cornage* tenancy, and is considered to have been comparable to the *commorth* of Wales, the *cain* of Scotland and the *pecunia* of the Isle of Man. In northern England, those holding land under *cornage* tenancy were obliged to accompany the king if he raided Scottish territory. They served as a vanguard during the advance and as a rear-guard on the way back; all of which suggests that such troops were regarded as local experts. Other men holding land through *drengage* in ex-Danish areas, or *thanage* in other places where Northumbrian Anglo-Saxon military traditions persisted, appear to have been responsible for both organising and leading local infantry or light cavalry in Border warfare.

An active form of Anglo-Norman feudal military obligation persisted in other troubled areas, such as the newly conquered parts of Wales. It was particularly clear among the new Flemish settlers of Pembrokeshire in the far west. A slightly different system was found in the Welsh marches to the east where free but non-*knightly* 'riding men' may have consisted of light cavalry or of mounted infantry. As such they and their manner of fighting may reflect much earlier military systems; pre-dating the Norman Conquest. In the newly occupied Anglo-Norman eastern part of Ireland, new towns and villages had similarly been given heavy military burdens. These fell on both the few *knights* and on the larger numbers of non-noble settlers. The latter were, in fact, recorded serving as crossbowmen, archers and ordinary spear-armed infantry in the late 12th and 13th centuries. Once again, many of these colonists were of Flemish origin; perhaps including ex-mercenaries who had been given land in return for loyal service. They were clearly effective enough to be summoned to serve the English king both in Wales and in France.

Among the real mercenary troops of England, those in the *Familia Regis* or Royal Household were of élite status, but their origins were often lowly. They also provided a vital professional element in the king's army and could be drawn from many different countries such as Normandy and Anjou in France, both of which were still under the English crown, or from Flanders, Hainault or Brabant in what is now Belgium.

Mercenary infantry were recruited from an even wider area; ranging from Wales and Scotland, both of which were by then under English suzerainty, from the English-ruled regions of France, from among the spear-armed infantry of Flemish cities, from Spanish Navarese, Aragonese and Basque spear or javelin troops; perhaps even from among the Muslims of the Norman kingdom of Sicily. The *Cotteraux* and *Routiers*, who were at this time earning a savage reputation in France, were similarly enlisted by the English crown; as were skilled military engineers from several sources.

Celtic States

The only part of the British Isles and Ireland that did not recognise Angevin English suzerainty during the late 12th and early 13th centuries was the Norse 'Kingdom of the Isles'. At the time this included the Northern Isles, the Hebrides and the Isle of Man. But in many areas English suzerainty was so distant as to have no impact on local military systems of recruitment. In 12th century Wales, for example, almost every man was now a warrior – not merely the old Celtic military aristocracy. The country still consisted of several Welsh principalities, in addition to those areas under direct English rule. Each prince had his own élite *teula* of both horse and foot, some of whom were recruited from wandering adventurers. In addition such rulers could call upon a general infantry levy, summoned from freeborn land-owners on a household basis as had been the case in earlier centuries. Men would apparently be summoned from the age of fourteen onwards and they were expected to serve for the usual feudal period of forty days. Unfree men, comparable to the peasant serfs of England, could volunteer and they seem to have been paid though this was more characteristic of the 13th and 14th than the 12th century.

The Scottish army was still a peculiarly hybrid organisation, consisting of a native levy of extremely mixed origins plus a Royal Household largely made up of recent Anglo-Norman settlers. The way in which the Scottish king addressed his subjects indicated their relative military importance. At the top of the hierarchy were the so-called 'French' or Anglo-Normans. Next came the English or Anglo-Saxons of south-eastern Scotland; then the Scots of the north, who also included the otherwise separate men of the Moray region in the far north; the 'Welsh' of an area stretching from Loch Lomond to Carlisle; and finally the mixed Celtic British-Norse Galwegians of the far south-west. Scotland was also a very poor kingdom whose rulers were rarely in a position to employ professional mercenaries. Nevertheless, Flemish siege engineers were reported in 1173.

The armies of Celtic Ireland, largely consisting of the western two-thirds of the island, seem to have been recruited on the same traditional basis as in earlier centuries. The only really new military group were the largely urban *Ostmen* of Dublin who were of mixed Norse-Irish origin. They, however, soon found themselves at the centre of the new Anglo-Norman administrative system imposed on eastern Ireland. In the mid-12th century one Irish 'sub-king' hired a war-fleet from the Norse Kingdom of the Isles during one of the many petty wars which still plagued Celtic Ireland. A few years later another such 'sub-king' enlisted a small but highly effective mercenary force from among the Norman and Flemish settlers. *Galloglass* professional infantry, originally stemming from western Scotland, also began to appear from the mid-13th century onwards.

Scandinavia and the Baltic

The 12th and 13th centuries were a period of considerable change in Scandinavia. During this period Denmark, Sweden, Norway and even to some extent Iceland, were gradually drawn into the mainstream of western European culture. Meanwhile a simple form of feudalism, largely based upon that of Germany and perhaps the Low Countries, spread across Denmark and the more densely inhabited southern parts of Sweden and Norway. All these regions were, however, old fashioned and somewhat backward by the standards of the rest of western Europe. Even so, Denmark was far ahead of the others. In the early 12th century its military aristocracy was still basically in the old Norse-Viking mould. But now that the Viking Age itself had ended, there were far fewer outlets for the Scandinavians' warlike energies. At first these could be focused on resisting a series of ferocious naval raids by the Slav peoples of the southern Baltic coast. At the same time some of the Scandinavian military élite could find a military role as mercenaries in Russia and the Byzantine Empire. Even the Christian Slav ruler east of Lübeck in what is now northeastern Germany recruited Danish and Saxon mercenaries during the early 12th century.

Then, in the mid-12th century, Scandinavian Christianity took the offensive; first against the remaining pagan

Carved wooden chair from Blaker gård, Lom Oppland; Norwegian, c.1200. The ancient Scandinavian art-form in which animals and patterns were interlaced with one another to form an almost abstract pattern still seems to have influenced this later carving; the swords and shields of the two warriors having become entangled. Nevertheless, the picture is realistic enough for a horrible wound to one man's arm to be shown very clearly. To the right another figure appears to be juggling with swords – unsuccessfully! (Universitetets Oldsaksamling, Oslo)

Slavs of what are now northern Germany and northern Poland; then, at the end of the century, against the pagan Balts and Finns of what are now Lithuania, Latvia, Estonia and Finland itself. This marked the start of the Northern Crusades. The forces involved in these less well-known crusading enterprises were organised along essentially German lines.

Meanwhile, the pagan Baltic victims of these Northern Crusades were still tribal societies in which each freeman was also an active warrior. Even after being forcibly converted to Christianity, a large proportion of the Prussian population continued to live in a traditional manner. As a result the Prussian warriors were still capable of providing useful auxiliary troops to the German Crusading Order of Teutonic Knights who ruled over them. Farther north the Estonians and other peoples of Estonia and Latvia accepted Christianity more readily, although they continued to supply perhaps less willing auxiliary conscripts to the armies of the Crusading Orders in the 13th century.

Eastern Europe

Military recruitment in Poland seems to have been almost entirely internal and rural, there being still very few towns in this area. Slav Bohemia and Moravia were now firmly within the German Empire, their military recruitment and organisation reflecting this fact in being virtually identical with those of neighbouring Germany.

In almost complete contrast, Hungary was, and remained, very distinctive in almost all its military systems. Of the twenty-six recognised aristocratic clans in early 13th century Hungary, seventeen were described as being Hungarian, though not all of these traced their origins back to the first Magyar conquerors. Six others were of German origin and the rest came from France, Italy and even Spain. All appear to have been almost completely 'westernised' in military terms; their warrior élites presumably serving as *knightly* cavalry. Yet there were still many other sorts of troops in the Hungarian kingdom, most apparent perhaps in the eastern provinces of Transylvania where archers, probably meaning horse-archers, continued to predominate.

Transylvania was also the main centre of the *Szekler* community which, though its precise origins remain unclear, served as light cavalry throughout the Middle Ages. They, and the more recently settled Pecheneg Turks, acted as

cavalry advance-and rear-guards for the early 12th century Hungarian army. The Pechenegs had, in fact, crossed the Carpathians from the steppe regions to the east into Hungary in the 11th century and, having been defeated by the Hungarians, were then settled in military colonies throughout the kingdom. Other Turkic nomadic peoples followed, including some Muslim Bashkirs from the Ural mountains much farther to the east. They proved to be loyal troops but, like Sicilian-Muslim troops in the Italo-Norman kingdom of southern Italy, were not expected to serve against fellow Muslims.

A larger and militarily more significant wave of Kipchaq Turkish refugees similarly invaded Hungary in the early 13th century. Once defeated, their leaders were executed. But the rest of these Kipchaq nomads were again settled into military colonies where they mostly served as frontier garrisons. A large number of them, however, was massacred by German troops during a civil war only a few years later, which deprived the Hungarian army of vital light cavalry just before the even more terrifying Mongols invaded central Europe.

Various groups of German troops were found in early 13th century Hungary. They included the Crusading Order of Teutonic Knights who were given large estates along the southern Transylvanian frontier; an area which was only nominally under the control of the Hungarian crown. But these were expelled in 1225 after extending their authority across the Carpathian mountains and attempting to establish their own independent state in the area. In 1260 there were even reports of Byzantine Greek troops in the Hungarian army. By then, of course, the Kingdom of Hungary had extended its frontiers southwards as far as the Adriatic; incorporating Slav Croatia and Bosnia, both of which areas now contributed their own troops to the Hungarian army.

The only remaining independent Slav states in the Balkans were now Serbia and the revived kingdom of Bulgaria. The little that is known about Serbian military structures suggests that its armies were recruited on a largely tribal or clan basis. The regions immediately south and east of the Carpathian mountain range were still dominated by various steppe peoples; first by the Pechenegs, then by the Kipchaqs and finally by the Mongols. The indigenous Vlach or Romanian-speaking peoples of the area largely seem to have been confined to the mountains or at least the higher land. Vlachs remained, in fact, numerous in both the Carpathians north of the Danube and in the Balkan and other ranges to the south.

The Vlachs themselves were a semi-nomadic or transhumant people who could be found in almost all the upland regions of south-eastern Europe from the Russian Principality of Galich in the north to Greece in the south. They were also warlike, being recruited by almost all the armies of the area and generally being used as what might now be called Alpine troops. The Vlachs of what would become the Principality of Wallachia in southern Romania fought for the militarily dominant Turkic nomads of the neighbouring lowlands and, together with them, played a significant role during the uprising against Byzantine imperial rule which in turn led to the creation of the second Bulgarian Kingdom south of the Danube.

The Turks involved in this uprising largely seem to have consisted of those assimilated Kipchaqs who had formed a local military élite in Byzantine service. They then continued to form perhaps the most important element in the army of a revived Bulgaria, with the Vlachs also playing a major role. Although the Slavs now formed a majority of the Bulgarian population, they seem as yet to have had only a secondary military role.

The 13th century similarly saw perhaps the first independent appearance of another Balkan people; the Albanians, who claimed descent from the ancient Illyrians of Roman and even earlier times. Their independence was only sporadic and generally short-lived. In fact it usually resulted from a broader struggle between the Byzantine Empire, which had long ruled what is now Albania, and the Angevin rulers of southern Italy. They in turn had inherited their Italo-Norman predecessors' territorial ambitions in the western Balkans. The Albanians themselves, like the Vlachs, were still a tribal people. The fighting forces of those regions which did achieve independence were, naturally enough, recruited on this tribal basis. The warriors involved also fought for the Italian Angevins as they struggled to set up their own autonomous principality along the Albanian coast.

ORGANISATION

France was viewed by most of its neighbours during the 12th and 13th centuries as the fountainhead, not only of chivalric culture and values but also as a military model. In many ways the organisational terminology used in the army of the French crown can be taken as a model, but each other state developed its own variations according to its particular circumstances.

France

During the 12th century the French would divide a field army into *batailles* or divisions; these then being subdivided into *echielles* or squadrons. The most typical of all such units would have been the cavalry *echielle* which, in turn, consisted at its most basic level of *knights*. Each *knight* would have his own *squires*, war-horse, riding horses, riding mules and pack mules or pack horses. During the 13th century this system appears to have been further formalised until its basic fighting unit emerged as the cavalry *lance*. This, in turn, remained the essential building block of 14th century armoured cavalry armies.

In northern France the role of the 12th century *squire* was as yet largely non-combatant; though these men would take a much more active role in later years. Most seem to have acted as military servants; almost as a separate group immediately behind the battle lines, but close enough to supply their particular *knight* with a spare horse or lance if these were needed. The second *squire*, which most *knights* also appear to have had among their followers, remained further to the rear under the command of a senior officer such as the *gonfanonier*, and could perhaps have formed a military reserve in case the *knights* suffered a setback.

On other occasions the *squires* seem to have been more closely associated with the infantry *sergeants*; suggesting that they could have had a proper, though still subordinate, military role. A great many such *sergeants* formed a substantial part of the urban militias. These were in turn organised, and often also led, by the local feudal lord or his *seneschal* governor in the town, or of one of the king's *seneschals* if the town were a royal possession.

The differences between northern and southern France were as obvious in terms of military organisation as they were in their methods of recruitment. This was even more the case when it came to military attitudes. A new military aristocracy had arisen in the Midi, or south, just as it had in the north. But in the south of France Roman social systems had survived to a greater extent and, largely as a result, feudalism was seen more as a matter of status than as a system of military organisation. Even *knighthood* itself was regarded as a matter of professionalism, rather than having the chivalric and quasi-religious overtones that were fast appearing in northern France. There seems, in fact, to have been remarkably little interest in the abstract concept of individual 'glory' in the south, and even the term *adober*, to 'dub' or 'make' a *knight*, simply meant providing him with proper cavalry equipment rather than involving an elaborate and religious *knighting* ceremony.

Nevertheless, the Church continued to play a significant role in the organisation of local military forces which included *knights* as well as professional infantry and large numbers of local militiamen. Naturally the *milites*, *knightly* class, regarded itself as superior both socially and militarily to the infantry. Yet there is also clear evidence that the *knights* of the French Midi could treat infantry crossbowmen as fellow professionals, even if this did not extend to other foot soldiers.

The Albigensian Crusades of the early 13th century led to a northern French conquest and occupation of southern France. Yet the military and organisational changes that resulted from the Albigensian Crusades were more obvious at the higher military levels than at the lower. Fortified cities and important castles were, for example, now firmly held by royal *baillis* or *seneschals*. Meanwhile many of the old southern attitudes to war and to the military way of life remained much as they had before.

The Empire: Germany

In western and central Europe, the military circumstances of the Empire were almost unique. The state itself was not only vast, but was divided by the Alpine massif into two quite distinct cultural and geographical areas; namely Germany plus its Slav dependencies to the north, and Italy to the south. Separate laws governed campaigning north and

Carved tympanum; German, c.1220. The construction of an early German great helm, and its decorations, are clearly shown in this little carving of a stricken knight. The flat-topped helmet itself had an almost D-shaped face-mask or fixed visor. Over it there is a kind of hat, while the broad decorated guige of his shield hangs around his neck. (Wartburg Castle Museum, Eisenach)

south of the Alps. By the 13th century various parts of even the German regions had extracted clearly specified limitations on their military obligations to the Emperor. One of the most obvious examples was the Duchy of Austria which was soon virtually exempted from operations in neighbouring territories.

The concept of *knighthood* came late to Germany where it also remained rather different from the *knighthood* of northern France or England. In the early 12th century the German term *riter*, which is normally simply translated as *knight*, appears to have meant 'one who went ahead'; not even necessarily a horseman. Sources written in Latin rather than German similarly still included references to *milites pedites*, 'infantry *knights*', as well as those on horseback. But by the early 13th century the *riter* was clearly a member of the military élite and the term would gradually also come to mean an aristocrat. Nevertheless this new German military aristocracy largely evolved from the minor vassals of earlier years and even from the originally unfree *ministeriales*.

The Empire: Italy

Very little is known of the structure and command systems of 12th century northern Italian armies. Yet it does appear that the *squires* took a more prominent and active combatant role than they did in France. *Squires*, for example, were recorded as forming a rearguard during a retreat – a tactic regarded as shameful by some French observers.

More information is available when it comes to the urban militia forces of northern Italian cities. In later 12th century Florence, for example, each quarter or section of the city, and subsequently also each of the main professional and craft associations, was headed by a *consul*. The first 'professional' *consulate* to appear in the written records was that of the *milites* or *knights*. This was soon followed by a *consulate* of the merchants. Each *vicinanze* or neighbourhood also had its own civic military unit within the overall militia structure. Some of these were also responsible for the defence of the many *torre*, tall tower fortifications, which were fast becoming a feature of medieval Italian cities.

The Papal provinces of central Italy were rather less urbanised that the regions farther north, but they were still considerably more urbanised than the German lands beyond the Alps. Here in central Italy a long-established

'Virtue jousting with Vice', carved wooden choir stalls; German, late 13th–early 14th centuries. Vice on the right is unarmed, wears a Jew's hat but rides upon a pig. Virtue on the left may have neither a helmet nor armour. Yet the figure charges forward with a lance in the couched position tight beneath the arm, a small form of later medieval shield, and firmly sitting in a war-saddle with a high protective pommel, high supporting cantle, and a fully developed straight-legged riding position. (Cathedral, Erfurt)

paid professional, though not necessarily strictly mercenary, *masnada* remained responsible for papal security until the mid-12th century. Thereafter, this *masnada* was gradually replaced by feudal forces raised in the Papal States. These, in turn, were commanded by *marshals* whose role was similar to that seen in France. The Pope himself and his leading churchmen had, in effect, now become feudal lords.

Southern Italy

The very mixed military heritage of southern Italy and Sicily naturally had its impact on the military organisation of the 12th century Italo-Norman kingdom. On the mainland the *masnada*, or military following, of a great lord had been the normal military structure under the previous Lombard rulers of the south. A more overtly feudal military system was then imposed by the Normans themselves; though the fortified towns with their own garrisons largely remained outside this system. In many areas a *Master Captain* and *Master Constables* had both civil and military functions; commanding the lesser *constables* of the region for which they were responsible and also leading armies in the field. In Sicily, however, much of the old Islamic system of *iqtāᶜ*, military estates, remained in place. Many of these seem, in fact, to have been converted almost directly into small *fiefs* for the conquering Norman knights. The Sicilian Muslim troops who formed so important a part of the Norman army also retained some of their old *jund* territorial organisation.

England

Norman England was very different from Norman southern Italy, though there were of course some similarities. The Norman rulers of England, and their successors the Angevins, took the kingdom of France as their military model. At the heart of the English military system was the *Familia Regis*, the Royal Household, which provided a large and effective fighting force. Those soldiers actually serving at court included a unit of professional archers or crossbowmen. Other household troops garrisoned important royal castles and cities.

The Anglo-Normans do not seem to have imposed any radically new military structure on the region bordering Scotland. Here local defence seems largely to have remained the responsibility of local Anglo-Saxon *thanes* and *drengs* who perhaps led local militias, rather than being the responsibility of the small number of Norman knights in these border areas. This situation did not, of course, mean that northern England and the Borders remained militarily backward. Rather it indicated that the existing systems worked well and needed minimal change. It is also important to note that the Anglo-Scottish Borders were not yet the war-ravaged regions which they would become in the 14th and 15th centuries.

Further military changes did come about under the Angevin-Plantagenet ruling dynasty of England. Henry II, for example, was so shaken by a widespread rebellion that he ordered thorough reviews to be made of the kingdom's entire military obligations. These resulted in the highly detailed *Assize of Le Mans* in 1180 which dealt with some of the king's French possessions, and the *Assize of Arms* in 1181, dealing with England. Both of these series of military laws or regulations attempted to impose some degree of uniformity on the equipment expected of each group owing military service to the Crown. This was in turn judged according to an individual's wealth rather than merely reflecting his military or social status. As such these *Assizes* were essentially non-feudal documents.

Under the Angevin kings of England, the *Familia Regis* was more than just a standing army. It now formed a pool of skilled and loyal men from whom the king could select *sherifs*, governors and other such key personnel. A man's country of birth was of little consequence if he were considered suitable for the job and this also applied to other aspects of military organisation. For example, Flemish knights commanded English *sergeants* in one early 13th century English army.

Beyond the standing élite of the *Familia Regis*, military obligations such as *castle guard* remained in existence; though in peacetime they were not much of a burden. Important strategic castles may always have had a full garrison, but when the kingdom was in a state of peace lesser castles are likely to have had only a gate-guard, a watchman and perhaps a couple of local knights on garrison duty. By the early 13th century such sleepy *castle guard* duties were widely used as an alternative to more burdensome service with the army. In wartime, of course, much more might be demanded of those who lived in the area surrounding a castle, and from those farther afield.

Celtic States

The 12th and 13th centuries were a time of change for the Celtic regions, just as they were for the rest of the British Isles, but the changes came about in different ways. The Scottish kings, for example, attempted to impose a military system based upon that of their Anglo-Norman neighbours to the south; but it proved to be a very slow process which involved many compromises. Scottish charters from the 12th century mention *knight* service, mounted *sergeants* who held small estates, mounted as well as infantry archers. Most distinctive of all, perhaps, were the feudal *fiefs* which were granted in western Scotland in return for the supply of ships and oarsmen for the royal fleet. The result may have been very mixed, but the Scottish kings could nevertheless field substantial armies, unlike the native princes of a fragmented Wales.

During the 12th century the Celtic rulers of Wales, though divided and often bickering, changed from being little more than tribal chiefs ruling men to minor princes controlling land. Their armies, though tiny, also reflected Anglo-Norman influence by the latter half of the 12th century. Yet the military terminology of Wales remained very largely traditional. Each Welsh prince had his own *teula* of household troops whose loyalty was owed directly to him as prince. The *penteula* or commander of the *teula* was normally one of the ruler's own sons or was at least a nephew. The *teula* itself now included both cavalry and infantry. Its élite clearly wore armour, much of which might have been captured from the Anglo-Normans, and by the 13th century there were even references to the use of horse armour in Celtic Wales. By then, some of the more prosperous local Welsh aristocracy, as well as the prince's own *teula*, were fully armed in much the same manner as their English neighbours – though always being regarded as rather old-fashioned.

Some parts of Ireland remained highly traditional, pastoral and almost semi-nomadic, longer than others. In northern Ireland, for example, the local sub-kings or princes remained for a very long time rulers of men rather than rulers of land. Elsewhere, state and military structures betrayed clear Anglo-Norman influence even before the Anglo-Norman invasions of the 12th century. This Anglo-Norman assault, however, led to a clear division between the eastern and western parts of the island of Ireland. In the east, the Anglo-Norman conquerors imposed a specifically military feudal structure, whereas traditional Celtic military systems survived in the west. Celtic Irish troops were, of course, still enlisted into the forces of the Anglo-Norman east of Ireland, but once the situation settled down the same pattern of commuting direct military service for the payment of *scutage*, 'shield money', which had been seen in England, was now also seen in Ireland.

Engraved gold belt-buckle plaque; Hungarian or German, 13th century. Only the musician beating a tabour or drum gives a slightly exotic flavour to this battle scene. Otherwise the heavily armoured horsemen, with their flat-topped great helms, almost triangular shields and full mail armour, are typical of the knightly élite of most of 13th century western Europe. The three helmeted riders also appear to have quilted cuisses over their knees and thighs. (Hungarian National Museum, Budapest)

Scandinavia and the Baltic

By the late 11th century the ruler of Denmark was a territorial king rather than merely the 'king of an army' as had largely been the case during the Viking era. As a result the 12th century Danish crown started to recruit and organise an army much like that of the rest of western Christendom. A similar process was seen in Sweden, though generally half a century later than in Denmark. Norway may have been even more backward, while distant Iceland, though not completely isolated from military and cultural trends within Europe, was the most old-fashioned of all.

Virtually nothing is known of the military organisation of the now well-established Norse colonies in Greenland, far across the Atlantic on the edge of the North American continent. Recent archaeological evidence indicates close but generally hostile relations between the Greenland Norse settlers and the *Skraelings* or Eskimos; an impression reinforced by the few surviving documentary sources from Scandinavia itself and by the more abundant though later medieval Sagas. The settlers were, for example, forbidden to trade iron weapons with these *Skraelings*, though other forms of exchange were almost certainly carried on. It also seems to have been necessary to fortify the Greenland North American settlements with palisades of some kind.

The Nordic peoples also had other neighbours, some of whom were at a similar cultural and social level of development to that of the Eskimo *Skraelings*. North of the Gulf of Finland the Finns remained only partially converted to Christianity as late as the 17th century. The coastal Finns appear to have been tribally organised, though this system only seems to have been relevant in times of war. Meanwhile the Karelian Finns to the east and the Lapps in the far north remained a nomadic and essentially 'pre-tribal' society with no identifiable military aristocracy. During the 13th century south-eastern Finland was occupied by Sweden, but it remained a poor and backward reflection of an already poor though not necessarily so backward Sweden. Here only a tiny Finnish military élite fought on horseback, the rest remaining on foot.

The Christian Slav rulers of Rügen and Mecklenburg on the southern coast of the Baltic Sea were now considered part of Christendom and soon joined in the Northern Crusades against pagan peoples farther east and north. By the late 13th century the surviving military aristocracy of Prussia had itself been largely Germanised; though some still clung to traditional ways even after becoming Christian. Their Lithuanian cousins remained both pagan and fiercely resistant to Germanic Crusader conquest well into the 14th century. Their traditional but highly effective forms of military organisation also remained little changed. The poorer regions of what are now the Baltic states of Latvia and Estonia were conquered sooner and with much less resistance. Nevertheless, little apparently

changed so far as the indigenous and still largely tribal warriors of these areas were concerned.

Eastern Europe
Some of the apparently old-fashioned features of the Polish army during these centuries may have reflected local military conditions as much as the kingdom's relative poverty. Polish military forces appear to have consisted of the ruler's own following of cavalry, plus a very large infantry force levied from the free peasantry, though only in emergencies. The majority of Polish *knights* apparent still lacked *squires* in the 12th century. Meanwhile the *knight's* relatively rare use of full western forms of armour might, however, have been a result of Poland's tactical need for large numbers of light cavalry in the forest warfare of the Baltic region; this being where the Polish army was so often engaged.

The military aspects of the Hungarian royal household were now consciously modelled on those of the country's western neighbours; at least from the later 12th century onwards. But at the same time the Hungarian kings tried to maintain adequate forces of light cavalry fighting in an essentially steppe–nomadic style. These included the *Szeklers* who were, however, commanded by non-*Szekler* officers. The *Szekler* communities themselves were divided into élite clans and 'lineages'; each clan supposedly sup-

plying a specified number of troops. In addition a more general militia could be levied from the *Szekler* commoners in time of need.

Each wave of nomadic refugees or invaders that entered the medieval kingdom of Hungary was gradually assimilated into the Hungarian military system; though this could take some time. The Pechenegs, for example, arrived in the 11th century, but it was not until the 13th century that their own military aristocracy came to consist of *Comes* or counts and *miles* or *knights*. Such a process could also leave the ordinary tribesman behind, in the sense that he retained traditional social and military structures which were seen as somehow inferior by the dominant feudal élite. A similar process took place among those Kipchaqs who entered Hungary in the 12th and 13th centuries.

The little that is known of the 12th and 13th century Serbian army indicates that it consisted of a small élite of horse-archers, apparently organised and equipped along a combination of Hungarian and Byzantine lines, plus a large levy of lesser warriors. The Bulgarian army, however, was both more advanced, probably better equipped, and was clearly under strong Byzantine influence where its military systems of organisation and command were concerned. To the north the Vlach tribes of the Carpathian mountains are said to have been still at a 'pre-feudal', essentially tribal, stage of social development. Military organisation and defence do appear to have been very localised on a separate valley by valley or even village by village basis. Much the same is understood to have been true of the tribal inhabitants of Albania. Here small local largely Albanian armies under local leadership appeared from the mid-13th century onwards. Later, many of these merged with, though not necessarily being absorbed by, the more advanced feudal or even post-feudal military structures of the Angevin forces which were attempting to occupy Albania. Southern Italian Angevin forces, meanwhile, fought long and hard though with very little success to conquer and hold Albania.

STRATEGY AND TACTICS

Armoured cavalry dominated warfare throughout most of western Christian Europe during the 12th and 13th centuries. Nevertheless, infantry continued to play a vital and perhaps increasingly important role. There were also several distinctly different strategic and tactical traditions in what might be described as the fringe or frontier areas of Christendom.

Broad Strategy
The classic, though not necessarily always typical, warfare of this period was most clearly illustrated in the Kingdom of France. Here armies usually mustered in late spring; assembling at an agreed rendezvous. There is clear evidence of broad strategic planning and forethought, and of considerable efforts to mislead an enemy as to precisely when and where an attack might be launched. Nevertheless, the nature of medieval warfare often made such campaigns rather predictable. Certain castles, such as Château-Gaillard in Normandy, were, for example, essentially built as forward bases and springboards for campaigns into specific enemy regions. So an army assembling in such a place would be seen as having a limited choice of potential objectives.

Campaigns largely focused on the ravaging and devastation of enemy territory; sometimes also with attempts to take key castles or fortified cities. The invading army would, however, normally try to avoid the main defending forces. Initially this would be done by misleading the enemy commanders about the invader's own intentions. But the invading forces might also attempt to catch the defenders unawares and at a disadvantage, whilst striving not be caught in the same way themselves. A graphic account of one such late 12th century invading force describes how it was preceded by scouts and incendiaries who set fire to the enemy's villages and captured the peasants. Then came the foragers who collected the spoils and loaded them into the army's baggage train. Meanwhile the primary role of the main fighting forces was to protect such foragers. Identical strategies were described in 12th

century Italy where this laying waste of enemy territory was known as *gualdana*.

While these destructive operations were being carried out, the élite armoured *knights* would not be riding their expensive *destriers* or 'war-horses', which were only used in battle. Nor would they normally wear full armour all the time; this being both heavy, tiring and limiting the endurance of men and horses. Instead these *knights* and other members of the mounted élite rode *palfreys*, ordinary 'riding horses'. If the men were in dangerous territory they would probably carry their shields, though these would normally have remained in the hands of their *squires* until needed. The *knights* would almost certainly not have put on their helmets until the enemy was either seen or heard. Normally such ravaging armies would move extremely slowly. Nevertheless, élite infantry could cover more than two hundred kilometres in a week and still be fresh enough to defeat enemy cavalry, while mounted troops could, of course, travel even faster.

Although major battles remained rare, just as they had been in earlier centuries, the small-scale skirmishing which characterised most warfare demanded considerable tactical skill as well as broader strategic thinking on the part of military commanders. The still widespread popular view that medieval military leaders lacked both interest and ability in strategy and tactics is totally at variance with the evidence. The normal image of medieval warfare largely consisting of brief but extremely violent clashes of arms was again clearly not entirely correct. In fact, during the 12th century, battles could consist of mutually entrenched camps bombarding each other with stone-throwing engines while small raiding parties attempted to cut the enemy's supply routes, attack his foragers if they ranged too far afield, block roads and defend bridges. In reality the basic imperatives of 12th and 13th century European warfare were essentially the same as they had been for many centuries, and would remain for centuries to come.

The most obvious differences between warfare in the heartlands of western Christendom and that on frontiers or backward regions was a relative lack of heavy cavalry in these most distant parts of Europe. In many cases such marginal warfare was characterised by an even less frequent resort to full-scale battle. The Anglo-Scottish Borders were, for example, a zone of transition with a low density of population. Although the exact position of the frontier itself was well-known to those involved, it had little bearing on local warfare. In fact the Anglo-Scottish Borders remained a relatively quiet area during these centuries, with little raiding by local people. The only major disruptions seem to have been caused by the royal armies of each kingdom either trying to move the frontier to their own king's advantage, or when passing through the Borders on their way to attack the enemy's main centres either to north or south. Even when larger campaigns took place, there seem to have been few attempts by the small local castle garrisons to attack the enemy's extended lines of communication. On the contrary, counter-invasion, counter-raid and retaliation were the normal responses to aggression. Within Scotland itself, however, internal warfare seems to have had a great deal in common with that of Celtic Ireland; with small-scale raiding, cattle rustling and relatively low casualties.

The Irish themselves used such harrying tactics. One sub-king or prince might attempt to dominate a neighbour, but his forces generally tried to avoid killing too many of the enemy. It was, in fact, precisely these people, rather than their land, whom the king was either attempting to dominate or from whom he was attempting to exact tribute. In such warfare the most effective strategy still appears to have been cattle rustling; the stolen beasts generally being returned to their owners once the latter submitted. Those on the receiving end of these tactics would rely on a highly developed *rabhadh* 'alarm' system, intended to provide time for the people and their herds to be taken to a place of safety. If this failed, the defenders would try to ambush the enemy as they made their way home, slowed down by the captured cattle. As a result the rearguard, rather than the vanguard, was generally regarded as a place of honour in traditional Celtic Irish warfare.

During the 12th and 13th centuries the main preoccupation of Welsh warfare was defence against English aggression. This resulted in the sort of prolonged guerrilla warfare that was otherwise rare in the Middle Ages. Welsh forces could attempt to harass and ambush the Anglo-Norman supply trains, particularly in wooded, marshy or confined mountainous terrain. But they rarely attempted to meet such heavier armed enemies in open battle. Above all the Welsh commanders tried to predict and then block an enemy's line of withdrawal, or to force him down a specific route by blocking all others. In response the Anglo-Normans attempted to lure the Welsh into their own ambushes, often by pretending to retreat in disorder. Meanwhile the Welsh also developed a talent for night fighting and adopted some more modern cavalry skills from their Anglo-Norman adversaries. Unlike the Irish, however, the Welsh sometimes adopted a scorched earth policy in the face of more determined English invasions. Bad weather was similarly used by the Welsh to their own advantage, it tending to confine the invaders to valleys and coasts. On the other hand, good weather could lead to the Welsh being trapped in their own relatively open and exposed mountains.

Warfare in the Baltic region had much in common with the Anglo-Welsh struggles. After an initial rush of relatively easy conquests, the Germanic and Scandinavian Northern Crusaders adopted much the same strategy of raid and ambush as their Lithuanian and other Baltic opponents had long used. The forces of all sides were again particularly vulnerable when returning home laden with booty and rustled cattle. By the 13th century, however, the crusading German invaders had developed a sophisticated system of small stone fortifications or blockhouses. From these they could launch raids, ambush enemy raiders, and gradually consolidate their hold over captured territory.

In response the 12th and 13th century Prussians, Lithuanians and other indigenous peoples made skilful use of light cavalry guerrilla tactics in marshes and forests. These were referred to as *latrunculi* or *strutere*, banditry or destruction, and were used both against the Crusader invaders and when the local warriors were serving as auxiliaries after having accepted Christian domination. Farther north, the nomadic Karelian Lapps were meanwhile noted for their skill in winter raiding. Under such circumstances small groups of Karelian warriors, wearing skis, attacked isolated enemy outposts though not the more densely populated centres to the west.

Within eastern Europe the armies of countries like Poland appear to have used a mixture of western and eastern, or more particularly Russian, strategy and tactics. Bohemia was now fully within the German western European military tradition. On the other hand Hungarian commanders seem to have tried to use western European strategies while still having to rely on a large proportion of troops equipped and skilled in their own non-western military heritage. The same was true of the Balkan states where Hungarian, western, Byzantine and Central Asian steppe influences all competed.

Troop Types

Although armoured cavalry remained the dominant élite in most western European armies, the strategy and tactics of this period necessitated the recruitment of a great many other military specialists. It would similarly be wrong to regard those non-élite, largely infantry troops who carried out the process of ravaging and devastation merely as a destructive rapacious rabble. On the contrary, they seem to have included men with recognised specific skills, such as foragers, incendiaries and heavier infantry to guard the supply train. The role of mounted troops could include equally specific skills, though a fully trained *knight* would presumably have been capable of undertaking all duties such as reconnaissance, escort and guarding the foragers. In reality, the armoured cavalry might have dominated battle, but they did not dominate warfare as a whole. By the early 13th century the French king's army, which was widely regarded as an ideal pattern by other rulers, included such military professionals as the *knights*, the mounted *sergeants*, mounted crossbowmen, infantry *sergeants*, infantry crossbowmen and sappers or engineers.

The very obvious increase in the important of infantry throughout most of western Europe was not a consequence of lessons learned during the Crusades. In fact the role of such infantry was basically a development of what had been the case during the preceding 11th century. A clearly increasing importance of archers, and more particularly of crossbowmen, may actually have been in response to the increasing effectiveness of the armoured cavalry charge; even though crossbowmen had initially appeared as a consequence of increased siege warfare. Such infantry were also more effective than is generally recognised. Nevertheless, in open battle they still usually needed the sup-

Right: Tactics, 1100–1275

1. Battle of Tenchebrai, 1106.
The numerically inferior
Norman forces attempted to
win by a sudden charge, but
were struck on their left flank
by a counter-charge by King
Henry's allies from Maine
and Brittany (after Oman)
Norman forces:
A. Robert of Normandy
B. Robert of Bellême
C. William of Mortain
Royalist forces:
D. Ralph of Bayeux
E. William of Warenne
F. King Henry
G. Hélie de la Flèche

2. Battle of Bremûle, 1119.
A very small-scale battle
involving few troops, in which
the first two French divisions
charged into the Angevin
army, breaking through the
first Angevin division only
to be over whelmed by the
dismounted second Angevin
division (after Oman)
Anglo-Angevin forces:
A. King Henry of England.
B. Robert and Richard, sons
    of Henry
French forces:
C. William Crispin
D. Guy de Serranz
E. King Louis of France

3. Battle of the Standard,
1138. An almost entirely
infantry battle in which
several Scottish charges were
driven back by English
archers; after which a cavalry
charge by Prince Henry
pierced the English line but
failed to attack again from the
rear. The Scottish army then
collapsed (after Beeler)
Scottish forces:
A. King David of Scotland
B. Cumbrians and Teviot
    men
C. Prince Henry
D. Galwegians

E. Lothian men and Western
    Highlanders
English forces:
F. Archers and dismounted
    knights
G. Dismounted knights
H. Shire levies
I. The Standard
J. Reserve of mounted men
    with knights' horses

4. The First Battle of
Lincoln, 1141. A direct clash
of cavalry charges in which
the rebel forces succeeded
because they fought with
desperation rather than merely
hoping to take captives for
ransom. The royalist left
scattered the Welsh but were
checked by rebel infantry in
the centre (after Beeler)
A. Walled city of Lincoln
B. Lincoln castle
C. River Witham
D. Brayford pool
E. Fosdyke stream
F. Advance by rebels
Rebel forces:
G. 'The Disinherited'
H. Ralph of Chester
I. Robert of Gloucester
J. Welsh
Royalist forces:
K. William of Aumale and
    William of Ypres
L. King Stephen
M. The Earls (various
    contingents)

5. Battle of Muret, 1213.
An unexpected sortie by the
defenders of Muret challenged
the besiegers' front while a
third division under Simon de
Montfort crossed the supposed
barrier of a marsh to hit the
enemy's rear echelon. (after
Oman)
A. River Garonne
B. Marsh
C. River Louge
D. Citadel of Muret
E. Town of Muret
Allied forces:
F. Aragonese camp

G. Toulousan camp
H. King Peter of Aragon
I. Count of Foix
J. Allied river fleet
De Montfort's forces:
K. William d'Encontre
L. Earl Simon de Montfort
M. Bouchard de Marly

6. The battle of Bouvines,
1214. A large-scale and
protracted pitched battle in
which the French took the
initiative. Several cavalry
charges were delivered by both
sides, followed by a general
mêlée involving cavalry and
infantry. This continued for a
long time until the Allied
forces gradually fragmented
and fled (after Oman)
A. River Marque
B. Marshes
C. Village of Bouvines
D. Forest
Allied forces:
E. Earl of Salisbury and
    Reginald of Boulogne
F. Emperor Otto of Germany
G. Count of Flanders
French forces:
H. Troops of Ponthieu,
    Dreux, etc
I. King Philip of France
J. Troops of Champagne
    and Burgundy

7. Battle of Benevento,
1266. Infantry opened the
battle and the Muslim foot
soldiers drove back the French,
after which the cavalry of both
sides took over. The Germans'
heavier armour initially gave
an advantage until the
Provençals and French started
to thrust rather than cut with
their swords, after which the
Ghibelline army collapsed
(after Oman)
A. Steep hills
B. River Calore
C. City of Benevento
Ghibelline forces:
D. King Manfred of the Two
    Sicilies

E. Lombard and Tuscan
    mercenaries
F. German mercenaries
G. Italo-Muslim infantry of
    Lucera
Guelph forces:
H. French infantry
I. Provençals
J. Charles of Anjou
K. Robert of Flanders

8. Battle of Tagliacozzo,
1268. A flanking attack by
the second and third divisions
of the Ghibelline army caught
the Guelphs in flank; a
frontal attack by the first
Ghibelline division then
completing the rout. As both
forces sped past, the Guelph
reserve charged into the
Ghibelline flank, forcing
Conradin to flee the field.
Charles' tactics may have been
inspired by a similar Mamlūk
victory over the Mongols in
Palestine eight years before,
which was said to have been
witnessed by some men in the
Guelph army (after Oman)
A. River Salto
B. Marsh
C. Steep hills
D. Village of Scurcola
E. Village of Capelle
Ghibelline forces:
F. Conradin of Hohen
    staufen
G. Galvano Lancia
H. Don Henry of Castile
Guelph forces:
I. De Cusances
J. De Clary
K. King Charles of Naples

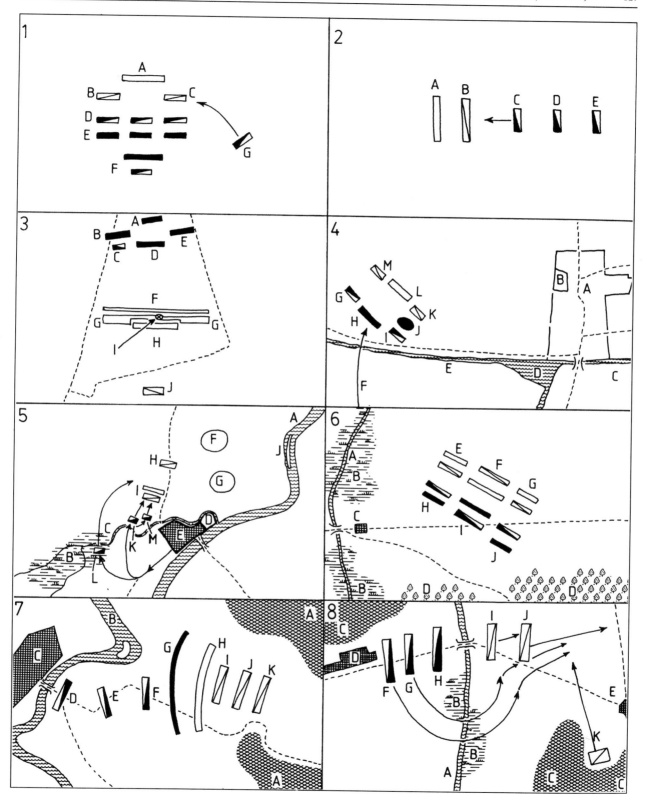

port of cavalry and their morale often needed stiffening by the presence of dismounted élite *knights*.

Whereas armoured *knightly* cavalry remained dominant in most of Europe, there were again clear variations in several border or backward areas. In Poland, for example, contemporary descriptions indicate that the military élite in the west of the country differed from that of the eastern provinces; largely in its greater number of spear-armed and armoured horsemen. In Hungary an élite trained in western modes of warfare may already have formed a majority of cavalry by the end of the 12th century, while in Croatia to the south, western European military styles dominated completely.

In some other areas, light cavalry continued to predominate both numerically and tactically. Those of Wales soon adopted some aspects of Anglo-Norman horsemanship but, like their enemies, were fully prepared to fight on foot when necessary. Tactically they seem to have used sudden and repeated attacks and withdrawals, much like Middle Eastern Islamic and some Byzantine cavalry. Yet it must be remembered that precisely these same tactics had also been used by the late Roman cavalry on whom the Romano-British predecessors of Welsh light cavalry surely modelled themselves. Perhaps such tactics had never died out in the Celtic west of Britain. Small groups of lightly equipped cavalry, riding ponies rather than horses, also provided the main striking power in Celtic Irish armies.

More surprising, perhaps, is a reference to some mid-13th century Norwegian knights who are described as being skilled archers on horseback – though in hunting rather than warfare. Quite how that skill reached Scandinavia remains unknown, but it might have been brought back by Norse-Viking warriors who had earlier served in the Byzantine Emperor's *Varangian Guard*. The renowned light cavalry of the early 12th century Baltic coastal Slavs, and of other eastern Baltic peoples such as the Lithuanians and Prussians, rode lighter horses than their German and Scandinavian Crusader foes. Little is known of their combat skills, at this time, though the mid-13th century Lithuanians are said to have fought much like the Mongols. They, however, harassed their enemies using the javelin rather than the bow used by Mongols and Turks.

Similarly, relatively little precise information survives about the tactics used by the remaining Hungarian light cavalry. Nevertheless, their continued use of traditional weapons such as the composite bow and their wearing of either light armour or no armour at all, suggests that they too relied on traditional harassment tactics.

There was a less clear-cut difference between heavy and light infantry during the 12th and 13th centuries than would be the case in the 14th century. Even so, well armoured men would presumably have been better suited to static tasks such as defending river crossings and fixed positions, or in providing a defensive shield for lighter equipped foragers. In such cases, the infantry were normally supported by cavalry. It is also clear that the mercenary infantry hired by the rulers of more backward parts

of Europe would normally have been classed as heavy infantry. It was, of course, precisely these troops that were lacking in marginal areas like Celtic Ireland.

But the most prestigious and most highly paid infantry of this period were undoubtedly the crossbowmen. The first crossbow mercenaries to be recorded in substantial numbers during the 12th century appear to have been Genoese from northern Italy and Gascons from southwestern France. As yet they were still often associated with ordinary hand-bow archers; Genoa itself sending only ten crossbowmen accompanied by two hundred other archers to support neighbouring Alessandria in 1181. In France, the longbow was not ousted by the crossbow until the early 13th century; nor did the longbow ever disappear in England. By that time, the élite of professional crossbowmen were already mounted, though they probably fought on foot and should thus be classed as mounted infantry.

During the 12th century the Slav tribes of the southern Baltic coast made great use of infantry archers, but these soon found themselves outclassed by the larger longbows and more powerful crossbows of their Danish foes. Perhaps these Slav archers were using a form of short or 'flat-bow' such as was typical of the Lapps, far to the north. Flat-bows are also said to have been used by Welsh infantry. Poisoned arrows, however, were only recorded in the hands of Serb archers.

Other light infantry still used javelins; particularly the *dardiers* of Gascony and several other parts of southern France. Light infantry axes appear to have been characteristic of the Lithuanians, while many Irish foot soldiers still used slings to good effect, particularly against Anglo-Norman cavalry horses. As had been recorded in the 11th century, women were still sometimes expected to help operate stone-throwing *mangonels* in defence of their own fortified home-towns. But such an obligation presumably declined or died away as these early forms of *mangonel* were replaced by the counterweight version known as a *trebuchet*.

Battle Tactics

As has already been pointed out, battles fought entirely by cavalry were extremely rare in the 12th century, yet they may have become slightly more common in the 13th century. Even so, most battles still relied upon both horse and foot. Tactics, of course, varied according to circumstances; but in Anglo-Norman warfare it seems to have been normal for the cavalry to advance in very close-ordered ranks with infantry archers and crossbowmen on their flanks. The role of such infantry was to injure as many of the enemy's horses as possible. When fighting in a defensive manner against a cavalry attack, the infantry were still normally supported by their own fully armoured but dismounted *knights*. Under some circumstances these *knights* would also advance against the enemy on foot and in close-ordered ranks.

Other evidence indicates that, again in a defensive situation, the archers could be placed in front of dismounted *knights* with mounted *knights* behind them; sometimes also with mounted archers on their left flank. The latter were expected to remain ready to hurry to a new position from which they could shoot at the advancing enemy's unshielded right side. The similarity between such tactics and that of traditional pre-Turkish, Arab-Islamic armies such as those of 11th and 12th century Egypt, or pre-Norman Sicily, North Africa and southern Spain, is so striking that some degree of Arab-Islamic influence seems likely. Perhaps it reached the Norman lands the north via Spain or Sicily. Similarly the death of the standard-bearer or the fall of his flag almost invariably signalled defeat in Anglo-Norman or French battles; precisely as it did in Arab-Islamic warfare.

Traditionally, French or Anglo-Norman cavalry were deployed in divisions according to their place or province of origin. They would then normally be under the leadership of the senior count or duke of the area in question. These large divisions would, in turn, consist of *échelles* or squadrons. The exact relationship between an *échelle* and a *bataille* or operational battalion is unclear; though the *batailles* were certainly subdivided into small *conrois* sections, as they had been since Carolingian times. The *conrois* itself now normally consisted of about twenty to twenty-four *knights* in two or three ranks, riding very close together, shoulder to shoulder in a manner described as *seréement*. The *conrois* also appear to have been quite close to one another. Whether a theoretical tactical unit of ten men, known in early 12th century England as a *constabularium*, was actually used in battle is again unknown.

The tactical function of these densely packed cavalry units was to act as shock cavalry; the 'shock' that their charges delivered being largely psychological, as was almost always the case throughout the history of cavalry warfare. They charged at a relatively slow speed and, if they succeeded in breaking the enemy's formation, they would then fight individually in the resulting *mêlée*. Ideally a 12th or 13th century heavy cavalry charge hoped to break right through an enemy line, then turn and charge once more from the rear.

There was also clear use of operational reserves, intended to take advantage of any such break in the enemy's front. Such reserves were, like most other ambush forces in the typical tactics of the French and neighbouring peoples during the period, almost always of cavalry. They could also be thrown against an enemy's flank if the opportunity arose; particularly if this could be done unexpectedly and from cover. Franco-Norman and Anglo-Norman cavalry of the 12th century certainly continued to make use of feigned retreat. Meanwhile the cavalry of 12th century Milan in northern Italy earned widespread praise because of their discipline and restraint in remaining to support their infantry, instead of charging off in pursuit of broken enemy horsemen.

Infantry tactics are recorded in less detail. The little that is known largely deals with heavy infantry; the evidence for lighter foot soldiers indicating that their main role would have been to harass an enemy and perhaps launch ambushes, sometimes in conjunction with the cavalry. Evidence from the 12th century describes heavier infantry being drawn up in three divisions behind a defensive ditch, but still remaining vulnerable to flank attack by enemy cavalry. To defend themselves from this danger, infantry would try to secure their flanks against natural obstacles or topographical features. Or they would adopt a 'crown' formation which faced in all directions, or their flanks would be covered by their own cavalry forces.

This was normally the case in Italy where infantry warfare was more advanced, more disciplined and also more effective than elsewhere in Christian Europe; their only real rivals being found in Muslim Spain. Northern Italian militia forces were described as fighting in close-ordered ranks with their city's *carroccio* or 'banner-wagon' forming a rallying point and a refuge for the wounded. These men used their long spears almost as pikes against the enemy's largely unarmoured horses; a tactic which demanded considerable discipline, and which was often fully capable of withstanding a cavalry charge. Nevertheless, even the highly disciplined infantry of the northern Italian cities needed the support of armoured cavalry. Here horse and foot clearly fought as an integrated team. A noted example was at the battle of Legnano in 1176, where the Milanese infantry militia fought the Emperor's German cavalry *knights* to a standstill, thus giving their own cavalry time to reform and successfully launch a counter-attack.

Fringe areas, where the bulk of troops still fought on foot, developed their own infantry tactics; though few were as effective as those of northern Italy. The Scots, for example, used the *schiltron* in open terrain. Here their characteristic massed spearmen all faced outwards in an essentially circular formation. But this was not as disciplined as the manoeuvre seen in Italian infantry warfare, and their spears were not yet as long as real pikes. Northern Welsh spear-armed infantry fought in much the same manner. Elsewhere, Welsh forces are described as placing their cavalry either at the centre or on one flank, or on high ground ready to swoop on the enemy should an opportunity arise.

The military theorists of the mid-13th century do not appear to have been hidebound or blinded by tradition. Following the devastating Mongol invasion of central Europe, one such theorist suggested dealing with the Mongols' unfamiliar horse-archery harassment tactics by using massed crossbowmen. As an alternative he suggested placing heavily armoured cavalry, riding fully armoured horses, in the front ranks; apparently with large shields with which they hoped to protect their horses' heads from the Mongols' arrows. There is, however, no evidence that such ideas were put into practice.

Combat Styles

Basically, there was very little change in the skills demanded of cavalry or infantry during this period. The heavy horsemen now relied overwhelmingly on the *couched* lance; the armoured *conrois* now having become a battle-field 'projectile' in its own right. The *conrois* could, in fact, be regarded as the only real projectile available to a 12th or 13th century western European military commander. The many references to apparent individual combat between champions is likely either to have been a mere literary convention, or it might have referred to the leaders of small units whose followers were also involved in such combats.

Meanwhile, a crossbowman's skills remained what they had always been; though his weapon was clearly increasing in power. When fighting on foot, at least in 13th century Germany according to literary sources, even the *knights* continued to use javelins. Elsewhere this weapon was rarely regarded as suitable for a member of the military élite. On the other hand, *knights* were fully prepared, if necessary, to break the shaft in order to have a shorter spear suitable for use on foot. Under such circumstances they were described as advancing on foot in essentially the same close-ordered *conrois* formations as they used when on horseback.

Field and Camp Fortifications

The little detailed information available concerning field fortifications suggests that there had been no great changes since the 11th century. Such defences still consisted of ditches, earth banks or ramparts, wooden palisades or iron-pointed wooden stakes. The existence of the latter, however, clearly indicates forethought, planning and the preparation of perhaps re-usable field fortifications before the start of a campaign.

WEAPONRY AND HARNESS

The pace of change in the development of western European arms and armour quickened during the 12th and 13th centuries. Archery was probably the main stimulus; particularly the development and wider use of crossbows which alone were capable of challenging the armoured *knight's* domination of the battlefield. The crossbow may, in fact, have been largely responsible for the adoption of face-covering helmets, heavier body armour and also horse armour. Partly as a result of such developments, there was an increasingly clear separation between the arms and armour of cavalry and infantry. Climate did play its part, though largely in the way in which such new challenges were met and in the materials used by the armourers in question. It is also interesting to note that many new aspects of armour design and construction were first seen in southern Europe, including Spain and Italy; areas under close Byzantine or Islamic influence where archery had long played a dominant role in warfare.

Archery

There were no significant changes in the design of hand-held bows. The simple longbow remained much as it had

for centuries throughout most of north-western and central Europe, while an essentially sub-Roman form of semi-composite bow with bone stiffening appears to have remained in use in parts of the Balkans and Italy.

The really important technical developments concerned the structure and mechanism of crossbows. Efforts by the Church and by the German Emperor to ban or restrict the use of crossbows in warfare among Christians failed. Instead this weapon was positively encouraged in France and England. Nevertheless, the crossbow as a war-weapon remained more common in southern than in northern Europe until the end of the 12th century. The 13th century then saw its dramatic spread to almost all corners of Europe, including Scandinavia. But the military impact of the crossbow was most obvious in the prosperous autonomous cities of Italy and, only a short while later, in the cities of western and northern Germany. Shooting guilds seem to have sprung up quite suddenly, with Saints Sebastian and Mauritius as their patron saints. Similarly, shooting competitions began to be recorded in large numbers; again south of the Alps at first, but by the late 13th century also in the German Empire.

Crossbows of composite construction had probably been known in the Islamic world for some time, but were first recorded in Europe in the second half of the 12th century. The system of combining wood, horn and sinew in these composite crossbows was, however, very different from the system used in the making of an Asiatic composite hand-bow. It was also technically much inferior; the reasons for this discrepancy remaining unknown. Nevertheless, such composite crossbows provided greater power for the same weight.

On the other hand they correspondingly needed greater strength to *span* or pull back the bowstring. The first consequence of the greater strength of such 12th century crossbows was the attachment of a metal stirrup to the end of the *stock* or *tiller*. This feature may also have been associated with the use of a *spanning hook* attached to a waist-belt, which also appeared at about this time. By the beginning of the 13th century a normal-sized war crossbow had a draw of about 85 centimetres. But as the weapons grew stronger, the bow-arms shorter and the methods of *spanning* them more effective, this long pull was considerably reduced. The crossbow's ability to shoot shorter *bolts* or *quarrels* had other advantages since these missiles were not only aerodynamically superior to a full-length arrow, but would also soon evolve into a relatively stout armour-piercing missile with a heavy, sometimes specially tempered, steel head.

The larger crossbow for use in the static defence of fortifications was certainly known by the 13th century. This was not necessarily the huge frame-mounted device of earlier years, but simply a heavy crossbow which could be rested on a wall or parapet, or on a cart in open battle. The terminology is varied and far from clear, but many of these larger weapons may have been classed as *ballista de torno* in

Italian, with comparable names in other languages. They would probably have been *spanned* by a windlass, a device normally too complicated for use in mobile warfare. In some areas the crossbow achieved an almost mystical status, perhaps because it arrived quite suddenly amongst hitherto militarily primitive peoples. In Finland, for example, the *Kalevala* national epic may have developed at about this time. In these verses the hero has a magical metal crossbow with a bowstring of elk sinew, bolts with oak shafts and pinewood heads, but tipped with primitive bone – an extraordinary mixture of late medieval and virtually Stone Age technology.

'Huntsman', carved relief by Master Radovan; Dalmatian, 1240. Although the style of art of these 13th century carvings from Dalmatia are typical European, some of the subjects illustrated differ from those seen across the Adriatic sea in Italy, or elsewhere in western Europe. This huntsman is drawing an early medieval form of composite bow, such as was used in the rest of the Balkans and the Byzantine Empire. His quiver, however, is like a later quiver for crossbow bolts and may have been developed from the Central Asiatic or nomad form of quiver which fully enclosed its arrows. (West door of Trogir Cathedral, Croatia)

Swords

Whereas the 12th century saw greater uniformity in the design of western European swords than had been seen before, the later 13th century witnessed the early development of a number of divergent types. In the normal 12th century weapon the emphasis was still on cutting rather than thrusting; though not to the exclusion of the latter. Most swords appear to have weighed from one and a quarter to one and a half kilograms. During the mid-13th century there was a gradual separation of specialised cutting and thrusting weapons; the former often increasing in size to a substantial extent. References to horsemen carrying two swords were widely recorded – from the Crusader States of the Middle East to Iceland in the far north-west of Christendom, but this feature appears much more rarely in late 13th century art. Nevertheless, the weapons involved are likely to have consisted of a heavy slashing weapon and a lighter thrusting one. Meanwhile, use of the curved sabre which had early been common in some parts of nomad-occupied central Europe, seems to have died out. The only remaining exceptions were the most recently arrived refugees or invaders from the steppe lands to the east.

Spears

The ordinary cavalry lance of the *knight* saw a continuing adoption of smaller but stronger, shield or armour-piercing, spearheads. The lance itself was sometimes described as being of ash wood, about three metres long or slightly more.

An increasing specialisation among infantry weapons and their increasingly varied terminology again reflected the growing importance of infantry, despite their still subordinate role. The spears of those feared 12th century Brabançon infantry were described as being longer than those of French cavalry; thus almost rating as *pikes*. Half a century later, foot soldiers from neighbouring Flanders wielded similarly long spears which now also incorporated hooks for dragging a horseman from his saddle; a device which might almost be classed as a *staff weapon* or *pole-arm*.

Other Weapons

The development and use of true *staff weapons* refers to those which could cut, thrust and perhaps also drag down a cavalryman. Their emergence virtually presupposed the existence of disciplined professional foot soldiers. The first apparently new weapon to be mentioned in such a context was the *gisarme*, *jusarme* or *guizarme* which may have originated within the Iberian peninsula. It was a distinctly 'non-noble' weapon that could be used in open battle or in the most confined street fighting; probably having a curved blade with or without a hook at the back.

The *halberd* form of long-hafted axe with a thrusting blade at the top had yet to appear, but the process which would lead to its development may already have started by the late 12th century. By then, for example, in an area such as the Scottish Borders the old Viking-style war-axe

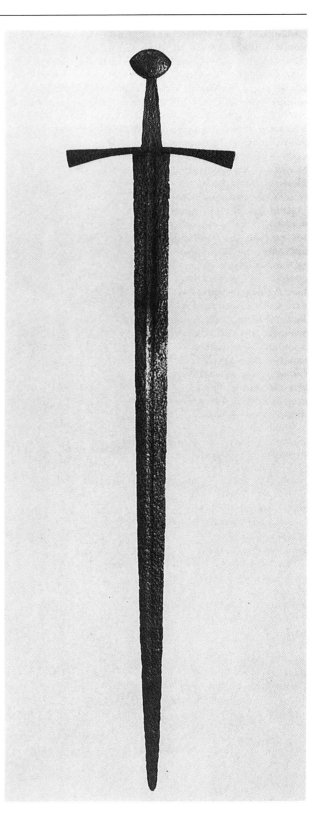

had lost its downwards curving 'beard'. Instead it was developing an upwards curving tip to the blade; presumably to enable its user to thrust as well as chop at his opponent. In Scotland this particular weapon would evolve into the *Jeddart Axe* of the late Middle Ages. In Ireland a very different process led to the evolution of the equally famous *Galloglas Axe*, a fearsome long-hafted infantry weapon which first appeared in western Scotland.

The use of the *mace* as a *knightly* weapon in 13th century western Europe was one of relatively few ideas that clearly stemmed directly from military experience during the Crusade. Nevertheless, the armour-breaking flanged *mace* of Europe took the rudimentary flanges of the original Islamic weapon to extreme lengths; clearly in an effort to break the increasingly effective and heavy armour used in western Europe. Meanwhile, in eastern Europe an almost opposite process was taking place. Here the light cast-bronze, lead or iron studded *mace*, known as a *buzogány* in Hungary, had originally been introduced by lightly armoured warriors of steppe nomadic origin. This, however, was now being rapidly abandoned, it being ineffective against heavily armoured European foes. The light *mace* did survive among light cavalry in some areas, and would eventually be reintroduced in a slightly heavier form by the Ottoman Turks at the end of the Middle Ages. In all cases its name reflected its Turkish origin, and probably came from the Kipchaq dialect term *buzgan*, meaning 'crusher'.

Shields

At first, the general adoption of the *couched* lance and close-formation *conrois* cavalry tactics led to a considerable increase in the size of a *knight's* shield. These were generally known as *targes* and normally made of leather-covered wood. Entirely leather shields seem to have been reserved for infantry and even then only in limited areas such as

Left: French sword, 1150–75. This rather rusted sword is a very typical weapon of the later 12th and early 13th centuries. There is a small amount of gold inlaid inscription in the fuller or groove along the blade and the tang between the quillons and pommel would, of course, originally have had a comfortable wooden grip, probably covered in leather. (Private collection; photograph, P-R. Royer)

Right: The interior of a small wooden shield or buckler made of willow and poplar, as found during excavations in Amsterdam; Dutch, 13th–14th centuries. The shield is basically flat, with a substantial wooden reinforcing cross-bar which also forms a hand-grip inside the metal boss. The outside of the shield was strengthened by a circular metal strip near the edge. (Photograph, DOW/AHM-Afd. Archeologie, Amsterdam)

southern France where they were clearly a result of Islamic influence coming northwards through Spain. Leather shields also seem to have persisted in some Celtic regions.

The wear and tear on such shields meant that a member of the armoured cavalry élite went into battle with several spares being carried by his *squires* or servants. The infantry often also used a very large shield during the 12th century; this also being known as a *targe* or as a *talevas*. The latter term was perhaps a pun, suggesting that it was the size of a 'table'. In some parts of Europe this very large cavalry shield remained in use even beyond the mid-13th century, particularly in Italy where it was known as a *tavolaccio*. Elsewhere, cavalry shields steadily shrunk in size, though perhaps becoming thicker in construction. This almost certainly resulted from the adoption of new forms of semirigid body armour which tended to make the large shield redundant.

Helmets

Whatever the shape of a helmet, it was considered necessary for a *knight* to cut his hair before going to war; both to ensure that his helmet fitted snugly, and to show proper respect for his foe. Over and above such social attitudes, however, changes in the design of helmets reflected the increasing threat from the crossbow and the *couched* lance.

The most obvious development was that of the *heaume* or *great helm* which, in its final form, completely enclosed the wearer's head. During the 12th century some long-established forms of both pointed and rounded helmets, of both one-piece and segmented *spangenhelm* construction, were given a very long and broad nasal. This virtually obscured the wearer's face and, in effect, served as a face-mask; particularly when the sides and lower part of the face were also protected by a mail *coif*. The earliest examples of such helmets were seen in the Iberian peninsula where, again, they are likely to have reflected Andalusian Arab-Islamic influence as well as both a traditionally greater importance of archery and a precocious development of the crossbow for use in war.

Helmets known as *great helms* existed in the kingdom of France by the 1160s. At about this time the Count of Loos requested some of these new protections from the French king, since they were not available in his part of northern France. Within a few years various early face-mask forms of

great helm were appearing in pictorial sources. Most were of the flat-topped type, but complete face-masks were also shown, attached to both rounded and pointed helmets. The true *great helm*, which also protected the sides and back of its wearer's head, appeared by 1220. The late 13th century similarly saw the first references to a *heaume à visère*, which perhaps suggests a movable visor, though this would not appear in pictorial sources until the early 14th century. The re-appearance of elaborate helmet crests and flowing cloth *lambrequin* helmet decorations from the late 12th century onwards was also closely tied to the development of the *great helm*.

The brimmed war-hat or *chapel de fer* had been known for some time, but it now saw a considerable and quite dramatic increase in popularity, particularly from the later 12th century. This was not seen among infantry *sergeants* only, but also among the *squires* and *knights* of southern Europe where heavy and stuffy *great helms* must have been exhausting to wear, particularly in summer.

Plain round and pointed helmets without *nasals* continued to be used in the second half of the 12th century, but whereas the latter soon faded from fashion in most areas, the simple round helmet seems to have become lower in outline and probably evolved into the close-fitting *cervellière* of the 13th century. The true *cervellière* was used by all classes of soldier and could be worn over or beneath a mail *coif*. It could also provide an additional protection beneath a *great helm*; some sources specifically referring to otherwise unexplained 'doubled helmets'.

When worn on its own over the *coif*, the *cervellière* may in addition have evolved into, or contributed towards the development of, the later *bascinet* form of helmet. This in turn first appeared in mid-13th century Italy. It normally extended to protect the sides and rear of the wearer's head, though leaving the face largely exposed; at least until movable visors were attached to such *bascinets* in the 14th century. It has been suggested that the early *bascinet* almost certainly reflected Byzantine, Mongol or more specifically Middle Eastern Islamic influence. Although the evidence remains circumstantial, the theory is quite convincing.

Other types of helmet were still to be found in central Europe and again they reflected both residual earlier fashions and newer eastern influence. In 12th and 13th century Poland, for example, a helmet of directly riveted segments but lacking the frame of a *spangenhelm* was known as the 'Great Polish' form. This was a direct descendant of those helmets, of ultimately Central Asian stylistic origin, that were also used in Russia and perhaps Byzantium. Comparable types were found in Baltic Prussia and in Hungary. Several helmets that appear in Hungarian art, in addition to a few surviving fragments, were of more recent Central Asian origin or inspiration. They would, presumably, have been used by troops of relatively recent steppe origin.

It had long been normal in western Europe for a soldier's head to be protected by a mail *coif*. The separate form of coif may have been known in earlier years, but it only became common in the late 12th and early 13th centuries. A mail flap called a *ventele* or *ventaille*, which was laced across the lower part of the face in battle, had again come into general use by the 12th century. Like helmets themselves, the mail *coif* would invariably have been worn over a padded non-metallic *coif* or *arming cap*. Some of these included a substantial ring of quilted material around the top of the head; clearly to support a flat-topped form of *great helm*.

By the late 13th century separate mail *coifs* were sometimes extended to cover the entire shoulders and even part of the upper arms, chest and back. These could be regarded as an early form of *tippet*, though in its fully developed form the latter would normally lack a head-piece. Instead it would consist of the shoulder element plus a semi-rigid or stiffened collar; or could consist of an extended form of mail *aventail* extending beneath the rim of a helmet rather than being attached to this rim. Other perhaps overlapping terms for such neck and shoulder defences, most of which date from the late 13th century, include the *capmalh*, *cols sfrachis* and perhaps *cuychals* of southern France, and the *gorgieri* of Italy. *Ailettes* worn on the shoulders were, of course, solely a means of heraldic display and had no protective function. They were often made of painted paper stuck on a slender piece of wood.

Body Armour

The mail *hauberk* remained the main form of armour throughout the 12th and 13th centuries; though by the end of this period it was widely supplemented with other forms of protection. It normally weighed slightly more than ten kilograms and, with proper padding, was quite comfortable even in hot weather. The *hauberk* already came in several forms: from the *jazerenc* of Middle Eastern origin which incorporated its own quilted lining and could also have a decorative fabric cover, to the lighter *aubergel* or *haubergeon* used by poorer troops. This is believed to have had short sleeves, or at least to have lacked the hand-protecting integral mittens or *mufflers* which came into use in the later 12th century.

A quilted or padded garment would almost certainly always have been worn beneath a mail hauberk. Otherwise any strong blow from a weapon would simply have driven the mail links into the wearer's flesh, or at least have broken some bones. This padded garment, rather than the

Iron chapel de fer 'war hat' helmet; probably German or Scandinavian, late 13th–early 15th centuries. This kind of brimmed helmet with a slightly bulbous bowl was characteristic of late 13th and early 14th century Scandinavia, but continued to be used by ordinary infantrymen for many years later. Its construction is essentially of the segmented spangenhelm form, though the bowl basically consists of two pieces; not four as might at first appear. (Museum of Estonian History, Tallinn)

Opposite page: Statues from Hereford; English, early 13th century. The two typical seated knights in these carvings portray three interesting features: the flat-topped great helm which still does not extend to cover the whole of the back of the wearer's head; the almost flat-topped outline of the other figure's mail coif, indicating some kind of arming cap beneath to support a great helm; the very thickly padded shoulder between the surcoats and mail hauberks of both men. This may indicate that they are wearing the otherwise not fully understood spaulder or espalier form of shoulder protections. (On loan; Cloisters Museum, New York)

Below: 'Massacre of the Innocents', relief carving; Swedish, late 13th century. The soldiers in this carving are shown in the same manner as other such carvings from Germany, France and England —except for the man closest to King Herod. He has a form of scale cuirass over his surcoat and also protecting his upper arms. This might be regarded as the artist's effort to make the soldier look oriental and thus 'wicked', but various forms of body protecting cuirass were being used in the later 13th century. And scale armour comparable to this appears in a more realistic manner in Italy, where it almost certainly did exist as a genuine form of protection. (Linköping Cathedral; photograph, Colette Nicolle)

hauberk itself, would have accounted for the bulky broad-chested appearance of late 12th century armoured men, even when they were attempting to hide their armour beneath other clothing. At about this time, references to other specific forms of *soft armour* also appear; though it is often difficult to differentiate between the various types.

The *aketon*, for example, was almost certainly quilted; its name stemming from the Arabic word for cotton. Meanwhile the *gambeson* or *wambasia* may have been a larger, perhaps finer-looking garment with longer sleeves. The term *pourpoint* was perhaps applicable to them all, and reflected their method of construction rather than any particular shape or cut. The effectiveness of such *soft armour* was clearly sufficient for the *gambeson* widely to replace the old mail *haubergeon* among 13th century infantry. It was also considered suitable for non-élite cavalry *squires* or *sergeants*. Whether the decorative and, soon heraldic, *surcoat*, worn over armour and first introduced to western Europe in the mid-12th century, was also padded or quilted remains unclear.

Tests have shown that mail can absorb arrows shot from a reasonable distance, but it could not prevent them causing minor wounds. *Lamellar* armour, however, was much more effective against arrows. But *lamellar* is very rarely found in medieval Christian western Europe, either in the archaeological records or in documentary and pictorial sources. The only 12th and 13th century exceptions

appear to have been the Baltic, Scandinavia and perhaps the Norse-Viking settlers of eastern Ireland. Nevertheless, the 14th century western European *coat-of-plates*, and probably its varied 12th and 13th century predecessors, almost certainly evolved from – or was inspired by – the Asiatic and Islamic lamellar *jaw̱shan* body protection; particularly by the smaller abdomen- and torso-covering versions of the latter oriental armour. It is similarly worth noting that some of the earliest illustrations of a form of western European *cuirass* which could be interpreted as an early *coat-of-plates*, come from northern Spain and Germany. In the former instance Andalusian-Islamic influence can be assumed, while in the case of Germany some influence could well have stemmed from eastern Europe and the Baltic region.

The *curie* was the first such semi-rigid *cuirass* of the late 12th century. It was probably made of hardened leather and would have been worn either over or beneath a mail *hauberk*. The *coirasses* of early 13th century Provence were probably much the same, and by the late 13th century a 'poncho-like' *pair of plates*, *coat-of-plates* or simply *plates* could clearly be worn over a hauberk. Nevertheless, a reference to iron plates being riveted inside a piece of cloth and worn beneath a hauberk in France in 1185 is likely to have been an unusual experiment at such an early date.

Another less clear form of body armour was the *panceriam* or *pansieri* of early and mid-13th century Italy; the term perhaps stemming from the German *panzer*, meaning armour. In 1219 one such protection was described as having a mitten on only one of its sleeves, though it did incorporate a coif. In 1260 a *panceriam* was clearly stated to be different from both the ordinary mail *hauberk* and the *lamieri* cuirass or *pair of plates*. It may, in fact, have been a special form of padded, cloth-covered mail or even scale-lined hauberk, though as yet the question is unresolved.

Limb Defences

Most 13th century mail *hauberks*, and many *soft armours* such as the *gambeson*, incorporated *mufflers* or mittens to protect the hands. But separate glove-like gauntlets did not reach the west until the late 13th century, when they may at first have been known as *pons*. In fact they probably arrived from Byzantium where they seem to have been known several decades earlier.

Separate leg armour had probably never dropped out of use entirely and it began to be increasingly popular again in about the mid-12th century; particularly for armoured cavalry. This again suggests a growing threat from infantry forces. These mail *chausses*, *cambieras* or *stivaletti* could cover the entire leg from mid-thigh to foot like stockings, or they could be laced around the front of the leg and over the top of the foot. In each case they appear to have been held up by straps to a *braquier* girdle worn beneath the *hauberk*. Quilted and possibly sometimes scale-lined *cuisses* for the thighs appeared in the later 13th century. The first pieces of plate armour for the limbs to re-appear in western Europe were hardened leather knee-cops

attached to such *cuisses*. Comparable small pieces of plate protection for the arms had to await the end of the 13th or even the first years of the 14th centuries.

Horse Harness

Few changes were apparent in horse harness, the fully developed curb-bit not being reintroduced into most of western Europe until the late 13th century. Once again it was probably a result of Islamic or Byzantine influence. Meanwhile, the influence of the nomadic peoples of the Eurasian steppes continued to be felt in the horse harness of Hungary, the Balkans, the eastern Baltic regions and perhaps Poland.

The deep seated or 'peaked' saddle associated with the *couched* lance technique of warfare had become standard equipment for the *knightly* war-horses of western Europe by the early 12th century. But a tall protective pommel at the front and a tall supporting cantle at the back were not sufficient, on their own, to withstand the jarring impact when delivering or receiving a direct blow with a *couched* lance. The saddle itself had be attached more securely to the horse. For this reason a broad *poitral* breast-strap was just as vital for the heavily armoured cavalry of western Europe. But even this could burst, and so by the 13th century such wide breast-straps were sometimes wrapped around the rear of a saddle, rather than merely being buckled to its front.

Horse Armour

Horse armour re-appeared in western Europe in the late 12th century, though it remained rare until the mid-13th century. By then, rich states such as Milan could field a large number of 'iron-clad horses'. Elsewhere, the fabric *caparisons* shown in many pictorial sources may also have covered mail or quilted *trappers* and *bards* of *soft armour.*

Protection for the animal's head may not have re-appeared until the mid-13th century; with the possible exception of earlier references in the Iberian peninsula. Written sources then began to refer to *testières de cheval* and hardened leather *coopertus* or *copita*; sometimes with a neck-protecting extension or *poll* at the back.

FORTIFICATION

The 12th and 13th centuries saw a huge upsurge in fortification across most of Europe, both in urban defences and isolated castles or fortresses. In many parts of the north the old wooden stockades and wooden keeps were replaced by strong stone structures. Nevertheless, these usually remained refuges rather than habitations. Defence remained essentially passive and static, with an emphasis on frontal fire and with little effort being made to provide flanking fire. There was, in fact, little apparent effort to return fire at all during the 12th century; the defenders largely relying on the strength, height and, where possible, the sheer inaccessibility of their walls.

The 'Nikolaitor' of Eisenach, the oldest surviving fortified city gate in Germany, c.1200. Once again the German bergfried principle, in which a single tall tower formed the focus of defence, was reflected even in the design of a city gate. The concept continued throughout the medieval period in Germany, with later such tower gates becoming even higher. The larger arch through the city wall on the left was enlarged in more modern times; the small archway to the right of the tower perhaps being medieval though probably later than the Nikolaitor itself.

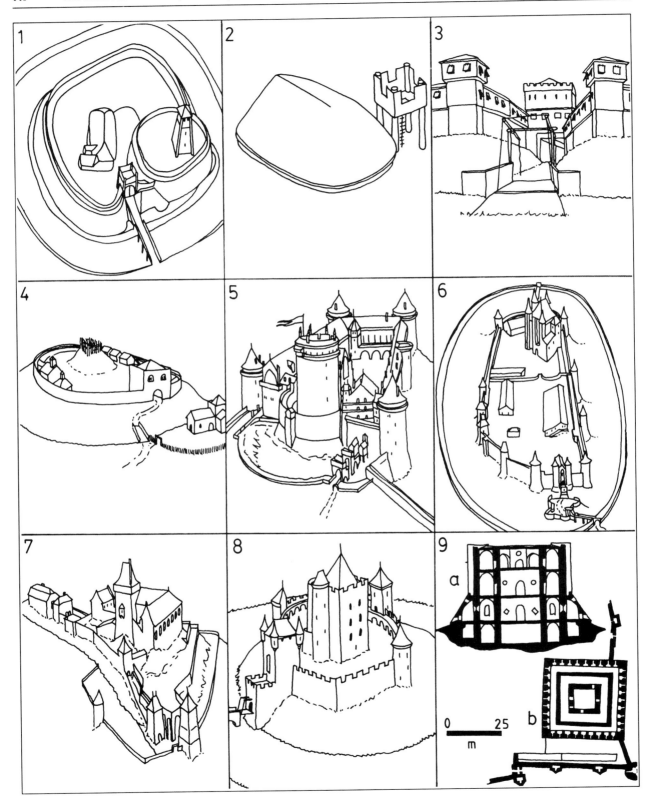

Left: Fortifications, 1100–1275

1. Reconstruction of Goltho Castle, Lincolnshire, England, as it might have appeared c.1125–1150. The raised motte has a tall timber tower, a dwelling-hall nestles in the bailey, the gate is defended by a smaller wooden tower and a moat surrounds the entire complex (after Higham and Barker)

2. Reconstruction of the fortified dwelling at Lismahon, County Down, Northern Ireland, c.1200. A large, low dwelling building occupied the summit of a mound and had a turret mounted on four stout posts attached to one side (after Higham and Barker)

3. Reconstruction of the gateway to the inner bailey of Stafford Castle, Staffordshire, England, as it might have appeared in the late 11th century. This very large complex of walls, towers and dwellings was built entirely of timber (after Hill)

4. Reconstruction of Bramber Castle, West Sussex, England, early 12th century. The castle is shown at the time when the original timber tower on top of the conical motte had been abandoned, to be replaced by a curtain wall with a massive gate-tower (after Sorrell)

5. Reconstruction of the Château of Coucy; France,

13th century. Coucy was regarded as the most elegant castle in the country; the pride of its owner being summed up in his motto, 'I am not a king, nor am I a prince. I am the Sire de Coucy.' (after Tuulse)

6. Reconstruction of the Castle of Arques, France, early 13th century. The 12th century donjon or keep remained at one end but the castle was extended with outer walls and tall slender turrets (after Tuulse)

7. Reconstruction of Trifels Castle, western Germany, 13th century. The main bergfried tower remained central, while the outer walls made full use of the castle's position on top of a rocky summit. (after Tuulse)

8. Reconstruction of Oost-voorne Castle, Netherlands, late 12th–13th centuries. Because of the low-lying and flat nature of the country, Dutch and Flemish castles made great use of water-filled defensive moats (after Tuulse)

9. Section and plan of the Citadel of Lucera, southern Italy, early 13th century. Apart from being the garrison base of the famous Italo-Muslim troops of Lucera, this citadel was also built in a style strongly influenced by the Mamlūk military architecture of Syria (after Tuulse and Hohler)

domination or ownership as it was an effort to provide a local refuge.

This symbolic aspect of the castle also accounted for the high degree of decoration given to castle gates, which could include helmets and heraldic shields. The same would have applied to the élite status and probably splendid appearance of those charged with guarding such gates. Then there was the function of the *guette* or watch-tower as a high place from which the hours of the day, the duties of various officials, and timing of hunting expeditions were announced. Hunting was itself, of course, a somewhat symbolic activity which demonstrated the local aristocracy's dominance over their own territory. In France it was said that only a nobleman was permitted to erect a weather-cock on the tower of his castle. It should also be pointed out that the dark and sometimes dank lower floors of a castle were normally used for storage, rather than for the imprisonment of starving captives.

France

Each part of Europe developed its own characteristic styles of fortification in this Golden Age of castles; though again there were several 'centres of fashion' which influenced a wider area. One of these was, of course, France. There was remarkably little clear evidence of eastern influence, via the Crusades, on the design of fortifications in northern France. This was, however, an area which generally lacked high rocky hills to provide naturally defensible features. Instead isolated castles of the 12th century could be placed behind rivers or forests, which gave them some degree of defence in depth. The sites themselves often consisted of strengthened earlier *motte and bailey* castles. Others were early examples of the concentric principle, with a main *donjon* or tower surrounded by one or more circuit walls. From the later 12th century onwards, smaller towers were generally added to such outer walls. This latter development indicated an increasing concern to defend the walls by providing flanking fire and, perhaps more importantly, to serve as firing points for new forms of stone-throwing engines.

In southern France isolated castles were increasingly sited for commercial or trade reasons, rather than to dominate agricultural areas. Fortified towns and churches, for example, became a feature of the Rhône valley in the 12th century, this being one of the main arteries of European trade. The re-appearance of brick in some of these fortifications may have reflected Italian or perhaps Spanish influence. Widespread efforts to restore and greatly strengthen old city walls, many of which were of Roman origin, was yet another characteristic of 13th century southern France. It partly resulted from the Albigensian Crusades and was partly an effort to consolidate northern French authority in the wake of these events. The fortification of some great churches and associated bishops' residences similarly reflected a situation where the northern French, and the Catholic Church, were widely seen as forces of alien occupation. During these centuries, many

The role of isolated castles is also a matter of debate at this time, since they could almost invariably be bypassed by an invader. In general such small castles also seem to have had garrisons that were too weak seriously to threaten an invader's lines of communication. Within powerful kingdoms such as France, the castle almost seems to have been more important as a symbol of either royal or local aristocratic power. The symbolic nature of much fortification during the 12th and even 13th centuries may also have contributed to the secular aristocracy's interest in fortifying churches in many parts of southern Europe, and in the Church hierarchy's considerable efforts to stop this practice. Perhaps such fortification was as much a mark of

simple village fortifications were also erected across the south; often as a protection against rapacious local lords in a time of political uncertainty when law and order failed.

The Empire: Germany

Considerable use of naturally rugged sites continued to be typical of German castles, at least in the south. At the same time there was further development of the *bergfried*; the tall and often slender tower with a surrounding wall which had become widespread in 11th century Germany. In some cases it is said that the upper floors of such towers could hold out, even after the lower floor had been captured. This traditional German *bergfried* principle was again reflected in the single great tower of even quite large fortified enclosures, the subordinate towers being far less prominent. One very notable feature of 12th century German military architecture was a series of great fortified imperial palaces. In addition to the main *bergfried* towers which characterised these palaces, many also included very large ceremonial halls as well as a church. In fact, the magnificent imperial palaces of Germany served as major cultural centres for the northern part of the Empire.

The Empire: Italy

Tower castles of German type were widespread in the sub-Alpine north of Italy. Meanwhile a superficially similar, though probably quite separate, tradition of tall

Opposite page: Some of the torre or 'family towers' of San Gimignano in the Piazza della Cisterna; central Italian, 13th–14th centuries. Only a few of these towers survive, even in the little medieval town of San Gimignano which has more than any other Italian city. During the 13th and 14th centuries some Italian cities were described as looking like brick and stone forests, their towers being densely packed and often much taller than those seen here.

urban towers became typical of the northern and central Italian cities. Few of these now survive, but at one time they were described as giving such cities, and even many small towns, the appearance of brick-built or stone forests. Only a few such *torre* had, for example, been built in Florence by the end of the 11th century; but there were more than one hundred and fifty of them crowded into the still largely wooden medieval city a hundred years later. Some were described as being almost ninety metres high.

These *torre* were normally owned by a clan or a set of families with a shared lineage; such clans dominating the life of the early Italian city communes. They came in two types: the purely military *torre* which consisted of a plain shaft with few apertures but normally having battlements at the top, and the lower *casa-torre* which was essentially a large fortified house in which the defences often seem to have been more symbolic than real. The

The Dalmation coast of Croatia was dominated by Venice during the latter half of the Middle Ages. It is still studded with fortifications, most of which were built by the Venetians to protect harbours or coastal villages where their ships could find water and shelter. Some consisted of great fortresses but others, like this simple tower at, Klek, were more rudimentary.

Above: The east gate of the Château Comtal of Carcassonne, southern France, 13th century, heavily restored in the 19th century. The early 19th century French historian, Viollet-le-Duc, who supervised the restoration of Carcassonne's fortifications, has been strongly criticised in later years. But he virtually invented the idea of accurate rather than romantic restoration; and without him these wall towers would probably have disappeared long ago. His work is also remarkably correct, considering the period in which he lived. Note the tiled roofs which are now missing from almost all other medieval castles, and the wooden hoardings overlapping the top of the walls; enabling defenders to shoot down on attackers from relative safety. It was these hoardings that the stone-throwing siege engines of the period were intended to destroy, rather than the stone walls themselves.

Opposite page: Arrow-slit or observation position in the donjon or keep of Lillebonne castle; Norman French, early 13th century. This is a very typical embrasure of the 13th century. An archer or cross-bowman could have fired through the aperture, though it would not have been easy, whereas the stone benches on each side strengthen the idea that these were primarily observation posts.

upper floors of the slender military *torri* were normally of wood; usually being reached via ladders and trapdoors, though some had fireproof stone stairs. Some *torri* were erected for communal rather than private family defence and even the private ones often seem to have been concentrated at strategic spots, such as bridgeheads, where they would have strengthened the defences of the city as a whole. Meanwhile, the *casa-torre* generally seems to have had several features in common with the late Roman fortified villa. They were often built around a courtyard with the family's shops beneath the living quarters which were situated above. Sturdier towers stood at the corners and the entire complex was

capable of being sealed off from the surrounding streets in case of trouble.

A comparable process of widespread fortification could also be seen in the Italian countryside, with many villages being walled as *castelli*, while rural towers or *rocche* dotted surrounding hills. Towers known as *saraceno*, probably because they were modelled on the earlier coastal defences of Muslim Sicily and North Africa, similarly sprang up around Italy's coast. The larger, often imperial, fortresses that were built in many parts of 13th century Italy showed a mixture of local, Germanic and eastern Mediterranean influences in their design. The latter probably accounted for the designers of several such imperial fortresses showing an increasing preference for geometrically regular plans, some of which almost rated as works of abstract art.

Southern Italy

The main difference between the military architecture of southern Italy and that of the rest of the country was an even stronger Byzantine, Islamic and, by the 13th century, classical Roman influence upon their design. The early Norman conquerors may have brought some northern ideas with them, but these seem to have faded away very quickly. Instead Arab-Islamic influence grew particularly strongly under the Normans; partly as a result of their employment of Sicilian Muslim military engineers and architects. Meanwhile the Norman rulers of Sicily and southern Italy enthusiastically modelled many aspects of their court and kingdom upon the Fāṭimid Caliphate of Egypt, which again had a distinct influence upon both the shape and the decoration of several of their most famous buildings.

This fascination with the sophisticated civilisation of Middle Eastern Islam continued very strongly under the Emperor Frederick II during the early 13th century. It was largely disowned by the subsequent Italo-Angevin dynasty, yet to some degree the influence of Muslim Middle Eastern fortification remained; perhaps most obviously in the massive and strongly garrisoned citadels which typified the strongly centralising state-structure of southern Italy during this period. Under the Italo-Angevins, however, several novel designs of castle also appeared, the origins of which remain a matter of debate. At the same time a use of classical Graeco-Roman decoration on the gates of certain buildings, including fortifications, may have been a precocious forerunner of Italian Renaissance architecture.

England

Compared to what was happening in the deep south, the development of military architecture in England seemed both rudely practical and often merely a reflection of French fashions. By and large, England itself was a peaceful land. The small, rapidly erected and sometimes even apparently prefabricated wooden castles of the Anglo-Norman early 12th century largely disappeared under Angevin-Plantagenet rule. Yet they had been highly effective in the circumstances of their time. Most had a ditch and palisade of wood or interlaced wattle. The most formidable included a timber gate, crenelations and *bretesches* or covered hoardings on top of stronger stone or timber walls. Prefabricated castles could even be carried by invading armies, to be erected within days or weeks and disassembled when no longer required. The many timber castles which the Anglo-Norman invaders built in Ireland were probably of a similar type but were abandoned after a generation or so, the Celtic Irish raiding armies posing little real threat of siege. On the other hand, some of the newly established or settled Anglo-Norman towns in Ireland were given quite strong walls; these being built and maintained

Right: 'Defeat of Satan's army outside Jerusalem', in an Apocalypse; English, c.1270. Apart from a couple of 'oriental' features of costume and a coat of arms consisting of toads among Satan's army on the right, the arms, armour and costume in this manuscript illustration are entirely Anglo-French from the later 13th century. The helmets are of the brimmed chapel de fer type, the armour consists of mail hauberks with quilted cuisses for the upper legs, plus two high-necked surcoats which must therefore include some kind of padded soft armour or perhaps some form of semi-rigid protection, perhaps a felt or leather gorgerete or spaulder. (MS. Douce 180, f.88, Bodleian Library, Oxford; photograph, The Bodleian Library, University of Oxford)

by work-gangs recruited from the town's quarters or trades.

Within England itself, the larger royal castles and some urban fortifications were strengthened in the late 12th and 13th centuries, though the lack of any obvious serious military threat suggests that these defences were even more symbolic than comparable examples in France. Relatively close-spaced D-shaped turrets were typical of such 13th century curtain walls and in general the design of 13th century English fortifications continued to mirror those of France. The only major exceptions were the extremely advanced and business-like, though at the same time still highly symbolic, concentric castles built by King Edward I to overawe the Welsh in the late 13th century. Some degree of influence from the equally powerful and sophisticated castles of the Crusader States in the eastern Mediterranean might, however, be assumed here, as Edward himself had gone crusading as a younger man.

Celtic States

Norman-style *motte and bailey* castles appeared in Lowland Scotland during the 12th century, and the traditional wooden fortifications of many other parts of Scotland were largely replaced by stone structures during the 13th century. The only exception to this trend seems, rather surprisingly, to have been the region bordering England. Farther south, the traditional *llys*, fortified residence of a Welsh lord, had only a stone or wooden palisade. Some Norman influence may perhaps have been felt during the 12th century, with the appearance of small *motte and bailey* castles or *mottes* associated with separate ringworks. Nevertheless, no larger Celtic fortresses seem to have been built in Wales before the English conquest was completed. Similarly in Celtic Ireland, earthworks with ditches and stone walls continued to be used; but no more modern castles were built except for those of the Anglo–Norman invaders.

Scandinavia and the Baltic

The huge late Viking fortresses of Denmark seem to have been largely abandoned during the first half of the 12th century. Instead, these remarkable bases for overseas aggression were replaced by many smaller towers sited to

defend Denmark's own long and vulnerable coastline against Slav naval raiders coming from the southern Baltic. Many appear to have been wooden *motte and bailey* constructions; a fashion which also spread northwards into Sweden which was similarly threatened by Slav naval raiders during the early 12th century. A completely new form of brick and stone fortification began to be erected in mid-12th century Denmark under King Valdemar the Great; a style which, however, showed much less German influence than might have been expected. Sweden and Norway were apparently slow to adopt these new styles in the 12th and 13th centuries, but turreted fortresses did spring up along the Swedish coast.

The massive castles which the invading German Crusaders built as they consolidated their hold on the southern and eastern shores of the Baltic Sea were mostly built in the late 13th century. Not surprisingly, they generally mirrored many aspects of northern German fortification. This was particularly the case where urban defences were concerned, whereas the massive citadels of the German Crusading Orders were as much a reflection of their wealth and power as anything else. Once again the vital symbolic aspect of castle-building had come to the fore.

Eastern Europe

As yet the fortifications of Poland remained extremely old fashioned and even backward; still relying almost entirely on timber and earth. Farther south German styles of military architecture completely dominated Bohemia and to a great extent Hungary. On the other hand there was also discernible French and Italian influence in Hungarian military architecture.

Timber fortifications remained the norm in 12th century Serbia, though stone structures of essentially Byzantine design began to re-appear during the second half of the 12th century. Byzantine military architecture also naturally dominated Bulgaria. More surprisingly, perhaps, was the Arabic origin, introduced via its Turkish version, behind the word *galati* or castle as used in the Vlach-Romanian regions of Wallachia and Moldavia north of the Danube.

SIEGE WARFARE

Developments in siege techniques were almost as dramatic as those in the design of fortifications during the 12th and 13th centuries. They were, of course, related. Most importantly, there was a considerable increase in the use of more powerful stone-throwing machines. But this did not mean that sieges necessarily got faster or more decisive. Sieges often dragged on for a very long time, which tended to have a serious effect on the morale of the attackers; perhaps more so than upon the defenders. Yet such sieges remained necessary, the capturing of towns being often the main reason for a campaign, while there was a natural fear of leaving any strongly garrisoned enemy position in the rear of an invading army.

The preferred method of taking a fortified place was, wherever possible, a sudden expected assault in the hope of catching the garrison unawares, or even with its gates open. In any case the attackers hoped to invest the place before its garrison could be strengthened. If this failed, a careful assessment would be made of the fortifications themselves. Threats might be made to execute or muti-

late captives the attackers might already be holding; threats all too often carried out. The heads of slain defenders, their friends or allies, could be tossed into a castle or fortress, and child hostages might be tied to wooden siege engines to deter the defenders from trying to set them on fire.

Hungry garrisons were taunted with the attackers' own food supplies, potential traitors would be bribed, water sources either diverted or polluted with corpses. One way or another it was clear that western European siege warfare often degenerated into forms of savagery rarely seen elsewhere, except in the savage Mongol wars of the 13th and 14th centuries. At the same time, however, the besiegers' own stinking camps frequently became riven with dysentery and other diseases as a result of the Europeans' habitual lack of hygiene.

Larger fortified areas, such as towns or cities, could rarely be completely surrounded. In such cases a blockade

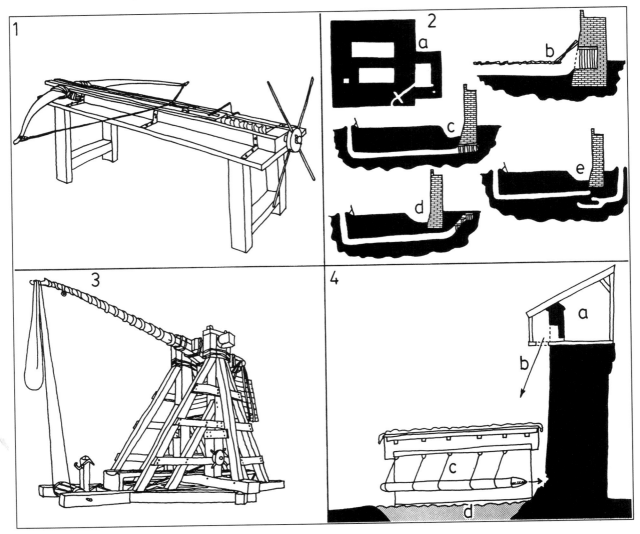

Opposite page:
Siege Warfare, 1100–1275
1. *Great Crossbow; mounted on a bench and spanned by an integral winch system. In reality there must have been some means of raising or lowering the bench in order to aim such a weapon (after Gravett)*
2. *Mining operations*
a *Few examples of medieval mining tunnels survive. The unfinished galleries which threatened to bring down one corner of Bungay Castle in England in the mid-12th century have, however, been cleared and are shown in this plan (after Braun)*

b *Attackers dig a covered trench to the base of the wall, remove part of the wall which is then shored up with timber; to be burned when ready*
c *Attackers dig a tunnel to the base of the wall which is then shored up with timber; to be burned when ready*
d *Attackers dig a tunnel with a camouflaged exit, ready to launch a raid inside the defences*
e *Defenders dig countermines in an attempt to destroy the attackers' tunnel*
3. *Counterweight trebuchet. In*

this reconstruction the arm is drawn down by a winch at the centre of the structure and released by a trigger at the rear. The sling and its missile lay in a large trough prior to release (after Quennell)
4.a *Wooden hoarding on top of the defensive wall.*
b *Rocks, fire-brands or other missiles dropped or shot at the attackers' ram*
c *Attackers' ram swung against the base of the wall; inside a protective wooden shed often also covered by a protective layer of earth*
d *Defensive ditch filled by the attackers*

Above: *Relief carving said to portray 'The Crusader siege of Albigensian-held Carcassonne', perhaps originally from the tomb of Simon de Montfort; southern French, early 13th century. Most of the attacking forces wear flat-topped great helms, probably to indicate their knightly status, whereas the defenders are shown as an ill-armed 'low-class' rabble. One of the outworks of the fortified city is seen on the right, while in the lower right-hand corner a team operates an early form of man-powered mangonel, another man placing a large stone in its sling. (Basilica of St Nazaire, Carcassonne)*

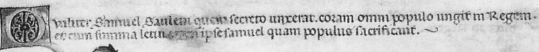

Left: 'Saul destroys Nahash and the Ammonites', in the Maciejowski Bible; French, c.1250. A man-powered mangonel is also shown in this page from a northern French manuscript, though the team actually pulling the ropes is hidden behind the carnage going on in front. The individual holding back the sling of the mangonel appears in several such pictures; his role probably being to give an added spring to the beam-sling or arm of the mangonel. The archer in the tower may be using a rather archaic Mediterranean form of composite bow, perhaps descended from that used in late Roman times. The weapons used by the horsemen include swords, maces and even axes; both the latter weapons being wielded with two hands. (M. 638, f.23v, The Pierpont Morgan Library, New York)

was usually the only answer, unless the walls were attacked directly. But this latter tactic tended to be expensive in lives and was resorted to only in the most pressing circumstances. Instead, the steady wearing down of one section of the wall, a tower or gate, was the standard way of conducting a lengthy siege.

The first step was normally to try to fill the defensive ditch, so that the attackers' movable wooden siege-towers, *belfreys* or *berfriez*, could approach the defenders' wall. This would also enable the sappers and miners to attack the foundation of the wall without having to tunnel too far. Siege towers similarly served as vantage points from which archers and crossbowmen could shoot down on the defenders. Under the best conditions they could even permit direct access to the top of the wall itself. Consequently the defenders would try to destroy these wooden towers' before they reached the fortified wall. Here they could use the various forms of *Greek Fire* which were now known in western Europe. The defenders not only attempted to kill their attackers, but even to 'fish' them from the base of the wall or from their wooden towers, using long pivoted poles with hooks at the end known as *crows*. The attackers similarly used this device against the defenders. Meanwhile the garrison's best defence against mining beneath their walls was counter-mining.

The single most notable technological advance in siege engines during this period was the introduction of a counterweight *mangonel*, normally referred to as a *trebuchet*. It originated in the eastern Mediterranean region and appears to have been invented earlier in the 12th century. Before the *trebuchet*, the only available stone-throwing machines were man-powered *mangonels* and torsion-powered devices generally known as *petrarias*, *perrieres* or *pierries*. Such terminology, however, often appears to have been interchangeable. Some torsion devices may have been mounted on wheeled carriages, since they were smaller than the great majority of both *mangonels* and *trebuchets*. The *boves* of later 12th century southern Italy and the 13th century Crusader States may have been a form of *trebuchet* with an adjustable counterweight; essentially the same as the slightly later *biffa*.

These siege engines could maintain a remarkable rate of fire, being operated by shifts of men working day and night. The counterweight type was not only more powerful than the earlier man-powered versions, but could be considerably more accurate. So much so that in the 13th century they were often shot from under cover, scattered over a wide area and at greater range due to the threat of accurate counter-bombardment by the defenders' engines. The best wood for the great beam-sling arms of such *trebuchets* was cherry or cedar; their ranges being from a stated minimum of eighty metres to a maximum of one hundred and twenty metres for the largest types.

The *espringal* was smaller but even more accurate. It consisted of a torsion-powered device with two separately powered arms which could shoot a large crossbow bolt-like missile, a small stone shot or a container of inflammable material. Unlike the *mangonel* and *trebuchet*, which lobbed their larger missiles high rather like a modern mortar, the *espringal* shot its missile along a near-horizontal trajectory like the more primitive *ballistas* which it largely replaced. It was at first known as a *petraria turquesa*, indicating its eastern Mediterranean though not necessarily Islamic origin. During the 13th century the *espringal* came to be known as a *spingarda*, *spingala* or *springolf* in various parts of Italy and Germany. The best were made from beech, elm or oak; their torsion power coming from twisted skeins of horse or cattle hair, rather than from the twisted animal tendons as had been, and probably remained, the case in the Byzantine Empire and Islamic regions. The power of the normal-sized *espringal* may have been as much as 1,800 kilograms. It could shoot an iron-tipped wooden *tongue* which was up to eighty centimetres long; this being capable of picking off individual enemies at a terrifying range.

In addition to the *espringal* large numbers of large and now apparently often frame-mounted *great crossbows* and *ballistam ad tornum* were still used to defend walls or towers.

Though there was no scientific study of ballistics in western Europe until the 16th century, there was clearly a great deal of practical knowledge. At the same time, however, some moralists – though rarely military theoreticians – derided the increasing popularity of mechanical siege engines in the 13th century. This was no longer because they ran counter to the *chivalric* ethic of man-to-man combat, but because they had not, it was erroneously believed, been used by the great heroes of antiquity.

France

There was considerable similarity in the tactics of siege warfare throughout western Europe, and indeed across many neighbouring lands, during the 12th and 13th centuries. As a consequence, detailed accounts of sieges in one particular country could probably also apply elsewhere. In one minor northern French siege of the early 12th century, for example, we hear that several small wooden siege-towers were pushed towards the enemy's wall by armoured men, while armoured *knights* stood ready in these towers to fight those who defended the summit of the enemy's wall. The wooden towers were, however, rapidly smashed by defending *mangonels* operated, much to the chagrin of the attackers, by women. Whereupon the defenders came out of their fortifications and gathered up the timber from these now abandoned wooden siege-towers.

A much larger siege of Château-Gaillard in Normandy early in the 13th century involved the French attackers digging their own ditch to isolate the English-held castle. The French defended this new ditch with no less than fourteen wooden towers. They then attacked the castle itself by filling the castle's ditch, and rolling forward movable towers which enabled them to smash the wooden hoardings on top of the castle walls. At the same time French miners threatened to bring down one of the gates in the castle's outer wall. Not surprisingly, there being no sign of an English relieving army anywhere near, the garrison then surrendered.

In early 13th century southern France a powerful fortified base-camp could be built near a besieged city. From this the attackers could maintain their siege in relative safety. Several of the new *trebuchets* could concentrate on a single tower in the defenders' fortifications, rendering it virtually untenable. The defenders would retaliate with clay 'firepots' in the hope of burning these *trebuchets*; the attackers would counter this by protecting their vulnerable wooden engines with layers of felt padding. The defenders might then sortie in an endeavour to reach the *trebuchets* and burn them, using animal fat, bales of straw and baskets of flax as fuel.

The Empire: Germany and Italy

Evidence from Germany again describes tactics virtually identical with those seen in France, though making it even more clear that the simpler or earlier forms of man-powered *mangonel* were more effective at clearing the defenders from their walls than damaging the walls themselves.

Urban warfare in northern and central Italy probably more frequently involved strife within a city than attacks upon its walls by an external enemy. Such struggles, however, were more than mere street brawls between clans or political groups. They involved attacks on rival *torri*, street warfare with barricades and considerable use of various stone-throwing siege engines. In fact the phrase 'arming the towers' may have meant placing small *mangonels* or *ballistas* on the summits of such *torri*.

The most advanced and experimental weapons in 12th century western Europe were, perhaps not surprisingly, recorded in Venice which was in close commercial and indeed military contact with the advanced Islamic and Byzantine states of the eastern Mediterranean. One such device was a multi-shot crossbow which was said to be capable of shooting fifteen darts at a time. The brief surviving description is almost the same as a series of equally experimental, and apparently equally impracticable,

Right: Shipping, 1100–1275
1. Reconstruction of a small Baltic coastal vessel with a stern rudder, 13th century (after Landström)
2. Reconstruction of an English warship or merchant vessel with fighting castles
added for use in war; early 13th century (after Landström)
3. Reconstruction of an Italian round ship or merchant vessel with integral fighting castles forward and aft, 13th century (after Landström)

multi-shot crossbows in a 12th century Egyptian military treatise.

Southern Italy

Once again it was the Norman Kingdom of Sicily's élite Muslim troops who seem to have taken the lead in siege engineering. They were particularly active when it came to building movable wheeled siege towers during the 12th century. In so doing, they presumably still drew upon the highly sophisticated tradition of Islamic siege warfare. Other Siculo-Norman engineers must in turn have learned from them. For example, the Norman fleet which attacked Alexandria in 1174 is said to have brought such towers with them in pre-fabricated form. The Italo-Normans' own Muslim troops were not, of course, used during such campaigns against fellow Muslims.

Other Regions

The techniques of siege warfare in England were exactly the same as those in neighbouring France, and the Scots learned a great deal from the English. The Welsh and Irish, however, made very little use of siege engineering techniques, and even then only of the most rudimentary kind.

Similarly, in the north of Europe the Scandinavian peoples appear to have adopted German siege techniques, and these were being used by the still pagan Lithuanians in their struggles against invading German Crusaders in the 13th century. Much the same was true of eastern Europe, though Italian influence may have been as important as German where Hungary was concerned. The eastern Adriatic city of Zadar in Dalmatia, for example, already employed the most advanced available siege engines against a Venetian attack early in the 12th century.

NAVAL WARFARE

One small weapon led to a significant revolution in naval warfare during the 13th century. This was the hand-held crossbow. In previous years a large crew had been needed to defend medieval ships; far more than was necessary simply to sail such vessels. A Mediterranean galley, of course, already needed about 140–180 men, some 100–120 of these being oarsmen. In the early years several hundred men would be embarked in even a moderately large mer-

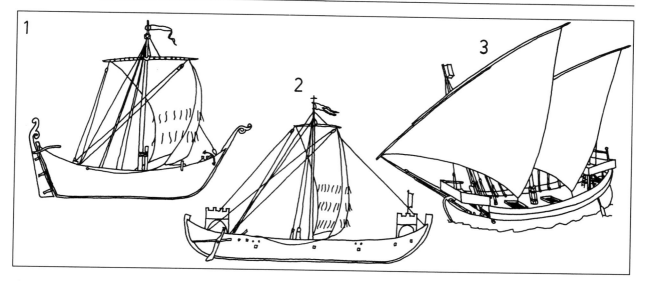

chant ship if there were any danger of meeting pirates or enemy vessels. This was a direct consequence of the fact that naval warfare still largely consisted of grappling and boarding after some use of short-range archery and javelins.

Crossbows had, of course, been used since at least the 11th century, particularly by Mediterranean Islamic fleets; but the real changes came in the 13th and 14th centuries with the enlistment of highly skilled professional marines, largely armed with hand-held crossbows, and the subsequent widespread disappearance of large defensive crews. Other new weapons also played their part, though to a much lesser degree. It is interesting, however, to note that the heavy or even pedestal-mounted *great crossbow* was still preferred to the *espringal* at sea, as it was less susceptible to humidity and sea-spray.

The Mediterranean

The 13th century also saw significant improvements in the design of Mediterranean fighting galleys. Whereas those of the early Middle Ages appear to have had their oars evenly spread along two levels, rather like the smaller types of ancient Greek or Roman galleys, the 11th and 12th centuries saw the grouping of such oars. In this new system two or three men, each pulling his own single oar, shared one rowing bench. This was known as a *galee alla sensile*, 'galley in simple fashion', and it would remain the normal pattern from the 13th century until the introduction of the *galee al scaloccio*, in which several men pulled a single larger oar. But this latter system was not seen for several more centuries. The *galee alla sensile* may also have been more suited to the highly motivated, disciplined and above all free galley oarsmen; whereas the latter might have suited the use of galley-slaves who were virtually unknown in the Middle Ages. Some surviving mid-13th century maritime contracts indicate that a medium-sized galley could be armed with small *mangonels* at the prow, a

fighting top on the mainmast, and large *pavise* type shields to protect the defensive force of crossbowmen.

The frame-first rather than skin- or hull-first system of ship-building was by now fully established. It may have been one reason why the powerful mercantile republic of Venice gathered the previously scattered shipyards of the Venetian Lagoon into its soon to be world-famous *Arsenale* at the start of the 12th century. The Venetians would rapidly become the most advanced, though not as yet clearly the dominant, naval power in the Mediterranean. Their trading empire consisted of strategically placed outposts each linked to the mother-city by a chain of islands and additional outposts. These enabled the relatively short-range ships of the period to maintain communications between Venice and her overseas colonies, particularly the war galleys with their large crews and need for frequent watering places. In the early 13th century we hear of a single small Venetian ship being sent on a month-long patrol, perhaps to gather intelligence about pirates. Larger expeditions would consist of many galleys and other ships, big and small, the commander of this fleet paying half the cost of arming the crew, with the Venetian republic paying for the other half. Presumably the man in charge expected to reap some reward for such a substantial financial outlay. Some of the ships involved were already known as *galleons*, though they seem to have had nothing in common with the famous Spanish *galleons* of a later century. Instead these early Venetian *galleons* were small galley-like vessels with perhaps twenty-five oars each side.

Naval tactics still mirrored those of warfare on land. For example, a fleet would normally try to keep close together, with galleys and merchant *round ships* supporting one another. Lime was thrown to blind an enemy crew; soap also being thrown to make his decks slippery. Ambushes would be launched by galleys from behind headlands or islands, usually against small enemy convoys since major fleet actions were extremely rare. In fact, combined operations and the landing of troops on an enemy shore remained the single most important element in Mediterranean galley-warfare throughout the Middle Ages.

The Northern Seas

Naval warfare was far less advanced in northern waters, such as the English Channel, North Sea and Baltic. Nevertheless, some of the same weapons and similar tactics as seen in the Mediterranean were being used during the 12th and 13th centuries. The sturdy but far from swift merchant *cogs* of the north were often converted to warships, though many may have had wooden *fighting castle* structures on prow and stern as permanent features. They seem to have been lightened to ride higher in the water when being used specifically as warships; this gave the crew an advantage when boarding and shooting down at an enemy, but it may have made the ships less seaworthy. Pots of chalk or lime were thrown in an endeavour to blind an opponent. A Danish law of 1241 specifically stated that a steersman must have a crossbow with thirty-six arrows, or be supported by a man so equipped, which rather suggests that crossbows had not yet been universally adopted by Scandinavian naval crews.

Western Slav fleets had already raided beyond the Baltic by the 12th century. They even reached out into the North Sea, showing that they were a formidable foe. The ships involved in Baltic warfare were soon quite large; including, perhaps, the specially commissioned large warships used by the German Crusading Order of 'Sword Brothers' in the early 13th century Baltic. Nevertheless, the climate ensured that northern naval warfare remained a summer occupation. A Mediterranean influence may have lain behind the introduction by King Richard I of England of the *calcar* or beak to northern war-galleys. This was no longer the hull-breaking ram of ancient times, but was placed well above the water. The *calcar* was, in fact, designed to ride over an enemy's bulwarks and thus enable men to board the enemy vessel.

River Warfare

Remarkably little is known about river warfare during these centuries, though the major rivers of Europe certainly remained essential arteries of communication; particularly for trade. Generally speaking, it seems that they now played a less significant role in warfare than they had done in earlier centuries, with the possible exception of the Danube.

'The Story of the Wicked Knight Milo,' illustrated in a series of relief carvings from around 1200 AD. Moral stories were common subjects of art in churches at a time when the bulk of the population could not read, but few showed the dangers posed by young and doubtless often arrogant young knights to a lady's virtue as this scene on the outside of Fidenza Cathedral in northern Italy.

IV
LATE MEDIEVAL
EUROPE (1275–1400)

LATE MEDIEVAL EUROPE (1275–1400)

Two competing trends characterised warfare in late 13th and 14th century Europe. On the one hand, many armies were increasingly dominated by professional soldiers, normally referred to as mercenaries. But in many cases these mercenaries were largely recruited from within the state that employed them. Partly as a result of this, such armies gradually took on an almost national character. Increasing 'national awareness' of a kind recognisable to the modern mind was another very important feature of 14th century European history.

On the other hand, there were important exceptions to this trend; the most obvious being in Italy where the professionalisation of military recruitment led to widespread enlistment of foreigners. The troops in question could be Germans, French or English from outside Italy, or be Italians from a different state within a politically very fragmented part of western Europe. In several countries non-professional, feudally recruited troops maintained a vital role, while even in France, Germany and Italy part-time urban militias continued to have an important military function. In general, however, late medieval European warfare normally involved a professional minority of volunteers rather than the bulk of the population; at least as active participants though not as victims of such conflicts.

If there were partial exceptions to this trend in western Europe, there were even more in central Europe and the Balkans. Yet even here a process of military professionalisation could be seen. It often tended to focus on particular 'warrior peoples', rather than social groups or individual volunteers as in 13th and 14th century western Europe. As such, it had a great deal in common with patterns of warfare and recruitment that had long been common in neighbouring Muslim countries. By the mid-14th century a great many states and peoples were involved in the struggle for domination of the Balkans. These not only involved professional Hungarian armies of basically western European character, but also local Slav and Vlach or Romanian forces, as well as Turco-Mongol groups from the steppes. Another 'warrior people' who played a leading role in Balkan armies, as well as in Venetian colonial forces, were the Albanians. The mass migration of Albanians into Greece, which began early in the 14th century, was in some ways a throwback to the 'folk wanderings' of the early Middle Ages.

Just as there were large-scale population movements in the Balkans, so new national identities and even new peoples were emerging in north-eastern Europe. While the Prussians were assimilated and disappeared as a distinct or separate group, the Lithuanians were converted from paganism, and thus drawn into Christendom. By this time the rest of the European continent, with the sole exceptions of the far north of Finland, Norway and Sweden, plus some isolated valleys in the northern Caucasus mountains, had been Christian or Muslim for centuries. These fearsome Lithuanians had, of course, maintained a distinct and separate identity since ancient times; as had the Finnish Estonians farther north. But between the Lithuanians and Estonians a third new people now emerged. These were the Latvians who evolved out of previously competing tribes as a result of the social and cultural pressure imposed by German and Scandinavian Crusader conquest.

Major Campaigns

1278: Defeat of Bohemia by Austrian and German princes.

1282–3: Aragon conquers Sicily.

1284: English conquest of Wales.

1285: War between Aragon and France.

1296: English invasion of Scotland; Scots defeated at Dunbar.

1298: English invasion of Scotland; Scots defeated at battle of Falkirk.

1299: Franco-Italian Angevin fleet defeats Aragonese in naval battle off Cape Orlando.

1303: Flemish revolt against French crown, defeat of French at battle of Courtrai.

1303–4: English invasion of Scotland.

1306–7: Papal Crusades against 'heretics' in north-western Italy.

1306–10: Civil war in Sweden.

1308–9: Crusader Teutonic Knights occupy Pomerania and Gdansk; start of a 'perpetual Crusade' against the Lithuanians.

1314: Scots defeat English at the battle of Bannockburn.

1315: Swiss defeat a Habsburg army at the battle of Morgarten.

1315–18: Scottish invasion of Ireland, defeated at battle of Faughart.

1321–4: 'Crusade' by Guelphs (faction in favour of papal temporal authority in Italy) against Ghibellines (faction against papal temporal authority in Italy).

1322: Civil war for the imperial crown within Germany, resulting in the battle of Mühldorf.

1323: Norwegian Crusade against the Russians in Finland.

1323–8: Renewal of the Flemish revolt against French rule.

1330: Serbia defeats Bulgaria at the battle of Kustendil; Wallachia defeats Hungary at the battle of Posada.

1337: Start of the Hundred Years War between England and France.

1340: English fleet defeats French fleet at the battle of Sluys; Crusade against heretics in Bohemia; Jutish uprising in Denmark.

1343: Last uprising by Estonians against Crusader rule.

1343–52: Serbia conquers most of Byzantine Greece.

1346: Scots invasion of northern England defeated at the battle of Neville's Cross.

1346–7: English defeat French at the battle of Crécy; English capture Calais.

1348: Swedish Crusade to Finland.

Mid-14th century: Ukraine gradually occupied by Grand Duchy of Lithuania.

1353–60: Guelph-Ghibelline wars in Italy.

1356: English defeat the French at the battle of Poitiers.

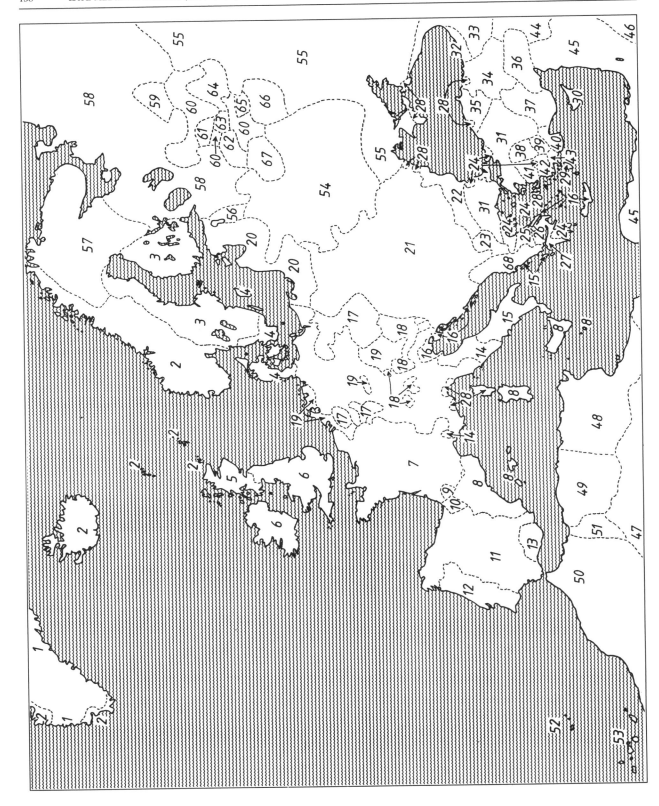

Left: Europe, c.1382

1. Inuit-Eskimos	30. Cyprus
2. Norway and depen- dencies	31. Ottoman Sultanate
3. Sweden	32. Byzantine 'Empire' of Trebizond
4. Denmark	33. Georgia
5. Scotland	34. Eretna
6. England and	35. Candaq
dependencies	36. Dhū'l Qadr
7. France	37. Karaman
8. Aragon	38. Germiyan
9. Béarn	39. Hamid
10. Navarre	40. Teke
11. Castile	41. Saruhan
12. Portugal	42. Aydın
13. Granada	43. Menteşe
14. Papal States	44. Jalayrids
15. Naples	45. Mamlūks
16. Venice and overseas	46. Arab tribes
territories	47. Berber tribes
17. Luxembourg lands	48. Ḥafṣids
18. Habsburg lands (plus	49. Ziyānids
several smaller	50. Marīnids
enclaves not shown)	51. Neutral territory
19. Wittelsbach lands	52. Uninhabited
(plus several smaller	53. Guanches
enclaves not shown)	54. Lithuania
20. Teutonic Military	55. Golden Horde
Orders	56. Pskov
21. Hungary and vassal	57. Saomi-Lapps
states	58. Novgorod
22. Bulgarian	59. Veliki Ustyug
principalities	60. Muscovy
23. Serbian principalities	61. Yaroslav
24. Byzantine Empire	62. Tver
25. Megalo-Vlachia	63. Rostov
26. Duchy of Athens	64. Suzdal-Nizhegorod
27. Achaia	65. Murom
28. Genoa and overseas	66. Ryazan
territories	67. Smolensk
29. Knights of St John	68. Albanian rulers

1357–8: 'Jacquerie' revolt against the French crown and aristocracy in France.

1361: Danes occupy the island of Gotland following the battle of Visby.

1366: Lithuania conquers Ruthenia and Galicia.

1367: Rival French and English interventions in Castile.

1369–77: French conquer Normandy, Poitou, Aunis, Saintonge and part of Aquitaine from the English.

1371: Baronial war in Germany resulting in the battle of Baesweiler.

1372: English fleet defeated by the Castilian fleet in a naval battle off La Rochelle.

1379: Clash between Norse Greenland settlers and the *skraelings* (Eskimos).

1382–3: Urban revolts in France; Crusade against heretic-rebels in Flanders.

1385: English invasion of Scotland.

1386: English 'Crusade' against Castile; Swiss defeat a Habsburg army at the battle of Sempach.

1386–9: Civil war in Sweden, involving Norway and Denmark; ended by Danish-Norwegian victory in Västergötland.

1388: Scots invasion of England; defeat of English at the battle of Otterburne; war between Rhenish League and League of Princes in Germany resulting in the battle of Döffingen.

1391: English Crusaders raid Lithuania from territory of the Crusader Order of Teutonic Knights.

1392: French invasion of Italy.

1396: Start of a baronial civil war in France.

1397: Lithuanian occupation of Moldavia.

1398–9: Irish king of Leinster rises against the English governor of Ireland; inconclusive English campaign to restore authority.

ARMY RECRUITMENT

The continuing growth of a money economy in western Europe during the 13th century led to radical changes in military recruitment in the 14th century. Rulers and great feudal barons had long trusted professional mercenaries more than their own feudal troops, and now the wealth of many states led to these being recruited in ever larger numbers. The great majority found employment within their own countries, though there was also a remarkable degree of foreign enlistment. This, plus the fact that militia conscription systems continued to operate in most areas, even if in new guises, probably contributed to the rise of 'national consciousness' which characterised many parts of 14th century western Europe.

The dividing line between feudal and mercenary, or at least paid, soldiers was very blurred. For example, it was now quite normal for urban militias to be paid wages after the first few 'feudal' days of their service in a major campaign had expired. Many late 13th and 14th century Italian and Flemish cities could also raise thousands of troops which, in many ways, now became available for hire. On the other hand, in certain areas such as Brabant local spear-armed infantry forces, which had once been widely employed as mercenaries, only seem to have operated locally in defence of their own districts. Other groups, such as Navarese and Basque javelin-armed light infantry, continued to find foreign employers into the early 14th century, but then they also largely fell from favour. Instead it was crossbowmen, above all those from northern Italy, who were in greatest demand. Other less élite mercenaries tended to be drawn from poor or marginal parts of Europe, such as Ireland, Scotland, Switzerland and some parts of the Iberian peninsula.

'Siege of Constantinople' in a copy of Cassydorus manuscript; French, early 14th century. While the two heavily armoured crossbowmen on the left have later conical forms of great helm, those of the horsemen on the right may be early forms of heaume à vissere with movable visors. The man on the far left also wears a scale cuirass; perhaps the artist's attempt to indicate an alien or 'oriental' figure, or perhaps reflecting current experimentation in armour. (MS. 9245, f.254r, Bibliothèque Royale Albert 1er, Brussels)

At one end of the mercenary pay-scale were skilled military engineers and other technical specialists who were always in short supply. Some earned the title of 'master engineer' and even rose to the status of *knights*. At the other end were those professional trial-by-battle 'champions' who hired themselves out to the highest bidder. These unfortunates may have been drawn from disgraced or otherwise ruined mercenary soldiers and were widely regarded as the male equivalent of prostitutes.

France

The unwillingness of a large part of the lesser nobility to fulfil their feudal military obligations in person had led the rulers of both France and England to try to insist that men of certain wealth become *knights*, whatever their social origins. This was clearly an unsuccessful stop-gap measure, whereas the expanding French towns gradually became an increasingly important source of both wealth and troops, though of only few *knights*. By the late 13th century the French crown seems to have accepted the new socio-military situation within France and had apparently come to rely on cash instead of direct feudal service. With such financial resources the crown could hire the best available professional mercenary soldiers.

The ordinary inhabitants of French cities or communes, however, remained responsible for the maintenance and guarding of their own fortifications. Such communes could raise large numbers of skilled but non-noble *sergeants* in time of need. Women continued to be drafted when required in the mid-14th century. There were, for example, instances where women served in the night watch on a city wall if, for whatever reason, their husbands were not available. If such a town was attacked, all able-bodied people, men, women and clergy aged eighteen to sixty, had a role to play. Even smaller children were given some duties in an emergency. The only exceptions were beggars and foreigners. Citizens of noble rank were normally excused the tedious patrols of *guet* and *garde*, but instead they might form a troop of cavalry or play leadership roles. In fact many 14th century French towns could field a small army in their own right; including horse and foot with the normal forty days of feudal military obligation. Smaller contingents sent to serve in the king's own army were probably selected from among the poorer artisans who were paid for such duties, in addition to the town's own semi-professional force of crossbowmen or *sergeants*. At other times, such as the harvest, towns might hire professional mercenary *gens d'armes* cavalry or 'men-at-arms' to protect their food stores from local bandits or enemy raiders. Most such mercenaries would have been Frenchmen, but élite Italian crossbowmen were also recorded in the early 14th century.

Rural levies had declined by the early 14th century, though again, local village soldiers might be hired at harvest time. The general *arrière ban* remained in law, though it was rarely used in practice. Yet it would see a remarkable revival during the difficult years of the Hundred Years War against England. Despite several crushing defeats at the hands of English invaders, the French crown rarely had difficulty in raising large armies. The pay appears to have been good and there were plenty of volunteers – at least for the first few decades.

By the late 14th century things were getting more difficult for the kings of France. One consequence of this was the development, in France as in England, of what has become known as 'bastard feudalism'. The old feudal order had fragmented under new economic and social as well as military stresses. Instead its members now were held together with often-broken oaths of loyalty, or by financial contracts. Meanwhile 'mutual interest associations' sprang up, which in turn played their part in the fierce rivalry of factional court politics.

Military recruitment was increasingly carried by *indenture* and *contract*; a system again also seen in England. Here a recognised military leader, lieutenant or captain, received *lettres de retenue* from the king or from a senior baron. These specified precisely how many troops, and of what type, were required in return for a specific sum of money. Such a system in turn soon led to a whole hierarchy of sub-contracting right down to the level of the individual soldier himself. The main difference between the French *indenture* system and that of England was the less rigid character of French military contracts. Unlike most of the contracts seen in England, the French examples often specified no particular time limits, being reviewed or renewed at the end of each month.

The Empire: Germany

Rural militias had similarly declined in the German Empire, though they did remain in some areas and in some forms. Two examples were the *folgepflicht* of Germany itself and the *landrecht* of Austria. In certain cases these rural recruits owed service to a local city, rather as

the inhabitants of a *contado* did to its local city within Italy. The most important exception was still, perhaps, the *dithmarschen* peasant infantry of the bleak and most isolated parts of northern Germany. This remained a highly effective though localised force to the end of the 15th century.

Urban recruitment north of the Alps developed on similar lines to that seen in Italy, though more slowly. Many 'imperial' cities were dotted about Germany itself, but tended to be isolated from one another by the great baronial realms that lay between them. Such 'imperial' cities theoretically still provided the Emperor with *knightly* cavalry, though in reality few were doing so by the early 14th century. Instead, the Emperor relied on taxation money from these cities, in addition to that agreed by the imper-

'The militia of Ghent at the battle of Courtrai', on the Courtrai Chest; Flemish, c.1305. As in the much earlier 8th century Pictish carving from Aberlemno, the artist who designed this chest indicates the infantry tactics of the day by showing a section through their ranks. At the front, armoured pikemen incline their long spears or pikes towards the advancing enemy cavalry. They are supported by crossbowmen who shoot at the foe, while to the rear stand men ready to deal with any horsemen who break through. Here they are armed with goedendags, a crude form of mace with a spike at the end. (New College, Oxford)

ial *Diet* or parliament; money with which to hire professional mercenary armies.

Most urban troops fought for their city, not for a distant Emperor. Such communal militias were quite effective by the late 13th century, and over the next few decades the cities of the German Empire came to be divided into quarters; each furnishing a militia of citizens who also provided their own military equipment. Other militias were based upon various craft or merchant guilds and all were largely recruited from the class of craftsmen, plus the lesser and greater *bourgeois* or merchant citizens. Some of the most advanced of these urban militias were those of what are now the Benelux countries and eastern France. For example, the militia of Liège was famous for its sappers and miners; while that of Strasbourg had firearms by 1375.

Another distinctive characteristic of imperial Germany was the 'Leagues'. These initially consisted of cities who combined to defend their interests against various external threats. In so doing they pooled resources and hired élite cavalry forces known as *knechte der freiheit*, or 'knights of freedom'. A particularly powerful and effectively permanent urban league was the Hanseatic League. This basically consisted of cities involved in overseas trade, largely through the Baltic and North Sea. The Hanseatic League even provided specialist marine infantry to the lesser vassal cities of the League; these apparently again being recruited from *knechte, knights* or other mercenaries. Urban leagues were then followed by Leagues of Knights, which were associations of the minor rural aristocracy who combined to defend their interests against the increasingly powerful towns. These Leagues of Knights would also sometimes hire themselves out as ready-made mercenary units. Additional exotic elements were provided by the *Cuman* light cavalry auxiliaries, who were in fact men of Kipchaq Turkish origin from Hungary. There were even references to Welsh infantry who served in Austria during the final years of the 13th century.

The Empire: Italy

No country developed a more characteristic form of military recruitment in the late 13th and 14th centuries than did Italy. This eventually evolved into the much-criticised but widely misunderstood *condottieri* system. During the late 13th century, however, communal militias continued to play a vital and perhaps dominant role in Italian warfare. The recruitment of such militias often continued to reflect archaic and by now largely irrelevant social divisions between cavalry *milites* and infantry *pedites*.

Much of the cavalry was still recruited from a war-oriented *feditori* class which consisted of the old feudal élite plus the wealthier merchant *bourgeoisie*. Those of real *knightly* or aristocratic status tended to take command or at least to be given leadership roles. They were also supposed to fight for their city without pay, in return for tax exemptions. Meanwhile many of the senior *feditori* aristocracy brought along their own *masnadieri* or paid retainers, though this word was already coming to mean ruffian or

assassin. The city's infantry force was drawn from ordinary *popoli* citizens who owed military service from the age of fifteen to seventy. An élite of better armed *pavesari* shieldmen traditionally fought in the front rank and were recruited from the more prosperous skilled craftsmen. Larger, but less well-equipped, forces of light infantry, pioneers or labourers were drawn from the surrounding *contado*; that part of the countryside politically dominated by the city in question. Powerful cities like Florence could also summon contingents from allied or vassal cities and towns; though the exact dividing line between allies, vassals and mercenary units was often rather blurred in the 14th century.

During this century, however, many of the richer citizens gradually came to prefer to pay money rather than serve in the ranks. This money was welcomed by the city government since it could be used to pay *soldato* troops recruited both from within the city and from its *contado*. Once again crossbowmen were most needed. Supposedly 'foreign' troops, particularly *knights*, were similarly enlisted in increasing numbers; the term 'foreign' then meaning anyone from beyond the city, whether he came from Italy or from another part of Europe.

Italian mercenaries remained a majority, large numbers being rural peasants who sought additional income either before or after their harvests. Tuscans were noted as crossbowmen and spear-armed infantry, men from Lombardy and the Campagna as horsemen. Other poorer or wartorn areas of Italy also became known as sources of mercenary cavalry; including the Emilia and Romagna regions. In fact, cavalry sometimes seem to have been in greater demand than crossbowmen; perhaps because many cities could still supply most of their own infantry. In addition to Italian knights from families which had long traditions of serving for hire, many French veterans of the Angevin campaigns in southern Italy were enlisted as mercenaries in late 13th century northern Italy. During this same period horsemen came from Friuli in the far northeast of Italy; an area where Germanic military fashions appear to have been particularly strong. Germans themselves were also hired in considerable numbers; though they usually seem to have been taken on in groups rather than as individuals. Other mercenaries included Picards from northern France, Gascons from the south-west of France and Provençals from the south-east, Brabançons from what is now Belgium, Navarese, Aragonese and Catalans from Spain, as well as mountain-men from what would later emerge as Switzerland. There were even Hungarian horse-archers by the mid-14th century. The first records of mercenary 'companies' stem from the 1320s. Such ready-made mercenary armies soon came to dominate 14th century Italian warfare, but this was largely a matter of military organisation rather than reflecting any changes in basic patterns of recruitment.

Somewhat outside this normal pattern were the many so-called Crusaders who served in late 13th and early 14th century papal armies in return for *indulgences* to wipe away

telur a retorne a alix. Coit
alir apoic te la dute dapir.

faire poz ce que la grant poz
tre apanist a loz anions et q

Histoire du Bon Roi Alexandre, manuscript, French, c.1300. Several new features appear in this manuscript; most notably the greaves which protect the front of the armoured king's legs, *the visors, and the heraldic ailettes on the horsemen's shoulders. Basically, however, their armour is still largely of mail. (MS. 11040, f.36v, Bibliothèque Royale Albert 1er, Brussels)*

their sins – in addition to their ordinary pay. Even more on the margins were the Armenian and other militia troops who helped defend isolated Genoese merchant colonies around the Black Sea.

Italy: Venice and the South

Genoa remained firmly within the Holy Roman Empire, but its great rival Venice was now truly independent. As such it is here treated separately because in many ways the military structures of later medieval Venice were developing along very different lines from those seen in the rest of northern and central Italy.

The Venetian militia remained a highly effective military and naval organisation for a very long time. Each resident of the city was entered in the register of his *sestieri* or quarter, and was expected to serve when needed from the age of seventeen to sixty. This could involve major campaigns, or simply be giving help to the *signori di notti* patrols who maintained law and order during their nightly rounds. Venetian troops were also enlisted from the Lagoon area and from Venice's steadily expanding *terra firma* territory on the Italian mainland, as well as by hiring mercenaries such as Catalan crossbowmen. Nevertheless, the city of Venice, the Bride of the Sea, always preferred to

rely on its own people whenever possible, either as volunteers or as conscripts. The men who garrisoned the far-flung and scattered elements of the Venetian mercantile empire were also sent from Venice; the men involved being strongly discouraged from intermarriage with the locals. The populations of such outposts were also largely Venetian and had the obligation of *angaria*, or defending the settlement's walls. Not until the late 14th century did Venice normally trust 'foreigners' to garrison its overseas possessions; and even then only as infantry, not cavalry.

On the other hand, there was a growing reliance on local troops from these scattered outposts and the neighbouring regions. For example, many redundant Byzantine *gasmouli*, marines of mixed Greek and western European origin, sought employment in Venetian Crete after the Byzantine navy virtually ceased to exist in the mid-14th century. Albanians and Dalmatians were recorded in Venetian garrisons along the eastern shore of the Adriatic Sea. As the Byzantine Empire crumbled in the face of Serbian and Turkish assaults, much of the Byzantine aristocracy, including some of the old military élite, fled to these Venetian colonial outposts. Others went to Italy itself, or to the remaining Byzantine outposts around the Black Sea, or to the rising Romanian principalities of Wallachia and Moldavia.

During the 14th century southern Italy, having once been re-united by its Norman conquerors, was again divided into an Angevin or French-ruled Kingdom of Naples on the mainland and a basically Spanish dominated Kingdom of Sicily in that great island. In both these areas armies seem to have consisted of the remaining feudal forces, plus indigenous mercenaries and a large number

'Saint George', wall painting; English, early 14th century. The great majority of ordinary early 14th century English and French knights still probably wore only mail armour, without any very obvious use of the newer and more experimental forms of plate armour even for their limbs. Such basic kit is shown in this painting from a small English country church. (Church of All Saints, Little Kimble, Buckinghamshire)

of foreign troops. The famous Muslim infantry of Lucera were, by the late 13th century, Muslim Italians with virtually no remaining links, either with their original Sicilian homeland or with the rest of the Muslim world. These troops were, however, still being sent to garrison the Angevins' ephemeral possessions in Albania. Then, in 1300, the Angevins finally obliterated this last vestige of Italian Islam; ending an extraordinary chapter in the military history of medieval western Europe. By then, however, the Italo-Angevins were also recruiting Albanian troops as well as Balkan Slavs. Large numbers of both these communities eventually settled in southern Italy itself. Hungarians had been recorded in southern Italy earlier in the 13th century, but in the 14th century French, northern Italian and Spanish mercenaries appear to have been more numerous.

England

The system of *contract* and *indenture* seen in 14th century France was also characteristic of England. Here, the old system of feudal military obligations still worked, up to a point, into the late 13th century; providing the king with armoured cavalry *knights*, *bachelors* and *vatlettes* of differing status and perhaps quality of equipment. Yet this traditional system seems to have been noticeably inadequate when it came to raising élite cavalry forces, though it did remain effective enough for local defence levies. Only in the far north, along the Scottish border, did traditional systems of feudal military service remain relatively untouched. However, it also continued to play a significant role in the English crown's remaining possessions in south-western France. During the late 13th century these were, in fact, largely defended by local Gascon troops whose reputation for unreliability was very unjustified. In fact, these southern Frenchmen loyally supported their English overlord, largely because he himself was not a northern Frenchman.

The old *fyrd* or *ferd* local levy also still existed in several areas. On the other hand, it was both rarer and less effective in England than in most other parts of western Europe for the simple reason that England had been so rarely invaded since 1066 that the habit of local military service had faded. Nevertheless, the legal obligation to serve in rural or urban levies remained on the statute books; each individual's role as an axe- or spear-armed foot soldier, or as an archer, being assessed according to his wealth and the place where he lived. Those men of northern England who were summoned against the Scots tended to include archers, crossbowmen, spear- or *gysarme*-armed infantry.

The men of Sussex and Kent were, however, the most noted archers by the mid-13th century; but at the same time it gradually became clear that many more archers came from forest regions. This was despite the fact that the possession of a longbow in such areas often raised suspicion that its owner was poaching the king's deer. In fact, some 14th century military regulations specifically stipu-

lated that longbows should be the weapons of those who live 'outside the forest'; crossbows being for those 'inside the forest'. The 14th century was, of course, the great age of the English longbowman and such troops soon became something of a professional élite. The best were recruited into the military households of the great nobility. At the same time the problem of recruiting sufficient numbers of good infantry remained serious, even for campaigns within the British Isles against the Scots. As a result men of highly dubious reputation were often enlisted from those suspected or convicted criminals that had sought sanctuary in various northern 'royal liberties'; including the notorious *grithmen* of Tynemouth and of Wetherall.

During the 14th century the Royal *Commission of Array* replaced the ineffective old *fyrd* levies, though the duties involved and the equipment required still were based on wealth and status. The main difference was that authorised *commissioners*, either from the *Royal Household* or designated by army commanders, now toured the *shires* and *hundreds* of England to select a specified number of suitable men from those eligible. Those chosen were, however, still usually summoned for local defence rather than overseas campaigns. Meanwhile the cities of England and Wales continued to provide the king with whatever number of soldiers their charters specified. Other more or less voluntary troops included pardoned criminals and better paid specialists such as miners from the Forest of Dean. Mounted archers were already a professional élite, these largely being drawn from southern England, whereas by the 1330s the bulk of ordinary longbowmen seem to have been recruited from the northern counties of England. As yet the Welsh largely remained spearmen rather than archers. For their part Irish troops consisted of assorted infantry, though not bowmen, plus the *hobelar*. These *hobelars* would, in fact, become an increasingly important and highly regarded form of light cavalry, clearly based on Celtic traditions of warfare.

A slightly different system applied in the more vulnerable coastal *shires* of southern and south-eastern England. These were exposed to French naval raids during the Hundred Years War. Here all men between sixteen and sixty could be summoned to the array; including those who held land within the area but lived elsewhere. On the other hand, these coastal militiamen were not normally expected to serve outside these specific regions. They were also backed up by militias from various inland *shires* which had special military links with a particular section of coast; for example, the connection between Surrey and Sussex.

Foreign mercenaries played a lesser role in England than in some other parts of Europe, though they did appear in élite specialist roles and in quite senior positions of command. During the late 13th century, for example, the *Royal Household* included soldiers from Scotland, which was theoretically under English suzerainty, Gascony, which was also under the English crown, Picardy, Flanders and Burgundy. Even men from Savoy far away in what is now south-eastern France, western Switzerland and north-eastern Italy, took their place in the English king's service.

The *indenture* system was already in use during the early 14th century. As in France, a military commander arranged with the government the total number and type of troops the king required. These generally consisted of armoured cavalry *men-at-arms*, *hobelar* light cavalry, archers of various sorts and other infantry; their cost and conditions of service also being negotiated. The commander in question was then responsible for raising this force; usually via sub-contracts with junior commanders, the lesser nobility, local gentry and their tenants. Unlike the men summoned by the *Commission of Array*, these soldiers could be, and often were, sent overseas for as long as their *contracts* stipulated.

Celtic States

Compared to England and France, the armies of the Celtic states and principalities remained very old fashioned and even primitive. On the other hand, they were also often highly effective. In Scotland, for example, rural levies faced the professional troops of invading English armies and won some notable victories. Yet these Scottish armies were still as extraordinarily varied as they had been for centuries. They included those claiming Norman descent who formed the feudal élite of the central Lowlands, occasionally some Flemish mercenaries, 'Northumbrians' from the Lothian regions, 'Picts' from Galloway, sometimes Cumbrians from the western Anglo-Scottish Border region, Highlanders from the Isles, and 'Danes'; the latter perhaps also stemming from the northern and western islands. Those drawn from the Scottish Highlands still included peasant warriors who were virtually tribesmen and who followed their own regional earls.

Following the completion of the English conquest of Wales in the late 13th century, the traditional Welsh warrior class gradually disappeared. In its place a local gentry, much like that of England itself, slowly emerged. This, however, continued to play a significant military role in 14th century English armies. Changes were slower and more limited in Ireland, despite the imposition of theoretical English rule over the whole island. In reality, many local Anglo-Irish lords continued to recruit their own forces. These often also reflected traditional Celtic military systems, though they could include outside mercenaries such as the traditionally axe-armed *galloglass* infantry brought in from western Scotland during the late 13th century.

Scandinavia and the Baltic

Scandinavia, though old fashioned in several respects, saw the development of military recruitment patterns similar to those recorded in parts of Germany. This was particularly the case in royal armies; above all that of Denmark and to a lesser extent of Sweden. Nevertheless, rural militias continued to play a role, specifically on the island of Gotland which, though it technically formed part of the

kingdom of Sweden, remained largely autonomous. Gotland was, in fact, only required to contribute six or seven ships to the defence of the Swedish kingdom, and then only in campaigns against heathen rather than Christian foes. Urban militias similarly developed in some Baltic merchant cities; a classic example being the prosperous but perhaps militarily backward city of Wisby on the island of Gotland.

On the other side of the Baltic sea Prussian tribal troops continued to serve as auxiliaries and as guides in Germanic Crusader campaigns against the still pagan Lithuanians. Estonian, Semgallian, Kur, Liv and Lett tribes to the north similarly served, often under their own tribal leadership, in the armies of the Germanic Crusading Orders. Whereas the Estonians often rebelled, the last such uprising being in 1343, the Livs and Letts were the most loyal to their new masters. It was largely from these two previously weak and oppressed tribes that the Latvian people evolved during the 14th century.

Between German-ruled Latvia and Prussia lay the remarkable Grand-Principality of Lithuania. This not only survived constant military pressure from its Christian neighbours but went on to carve out its own huge empire to the south and east during the 14th century. The Lithuanian *karias* or army consisted of local *boyars*. These included aristocrats of Lithuanian, Byelorussian (White Russian), Russian, Polish and eventually even Ukrainian origin. In addition the Lithuanian *karias* relied upon the Grand-Duke's own castellans plus the local levies of these various and disparate regional powers.

During the 14th century Lithuania was reorganised as a *diarchy*; in other words two separate sections under their own governments, but forming one state. The western half gradually adopted many western European systems of military recruitment and organisation; meanwhile focusing its energies on resisting German Crusader and Polish aggression. In contrast the eastern half was in a position to conquer vast areas of what had been Russia, even reaching the Black Sea during the early 15th century. In fact an Act of Union with Poland in 1386 created the largest single state in Christendom; with the solitary possible exception of the sparsely inhabited Russian republic of Novgorod. This Act of Union also finally brought pagan western Lithuania into Catholic Christendom; the eastern half having already largely converted to Orthodox Christianity.

Eastern Europe

Before its union with the Grand-Duchy of Lithuania in the late 14th century, Poland had declined into a weak, backward and often divided area. Its armies were drawn from a large but often notably poor noble class. The resulting forces now largely seem to have consisted of light cavalry, many still unarmoured, supported by relatively few foot soldiers. During the early 14th century Poland was itself also under great pressure from the increasingly powerful and aggressive Margrave of Brandenburg in north-eastern Germany. Other small states had similar fears. So much so that in 1325 the Poles were able to summon the help of allied troops from Baltic Lithuania in the east, as well as semi-autonomous Slav Ruthenia to the south.

Generally ephemeral alliance and recruitment from a very wide area were, in fact, a common feature in central Europe during this period. For example, the late 13th century Bohemian army is described as including Bohemians themselves, as well as Moravians, heavy cavalry German mercenaries and light auxiliary horsemen from Silesia and Poland. On the other hand, such forces could be as effective and well-equipped as any in Europe; Bohemian cavalry having already been described as including many men riding fully armoured horses.

Hungary continued to expand during the 14th century; becoming a major military power, though also including the seeds of subsequent internal weakness and fragmentation. Its subjects included huge numbers of non-Magyars; mostly Slavs in the northernmost and southern provinces, but also Romanian-speaking Vlach people to the east.

Hungary was now ruled by a French–Angevin dynasty like so much of the rest of Europe. Its army was also almost entirely western European in character. Nevertheless, only the king seems to have recruited more than a handful of foreign mercenaries, largely Germans and Italians. Meanwhile much of the Hungarian military aristocracy still owed service to the ruler, though this was on the basis of personal 'fidelity' rather than the feudal possession of land. At the same time the increasingly powerful leading nobility had its own private armies or *banderia* consisting of paid retainers and vassal families. Other forces were provided by urban, rural and Church-led militias.

The Hungarian army did still have some light cavalry; these being recruited from the stock-raising though no longer nomadic peoples of the Great Plain of Hungary and from the Balkan provinces. Those who were of Kipchaq Turkish origin still, perhaps, fought as horse-archers. These Kipchaqs had fled into Hungary ahead of the all-conquering Mongols, and with few exceptions they proved to be fiercely loyal in the service of the Hungarian crown. In return, the favour which the king at times showed to his Kipchaq followers could lead to friction with the Hungarian nobility.

Other troops of eastern steppe origin who had settled in Hungary in earlier years included Turkic Pechenegs and Berends, some of whom probably retained their separate and even pagan identity throughout the 13th century. The Iasians, who were first mentioned in Hungary in 1318, were not Turks but were basically Iranian-speaking semi-nomads from north of the Caucasus mountains. They had also fled westward during the chaos of the Mongol conquests. Like their cousins, the Ossetians in the northern Caucasus, these Iasians seem to have been either highly unorthodox Christians, similarly unorthodox Muslims, or largely pagan.

The precise identities of these peoples was already confused in the 14th century. In fact, it has been suggested that the Iasians were, in reality, basically the same people

as those north Caucasian Alans who sought refuge in Byzantium. Many centuries earlier, of course, another wave of Alan military refugees had found service in the late Roman army. One way or another, the Iasians and Alans do seem to have been essentially the same people as the Ossetians who survive today in the Caucasus mountains. Like the Alans in Byzantine service, the Iasians in Hungary served as light cavalry alongside the Kipchaqs. Meanwhile Romanian-speaking Vlach light cavalry were similarly recorded a few years later in Hungarian-ruled Croatia, down on the Adriatic coast. All these 'alien' horsemen tended to be used as fast-moving and, for their western neighbours, visibly intimidating raiders.

Less exotic, but militarily just as important, were the varied militia forces available to the Hungarian ruler. They were drawn from the large communities of Saxon German settlers in the towns of Transylvania. The existence of these communities, so far from Saxony itself, are believed to lie behind the story of the Pied Piper of Hamelin. Other sources of militarily significant militias were the almost as mysterious Hungarian *Szekler* community of Transylvania, and the slightly more straightforward Romanian-speaking Vlachs of this same region.

The status of the earlier Orthodox Christian and perhaps Romanian-speaking military aristocracy of parts of Transylvania, however, had slumped by the 14th century. Those who remained largely became Catholic and were assimilated into the dominant Magyar culture. Others, perhaps wishing to retain their distinctive identity, migrated over the Carpathian mountains to strengthen the emerging Romanian principalities of Moldavia and Wallachia. The peasantry of Transylvania, meanwhile, also had a military role in this exposed part of the Hungarian kingdom. One-fifth of those eligible were summoned for offensive campaigns; one-third for defensive. The famous Hungarian *honved* local defence militia may also have been coming into existence, though this would be much more characteristic of the 15th century.

During the 14th century Serbia suddenly erupted from being a minor Balkan state to rivalling both the declining Byzantine Empire and the rising Ottoman Sultanate. This remarkable process had much in common with the sudden rise of Lithuania, but was even more ephemeral. During these brief conquests much of the existing Byzantine military aristocracy, as well as many garrisons, simply transferred their allegiance without much resistance from the Byzantine Emperor to a Serbian ruler who came to style himself Tsar of the Serbs and Greeks. The renowned Vlach cavalry who dominated much of central Greece in the late 13th century did the same; fighting for the Serbs as *voynik* semi-feudal provincial cavalry forces. So did many Albanian mountain chiefs.

Serbia, meanwhile, was growing in wealth, partly from new mines run by German immigrants; this providing the money that enabled Serbian rulers to recruit an élite royal force of mercenaries. Some were Germans, but many others were Hungarians or Poles. Above all, Spaniards seem to have been welcomed beneath the Serbian banner; as were Kipchaq Turkish refugees from the Mongol onslaught. Whereas the Kipchaqs naturally fought as light cavalry and horse-archers, the Spanish Catalans and Aragonese largely consisted of infantry who were employed as garrison troops in several newly conquered cities. Nevertheless, the bulk of the 14th century Serbian army almost certainly remained locally recruited Serbs, Bosnians, Albanians, Bulgarians and Vlachs. Troops of mixed Greek and Turkish origin, known as *murtat*, were similarly found in Serbian ranks. Some of these may have been of Turkish prisoner or slave origin and their numbers are likely to have been few.

The 14th century saw a brief period of Bosnian independence and even of expansion at the expense of neighbouring states. The little that is known of recruitment in Bosnia suggests that it remained largely internal, as was also the case in the independent Adriatic Slav city-state of Ragusa, now known as Dubrovnik. Here, however, the dominant political and military élite were very Italianised. The main external source of troops for the Republic of Ragusa seems to have been light cavalry from the semi-nomadic Vlach tribes of the hinterland.

The Italo-Angevin feudal lords of Albania, to the south, owed allegiance to the Kingdom of Naples in southern Italy and were supported by garrisons recruited from local Albanians, Greeks and Serbs as well as mercenaries from Italy itself. The Albanians were already earning a reputation as excellent light cavalry *stradiotti*. Such troops would subsequently be found in the armies of various 15th century Italian states, most notably that of Venice.

The Kingdom of Bulgaria similarly recruited non-Bulgarians, including large numbers of semi-feudal Vlach *voynik* cavalry under their own *voivode* commander. Turkish Kipchaq horse-archers, large numbers of Tartars who were, in reality, probably Mongol mercenaries, as well as some Iasians or Alans, were also enlisted by the rulers of Bulgaria. North of the Danube two new Romanian states now emerged during the 14th century – Wallachia and Moldavia. The former consisted of Oltania and Muntania which had themselves grown out of the previously autonomous Hungarian regions of Severin and Cumania; the latter region having been known as 'the Land of the Kipchaqs'.

During the late 13th century such areas had been under local lords known as *knézats* and *voivodes*; each with its own troops led by the local nobility. Some parts of Moldavia and Wallachia also included settlements of German Saxons and basically Iranian-speaking Iasian semi-nomads as well as *Szeklers* and other Hungarians. Semi-nomadic Kipchaq Turkish tribal groups meanwhile still inhabited some low-lying regions of open grassland.

The Hungarian king had at first encouraged the development of the Principality of Moldavia as a bulwark against the vast Mongol Golden Horde which controlled the steppes to the east. However, the local Moldavian rulers soon co-operated with these Mongols while many of their troops adopted Mongol styles of warfare. Nevertheless, an essentially western European style of feudal military structure came to dominate both Wallachia and Moldavia, with urban and rural militias as well as a mass levy of all freemen remaining throughout the 14th century. The massed levy constituted what was known as the 'big army', which was only used in emergencies; the 'little army', which consisted of the feudal and tribal élites supplemented by foreign mercenaries, was used during more normal campaigns.

ORGANISATION

Changes in military recruitment and weaponry during the 14th century led to significant changes in military organisation. In broader terms, the *indenture* system seen in France and England, and the increasing use of professional mercenaries in Italy, both resulted in better discipline, longer terms of service and thus more permanent and effective command structures. At a more personal level, the use of increasingly powerful crossbows, which were in general slow to *span* and load, necessitated a new corps of *pavise* or large mantlet shield-carrying men to protect these crossbowmen as they loaded their weapons.

France

Although there was no really permanent French army, even in the late 13th century, there was a permanent command structure. At the head of this were those Princes of the Blood, close relatives of the king, who commanded both national and provincial armies. A professional *Constable* and two *Marshals*, also drawn from the military aristocracy, were another permanent feature of the French Court. So was a *Master of Crossbowmen* who may, however, often have had humbler origins. Other senior men, permanently 'on call' if not permanently 'on duty', included the royal *seneschals* who served as provincial military governors and army commanders. Then there were those senior members of the French nobility who took leading roles on specific campaigns, not as a lifetime career but as a matter of honour.

Whereas the *Constable* and *Marshals* had other non-military, often political, duties, the *Master of Crossbowmen* held a more specifically military position. In fact, there appear to have been separate chains of command for cavalry and infantry forces. The cavalry could, of course, be mustered far more quickly than was possible with foot soldiers. Even in the late 14th century, both feudal and paid volunteer cavalry were still mustered before one of the *Marshals* or his deputies, whereas on many occasions the *Master of Crossbowmen* seems to have been responsible for all infantry forces, not merely those armed with crossbows. Sometimes the *Master of Crossbowmen* also commanded some cavalry forces. Generally, however, mercenary cavalry from outside the Kingdom of France were commanded by *knights* or barons while on active campaigns. In effect

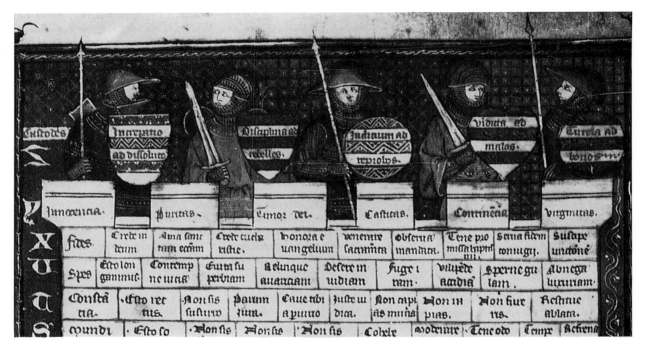

'Allegorical warriors', in the Speculum Theologiae; French, early 14th century. At one time the inaccurate date given for English effigies and monumental brasses made early 14th century England look far more advanced than neighbouring parts of Europe, in terms of its armour. In reality it now appears that peaceful England was, not surprisingly, rather old fashioned compared to its more war-torn western European neighbours. Here, for example, a series of armoured figures in a French manuscript wear a variety of types of brimmed chapel de fer, mail coifs and mail hauberks. But the man on the far left has a very advanced form of plated neck-protecting gorgerete. (MS. Ars. 1037, f.3, Bibliothèque Nationale, Paris; photograph, Bibliothèque Nationale)

these *knights* and barons formed the middle ranks in the chain of command.

The process of mustering armies was given different names depending on the type of campaign envisaged. An *ost*, for example, was normally an offensive force intended to operate outside its own immediate region, usually under the command of the king, a prince or baron. A *chevauchée* was normally considered defensive, being designed to operate within its own area of mobilisation. In fact, the extreme military pressures imposed by the Hundred Years War led to a considerable devolution in the defences of the French kingdom; largely as a result of the distances involved in these campaigns and the inadequacy or slowness of 14th century communications.

Within these forces the status of individual troops was largely a matter of wealth rather than solely of birth. This clearly reflected the fact that the arms, armour and above all the horses required of a properly equipped *knight* were now extremely expensive. A *knight* was generally expected to have five such horses, though not all were *destrier* warhorses. A 14th century *squire* probably had fewer. On the other hand, he was now a fully-fledged combatant rather than a mere servant. Among these *squires*, the *armigeri* may have formed a group with more aristocratic origins. Similarly, non-noble *sergeants à cheval* were now front-rank armoured cavalry, though generally with only three horses: a *destrier* for battle, a *palfrey* for ordinary riding and a pack-horse.

The military significance of similarly non-noble mounted crossbowmen was indicated by the fact that they were actually paid more than a *sergeant à cheval*. Overall there was a notable increase in the importance of all such professional soldiers, some of whom formed a permanent royal bodyguard in the later 14th century. This unit, incidentally, was certainly not merely for parade or display purposes, as some earlier court units seem to have been.

The Hundred Years War itself stimulated an increase in the importance of French urban forces; both royal garrisons and local militias. This was particularly apparent in the war-torn south of the country, where two forms of garrison were recorded. These consisted of the *establida*, which was theoretically responsible for defending a whole region, and the *garniso*, which merely defended the town where it was stationed. Indigenous militias of towns or cities were supposed to maintain a daily watch and guard. In wartime they were placed under the command of *captains* selected by the crown in northern France or by local barons in the south. Such captains were themselves normally outsiders, supposedly free from the pressures of local interests. Otherwise the militias were commanded by the town *consul* or by a *captain* selected from among the most prominent citizens. They had their own banner and a standard-bearer, and during the second half of the 14th century many such militias were strengthened by the addition of some professional *sergeants*. Fortified cities in an important strategic military location might also have their own siege technicians; including carpenters, rope-makers and their assistants.

The main duties of an urban militia were known as *garde*, *guet* and *arrière-guet* in the north; *garde*, *gach* or *gag*, and *reyregach* or *estialgach* in the south. *Garde* basically meant sentry-duty at the town gates in daytime; this being the most important duty of all. *Guet* was mounting watch on the ramparts, usually at night, while *arrière-guet* was patrolling the streets and checking on the *guet*; again usually at night. *Garde* was normally undertaken by full-time paid gate-keepers who would be supported by professional soldiers or by the town's more prominent citizens in time of war. *Guet* duty could be imposed on every married man once a week. It was organised in two watches, the first being summoned by a bell or trumpet as night fell. Each watch was also under its own 'captain of the watch'. If danger threatened, the whole militia would be mobilised, usually in companies of fifty men and squads of ten, with a pre-arranged command structure. Ordinary foot soldiers manned the ramparts; archers being stationed at lower embrasures. If necessary a militiaman's entire family could join him at his post. Wealthier citizens who possessed horses might generally have remained in the streets below, ready to ride off and reinforce a vulnerable stretch of wall or to sortie against the attackers.

Where effective rural militias still existed, they were organised into *constabularies* or *companies* based upon their villages of origin. Again, each was led by a *constable* who received twice the pay of ordinary men. If such local forces were sent to strengthen the defences of a nearby town, they were naturally placed under the authority of that town's commander. But what happened when they joined an army in the field is less clear.

The Empire: Germany

The old-fashioned feudal systems of military organisation continued to exist in several parts of Germany well into the 14th century, particularly in the east. Meanwhile the west of the Empire gradually adopted structures similar to those seen in neighbouring France. The élite armoured cavalrymen of Germany, however, came to be known as a *panzerati* or *renner*, 'men-at-arms', rather than *knechts* or *knights*. At the same time this latter term generally came to mean a military servant. Such armoured horsemen were normally organised into *gleven*, which were comparable to the *lances* of France and Italy. As such they usually consisted of the *man-at-arms* and his followers. At first such a military following generally consisted of three armoured *sergeants*, but later it consisted either of *diener*, lightly

armed servants, or of three hired mercenaries. One would have been an armoured cavalryman like the *man-at-arms* himself; the second being a light cavalryman or mounted crossbowman; the third a servant or page, though this system could clearly vary to a considerable extent.

Urban militias played an increasingly important military role as the German part of the Empire fragmented into innumerable minor principalities, Church estates, free and 'imperial' cities. Urban militias in what are now the Benelux countries consisted of *constabularies* often based upon, and equipped by, the craft and merchant guilds of their particular city. They included fighting troops and their servants. A unit known as a *voud* seemingly consisted of about ninety-six armoured horsemen drawn from the richer citizens, plus five hundred and eleven guildsmen on foot. In Germany itself, such towns were divided into quarters, each with its own gate. The militiamen were actually led by a *viertelmeister* appointed by the city council. He in turn could be supported by other officers, a trumpeter, perhaps semi-professional watchtower guards and, towards the end of the 14th century, even a *büchsenmeister*, master gunner. The richer citizens served as cavalry, as was seen elsewhere in western Europe, and were organised into *gleven* units; particularly when supplemented by professional mercenaries. Many if not most German cities also had a wagon in which their banners were mounted, just like the better-known *carroccio* of an Italian city.

The Empire: Italy and the Papal States

Urban militias dominated warfare in northern and central Italy to a degree not seen anywhere else in western Europe; just as the cities which they served came to dominate politically and economically. Even though these militias declined in favour of *condottieri* mercenary 'companies' during the 14th century, the cities which now recruited the *condottieri* remained militarily dominant.

By the late 13th century titles such as *knight* and baron had become largely honorific, having little real military meaning within northern and central Italy. The old city armies had traditionally consisted of three distinct elements: the urban militias themselves, the auxiliaries from neighbouring or allied areas, and the mercenaries. This, however, was also changing. The *societas peditum*, 'associations of infantrymen', in such cities as Florence evolved into *societas populi*, 'associations of the people', whose political power grew even greater as German imperial control over Italy collapsed. In Florence, for example, a 'popular' regime had taken control in the mid-13th century, being supported by the militias of the six *sesti* or quarters of the city. This regime soon abolished the older aristocratic *societas militum* or 'society of knights' and limited the height of private *torri* urban towers to twenty-nine metres.

Political power fluctuated in such Italian cities, different noble or 'popular' groups winning power at different times; but during the late 13th century another *popolo* government in Florence radically reorganised the city's militia. This was now divided into twenty *gonfali* companies based upon specific parts of the city; each having its own banner. The members of these *gonfali* had to keep their weapons with them in time of trouble, and heavy fines were imposed on anyone who hindered a militiaman in the performance of his duty. These fines were particularly harsh in times of riot or internal disturbance. Members of the *gonfali* were themselves forbidden to help a member of the aristocracy in any way, were bound by oaths of loyalty to one another, and were led by the *Capitano del Popolo*. Echoes of the passions as well as the heraldry involved in this remarkable military system can still be seen in Italy; most magnificently during such events as the fiercely competitive annual Palio horse-race in Siena.

Troops drawn from the surrounding rural *contado* were similarly grouped into *pieve* detachments from a collection of villages, these apparently being subdivided into, or otherwise referred to as, *vessilli* from their *vexilla* banners which would themselves be carried by a veteran soldier. Infantry often outnumbered cavalry by ten to one in such Italian city armies. Nevertheless, the cavalry remained an élite, organised in squadrons. The best foot soldiers were similarly grouped into squadrons of *pavesari* shield-bearers and crossbowmen. Again, each had its own *vexillum* banner which was held by a *gonfalonieri* for the crossbowmen, a *bandifer* for other infantry. In addition there were two officers known as *distringitori* or 'explainers' and a senior *consigliere* or 'consul'. At the heart of the communal army stood the *carroccio*, a symbolic wagon with its banners and a *martinella* bell which presumably had some communication function.

'Infantry of allies and friends', wall-painting; northern Italian, mid-14th century. The wall-paintings at Avio may not be fine examples of early Renaissance art, but they provide a huge amount of detailed information about the arms and armour of 14th century Italy; above all that used by the infantry soldiers who tend to get pushed into the background of more aristocratic art. Here typical Italian light infantrymen are armed with large shields and spears, crossbows and large daggers or short swords. They have tall forms of bascinet helmets which also protect the sides and rear of the head, but most wear only thickly quilted forms of soft armour over their bodies; in many instances two being worn, one over the other. (Casetta dei Soldati, Castle of Sabbionara di Avio)

A number of military setbacks did much to undermine the reputation of urban cavalry militia forces in late 13th century Italy. In contrast, the reputations of infantry militias remained intact or even enhanced. As a result, the first large-scale recruitment of 'foreign' mercenaries involved armoured horsemen rather than foot soldiers. These were generally grouped into *conestabilaria* units under their own leaders, with rarely more than fifty men in each such formation. During the 14th century Italian cavalry formations were described as consisting of smaller units or 'lances', each under a *caporale*. They in turn were grouped into larger *bandiera* companies with a trumpeter, fifes or drums. Some surviving mercenary contracts indicate that infantry and cavalry were checked at a weekly muster or review.

The self-contained mercenary 'companies' which offered themselves for hire as ready-made armies in 14th century Italy were themselves remarkably disciplined institutions. Many were clearly governed by their own rules with agreed systems for sharing booty, provost marshals to maintain order, their own recognised judges and even a portable gallows to punish those who broke the regulations.

To some extent the military systems of Italian merchant colonies overseas mirrored those seen in Italy itself.

So-called 'Effigy of Charles II of Anjou'; southern Italian, early 14th century. Highly decorated sheets of hardened leather and perhaps partially gilded armour for the arms and legs were a characteristic of southern and some parts of central Italy during the early and mid-14th century. The technique probably reflected influence from the Balkans or eastern Mediterranean, and it was clearly suited to the hot climate of the south. Over his mail hauberk and mail chausses, this figure has cuir-bouilli hardened leather greaves on his legs, probably leather cuisses over his upper legs with some sort of internal bulbous poleyns for his knees, rerebraces on his upper arms, circular besagews on his elbows. He probably has vambraces for his lower arms beneath the mail sleeves of his hauberk. A typical Italian form of large dagger hangs from his belt. (Cathedral of Lucera)

Genoese outposts around the Black Sea, for example, largely administered themselves, under the authority of *podestas* or *consuls* sent by the mother-city. Pera next to Constantinople, and Kaffa in the Crimea, each had its own small military force. That of Kaffa defended the settlement both by land and sea under the command of a *capi-*

tanei. He himself was supported by subordinate *custodes* who were responsible for the gates, walls and towers, plus a *castellani*, a *vicarius* and a *capitanei gothie* who may have led local indigenous troops, and other officials in charge of the *arsenal.* Rising tension between Genoese Kaffa and the neighbouring Mongol rulers in the 14th century led to a restructuring of these defences under the direction of a *Baylia Officii Gazarie* who was now responsible for the gate-guards as well as the construction and arming of naval galleys to operate in the Black Sea.

Italy: Venice and the South
During the 14th century Genoa's great rival, Venice, developed into a land as well as naval power; though at first its main territories were in the Balkans and Greece rather than on the Italian mainland. Here Venetian armies were organised along basically the same lines as those of other Italian cities, each *knight* having one *destrier* war-horse, two other horses and three *squires*. The demands of 14th century colonial warfare also led to the abandonment of a 12th century law which stated that a Venetian nobleman was not allowed to lead more than twenty-five armed followers.

In Venice itself the city militia was restructured into units of twelve men, while in the city's far-flung trading outposts colonial captains commanded a strictly specified number of *banderie* companies led by a *comestabilis* officer; each unit averaging about twenty infantrymen and from fifteen to eighteen cavalry. A detailed description of a rather small company from the year 1400 stated that it consisted of one *comestabilis equester* commanding officer, one *banderarius* standard-bearer, nine *caporales* and seven *equitatores* horsemen. The numbers in this particular unit may have been small, but the proportions of different types of troops might be normal. The largest Venetian overseas possession at this time was the island of Crete which was divided into feudal *fiefs.* Each of these included a large number of serfs of basically Arab origin who could also be mustered for military service. Beyond the mountains, in the rugged and barely governed south of Crete, lived the Greek *Sfakiots.* When they were not in rebellion or operating as independent pirates, they were a useful source of highly skilled light infantry archers.

For many centuries southern Italy had been socially and militarily very different from the north of the country. These differences remained, and were to some extent even increased during the 14th century. During these years the southern mainland fell under the basically French Angevin ruling dynasty of the Kingdom of Naples, while the Kingdom of Sicily was ruled by an Aragonese Spanish dynasty. Each introduced several new military influences which in turn served to reinforce existing differences between these two parts of the south. Perhaps the most significant difference lay in the Aragonese Kingdom of Sicily's greater use of light cavalry. Here a Sicilian *knight* was expected to have a minimum of four horses, while in the Angevin Kingdom of Naples a *knight* had four horses plus a *squire* and two servants. The autonomous Neapolitan-Angevin possessions in Albania are dealt with in the section dealing with Eastern Europe.

England and the Celtic States
At the beginning of the 14th century English military organisation and command structures were very similar to those of France. Nevertheless, there had already been significant modernisation during King Edward I's Welsh and Scottish wars. During the 14th century itself, the unforeseen success of English arms in the Hundred Years War may have led English influence to be felt in France, rather than flowing in the opposite direction as it had done for several centuries. Paradoxically, however, such victories may have led to a self-satisfied military conservatism; resulting in England's military structures once again slipping behind those of France, Burgundy and Italy by the end of the century.

English military forces were now clearly divided into the king's army, built around the *Royal Household,* and a much larger array of local defence forces. The *knights* of the *Royal Household* not only formed a small but effective standing army, but also provided a core of élite experienced soldiers capable of providing military leadership. The *Royal Household* also provided the necessary administrative, organisational and indeed storage facilities to deal with the increasingly sophisticated weaponry of the 14th century. This was particularly important when it came to firearms, which were regarded almost as precious objects to be kept under strict government control. In about 1372 the English crown had its own gunnery department in the Tower of London; this department in effect still being considered part of the Royal Wardrobe.

Some changes in the organisation of armoured cavalry forces of England seem to have had more in common with developments in Italy rather than in France. For example, the term *sergeant à cheval* declined in favour of *damoiseau*, *ecuyer* or *man-at-arms*; there being about four such *men-at-arms* for every *knight* by the mid-1330s. Such troops still appear to have been in *constabularia* units of about twenty men; these being grouped in *acies* or *battles* while on campaign.

Some of the earlier local defence structures survived, particularly in northern England, whereas a coastal strip several miles deep was reorganised as the *terre maritime* during the 14th century. Its defences against pirates or privateers were separate from those of the rest of the *shire* in which it stood. As such they were the responsibility of a local bishop or nobleman. Here a *garde de la mer* coastal militia consisted of *posse comitatus* formations, which included local *men-at-arms* as well as light cavalry *hobelars* and infantry. They were led by the *constables* of the local *hundreds*; themselves being under the command of *Royal Commissioners*. Within this sophisticated system the cavalry were grouped into *constabularies*; the foot soldiers into units known as *millenaries*, *centaines* and *vintaines*. These infantry units supposedly consisted of one thousand, one

hundred, or twenty men each; the units in question being reviewed by the local *constables* twice a year.

Whereas the independent Kingdom of Scotland attempted to copy several aspects of English or French military organisation, at least in southern and lowlands regions, the old indigenous Welsh military structures disappeared during the 14th century. Instead they were replaced by an essentially English system imposed by the English crown. Much the same happened in those parts of Ireland under effective English rule, though clearly not in the Celtic west of the island which remained independent in all but name.

Scandinavia and the Baltic

The German influence on Scandinavian military organisation continued to be felt through the 14th century. This period also saw a great and widespread increase in the use of the crossbow by both professional infantry forces and urban militias. On the other hand, many of the ordinary rural levies of Scandinavia still consisted of longbowmen.

On the other side of the Baltic Sea the indigenous peoples were now largely dominated by Scandinavian or German rulers; often in the guise of Crusaders. In many such areas the Finno-Ugrian and Balt tribes continued to serve as local militias. Those of Livonia formed very useful frontier auxiliaries under the command of a small force of German Crusader *knights*. These auxiliaries, like the Crusader forces themselves, still faced both the Orthodox Christian Russian principalities and their still-pagan Lithuanian neighbours.

Only these Lithuanians retained a separate Baltic identity; the Principality of Lithuania being divided in 1345

Opposite page: Ivory chess-knight; probably English, c.1370. This little horseman's use of a large, reverse-curved shield suggests that he might be equipped for the tournament rather than for war. Nevertheless, his horse armour is of great interest. This is clearly of mail, though partially covered with sheets of probably heraldic cloth. The animal's head is also almost entirely covered with a chamfron; perhaps of iron though more probably largely of hardened leather. (Inv. 1968.68.95, Metropolitan Museum of Art, New York; photograph, Ministry of Works)

Below: 'King Louis the Great with figures representing the western European and nomadic elements of the state and army', in the Hungarian Illuminated Chronicle; Hungarian manuscript,

c.1360. The artist who painted this picture was clearly attempting to show, either by using real or symbolic costumes, that the ruler of Hungary was supported by a great variety of peoples of different ethnic origins and military traditions. Those on the more prestigious left are 'Europeans', though the helmet crest of the foremost figure and the pendant arm defences of two men may indicate the king's rule over parts of the ex-Byzantine Balkans. The figures on the right are portrayed as 'Asiatics' and represent those peoples of recent nomadic steppe origin who had either migrated into Hungary or over whom the king claimed suzerainty. Their costumes and weaponry are, in fact, remarkably accurate. (MS. Lat. 404, f.1, National Széchényi Library, Budapest)

into eastern and western *diarchies* under two ruling brothers. Each part had its own military administration, its own *karias* army and its own capital city. The ruling princes' efforts to turn Lithuanian tribal land-owners into feudal *fief*-holders owing military service on the western European model had led to civil war in the mid-13th century. But once the Lithuanian princes succeeded in these reforms, and had also imposed a European-style system of government, Lithuania was ready for that extraordinary wave of expansion which would eventually take it to the shores of the Black Sea far to the south.

Eastern Europe

Military and administrative reforms, as well as economic expansion, lay behind the remarkable rise of several eastern European states during the 14th century. Poland, though long established as a 'national state', did not take much part in this process and was, in fact, more of a victim than an aggressor. Nevertheless, the process of western feudalisation and the modernisation of *knight* service continued, even though it was several years behind comparable developments to the west. Meanwhile, some eastern regions of Poland such as Mazovia were now under very strong eastern and even Mongol military influence. This was very apparent in their arms, armour and tactics, though it is less clear in terms of organisation.

The local 'great power' status of 14th century Hungary was also based on that kingdom's military effectiveness;

not only in relation to its eastern and southern neighbours but also in competition with such advanced societies as that of Germanised Bohemia to the north, Germanic Austria to the west and even Italy to the south-west. Hungarian armies campaigned in all these areas with considerable, though varying, success.

Early in the 14th century the Hungarian army was reorganised into regional *bandiera* forces, the most important being that of the king himself. The others were controlled by barons known as *voivodes*, *báns* or *ispáns* depending on which linguistic region of the Kingdom of Hungary they governed. In addition, there were royal garrisons under various *castellans*, some of whom were in fact *ispáns*. Several of these increasingly powerful Hungarian barons also held castle-estates in many different parts of the kingdom. The system of *bandiera* forces was further refined in the mid-14th century as a result of the experience of campaigning in Italy. One of the most obvious and immediate effects of such experience was the adoption of heavier arms and armour by Hungary's Kipchaq and other light cavalry units.

The free Kipchaq warrior tribesmen, like others who were of ultimately steppe origin, were still organised on a clan basis under their own, now-westernised, military élite. The military organisation of the *Szeklers* was slightly different. Though they apparently also often served as light cavalry, they were commanded by non-*Szekler* officers. All these Hungarian light cavalry, however, seem to have been organised in perhaps Byzantine-style squadrons rather than in western European military formations.

The late 13th and 14th centuries saw a slight shift away from Byzantine forms of military organisations and towards various western systems in Serbia. Here the local Slav *wojnuks* or *voyniks* formed a minor military aristocracy which would have a considerable influence upon their subsequent Ottoman Turkish conquerors. Soldiers who distinguished themselves in battle could also earn the title of *vitez* or 'knight'; this term later, apparently, only applying to an élite cavalryman. Another less clear military title was that of *paličnik* or 'mace carrier'. He, however, only seems to have been seen at court. Some regions of the wide but ephemeral 14th century Serbian empire were more westernised than others; Thessaly in northern Greece, for example, had been substantially feudalised in the 13th century. Nevertheless, the Serbian army remained more Byzantine than western right up to the Ottoman conquests; its commanders ranging in rank from the *Grand Voivode* at the top, down through other *voivodes* and *tisučniks* 'leaders of one thousand'.

'Hungarians pursuing Cumans, in the Ladislas Legend', wall-painting; Hungaro-Slovak , c.1370. The Christian or Hungarian troops on the left are equipped in typical late 14th century central European plate armour, though the fact that they only have bascinet helmets may reflect the relatively light cavalry traditions which persisted in medieval Hungary. The Cumans or Kipchaqs on the right are dressed and equipped in a mixture of European and steppe styles, as is also the case with their horse harness. This may, in fact, have been accurate, for various originally Turkish nomadic groups retained a separate military identity in 14th century Hungary, despite being gradually assimilated in other aspects of their culture. (Evangelical Church at Rimavská Bana, Slovakia; photograph, Státny ústav pamiat- kovej starostlivosti, Bratislava)

Another example of profound western European military influence, this time stemming directly from Italian military involvement and Neapolitan-Angevin rule, was found in 14th century Albania. The Kingdom of Albania, established in 1272, was under Italo-Angevin suzerainty. Crushed in 1286, it revived at the beginning of the 14th century with greater support from the local lords and military élite. These latter then won increasing political and military autonomy as the years passed. At the same time, the few towns of Albania, most of which lay on the Adriatic coast, were restructured along Italian lines, many probably having their own urban militias. The Neapolitan-Angevin army in this area had been commanded by a *Marshal of Albania* in the late 13th century. Subsequently, a local largely feudal nobility also raised its own small private armies. The Byzantine term *protostrator*, 'commander of troops', was also recorded. Although this may have reflected an actual existing rank, the continuing use of other old Byzantine terms such as *theme*, military province, no longer reflected reality. Instead the military administration of Angevin Albania, like neighbouring Byzantine-ruled Epirus, was probably based upon walled towns known as *kastrons*.

Whereas western European military influence was penetrating the western Balkans, Bulgaria in the east attempt-ed to copy the structures of the late Byzantine military. However, like the rump of the Byzantine Empire itself, Bulgaria soon collapsed before the Ottoman Turkish onslaught.

Hungarian military influence not surprisingly dominated north of the Danube, in the rising Romanian principalities of Wallachia and Moldavia. This was particularly apparent in terms of administration and organisation. In turn this process reflected the French or south Italian-Angevin military models which were influencing Hungary itself. On the other hand, residual Byzantine influence could be seen in the military organisation of certain areas which had earlier been under the Byzantine Empire. Here the local *hospodars*, the most powerful feudal land-holders, dominated military districts known as *ţinuturi* in Moldavia and *judeţe* in Wallachia.

In Wallachia the *voivode* or military lord of Argeş emerged as Grand Voivode in the early 14th century. His successors later became the Princes of Wallachia. The Grand Voivode, however, remained a Hungarian vassal, continuing to hold lands north of the Carpathian mountains even after Wallachia won effective independence south of the mountains. The Hungarian crown had, in fact, encouraged the development of local Romanian-Vlach forces in Wallachia as a forward defence against the nomads of the steppes; first against the Kipchaq Turks and then against the Mongols.

Early military formations in this area consisted of feudal levies raised by local *boyars* or barons, plus a few urban militias. A permanent or professional Wallachian army only seems to have emerged in the late 14th century; this still being based on old temporary *dorobanţi* formations whose primary function had probably been to guard the mountain passes against steppe nomad raiders. This new permanent force was known as the 'Little Army'. It consisted of *curteni* or members of the ruler's court, plus some foreign mercenaries. Wallachia's 'Big Army' remained the massed levy used only in times of emergency. Somewhere between these Big and Little Armies stood feudal forces consisting of *viteji* cavalry, *voinici* or *iunaci* infantry and frontier troops called *strājeri*.

Developments in Moldavia were similar. Initially it too had been encouraged by the Hungarian crown as a buffer against the Mongol Golden Horde, the Poles, Russians and Ruthenians, all of whom sometimes took a threatening pro-Brandenburg, pro-German, stance. Like Wallachia, Moldavia won autonomy and then, in about 1365, virtual independence from the Kingdom of Hungary. Meanwhile its military position was strengthened by the migration of much of the Romanian-Vlach military élite from north-eastern Transylvania, across the northern Carpathian mountains into Moldavia. It is also interesting to note that the *hospodar* or governor of Moldavia in the second half of the 14th century was assisted by a council known as a *divan*. This was an Arab-Islamic term which clearly reached Moldavia via the largely Muslim Golden Horde. Other minor aspects of both military administration and tactics in Romanian Moldavia similarly reflected strong eastern, rather than western, influence.

STRATEGY AND TACTICS

The later Middle Ages saw the development and use of more sophisticated battlefield tactics than had been seen for many centuries, at least in some parts of Europe. At the same time broader strategy remained essentially the same as it had been for a long time. As such, this broader strategy was still more important for the winning of wars than were large-scale clashes on the battlefield. The military differences between the more advanced countries at the heart of European civilisation and those on the fringes of Christendom similarly increased in military and tactical terms; just as they did in the economical and social fields.

Broad Strategy
Naturally enough, the climate of a particular area affected the traditional campaigning season. In Italy in the 13th and 14th centuries, for example, this season was normally from March to October, whereas it tended to be slightly shorter farther north. Other northern regions, however,

'Battle of Sinalunga 1363', wall-painting by Lippo Vanni; Italian, c.1370. The fact that the majority of cavalrymen in this picture still wear conical great helms may be an artistic convention, along with the elaborate crests on top of several of these helmets; these items of equipment having normally been relegated to the tournament field. The limited form of apparently quilted horse armour of the animals on the left seems to have been typically Italian, though the perhaps scale-lined, rivet covered, cuisses on the thighs of each rider clearly reflected current practice. (Palazzo Pubblico, Siena)

had their own distinctive traditions of winter warfare, not seen in the south.

In almost all cases raiding and the inflicting of as much devastation upon the enemy's economic base as possible, at the same time avoiding major confrontations with his forces, remained the primary offensive tactic. The defenders, meanwhile, still focused on harassing, ambushing and otherwise forcing such raiders to leave. Siege warfare seems to have declined in relative significance, though it was still by far the most important means of conquering territory. Some raiding forces could be very small, and often included a far higher proportion of infantry to cav-

alry than might have been expected. Two detailed examples from early 14th century France each concerned raiding forces which included from ten to seventeen foot soldiers for every horseman.

In defensive terms, the French appear to have learned the art of guerrilla warfare during the 13th century Albigensian Crusades in southern France. This may, in fact, have enabled their leaders to accept a very cautious, even wily, form of warfare which might previously have been regarded as almost dishonourable and certainly contrary to the chivalric ideal. Similarly it may have contributed to the 14th century French military aristocracy's greater will-

ingness to operate in close co-operation with élite infantry, such as professional crossbowmen. At the same time late 13th century French armies developed more offensive tactics against enemy raiders. This, however, came to grief during the early decades of the Hundred Years War by leading to major battles against English invaders who themselves had by now developed even more effective battlefield tactics. Later 14th century French armies, most notably those under the leadership of the *Constable* Bertrand du Guesclin, reverted to battle-avoiding warfare of an almost guerrilla type which proved very successful in wearing down the invading English. In response, 14th century English armies took raiding tactics to an extreme degree. Some of their *chevauchées*, as such raids were now called, burned and pillaged across the entire Kingdom of France, from English-held territories in the north and south-west.

Warfare in Italy in the late 13th and 14th centuries seemed, on the face of it, to be on a much smaller scale. Yet, in relative terms, it did quite as much damage to both lives and property. Italy was by now an exceptionally strongly fortified part of Europe. Sieges, as well as *gualdana* raiding and devastation, remained commonplace although the forces involved could be small. Major battles did take place, but they generally had even less effect on the final outcome of wars than did the great battles of the Hundred Years War between England and France. Striking an enemy army while it was on the march, preferably in the flank, was another favoured tactic in Italian warfare that does not seen to been used to the same extent north of the Alps. In Italy armies normally marched with archers and crossbowmen at their head; the *carroccio* banner-wagon in the centre, and cavalry in the rear to protect the baggage train. English armies appear to have marched in the same *battles* or divisions in which they fought; armoured cavalry *men-at-arms* and mounted infantry archers protecting the van and flanks.

Not surprisingly, the different climate and much larger distances often involved in eastern European warfare resulted in different styles of campaign. The Hungarians, for example, strengthened their castles but also attempted to barricade passes through the Carpathian mountains in an unsuccessful attempt to stop the Mongols breaking through from the vast Eurasian steppes beyond. The Northern Crusades against the Lithuanians largely consisted of rapid raids or *reysa* by each side, deep into the other's territory. Here the vital role of river communications led to a series of relatively small fortifications being built along the most important rivers. While the armoured cavalry of the western Crusaders involved in these struggles with the pagan Lithuanians preferred winter raiding, when the frozen ground was more suitable for their heavily laden horses, the Lithuanians' own light cavalry preferred the summer when the vast swampy forests hampered their enemy. To the south the Moldavians had also developed highly effective winter raiding tactics by the late 14th century; perhaps for the same reason. In all such cases, however, those involved could lose valuable horses to the ferocious cold of an eastern European winter.

In another fringe area of 14th century Europe, that of the Celtic kingdoms and peoples in the north and west of England, raids, counter-raids, guerrilla resistance and ambush tactics remained the basis of warfare. This was clearly the case in the struggle between the relatively backward Celts and an English enemy which fought in a manner basically the same as that of the French or Germans. Early, essentially Norse-Viking, tactics seem to have survived in the very small-scale internal warfare of the western Highlands and Islands of Scotland. English aggression rarely reached these areas, but within Ireland the indigenous Celtic forces brought ambush techniques, particularly in the woods and boglands of the west, to a fine art.

Troop Types

Three new, or at least now more clearly differentiated, types of troops characterised western European warfare in the 14th century. There was now a clear distinction between the increasingly heavily armoured *men-at-arms* cavalry and various types of light cavalry who were, by now, more than merely less well-equipped ordinary horsemen. At the same time clearly different types of élite infantry emerged in various countries. In many cases the best of the latter also appeared as highly mobile mounted infantry forces. Otherwise there were few changes except, perhaps, for a general rise in the importance of infantry in mid-14th century Poland, a part of Europe previously dominated by cavalry warfare.

In late 13th and early 14th century Italy and neighbouring areas, *men-at-arms* were protected by various forms of helmet, leg armour and three distinct types of body armour; ranging from the ordinary *hauberk* to forms of *coat-of-plates* and heavier *cuirass*. In some cases horsemen apparently wore all three, while their horses were increasingly given some form of armour. As yet Italian, and perhaps neighbouring, armoured cavalry still used either a small *ecu* or *scutum* shield, or a large *targiam*, or an even larger *tabolaccium amplum*. But as plate body armour grew more effective in the 14th century many cavalry abandoned shields altogether – except for *jousting* in tournaments.

Evidence of the spread of western European tactics in the 14th century Balkans is reflected in the Serbian cavalry's adoption of heavier armour. This came to include the *oklopa* mail *hauberk*, the *shenkela* (possibly a cuirass), the *kolariya* neck protection or gorget, the *barbata* Italian-style helmet, the traditional *shtitova* shield, as well as mail *coifs*, *greaves* and *cirotechas* which were probably gauntlets. Even the Lithuanian military élite wore full armour later in the 14th century, though such troops remained a small minority in the Lithuanian army as a whole.

As yet light cavalry were not a feature of Italy, these appearing later and largely as a result of Spanish influence in the 15th rather than the 14th century. In England, meanwhile, the originally Celtic Irish *hobelar* was a virtually unarmoured light horseman who played an increasingly important role. They often operated in close co-operation with fully armoured *men-at-arm*s and élite mounted infantry archers during deep penetration raids into Scotland and France. In some mid-14th century English *chevauchées* such *hobelars* may actually have been tactically more important that the famous English longbowmen. English mounted archers, of course, were solely mounted infantry since it was not practical, nor even perhaps possible, to shoot a two-metre longbow while on horseback.

'The trial and condemnation of Saint James', on a silver panel by Leonardo di Ser Giovanni; Italian, 1371. The soldier in the middle of this scene has a bascinet with a mail aventail. He also wears a fully developed form of one-piece iron breastplate, below which hangs the laminated fauld to protect his abdomen and groin. The man on the left appears to have a laminated neck protection attached to the rear of his bascinet. The arms and legs of both figures are largely covered by early forms of plated limb defences, though mail is still visible beneath. (Silver altar in Pistoia Cathedral)

Other parts of Europe witnessed a continuing major role for light cavalry, though this was sometimes a consequence of economic and traditional factors rather than a response to specifically military imperatives. In Poland, for example, the majority of horsemen would have been considered light cavalry simply because most were too poor to afford the new styles of western European heavy armour. Records similarly show that the same applied to a large proportion of the Venetian colonial cavalry in Crete in about the year 1332.

In Lithuania, and in German Crusader-ruled Prussia, light cavalry persisted for both economic and traditional military or cultural reasons. In both these areas native horsemen still fought in a manner that reflected a strong steppe or Central Asian influence; an influence perhaps recently reinforced by the sweeping successes of the Mongols in neighbouring Russia. The same might also have applied in Hungary where, however, Kipchaq and other originally steppe nomadic warrior communities steadily abandoned various traditional weapons such as their light mace. Meanwhile the military élite of such communities even adopted the armour-breaking heavy European flanged mace, the straight double-edged western *knightly* sword rather than the Turkish sabre, battle-axes, and even some degree of western plate armour. Nevertheless, traditional horse-archers wearing only light layered leather armour continued to exist. As such they remained tacti-

cally important enough for every Hungarian lance-armed *man-at-arms* to be ordered to bring two mounted archers with him on campaign.

Whether the appearance of such Hungarian light cavalry in Italy prompted the recruitment of mounted crossbowmen here is unknown. On the other hand, the sudden appearance of a highly distinctive form of hardened leather armour in southern Italy surely resulted from Neapolitan-Angevin campaigns in the southern Balkans. Mounted crossbowmen were probably known in late 13th century Italy; more clearly so in the Angevin south. These troops largely operated as mounted infantry but they were also occasionally described as using their crossbows from the saddle against static targets, such as ranks of enemy infantry. The appearance of mounted crossbowmen in the 15th century Hungarian army may, in turn, have shown

Effigy of an un-named knight; Venetian, mid-late 14th century. Here a bascinet form of helmet appears to be worn over a mail coif, unless the latter is an aventail fastened to the interior of the sides of the helmet. A particularly Italian and German form of protection was the flap of mail, or more probably piece of shaped iron, hanging from the chin of his coif or aventail. This would be lifted up and fastened by a turn-buckle to the brow of his helmet to serve as a visor. (Victoria and Albert Museum, London)

Italian military influence flowing in the opposite direction.

The crossbow itself also seems to have reached Slovakia, in the far north of the Kingdom of Hungary, from Hungary itself rather than from Germany to the west. Perhaps it arrived initially in these regions of central Europe from the south – in other words from Italy. The ex-Byzantine *mourtatoi* of Venetian Crete were also crossbowmen, some perhaps being mounted, and mounted crossbowmen had clearly been known in France since the late 13th century; though once again they appear to have operated as mounted infantry.

The English longbowmen were the most famous of 14th century infantry forces. Yet they remained something of a military curiosity which resulted from England's special socio-economic circumstances. Longbowmen were also known in France and the Low Countries, as well as Poland, Bohemia and Moravia; but only in England did they achieve the status of a military élite. Even here the longbow had been regarded as the weapon of poachers, bringing official suspicion on the head of its owner. In fact the longbow had been banned in areas of Royal Forest until its military potential was, rather grudgingly, recognised in the second half of the 13th century. The only other European country to give a similar status to infantry archery was Italy. This was partly as a result of the importance of crossbowmen in the militias of Italy's increasingly independent and powerful cities. Partly it resulted from the military impact of those originally Sicilian-Muslim light infantry archers of Lucera who played such a prominent role in southern Italian warfare until they were destroyed at the end of the 13th century.

The greatest impact of the fast-moving, fast-shooting Muslim archers of Lucera was, however, tactical. Their by now old-fashioned form of Arab-Byzantine composite bows do not appear to have been adopted, even in other parts of Italy. Where archers were concerned, it was the crossbowmen of northern Italy who were both copied and employed in large numbers as mercenaries north of the Alps. Such troops now wore quite substantial body armour. They normally operated in close co-operation with the *palvesari* shield or mantlet-bearers whose role was to protect these vulnerable crossbowmen from other archers as well as from enemy cavalry as they *spanned* and loaded their relatively slow-shooting weapons. A crossbowman and a *pavese*-man were, in fact, often paid as a team; though more than half the money went to the man with the crossbow. Such troops and tactics spread eastwards as well as to the north. The Italian-style crossbow become the dominant infantry weapon in Slav Dalmatia during the second half of the 14th century; largely ousting the traditional slings and hand-held bows of the area. Nevertheless a composite bow of perhaps basically Hungarian form remained in widespread use in the rural or upland areas of the Dalmatian coast.

Other infantry, of course, remained an essential ingredient within all western European armies; though they rarely received either high status or high pay. Their equipment varied; that in early 14th century northern England seems to have consisted of a helmet, mail *hauberk* and a selection of weapons that included spear, axe, *war-scythe*, *gisarm*, long knife or short sword, and the *aunlaz* or short dagger. The infantrymen of northern Wales still largely relied on spears, whereas southern Welsh foot soldiers came to include larger numbers of longbowmen. The Scots were particularly hampered by their lack of archers. Nevertheless, they had developed quite effective spear tactics; perhaps even using early versions of the long two-handed *pike*, though such tactics remained highly vulnerable to an enemy who had plenty of archers. Much the same applies to the Swiss *halberdiers* and the Flemish *goedendag*-armed infantry militias of the 14th century.

Battle Tactics

Despite the variations seen in different corners of Europe, 14th century battles normally began with archery or crossbow skirmishing. Archers and crossbowmen would also be positioned so as to protect the flanks of an army in battle-array. A military commander also attempted to secure these flanks on natural obstacles or natural cover. The army itself was usually drawn up in two or three semi-autonomous divisions.

In France during the early 14th century it remained normal for the bulk of the infantry to be placed slightly ahead of the commander, and to be divided, like the cavalry, into *battailles*. Despite this deployment, French infantry continued to play an essentially static role. The commander himself led by example, rather than conducting operations from a position of relative safety. This, at least, was normal practice until such a tradition led to a series of catastrophic defeats at the hands of the English. The French cavalry remained the only really offensive element; still relying on the traditional charge with *couched* lances.

Nevertheless, French infantry was more effective than is sometimes believed. Under certain special conditions, as when they faced an even more static and overwhelmingly infantry Flemish force at Mons en Pévèle in 1304, the French even used small stone-throwing siege engines to bombard the enemy. It should also be pointed out that the decisive defeat of the French army's Genoese mercenary crossbowmen at the battle of Crécy in 1346 was largely a result of their lacking their usual accompaniment of shield-bearers; thus being exposed to the as yet little known firepower of the English longbowmen. At Crécy the heavily armoured French *men-at-arms* tried to copy the English tactics of attacking on foot, but were still defeated.

The German battle of Marchfeld in 1278, in which a Habsburg army with Hungarian support defeated a Bohemian-led alliance, provides a good illustration of the more normal cavalry tactics of the late 13th and early 14th centuries. Here both sides adopted three wedge-shaped formations, one behind another. The Bohemian array had lighter cavalry in the first division, then heavier horsemen, and finally the lightest cavalry of all taking up the rear. For

Right: Tactics, 1275–1400

1. Battle of Campaldino, 1289. The Florentine forces were greatly superior in number and the Aretine attack was confined to a narrow front. The Aretine cavalry and infantry charged together; the infantry intending to kill the Florentine horses. This was initially successful but was held by the Florentine crossbowmen's counter-attack. A charge by the Florentine reserve then routed the Aretine main force while its own reserve took refuge in Poppi Castle (after Oerter)
A. Woods
B. River Arno
C. Castle of Poppi
D. Monastery of Cer tomondo
Florentine forces:
E. Reserve
F. Baggage train
G. Crossbowmen and their counter-attack
H. Other infantry
I. Cavalry
Arezzo forces
J. Reserve
K. Cavalry
L. Infantry
M. Direction of Aretine attack

2. Battle of the Marchfeld, 1278. The armies were similar, except that the Austrians had a corps of horse-archers which harassed the Bohemians' right flank. Meanwhile the armoured cavalry of each force exchanged charges and close combat melées which gradually turned in the Austrians' favour. The greater mobility of the Hungarians and Kipchaqs also caused the Bohemian reserves to flee when they feared becoming outflanked (after Oman)
A. Jedenspeigen village
B. Durnkrut village
C. Weidenback stream
D. River March
Bohemian forces:
E. Bohemian camp
F. Militias and reserve
G. Poles, Bavarians and Saxons
H. Bohemians, Mora vians and Thuringians
Austrian forces:
I. Kipchaq/Cuman horse-archers
J. Hungarians
K. Count of Schildberg
L. Austrians
M. Styrians and Swabians

3. Battle of Bannockburn, 1314. The Scots dug a series of hidden pits or cavalry traps called pottes ahead of their initial position, but the English attacked from the east, across marshy ground, rather than up the main road. A charge by English cavalry was held by the infantry of Moray. An attack by English archers was then ridden down by Scottish cavalry. Much of the English force seems to have been unable to deploy because of boggy ground, and as the Scottish infantry pressed forward the English cavalry gradually crumbled and fled (after Oman)
A. Marshes
B. Woods
C. Bannockburn village
D. Bannockburn stream
E. Mill Lade stream (later drainage ditch)
F. Pottes
English forces:
G. Infantry
H. Cavalry
I. Earl of Gloucester
J. Archers
Scottish forces:
K. Robert Keith, Marshal of Scotland
L. King Robert the Bruce
M. James Douglas
N. Earl of Moray
O. Edward Bruce

4. Battle of Crécy, 1346. The Genoese crossbowmen opened the attack but appear to have been operating without the protection of their shield-bearing pavesari and were rapidly driven back by the English longbowmen. The first French cavalry division under Alençon then charged over their own infantry but was halted by the English defensive line. Numerous such charges were made and almost broke the English line but each was driven back with great loss until the French army retired from the field (after Emerson)
A. Woods
B. River Maye
C. Village of Wadicourt
English forces:
D. English camp
E. King Edward
F. The Black Prince
G. Earl of Northampton
H. Archers
French forces:
I. Genoese crossbowmen
J. Count of Alençon
K. Count of Lorraine
L. Remainder of French forming up and in column of march

5. Battle of Poitiers, 1356. The first French cavalry charge under the Marshal of France was shattered by English archers. The dismounted French knights of the second division then attacked but were again halted. The Duke of Orléans' division fled. King John's division then advanced but was struck in the rear-flank by the Captal de Buch's cavalry as the Black Prince also counter-attacked, overwhelming the French king (after Emerson)
A. Forest of Nouaillé
B. Hedge
C. Hamlet of La Car dinerie
English forces:
D. Black Prince
E. Captal de Buch's flank attack
F. Earl of Warwick
G. Earl of Salisbury
French forces:
H. Marshal of France
I. Dauphin
J. Duke of Orléans
K. King John of France

6. Battle of Castagnaro, 1387. The Veronese attacked across the Castagnare drain, having filled this with bundles of reeds, but the assault was slow and fiercely contested. As the Paduans were driven back, the drain separated the Veronese foot soldiers from their cavalry support. The Paduan cavalry now swept around the flank, collecting infantry and artillerymen as they went. A counter-charge by Veronese cavalry was hampered by their fleeing infantry. The Paduan horsemen then captured the Veronese carroccio as the enemy's militia fled
A. River Adige
B. Castagnare drain
C. Marsh
D. Alveo canal
E. Village of Castagnaro
Veronese forces:
F. Militias and levies
G. Carroccio
H. Cavalry
I. Dismounted men-at-arms and initial attack
Paduan forces:
J. Artillery
K. Dismounted men-at-arms
L. Carroccio
M. Cavalry
N. Cavalry flank attack

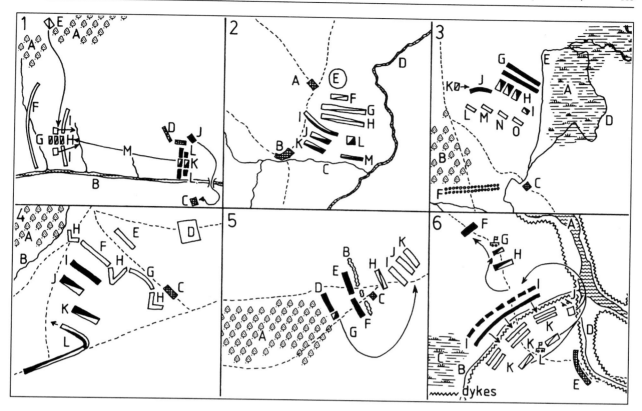

their part the Habsburgs varied this array by having a large force of light cavalry, including Hungarian horse-archers, in the van. Next came their heavy cavalry, and finally the heaviest troops they had available. The battle basically consisted of a series of cavalry charges, followed by close-combat *mêlées* with the Habsburgs also making more effective use of flank attacks and their small numbers of reserves. The Habsburg victory at Marchfeld has, in fact, been described as a brilliant combination of traditional western tactics and those of the still steppe-influenced Hungarians.

In complete contrast, the urban militia armies of Flanders relied on mixed forces of light infantry armed with small shields, swords and heavy single-edged *falchions*. These habitually stood behind a line of foot soldiers armed with long spears or pikes in addition to the fearsome *goedendag*, which was a combined mace and axe-like weapon. The Flemish light infantry were used to attack the enemy; the *goedendag* and pikemen forming a 'fortress' into which the others could retreat if necessary. The role of crossbowmen was to keep enemy archers away. It was, of course, always necessary to bear the threat of enemy crossbowmen well in mind when using the essentially static tactics adopted by the Flemings. Normally these Flemish infantry forces fought in a broad phalanx formation, but would form a circle if surrounded.

The same applied to Scottish infantry formations and to those of the Swiss who, however, seem to have fought in

deep columns rather than broad phalanxes; a tactic they probably learned either from their German or north Italian neighbours. A massed charge by such a *halberd-* and *pike*-armed Swiss infantry column could nevertheless be highly effective, even against élite cavalry if the latter allowed themselves to become caught in a narrow space such as a mountain valley. If such Swiss forces found themselves caught in the open, they were said to have adopted a 'hedgehog' formation. This was probably circular, with the Swiss infantry using their *pikes* to protect themselves from all sides. By the later 14th century, the pikemen had come to dominate Swiss armies, while the now reduced number of *halberdiers* dealt with those enemy who broke through the bristling *pikes*.

The widespread impression that later medieval Italian warfare consisted of battles with hardly any casualties is, of course, entirely inaccurate. It continued to be inaccurate even for the 15th century, when *condottieri* mercenary 'companies' dominated Italian warfare. In fact the changing tactics of 14th century Italian warfare led to a greater reliance on disciplined infantry who were expected to stand firm in the face of cavalry charges. As an inevitable consequence there were, in reality, higher casualties than had been seen in earlier years.

In the late 13th century Italian infantry were still, perhaps, the most disciplined of any in western Europe. Their normal tactics consisted of spear-armed infantry being drawn up behind men carrying large mantlet-like *pavese* shields, and supported by large numbers of crossbowmen. These troops generally seem to have adopted a crescent formation which, like so many other aspects of Italian warfare, might have resulted from eastern Mediterranean Islamic influence. This tended to constrict an enemy cavalry charge into a narrower space where they could be shot down by the crossbowmen; which was almost certainly the intention behind such a crescent formation, just as it always had been in the archery dominated armies of the Middle East. Even so, final victory still relied on a countercharge by the infantrymen's supporting cavalry. Here, however, the Italians seem to have been ahead of their northern neighbours in their greater use of tactical reserves; again perhaps learned from the east.

One very distinctive Italian infantry tactic, which undeniably resulted from the influence of Siculo-Muslim foot soldiers, was the offensive use of light infantry in close cooperation with cavalry. These men charged the enemy's cavalry alongside and among their own horsemen; then attacked the enemy's horses with short stabbing swords known as *coltello* or *corta spada*. Italian crossbowmen could similarly be used in an offensive capacity against enemy cavalry; skirmishing from a distance while aiming for the enemy's horses rather than their riders. In fact it was probably this tactic which failed at Crécy when the Genoese crossbowmen unexpectedly came up against English longbow infantry.

The battle of Campaldino in 1289 was a classic example of Italian tactics of this period. Here the Florentines may also have used their baggage wagons as a form of field for-

tification. Their *fedatori* cavalry élite were at the centre of the battle line, with spear and *pavese* infantry on either flank, perhaps some crossbowmen thrown forward as skirmishers ready to retreat behind their own horsemen if charged, and a substantial cavalry reserve to the rear. Unfortunately for the army of Florence, the light infantry of Arezzo got in among the Florentine cavalry and were able to wreak havoc upon their horses.

English tactics had remained essentially the same as those of France throughout most of the 13th century, but as the century closed the English adopted certain aspects of Scottish infantry warfare. To this they added their own higher discipline, better weaponry and above all their much greater numbers of archers. The resulting tactics were, in essence, those which crushed the flower of French chivalry during the first decades of the Hundred Years War. In its fully developed and most typical form, the 14th century English battle array consisted of a *herce* or 'harrow' formation. In this system the archers were either intermingled with dismounted heavily armoured *men-at-arms*, or stood slightly ahead of them; either immediately

'Jousting scene' on a carved wooden misericord; English, late 14th century. The fact that these men are fighting without visors to their bascinets suggests war or a joust à outrance ('with sharpened weapons') rather than a peaceful tournament. Nevertheless they are carrying the almost rectangular form of shield, one of which has the notch cut from its upper corner to serve as a lance-rest. (Priory Church, Great Malvern)

in front or as forward-thrusting flanks. The archers themselves usually sought protection behind ditches or natural obstacles. They often erected a forest of large sharpened stakes which were angled forward towards an expected enemy cavalry attack; the spikes of the stakes being at the height of a horse's chest.

Scottish infantry may have taught their English neighbours new, or perhaps in reality very ancient, forms of infantry warfare. Basically, however, the armies of southern and Lowland Scotland fought in much the same way as those of northern England. Their largely infantry *schiltrons* would adopt a close circular formation if menaced by enemy horsemen. But in so doing they presented an ideal target for English longbowmen to whom the Scots, with their few archers, could make little reply. In contrast, the other Celtic peoples, the Welsh and the Irish, rarely stood in open battle against the terrifying power of the English bowmen. Instead they generally relied upon highly effective harassment and ambush tactics.

Less detailed information survives, or has been published, concerning eastern European battles during the late 13th and 14th centuries. Yet it is clear that the Hungarian army's ability to combine eastern and western tactical traditions rendered it highly effective; not only against European foes but even against those from the east. Hungary may have been defeated by the invading Mongols, but even the battle of Mohi in 1241 had not been a completely one-sided affair. According to a Chinese chronicler, the Hungarians' combined light and heavy cavalry had at one point made the invading Mongol commander consider retreat.

The rising power of 14th century Serbia may similarly have managed to combine western European, Byzantine and Turkish steppe nomadic military ideas. At the battle of Velbuza in 1330, for example, the Serbian front line consisted of cavalry and the second of infantry; with additional infantry on the right to protect the Serbian flank which was next to the river Struma. These Serbian infantry forces probably included substantial numbers of archers. Nevertheless, it was a sudden and unexpected charge by the Serb armoured cavalry which caught the Bulgars unprepared and thus won the battle. The Bulgarians also appear to have placed their cavalry in the front line during this battle, with their infantry to the rear.

The Wallachians to the north of the Danube won recognition of their effective independence by trapping a Hungarian army in a narrow Carpathian valley at the battle of Posada, also in 1330. Here the lightly equipped Vlach infantry were able to maintain prolonged sniping at the trapped Hungarians with archery. They are also said to have rolled rocks down the mountainside before closing with *maces* and *halberds* to overwhelm their now demoralised foe; winning huge booty and taking innumerable prisoners.

Combat Styles

Individual combat styles did not fundamentally change during the 14th century. Even so, a significant difference did develop in the way cutting and thrusting swords were used. Two very distinct forms of blade also emerged in separate parts of Europe. This was partly a result of, and partly a reason for, these two distinct fencing styles. In Italy, for example, a preference for a thrusting rather than cutting style of swordsmanship is said to have had a long tradition. During the 14th century the so-called *Italian Grip* came into fashion. In this style of fencing the forefinger of the fencer's right hand was wrapped around one quillon of his sword's hilt. It was, in fact, of early medieval Persian or even Indian origin, and reached Italy via the Muslim Middle East or Spain. From Italy, this *Italian Grip* subsequently spread across most of later medieval and early modern Europe. At the other extreme, old-fashioned slashing rather than thrusting swords continued to maintain their popularity in, for example, Poland. This may have been because the troops of this relatively backward region lacked much in the way of body armour.

So little is known about earlier archery techniques in western Europe, it is impossible to say whether they had changed much by the 14th century. During the 14th century, however, the famous English longbowmen were using shower-shooting techniques, similar to those that had been used by the infantry archers of Byzantine and early Arab-Islamic armies. They were used even more effectively by the horse-archers of both the Middle East and Central Asia. Shower-shooting meant that archers did not aim at a specific individual target. Instead they loosed their arrows, normally with a high trajectory, into a predetermined 'killing zone'. The intention was to rain a storm of arrows on the heads of an advancing foe. For the English longbowmen this would normally have meant dropping thousands of arrows on the heads of a charge by French armoured cavalry during one of the great battles of the Hundred Years War. Even though the English longbowman would not normally achieve a rate of shooting much above fifteen arrows a minute, compared with the five arrows in two and a half seconds expected of a fully trained 13th or 14th century Egyptian Mamlūk archer, such shower-shooting probably caused relatively few mortal wounds. On the other hand it undoubtedly had a huge moral impact as well as wounding and probably panicking the enemy's horses.

Field and Camp Fortifications

Long-established traditional forms of field fortifications continued to be used throughout the 14th century and may even have been becoming more important as the period ended. The Hungarians, for example, had used baggage wagons as a primitive type of *wagenburg* against the Mongols at the battle of Mohi. The Moldavians defeated an invading Polish army in 1359 by trapping it in a dense forest; felling trees across the only feasible road ahead of the enemy, and also behind them.

English infantry archers may have been ordered to cut one pointed stake per man in order to make a thicket of such stakes; each stake being about a metre apart, six or seven stakes deep and angled towards an expected enemy attack. The infantry could then retreat into this thicket of stakes where a man on horseback would find it difficult to manoeuvre. By carefully erecting such thickets in certain positions, an enemy charge could be diverted away from the lightly armoured archers and towards an awaiting line of dismounted but heavily armoured *men-at-arms*. It is also possible that on at least one occasion the stakes were hidden from the approaching French cavalry by the archers themselves, who appear to have been standing in front of them. It has been suggested that the archers may have stepped back into the protection of the stakes almost at the last moment; thus causing the front rank of the enemy's densely packed cavalry *conrois* formations to crash into the stakes. This would have had appalling consequences for the horses, their riders and those coming so close behind.

The often huge casualties suffered by French *knights* at the hands of English archers usually seem, in fact, to have been inflicted by daggers, swords, pole-arms and even the mallets used to drive in the stakes. Presumably these massacres took place during or immediately after the horrific confusion which resulted from such a crash between heavily armoured horsemen and a line of sharp stakes. The impact would, however, have been more like a slow collision and pile-up than a single great crash, for even the most highly trained horse will not normally charge straight into a fixed obstacle if it can jump over it or see a way round it. On the other hand, the ability shown by English infantry longbowmen to face such cavalry charges, whose primary purpose was in any case moral rather than physical, says much for their initial discipline and their ever-increasing confidence.

WEAPONRY AND HARNESS

The 14th century saw a continuation of the arms race between the power of crossbows, and later also of small hand-held guns, and the protective effectiveness of increasingly sophisticated body armour. On the one hand, special armour-piercing steel-tipped crossbow *bolts* were developed; on the other, the élite heavily armoured cavalry of western Europe wore increasing amounts of plate armour covering not only the vital organs of head and body but also the limbs. At the same time it is important to point out that the fully developed plate armour of the late 14th and 15th centuries was little heavier than old forms of *mail* protection. What is more, its weight was so skilfully dispersed that a fully armoured man was entirely capable of running, fighting on foot and mounting his horse with no difficulty. The widespread idea that late medieval *men-at-arms* were rendered virtually immobile by such armour, particularly if they had fallen off their horses, is another myth.

The 14th century also saw an increase in regional variations in such armour, at least when compared to the remarkable degree of uniformity which had characterised

the 12th and 13th centuries. The clearest divergence was between the armours of Germany and those of Italy. To some extend these variations reflected climatic differences between north and south; but they also betrayed differing degrees of external influence, largely from the south and east. Not until about 1400 did, for example, Central Asian and Islamic fashions in arms and armour cease to have more than a very localised influence on specific areas such as the Iberian peninsula or eastern and south-eastern Europe.

Among the most visible examples of regional variations in body protection was the widespread use of hardened and often highly decorated leather armour in Italy. This perhaps initially resulted from the experience of Italo-Angevin armies in the Balkans. To some extent it later even seems to have become something a symbol of allegiance, being more prominent in those parts of Italy which supported the pro-Papal Guelph rather than pro-imperial Ghibelline political faction.

A greater amount of armour had been worn by cavalry than infantry for many centuries, but this distinction became even more pronounced with the rising importance of often virtually unarmoured light infantry forces. Late 13th century mercenary contracts from Italy similarly stipulated precisely what a cavalryman must wear. At about the same time a surviving highly detailed inventory of the possessions of a senior French nobleman, killed at the battle of Cortrai in 1302, lists the remarkable variety of equipment then possessed by the military élite. It consisted of: *arbalesres à tour* or windlass-spanned crossbows plus other ordinary types of crossbow; *couvertures à cheval gamboisés et pourpointée*, quilted forms of horse-armour in addition to iron *couvertures de fer*, *pieches de testières*, parts of chamfrons for the horse's head; *crupières* for the horse's hindquarters, probably of leather; *pieches de flanchières* for the animal's front or sides, probably again of leather; mail *hauberks* of various kinds including one *à gazerant* which could have incorporated its own padded lining, and others specifically for use in tournaments rather than war; *gorgerete pizaine* and *gorgerete de plates* for the neck and throat; *une plates* or *coat-of-plates*; *harnas de gaumbes fourbis*, leg protections to which rigid *grèves* or *greaves* were attached; *bras de fer*, which probably only protected part of the arms; and an *espaulière de balaunne* or 'whalebone' shoulder protection.

Archery

More is known about the English longbow, shaped from a single stave of yew, than about simple bows elsewhere in Europe. Ordinary arrows were of light aspen wood whereas the best war-arrows were probably of heavier but stronger ash. Many different arrow-heads were used for different targets and ranges; from the broadest hunting type of arrow-head to the slender armour-piercing forms. Yet these never reached the astonishing degree of variety and sophistication seen in Asian or Islamic archery where use was made of the composite bow.

Carved wooden statue of Saint George by Jacques de Baerze; Burgundian, 1390–9. This superb piece of French carving illustrates armour of the end of the 14th century in almost total detail. The bascinet now has a hounskull or 'dog-faced' visor. The mail aventail is attached by vervelles or laced studs to the rim of the helmet and is also fastened to the shoulders by a pair of knotted thongs. The Saint's bulbous breastplate and narrower fauld are covered by a large tunic or jacket whose full sleeves also cover his full plated arm defences. Only his plated leg protections can be seen, including the laminated sabatons on his feet. (Musée des Beaux-Arts de Dijon)

Composite bows were, in fact, still seen in a few parts of central, southern and south-eastern Europe; most notably in Hungary. Here a long-established and originally Central Asian tradition of archery survived, with the addition of needle-like armour-piercing arrow-heads in the late 13th century. These were specifically designed to penetrate heavier, European styles of armour. Composite bows, perhaps largely for infantry in the old Byzantine manner, continued to be made and used in the Balkans. These may have been of the Hungarian type but are just as likely to have been in the older Romano-Byzantine pattern. Whether this early form of infantry composite bow similarly survived in Italy is less clear. During the 14th century, however, warlike as well as trading contacts between Venice and the advancing Turks led to a revival or re-introduction of composite bows in some parts of Italy as well as in the Venetian colonial empire.

Nevertheless, the crossbow remained the primary missile weapon in most parts of 14th century western Europe. The bows were generally made of yew, the same as longbows. The best wood reportedly came from Italy where the climate was particularly suitable for the cultivation of yew. But by the late 13th century most of the bow-arms of the crossbow were now of composite construction. They incorporated sinew, horn and sometimes bone; the latter perhaps being shaped after prolonged soaking in milk.

The composite construction technique was, however, completely different from that used in Asiatic hand-held composite bows. In Europe, for example, the strips of horn were set edgeways in a technically far inferior manner, with the result that the greatest stresses were still taken by the wooden elements of the crossbow arms. The earliest written reference to crossbow arms of steel comes from 1314, but this is likely to have been an exceptionally rare and perhaps experimental weapon, and it would remain so until the 15th century. Some of the larger crossbows also shot heavy bolts with slender wooden rather than feathered flights.

The new, more powerful, forms of crossbow required stronger methods to *span* them. The earliest known clear reference to a spanning winch or *windlass* dates from 1297 and comes from Genoa; the earliest illustration of a *cranequin* rack-and-pinion system to *span* a crossbow dates from about 1375.

Swords and Daggers

Once again there was no firm dividing line between small swords and large daggers during this period, though it is clear that much larger 'swords of war' had come into use by the late 13th century. These were single-handed rather than two-handed weapons for use on horseback, with blades from 90 to 100 centimetres long, plus 15 to 20 centimetres of hilt. Clear distinctions between large and ordinary swords are recorded from the Balkans to Iceland, while in some parts of Europe there are also specific references to various types of short or small swords which were nevertheless larger than daggers.

Such shorter weapons were largely used by infantry; initially by those Siculo-Muslim light infantry of southern Italy. Here the weapon appears to have been known as a *coltello* or *corta spada*, which is normally translated simply as 'short sword'. But in Italian-influenced Dalmatia they were known as *corda*, which has sometimes been regarded as a derivation of the Turco-Persian and Arab word *kard* meaning a large, probably single-edged dagger. The French *couteau* was the same infantry short sword or large dagger, as were the 14th century English and Italian *coustell*, *custellerius* or *cultellus*. During the second half of the 14th century another term came into use for a short sword or large dagger in Italy and Dalmatia; namely the *stocco*. This, however, was specifically a thrusting weapon and was thus quite different from a relatively short slashing sword that was also coming into use in Serbia and other parts of the western Balkans. This latter weapon was known in late 14th century Dubrovnik as the *spade schiavonesche* or 'Slav sword'. It may, in fact, have evolved into the better-known *schiavone* or *stratiot* sword of 15th century Venice and Hungary, though the evidence for this supposition is flimsy.

Other distinctive or local forms of sword were similarly seen elsewhere in the 14th century. Those of late 14th century Celtic Ireland resembled the *jinete* weapons of Andalusian light cavalry, according to one Spanish traveller. In complete contrast, the late 13th century French and English infantry *faussart* and *falchion* were single-edged weapons of appalling power. The Bohemian *tesák* was said to have resembled a *falchion*, but it was clearly smaller than those seen in France. The curved sabre of Central Asian form seems to have been almost entirely abandoned in Hungary by the mid-14th century; yet it started to make a re-appearance in the Balkan regions at about this time. In this revived form it was known as a *sable* or *sabia*; almost coming back into use as a direct result of Ottoman Turkish influence. Thereafter the sabre also made a come-back in other parts of eastern Europe, though it only really become popular in the 15th century.

Smaller true daggers or knives had probably been carried by the cavalry and military élite for many years, but they only became accepted as gentlemanly weapons during the 14th century; those of the *dagues à rouelles* and *ballok dagger* forms being the most favoured. Whether the *baselard* should be regarded as a short sword or a large dagger is a matter of opinion. It was, however, clearly a popular and widespread weapon that may first have been seen in the late 13th century Crusader States, then in early 14th century Italy. The *baselard* was subsequently adopted throughout much of western Europe. It had a broad, tapering, almost triangular blade with a distinctive H-shaped hilt and was, like most other short swords, primarily an infantry weapon. In contrast, the less widespread early 14th century Italian *bordon* or *berdona* was a slender-bladed dagger comparable with the later *stiletto*.

Spears and Javelins

Spears or lances remained virtually unchanged during the 14th century and may have declined in relative importance as armoured cavalry made greater use of swords, maces and other close-combat weapons. Meanwhile western European infantry adopted a remarkable variety of *pole-arms* or *staff weapons* for cut and thrust. Javelins, meanwhile, virtually died out except in a few fringe areas.

Other Weapons

The main problem with late 13th and 14th century infantry pole-arms is the abundance of terminology, including several regional names for much the same

weapon. In addition there are names that have yet to be firmly associated with one or other of the great variety of weapons which appear in pictorial sources around this time. In England alone, foot soldiers used the *gaesa, godendac, croc, faus, faussa, pikte, guisarme* and *vouge*. The *gisarme*, which was basically a long-hafted axe, had declined in popularity by the late 14th century, often being replaced by the *halberd*. This in turn first appeared in mid-13th century southern Germany as the *hallenbarten*; the name perhaps originating from *halm* meaning pole and *barte* meaning axe. Such halberds were, in fact, essentially 'pole-axes'. Italian infantry seem to have preferred a lighter weapon which may have been more suited to their light infantry tactics; the most widespread of these being the *falco* or *falcione* which appears to have had a long, slightly curved single-edged blade, often with a substantial hook on the back for dragging a rider from his horse. The Swiss infantry *spiess* was rather like a pike, again with a hook at the back for the same purpose, whereas the English militia infantry *pykesteve* seems to have been a straightforward *pike* without a hook.

Some English local defence militiamen of the 14th century were armed with a *pale-axe* comparable to the early form of *halberd*. Others wielded the *sparth* or *spartha* 'Scottish' or 'Irish axe' which had an upwards-sweeping blade; or they might use the *secura* which seems to have been an ordinary battle-axe. More rarely the *wyax* double-bladed axe was also mentioned. The Italian heavy infantry's *ronco* or *roncone* remains rather a mystery; perhaps being a long-bladed axe.

Winged or flanged steel *maces* had been known in western Europe since the mid-13th century but they now became even more popular. So did the *war-hammer* which normally had a spike at the back and a hammer-head at the front. A light bronze mace with a small spiked or knobbed head continued to be used in a few parts of central Europe, Scandinavia and Finland, but only where few helmets and little body armour were worn. The *goedendag* of Flanders was a crude and very cheap infantry weapon which enjoyed a brief period of popularity as a direct result of a series of unexpected victories by Flemish militiamen over the pride of French cavalry during the early years of the 14th century. It was essentially a heavy, iron-bound wooden club with a vertical blade thrust into the end. This could inflict appalling wounds upon both men and horses, particularly when wielded by disciplined ranks of highly motivated infantry such as the men of Ghent at the battle of Courtrai.

The last decades of the 14th century saw the start of a revolution in weaponry which would eventually change the entire face of warfare. This was the appearance of small hand-held guns in relatively large numbers. Cannon of various sizes had been known early in the 14th century. But it was the large-scale manufacture and use of 'hand-cannon', as well as the lack of training or even skill needed to use them, that would gradually alter the entire military balance. These weapons were once again first seen in quite large numbers in Italy; Venice sending such *sclopi* to its Dalmatian allies who were fighting against the Hungarians in 1351. By 1375 the presence of such weapons in the hands of rioters in England indicates that they were, by then, commonplace.

Shields

Although heavy cavalry shields were gradually abandoned in war, they were retained for display purposes and in tournaments. Nevertheless certain specialised forms of shield did appear during the 14th century. The name *taboloccium anglum*, used in late 13th and early 14th century central Italy referred to a large shield with 'angled' corners; probably an early version of the rectangular cavalry shield with a cut-out notch in an upper corner which served as a lance rest. Rectangular cavalry shields were also a feature of eastern Europe, being used in parts of Poland, Lithuania and the Balkans where they subsequently became known as 'small Lithuanian *pavises*'.

In many areas large rectangular infantry *pavises* replaced earlier types which had looked more like flat-bottomed versions of the ordinary so-called 'Norman' kite-shaped cavalry shield. These were almost tall enough to cover a standing man. This tall infantry shield was, in fact, called a *setzschild* in Germany because it 'sat' on the ground. Large rectangular infantry shields of perhaps Italian form were similarly adopted in 14th century Bosnia, Bulgaria and probably other parts of the Balkans. At the same time much smaller hand-held bucklers, usually of wood but sometimes of leather, continued to be used by more agile light infantry forces in areas such as northern England and probably the Celtic regions.

Helmets

Although the *great helm* which fully enclosed the wearer's head continued to appear in art sources, it had been relegated to the tournament arena by the mid-14th century. During the early years of the century, however, such *great helms* could be worn over smaller close-fitting *cervellières* or visorless *bascinets*. Meanwhile some of the earliest 14th century illustrations of helmets with movable visors in fact look like a cross between a *great helm* and a large early form of *bascinet*. A fashion for decorating a *great helm* with a flowing piece of cloth called a *lambrequin* or perhaps *vrysoun*

Left: 'The Prankh Helm'; German, mid-14th century. This great helm would probably have been used in the tournament rather than in warfare. Nevertheless its basically flat-topped shape and form of construction had much in common with earlier warlike great helms dating from the 13th and early 14th centuries. (Inv. B.74, Waffensammlung, Vienna; Photograph Ministry of Works) Opposite page: Bascinet with a hounskull form of visor hinged at the sides of the helmet, and its original mail aventail; from Churburg Castle. This Italian helmet is believed to have been made in a Milanese workshop in about 1390. Similar bascinets appear in pictorial sources throughout most of western Europe. The best would probably be of northern Italian manufacture, though similar helmets might have been made in many other centres. (Inv. IV.470, Tower of London Armouries; photograph, The Board of Trustees of the Royal Armouries)

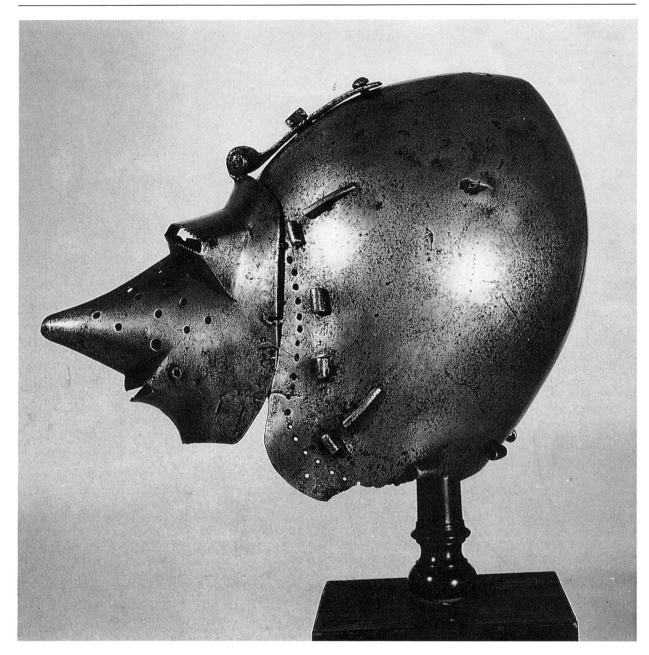

may have reflected Middle Eastern fashions which reached Europe via the Crusades. Nevertheless this was essentially a parade device for use in tournaments. The close covering of the bowl or body or a helmet with a layer of decorative cloth was more widespread during the 14th century and presumably evolved out of the earlier fashion for painting helmets in bright colours and with heraldic motifs.

The early 14th century was, in fact, a period of considerable experimentation during which the *great helm* declined as a real battlefield protection while the *bascinet* rapidly increased in popularity. Most *bascinets* had a mail *aventail* laced part way up their sides, unlike the Middle Eastern type of *aventail*, upon which they were probably based. In this Middle Eastern form the mail *aventail* was attached directly to the lower rim of the helmet bowl. The *barbuta* originated in Italy or the western Balkans during the first half of the 14th century. This was basically a special type of *bascinet* which came down to protect the sides, and even to some extent the front of the face. It became

Opposite page: Bascinet with a hounskull form of visor hinged at the front of the helmet; late 14th century. Several bascinets of this type survive in a number of museums. Their frequent appearance in art from Germany and its immediate neighbours suggests *that such a style of hounskull was essentially German, though again they may well have been made elsewhere. (Inv. T.4647, Tower of London Armouries; photograph, The Board of Trustees of the Royal Armouries)*

very popular in Serbia and surrounding areas in the 14th century, perhaps because of the continuing importance of light harassment archery in this part of eastern Europe. The broad-brimmed *war-hat, chapel de fer* or *cappelus de ferro* was still used by infantry in many parts of western Europe, but it seems to have become particularly characteristic of the eastern and southern Balkans during the late 13th and 14th centuries.

Written sources refer to soldiers wearing more than one armour or more than one helmet. This can also be seen on a carving of one of the sleeping guards at the Holy Sepulche dating from c.1330. In addition to his mail coif or perhaps aventail he has a bascinet and over this a brimmed chapel-defer. (In the Church of All Saints, Hawton, Notttinghamshire, England)

The full head-covering mail *coif* had largely died out by the 14th century, to be replaced by the neck- and throat-covering *aventail* attached to the outside of a helmet. Stronger neck and shoulder defences were similarly introduced in the form of the thickly padded mail and sometimes scale- or plate-covered or lined *gorgière*. The *espalier* or *spaulder* was probably a padded shoulder protection worn beneath other forms of armour, whereas the *pizaine* may have been a very large stiffened mail or scale-lined *tippet*. This covered not only the throat and shoulders but also part of the upper arms and chest.

Body Armour

Mail remained a vital aspect of body protection despite the increasing use of plate armour. It was naturally more important in poor or backward areas, or in those regions where light cavalry still played a leading role. In late 13th century Hungary, for example, some of the Kipchaq élite

added small shoulder plates to their limited forms of mail shirt; almost as a concession to western fashions. The *jazerant hauberk* with integral padding and perhaps a decorative fabric covering, made a belated appearance in early 14th century Italy where it was known as a *ghiazzerina*. Meanwhile the large *haubier* and smaller *haubregon* were still standard equipment for lesser military vassals in Hainault, in what is now Belgium, in 1336. The light cavalry élite of mid-14th century Ireland continued to rely on a plain mail *hauberk* over a quilted *acton*, to which they soon added a mail throat protection or *pisane*; this probably being the *sgabal* of Irish written sources.

Substantial quilted soft-armours such as the *gambeson* and *hoqueton* had, in fact, widely replaced heavier mail armour among many western European infantry during the second half of the 13th century. During the 14th century the militiamen of England and France, and probably other countries as well, were still expected to wear quilted soft-armour if they could not afford something of mail. Felt or felt-lined armour was used by the poorest soldiers of Hungary, some cavalry wearing leather armour described as being 'like a gambeson' even in the late 14th century. This was clearly no longer the hardened leather lamellar armour of steppe tradition, though real lamellar was introduced or re-introduced to several parts of eastern Europe in the wake of the Mongol conquest of neighbouring Russia. This was most visible in Lithuania, eastern Poland and even the Swedish island of Gotland. It has also been suggested that the Mongols' *khatangku dehel* large scale-lined fabric or felt coat lay behind the development of the 14th century western European *brigandine* and *jack*.

Before either the *brigandine* or the *jack* appeared, however, several other forms of semi-rigid body armour had been developed in western Europe. Some of them almost certainly reflected the influence of light Islamic armours such as the lamellar *jawshan*, the smaller versions of which protected only the chest and abdomen. Like the *jawshan*, most of these late 13th and early 14th century European body armours were often of hardened leather, though unlike the *jawshan* they were not of lamellar construction. Instead they appear to have consisted of pieces of hardened leather or, increasingly, pieces of iron, attached to the inside of sturdy fabric or soft leather broad girdles. The English and French *cuirie*, *cuirass* or *pair of cuirasses*, the Italian *corazza* and the Bohemian *thorax*, all probably came into this category.

Quite how the more advanced *coat-of-plates*, which was also sometimes simply called *plates*, evolved from these earlier armours is unclear. Its origins are claimed in Italy, Germany, Spain, Russia and even Byzantium, but it probably came from the south, rapidly improving and developing various local fashions as it spread across Europe. The earliest forms clearly did not protect the arms or arm-pits, since they basically consisted of a reinforced girdle with two or three rows of hoop-like iron plates or series of large scales riveted to the garment's interior. Italian sources once again seem to make the clearest distinctions between these various armours. They list the *asbergum* mail hauberk, the *panceriam* of perhaps mail or scale-lined construction, the *coraczas*, probably leather cuirass, and the newer *lameria* which was almost certainly an iron *coat-of-plates*. The presence of a *coat-of-plates* is not always obvious in the pictorial sources as it was normally worn beneath a *surcoat*; yet the guard chains, which had earlier run from the hilt of some swords to the user's belt in order to stop them being lost in battle, were now transferred to the chest of the *surcoat* in the early 14th century; this being a sure sign of semi-rigid body armour such as a *coat-of-plates* being worn beneath the fabric *surcoat*.

As the 14th century progressed, there was a general tendency for some of the plates in a *coat-of-plates* to get larger; this again being indicated by the now irregular spacing of the rivets across the external fabric which covered such armours. Basically the chest plates became larger while those for the abdomen became smaller; this providing extra protection above and increased flexibility below. A metallic loop or scale-lined *fauld* covering part of the belly and buttocks was also often added below the waist. By the late 14th century the upper chest-plates had essentially fused into one for the front and another for the back.

Not until later, however, did most of this series of body plates fuse into the rigid breast and back plates typical of fully developed 15th century plate armour. Such a gradual process of enlarging the plates also made it possible to dispense with the riveted fabric covering; thus leading to the polished bare metal 'white armour' of the later 14th and 15th centuries in which the plates were either riveted or buckled to one another, depending on whether or not the joint in question needed to be opened.

Fabric-covered armour remained in use and developed in a slightly different direction, basically to provide a lighter form of protection for infantry or light cavalry. The results were the *brigandine* and the *jack*, both of which were variations on semi-rigid, often decoratively as well as functionally fabric-covered, body armours. Here the protective element consisted of sometimes very small pieces of iron, remarkably similar in their shock-absorbent capability to the lamellar armours of the east and to modern bullet-proof jackets. The *brigandine* first appeared in mid-14th century Italy; the perhaps humbler and less decorated *jack* or *jack-of-plates* being more characteristic of English infantry during the second half of the 14th century.

Limb Defences

The development of rigid limb protections was slightly slower than that of body armour. Nevertheless *brassards* or additional pieces of armour for the arms did appear in late 13th century Italy, France and Spain. Separate *gants de fer* gauntlets and *manches de fer*, probably *vambraces* for the lower arms, also appeared at about the same time in Italy and France. Earlier 14th century *besagews*, circular plates to protect the elbow and shoulder, had been laced to the sleeves of a mail *hauberk*. But those on the elbows were soon replaced by wing-like extensions to the iron *couter*, which itself was basically a cup-shaped element over the joint.

Separate additional mail sleeves for the upper arms may have been used in several areas before the introduction of rigid arm defences; the latter at first being *cuirs à bras* of hardened and often decoratively tooled leather held in place by straps and buckles. Such hardened leather limb defences remained in use in many parts of Europe, most notably in Italy but also in England and the Low Countries, until the late 14th century. By the mid-14th century fully plated arm protections consisted of a *gauntlet* for the hand, *vambrace* for the lower arm, *couter* for the elbow, *rerebrace* for the upper arm, *spaulder* for the shoulder and, at the close of the 14th century, a larger plated *pauldron* for the front of the shoulder.

Separate mail, quilted and possibly scale-lined leg protections had been known for some time; the first clear examples of the addition of plate armour being knee-covering *poleyns* which came into use during the second half of the 13th century. These were at first almost certainly of hardened leather, though they were later made of iron, and they could be fixed to the thigh-covering *cuisses* or laced separately around the knees. It is possible that rigid pieces of leg armour to protect the shins and thighs were worn beneath *chausses* and *cuisses* before they began to be worn on the outside at the end of the 13th century. By then references to *demi-greaves* and *schynbalds* were increasingly common in England and Germany, while hardened leather leg armour commonly appears in Italian art from the very late 13th century onwards. Early 14th century Italian written sources also refer to the iron *stivalettos* worn by cavalry to protect the legs and feet. Laminated or segmented *sabatons* for the feet were as yet very rare in pictorial sources, but grew increasingly common as the 14th century progressed.

Horse Harness and Armour

The 14th century finally saw the curb bit adopted across most of western Europe; this type of bit having been known in the Middle East, most of eastern Europe, Hungary and the Iberian peninsula for several centuries. Rowel spurs, which consisted of a revolving spiked wheel rather than a single spike as in the prick spur, were also adopted; perhaps having spread from eastern Europe, Russia or Byzantium.

Full horse armour had been very expensive in the late 13th century when it largely consisted of mail over a quilted padding and sometimes also covered in a heraldic cloth *caparison*. The first piece of plate horse armour was for the animal's head; this initially being known as a *testière de cheval* in France. At first it protected only the front of the head, with the addition of a *poll* at the back to cover the top of its neck. An inventory of the French king's personal military gear in 1316 includes a variety of such pieces of horse-armour; including a *testière de haute cloueure de maille ronde* or mail *chamfron*, gilded *chanfreins* perhaps for parade purposes, and another of leather. Larger forms

of *chamfron* to cover the sides of the head only came into use during the second half of the 14th century.

The heaviest armour to protect the horse's body had previously consisted of two large pieces of mail. This system continued in use well into the 14th century, and included some of *jazeran* construction with integral lining and fabric covering. A few references to European horse armour of hardened leather date from the late 13th century, but probably referred to *testières*. The first clear reference to a *couvertures de plates* comes from 1338. It probably consisted of a *peytral* or *payttrure* for the front of the animal plus a *cropure* or *crupper* for the hindquarters, as would become normal by the late 14th century.

FORTIFICATION

The main elements in the fortifications of a town or castle remained essentially the same in the 14th century as they had been in the 13th, despite the gradual introduction of gunpowder artillery. In fact, the latter did not make its presence felt seriously until the 15th century. Defence, however, was increasingly active; shooting outwards at attackers from *battlements* and *embrasures* in walls and towers, vertically down on the enemy from wooden *hoardings* and stone *machicolations* on top of walls or towers, or from protruding *bretaches* part-way up a wall.

Embrasures had evolved considerably by the late 13th century but did not change much thereafter. Written sources suggest that these were more for use by crossbowmen than longbow archers. Nevertheless, *embrasures* of any type were rarer in those castles built in rocky places, relying on inaccessibility rather than active defence, than they were in fortifications more open to direct assault. Quite how such *embrasures* and other supposed archery positions were used remains a problem. They were often too small for a longbow, in addition to which an arrow shot from a hand-held bow yaws so much immediately after being released that it might not even have got through the hole of the *embrasure*. Similarly a crossbow, being held horizontally, was too wide to be used effectively inside such a confined space and must have had a limited arc of fire. Perhaps a crossbowman and an observer worked as a two-man team, as was clearly the case with a crossbowman and his shield-bearer in open battle. In such a system the crossbowman could have stood quite far back from the *embrasure* when shooting.

It was also impossible to shoot a crossbow downwards from the higher *battlements* or *machicolations* until the 'arrow-clip' was invented in Egypt during the 14th century; this being a device to hold the crossbow *bolt* in place until it was shot, a feature which does not appear to have reached Europe for many decades. Nor was it possible to fit the larger frame-mounted *great crossbows* or two-armed *espringals* inside the great majority of these supposed shooting positions, certainly not if they were to have any significant arc of fire. Instead these larger weapons were

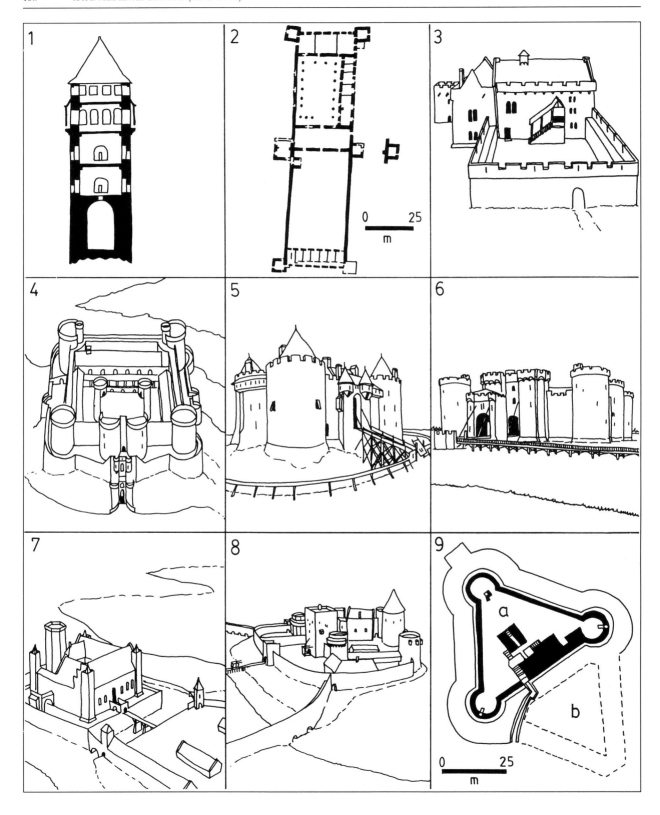

Left: Fortifications,
1275–1400
1. Pont Valentré, France,
begun in 1308. Section
through right-bank tower of
the fortified bridge (after
Mesqui)
2. Plan of the Rocca di Spol-
eto, central Italy, 1355–61. A
classic 14th century Italian
fortification (after Caciagli)
3. Reconstruction of Aydon
Castle, Northumberland,
England, late 13th century.
A fortified English manor
house (after Quennell)
4. Reconstruction of Harlech
Castle, north Wales, late 13th
century. A typical concentric
castle built for King Edward I
(after Quennell)
5. Reconstruction of Dirleton
Castle, Lothian region; Scot-
land, early 14th century (after
Sorrell)
6. Reconstruction of Bodium

Castle, England, late 14th
century. Though surrounded
by a broad moat and appear-
ing strong, Bodium had
already made substantial con-
cessions to the comfort of its
occupants (after Quennell)
7. Reconstruction of Rheden
Castle, western Prussia (now
Poland), late 13th–early 14th
centuries. A fortress of the
Teutonic Knights (after
Tuulse)
8. Kalmar Castle Sweden, late
13th–early 14th centuries.
Built on a small promontory
in a mixture of German and
French styles (after Tuulse)
9. Plan of the Fortezza of
Sarzanello, a classic example
of the Italian Renaissance
concern to use regular geomet-
ric forms (after Toy)
a   The keep built in about
*   1377*
b   Ravelin added in 1497

almost certainly placed on top of the towers, as is shown in most illustrations.

France

The Hundred Years War led to a considerable increase in all types of fortification in mid-14th century France. These varied from fortified manor houses and churches to huge castles and massive urban fortifications. The enormous power of the higher French nobility had already been reflected in their immense castles. Meanwhile, some castles remained purely military while others became little more than symbolic, though still strong, fortified residences. In general the old *donjon* or *keep* was now merely the most important of several towers, while the living quarters were grouped around a courtyard within the castle's outer walls. Defence was based upon these outer walls so that the interior buildings now sometimes had enormous

Below: The city walls of Tallinn, the capital city of Estonia, largeley date from the late 14th century though they were strengthened in subsequent years. The dramatic difference between the crowded interior of the city, on the left
as seen here from the Paks Margareta or 'Fat Margaret' tower nest to the Great Coastal Gate, and the land outside, now consisting of the park to the right, is very clear.

decorated windows proclaiming both the wealth and the confidence of their owner. A splendid *grand salle* or *great hall* became the focus of an aristocratic castle's symbolic role and the centre of a 'neo-chivalric' culture based upon the still-admired myth of feudal chivalry, though rarely upon the reality of aristocratic life in a France now increasingly dominated by commerce, a money economy and factional political rivalry.

At the other, purely practical, end of the scale were small prefabricated wooden castles or forts such as the example shipped to England by a French raiding force in 1386 and erected outside Sandwich. Fortified bridges remained an important functional and symbolic form of small fortification in 14th century France, many being specifically royal structures. The *bastide*, however, was a new concept dating from the latter half of the 13th century. Most were small fortified 'new towns' built along strategic routes or near sensitive frontiers; particularly those which divided 'French' France and the substantial southwestern parts of the country held by the English crown. Their inhabitants had heavily military obligations, as did the *seigneur* in whose land they stood. Even if these *bastides* were not surrounded by a fortified wall, the houses on the edge of town had their back walls closed with wood and stone and their gates barred.

By the mid-14th century the cities of France had considerable political influence and even greater financial power. Although their populations were often decimated by plague, they were constantly renewed by peasants

The walls and towers of Montagnana near Padua, northern Italy; largely 13th–14th centuries. Montagnana's rather isolated position, and the fact that it fell under the control of more powerful neighbours at an early date, account for the survival of its early and simple forms of city fortifications. These consist of a plain wall with widely spaced, tall but not particularly sturdy towers, and a broad moat which may originally have consisted of soggy marsh rather than deep water.

fleeing a war-torn countryside as well as by more prosperous people and members of the aristocracy. The latter now migrated to the cities because this was where the fashionable life of the time was centred. This wealth enabled the French cities to erect massive walls and often elaborate gates and towers. But in general urban fortifications were more old fashioned than those of castles, with few *machicolations* and only simple forms of *embrasure* well into the 14th century. Once a city wall had been taken by an enemy, the place normally fell, but there were examples of chains and other barricades being placed across streets within a town to enable its garrison and inhabitants to continue their resistance.

The defensive arrangements of these French towns and cities were similarly highly developed. Garrisons could be remarkably small in peacetime; even strategic Saint Emil-

Opposite page: Château Chillon on Lake Geneva; Swiss, the oldest part dating from the 12th century but substantially strengthened in the 13th and 14th centuries. This castle is most famous for its romantic and beautiful locations, as well as its association with 19th

century poets. But Château Chillon is also interesting because its design is basically that of a German or Swiss mountaintop castle, placed on a rock next to the shore of a lake. As such it successfully combined two very different architectural traditions.

ion in Gascony having only one *knight*, eleven *squires* and fifty *sergeants* in the early 14th century. But such a garrison would be substantially increased in wartime. The town militia still had their duties of *guet*, *garde* and *arrière garde*. In times of tension *badas*, lookouts, would be posted outside the town, on vantage points such as neighbouring hills and church towers; these being replaced at night by *scotas*, scouts, who listened for suspicious noises. Both could raise the alarm with bells, flags, trumpets or beacons.

The permanent *arsenals* in castles and fortified towns naturally varied considerably. For example, the little castle of Sainte-Claire-sur-Epte had only one middle-sized crossbow, whereas the vital fortress of Pacy-sur-Eure had twenty-six small crossbows, thirty-eight middle-sized, five large windlass-spanned crossbows, plus a store of armour. Other castles had exceptionally large stores of ammunition and appear to have served as regional munitions depots. The numbers of crossbows in almost all such fortified places increased still further as the decades passed; many small cannon being added during the second half of the 14th century. In 1358, and again in 1367, probably at other times as well, the French king ordered a general inventory of all fortified places with a view to strengthening them.

The Empire: Germany

Most of the characteristics seen in France were also found in 14th century Germany. Here local conflicts were even

more widespread, though perhaps less intensive than the Hundred Years War between England and France. In general, castles made greater use of inaccessible positions and mountainous terrain than was seen in France or England, and consequently made less use of regular rectangular or other geometric planning. There may also have been less use of the principle of flanking fire against attackers as a consequence. Such positions included islands in rivers or lakes, as well as precipitous hills or mountains.

The old *bergfried* great tower principle developed into a type of castle which still had one major tower; though unlike French practice this tower now became the main residential part of the complex as living quarters were transferred out of the courtyard below. Great Halls, as centres of both castle life and provincial culture, were also as characteristic of German castles as they were elsewhere. The introduction of gunpowder cannon similarly led to massive, almost solid, round towers being added to many existing fortifications in the late 14th and early 15th centuries.

A fortified village church within an enclosing wall and gate-tower, west of Medias in Romania; Transylvanian-Hungarian, 13th–14th centuries. During the Middle Ages the Carpathian mountains not only marked the eastern boundary of the Kingdom of Hungary, but to a large extent also the frontier between western European Christendom and the vast Eurasian steppe-lands beyond; the land of the Turco-Mongol nomads which stretched beyond Mongolia. Not surprisingly it remained a turbulent and often-invaded part of world. As a consequence, Carpathian Transylvania was also one of the most heavily fortified parts of Europe; its defences ranging from small castles and fortified villages such as this, to some of the most impressive fortresses in Christendom.

The great tower principle was again strong in Austria, where a large number of urban towers also appeared, clearly reflecting Italian influence from south of the Alps. In complete contrast, the fortifications of the Low Countries in the north-west of the Empire not surprisingly made

The brick-built Castello Estense in Ferrara, begun in 1383; northern Italian, late 14th century. The spirit of the Renaissance lay behind some of the magnificent castles of late 14th century Italy; particularly, perhaps, those in the low-lying lands of the Po valley in the north. One of the most impressive is the Castello Estense, built of brick to a carefully planned and highly geometric design which makes full use of water as an additional means of defence. Within the castle, however, the sumptuous rooms around a central courtyard point to a sophisticated, rich and very comfortable way of life.

considerable use of water-filled moats. These were often dug around a highly developed form of the old ring-fort concept, but were now usually rectangular in plan with substantial corner towers and an additional massive gate-tower, plus a central *donjon* or *keep*.

The Empire: Italy

Though much of northern Italy theoretically remained part of the Empire, or Holy Roman Empire as it would come to be known, the country was in reality separate in terms of culture, economy, politics, warfare, as well as the design and defence of its fortifications. The most impressive 14th century fortifications of Italy were those most closely associated with cities; either as citadels attached to or overlooking them, or as an integral part of the defences of the city itself, or as large fortified palaces within the city. The latter could belong to a ruling dynasty or be a *Palazzo Communale* in a republican city. They usually consisted of a large courtyard building with very tall exterior walls, towers and turrets. Nevertheless the large exterior windows in many such palaces showed that their defences were more often than not as symbolic as they were businesslike. Massive use of sometimes decorative brick, as well as deep water-filled moats, were characteristic of the low-lying regions of northern Italy. Even more typical of 14th century Italian fortifications was the use of regular and very geometric ground-plans wherever possible; this clearly reflecting the spirit of the early Renaissance.

The major role of firearms also had a more noticeable impact on late 14th century Italian fortification than was seen in most other parts of Europe. Elaborate and experimental plans would largely be a feature of the 15th rather than 14th century. Nevertheless, the use of sharply angled walls and a clear concern for the provision of flanking fire against attackers in the fortress of Sarzanello, north of Pisa, was purely Renaissance in spirit. Here military solutions were already being sought through science and mathematics.

England and the Celtic States

The Hundred Years War between England and France largely took place on French soil. England itself remained largely at peace in the 14th century and as a direct consequence aristocratic, if not necessarily royal, fortifications became even more symbolic and even unreal than in France. A royal fortress like that of Dover, standing on the often raided southern coast of England, was grimly practical. But a castle like Bodium, also in southern England, looked stronger than it really was. Aristocratic military power and aristocratic comfort were now in competition, and by the end of the 14th century residential comfort was clearly winning.

Fortifications in the English-ruled regions of France were, however, as real as those of French-ruled territory. They also included the English crown's own *bastide*, fortified 'new towns' in Gascony. The garrisons of strategic outposts were, as might be expected, sometimes very substantial. That of Calais in 1356 included one nobleman

as *captain*, 29 *knights*, 348 *squires*, 162 mounted archers, 123 light cavalry *hobelars*, 395 infantry archers, thirteen 'day guards', 120 masons, carpenters and other workmen, but only five crossbowmen; plus 129 sailors – a total garrison of 1,216 men. Other such castles had a 'keeper' who was responsible for the *arsenal* of weapons and armour, as well as for the stocks of food, plus smiths to maintain the garrison's weapons, carpenters for the siege engines and farriers for the horses.

While English fortification remained under French influence, that of the Celtic regions was influenced by England. The English royal castles in Wales were as businesslike as those in France, though they largely dated from the later 13th century. By the mid-14th century it is also clear that some towers in such castles were either specially built to carry powerful *espringal* siege machines, or had been modified to take these weapons. Many castles were built in Scotland in the late 13th and 14th centuries, primarily as a defence against English invasion. Once again they largely used English or French defensive concepts. Unlike the castles of England, these were again businesslike and very real, though generally being small. The near-anarchy which characterised much of 14th century Ireland meant that few castles were erected here. The earlier Anglo-Norman structures remained in use, but new ones largely had to await the 15th century.

Scandinavia and the Baltic

Small-scale, utilitarian and rather conservative fortifications were similarly characteristic of Scandinavia; though here most outside influence came from Germany. Norway and Denmark appear to have been particularly old fashioned, relying on plain curtain walls and rectangular towers. The single tower castle or fortified manor house only became important in the 15th century.

Some of the fortresses erected by the crusading Teutonic Knights in the Baltic States and in what is now northern Poland were particularly massive. They made use of many of the latest ideas, mostly from Germany, though their frequent use of water-filled moats in these generally low-lying regions was distinctive. Meanwhile the German Crusader Knights, like their Lithuanian opponents, continued to make use of small fortifications that could almost be described as block-houses; though the native Baltic forts were, in general, even more primitive.

Eastern Europe

Most of eastern Europe had been behind the western countries in terms of defensive architecture since the 11th or 12th centuries. In some areas, though not in all, this difference had become even more noticeable by the 14th century. Poland, for example, had very few stone fortifications in the late 13th century, and not many more by the end of the 14th. Bohemia, on the other hand, was now fully within German imperial military and cultural traditions, relying on the same sort of great tower and subordinate turrets as were seen in neighbouring Germany and Austria.

Above: *Today the Dalmatian coastal town of Ston is little more than a sleepy village, but in the 14th-15th centuries when these long defensive walls were built it was an important outpost of the Venetian overseas Empire. The walls enclose the mountain-top, including the port of Mali Ston on the far side of the hill as well as the main settlement of Veliki Ston seen here.*

Below: *The dramatic Scottish castle of Tantallon stands on a rugged promentary overlook-ing the Firth of Forth. Most of what remains dates from the 14th century and faces inland, since there was little real threat of an attack up the sea-cliffs.*

With very few exceptions, stone castles only appeared in Hungary during the mid-13th century, despite the country's increasing regional 'great-power' status. Many more were built in the later 13th and 14th centuries, once again largely in the German rather than French or Italian traditions. These new stone fortifications were mostly concentrated in the Carpathian mountain passes of what are now Slovakia and Romania, as a front line of defence against feared Mongol, Russian or Polish threats. As yet there was no Ottoman Turkish menace from the south. Here Serbia's ambitions were directed against its southern, eastern and to a lesser extent western neighbours. The increasingly important military role of the higher Hungarian aristocracy did, however, lead to a wave of baronial castle-building across Hungary during the early 14th century.

Many of the early Byzantine stone fortifications of the Balkans appear to have been destroyed and not rebuilt by the Serbs during the second half of the 13th century. Even in the mid-14th century the only Serbian stone defences were in the far west, close to the Dalmatian coast; the rest still being simple structures of earth and a single wooden wall. But as the Ottoman Turks advanced in the later 14th century, rather old-fashioned fortresses and, above all, fortified monasteries began to appear in direct imitation of traditional Byzantine styles of military architecture. The few stone fortifications of Bulgaria before it fell to the Ottomans were again in an old-fashioned Byzantine style, which largely relied on the height of their often not very substantial walls and towers. Wallachia and Moldavia built in the same fashion, several Carpathian valley towns being fortified; though here there was a noticeable degree of Hungarian architectural influence.

SIEGE WARFARE

Fourteenth century western European siege warfare saw more changes in the types of armies involved than in the tactics or weapons used. This was at least the case until a more widespread use of firearms at the very end of the 14th century. There was also an even greater degree of uniformity in the methods used during siege warfare than had been seen earlier. Efforts to capture a castle or fortified town still involved a great deal of diplomacy and considerable formality; the latter usually revolving around the time allowed for a relief force to arrive before the garrison of a fortified place surrendered. But there was, at the same time, a great use of stratagems, treachery, surprise attacks and above all the devastation of the surrounding countryside that formed the economic foundation of most fortified sites. Stone-throwing siege engines continued to play a prominent role, though mining still provided the most effective way of demolishing a defensive wall. Apparently the storming of breaches caused by mines was normally a job for low-grade infantry. Other tactics included polluting a fortification's water supplies and throwing dead car-

Early gunpowder artillery, 14th century
1. Reconstruction of a ribaud-equin, late 14th–early 15th centuries. This was an anti-personnel field artillery piece consisting of several small-bore barrels which could be fired simultaneously or in sequence (after Gravett)
2. Reconstruction of a bombard incorporating an original barrel and a hypothetically restored pezza cavalca 'riding piece' carriage; in the Armoury of the Knights of St John, Malta. Although the principel may be accurate, the supports for the barrel
which enable it to be raised, lowered and aimed appear to be too flimsy
3. Reconstruction of a bombard in the more normal earth mounting; late 14th–early 15th centuries. Once positioned, such weapons had a fixed aim (after Gravett and Michael)
4. Reconstruction of a small bombard or pierriere on a wooden elevation and turning mounting; late 14th–mid-15th centuries, now in the Metropolitan Museum of Art, New York. The dating of this device is highly debatable (after Gravett and Held)

casses over the walls in an endeavour to spread disease among the garrison.

Towers and 'Cats'

Whereas the sophistication of *Greek Fire* and other incendiary mixtures had virtually driven wooden assault structures from siege warfare in Asia and the Middle East, the latter still played a significant role in 14th century western Europe. Such devices included the *beffroi* 'belfry', *château de bois* 'wooden castle', *belette* 'weasel', *guérite* 'sentry-box' and *chats châteaux* 'cats'-castles'. Most of these could be rolled forwards against an enemy's wall. Some 14th century wooden siege towers were very large and complex structures with several floors, supposedly manned by a hundred or so crossbowmen. Others were described as being roofed with layers of absorbent earth and brushwood. The larger structures even appear to have had their own small stone-throwing and other engines, either mounted on top or inside. These sometimes enormous structures were inched forward by armoured men using wooden levers. The necessary timbers might be brought from a considerable distance. The operation might be carried out in sufficient secrecy for the sudden appearance of a massive tower, erected within a couple of days, to convince the defenders to surrender without further bloodshed.

Early 14th century sources still refer to small drawbridges being dropped across an enemy's battlements from such towers. In later years, however, the main purpose of these huge structures appears to have been to defend the attackers' ram or the entrance to his mineshaft. Some illustrations show wooden box-like containers being suspended from beams and cranes, apparently to lift attackers on to the wall or to a firing point with a height advantage. These devices may, however, have been more experimental than useful, although they had also appeared much earlier in Byzantine military treatises.

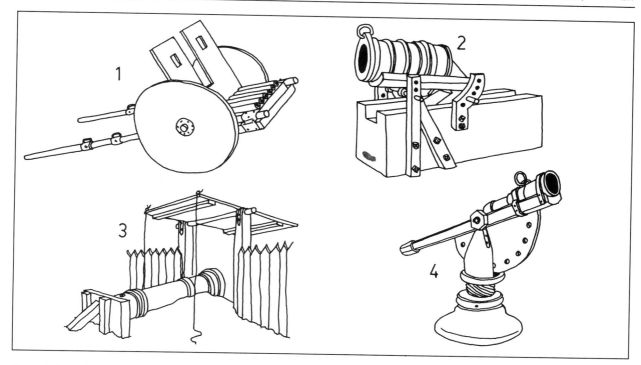

Stone-Throwing Engines

The more detailed information that survives concerning late 13th and 14th century counterweight *mangonels* or *trebuchets* indicates that some had counterweights consisting of lead bars. But since lead was costly, these *trebuchets* would surely have been of the smaller kind. Others had counterweights consisting of boxes of stones or earth. One 13th century Italian *trebuchet* was described as having a counterweight of ten *tonnellate*, and being capable of throwing a 100–150 kilogram rock one hundred and fifty metres. Modern experiments with replicas show that a single ton counterweight can indeed hurl a 15-kilogram missile to a maximum of 180 metres with remarkably consistent accuracy.

Essentially the same three versions of *mangonel* were still in use. These were of the relatively small man-powered type: the *biffa*, which had an adjustable counterweight, had probably been invented in Byzantium; the *tripantum*, which had a secondary movable weight, originated in the Muslim Middle East; and a large simple type with one fixed counterweight. The fact that the late 13th century European military writer Egidio Colonna thought that the accuracy of versions with adjustable weights was unreliable, whereas 13th and 14th century Arab-Islamic treatises categorically state that they were more accurate, suggests that Colonna was writing theoretically about weapons that were still little known in western Europe.

The largest *trebuchets*, in fact, were now very powerful devices. But still their primary role was to break *battlements*, *hoardings*, *machicolations* and gates of an enemy's fortification, and drive defenders from their positions; not to breach the main wall itself. These devices were also accurate enough to serve as anti-personnel weapons, while the engines of both sides engaged in duels in what can only be described as barrage and counter-barrage operations. All such engines were loosed or shot by pulling a trigger, not by cutting a valuable piece of rope, and their construction clearly included a considerable number of iron or copper parts.

Written sources even refer to 'boxes of spare parts' for assorted types of siege machine. Surprisingly, perhaps, man-powered *mangonels* also remained in use throughout the 14th century, even after the introduction of small gunpowder cannon, whereas the old Romano-Byzantine forms of single-armed torsion-powered small stone-throwing *petraria* gradually dropped out of use. The *caable*, *chadabula* or *chaablum* of northern France, and the *calabres* of the south were probably this type of simple machine.

Espringals, Great Crossbows and Cannon

The two-armed *espringal* was now a formidable weapon. *Spanned* by two men using levers and a winch, it may now have been released by a cast-metal *nut* like an oversized crossbow *nut*, rather than by the old system of release hooks. Its normal propellant power is estimated to have been about 1,800 kilograms. This enabled it to shoot a wooden *tongue*, 70–80 centimetres long, 4–5 centimetres wide and weighing about one and a half kilograms. The weapon had by now also spread to Germany, where it was known as a *springolfe*, two such devices being mounted above the city gates of Aachen in the mid-14th century.

The size of *great crossbows* often seems to have been exaggerated in the poetical sources of this period. In reality the bow of such a weapon normally seems to have been from one and a half to two metres long. The best were again made from yew wood, this time apparently imported from the southern Balkans; plus large amounts of horn, the best being that from billy-goats. Despite the increasing importance of cannon during the second half of the 14th century, these *great crossbows* still remained among the most important anti-personnel weapons. As such they seem, in fact, to have been more effective in defence of fortifications than in attacks upon them.

Rams, Mining and Scaling Ladders

By the beginning of the 14th century there had been a noticeable decline in references to rams and bores as methods of breaching a wall. On the other hand, picks, mauls, hammers, mason's axes, chisels, wedges and trowels continued to form a normal part of an army's siege train; all of which suggests that mining remained as important as ever. The basic techniques were largely unchanged, various types of strong wooden shed-like structures being used to protect the entrance to a mine-shaft, often fixed to the enemy's wall with iron pegs. The defenders' best defence against such attack lay in counter-mining from within the threatened fortification.

The great height reached by the walls of many 14th century fortifications must now have made the use of scaling ladders widely impracticable. Even so, there are continued references to such ladders having iron spikes at the bottom to stop them slipping, and being fixed to the enemy's wall with pegs. Both sides used forked poles, either to raise the ladders against the wall or to push them away.

Needless to say, the idea that defenders would waste large quantities of extremely expensive oil by boiling it and pouring it down on the besiegers is a myth. They used boiling water and heated sand; the latter apparently having the ability to penetrate the tiniest gaps in armour.

Incendiary Devices

Burning oil was, of course, used as an incendiary weapon. Small sacks of slow-burning sulphur could be thrown into enemy mines to smoke out or choke the enemy's miners. By now *Greek Fire* was known throughout much of western Europe, a book on *Fires for the Burning of Enemies*, by a Byzantine Greek or converted Arab named Marcus Graecus, having been written in about or slightly before 1270. This contains the earliest known recipe for *Greek Fire* in western Europe, though of course the substance had clearly been used in the west for many decades.

Fortified towns were much more vulnerable to attack by incendiary weapons than were castles, since most domestic buildings were still of wood. Barrels and other breakable containers of fat and pitch as well as sophisticated *Greek Fire* were hurled over the walls of various fortified places during a determined siege. Despite these available fire weapons, however, incendiary devices seem to have been less used in the 14th century than previously. Perhaps this reflected the increasing economic motivation behind warfare; the attackers now more obviously wanting to take a rich urban centre intact, rather than occupy a gutted shell.

NAVAL WARFARE

Several of the characteristics of medieval naval warfare that had been seen in earlier centuries became even more pronounced in the 14th century. Above all was the simple fact that the advantage remained firmly in the hands of the attacker rather than the defender. As a consequence naval fleets, where they existed in any recognisable form, were designed for offence rather than defence. Defensive measures, in fact, basically depended upon an individual vessel's ability to defend itself. As a clear consequence of this situation, all passengers as well as all members of a ship's crew were normally expected to be fully armed; the only exceptions being clergymen and sometimes pilgrims.

By the end of the 13th century naval or marine crossbowmen had become a professional élite. The larger galleys and merchant ships also had armourers to repair these men's crossbows. In fact it would be true to say that the crossbow caused a genuine naval revolution during the late 13th and 14th centuries. As the number of marine crossbowmen increased, so the need for numerous armed but militarily less skilled crewmen declined. The numbers of oarsmen needed in galleys, however, inevitably

Right: Naval warfare, 1275–1400
1. Reconstruction of a Hansa League cog, merchant and transport ship of the northern seas; mid-14th century (after Landström)
2. Reconstruction of a Baltic merchant or transport ship; c.1400 (after Landström)
3. Mediterranean galleys.
a–b   Schematic profile and midships section of galleys built for Charles of Anjou, according to a set of detailed orders dated 18 February 1275 (after Pryor)
c-d   Seating positions for the oarsmen of medium-sized and large galleys. Such vessels were sometimes known in written sources by the archaic and misleading terms bireme and trireme (after Galoppini)
4. Simplified reconstruction of the ship-building Arsenale of
Venice in the mid-14th century (after Pizzarelle and Fontana)
a   The Arsenale Vecchio or Old Arsenal
b   The Arsenale Nuovo or New Arsenal
c   The first Corderie or rope-making shed
5–6. Defeat of the Pisans by the Genoese in the naval battle of Meloria, 1284 (after Tangheroni)
5. Situation in the afternoon of 5 August
6. Situation on the morning of 6 August
a   Pisa
b   Porto Pisano
c   Island of Meloria
d   Livorno
e   Pisan fleet
f   Genoese fleet (commanded by Doria)
g   Genoese fleet (commanded by Zaccaria)

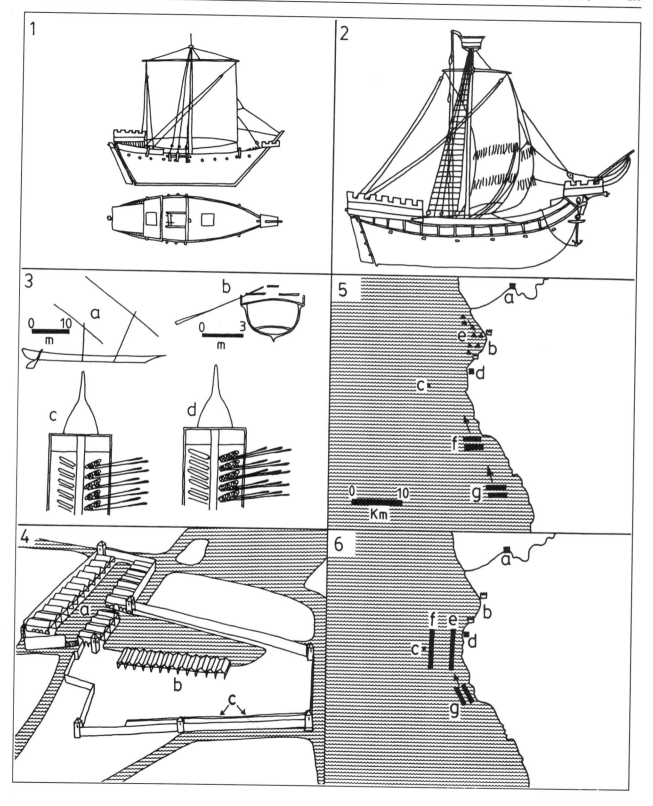

remained constant, but the numbers and status of ordinary sailors, particularly those aboard merchant ships, declined. This, however, was perhaps more characteristic of the Mediterranean than of the northern seas or the Atlantic. Nevertheless it was as pronounced in Muslim Egypt as it was in Christian Genoa. Meanwhile it is interesting to note that a slump in the status of sailors seems to have been seen earlier in the Muslim fleets of the eastern Mediterranean than in Christian fleets of the western Mediterranean.

The Mediterranean

The larger Mediterranean cargo ships used huge lateen sails. These in turn had needed a numerous crew, so the gradual adoption of various aspects of northern ships' design may again have been connected with the general reductions in the size of such crews. Square-rigged northern *cogs* had reached the Mediterranean during the 12th century, but do not seem to have had much technological influence before the early 14th century. It is also possible that the ships described as *cogs* by Mediterranean observers were, in fact, of the slightly different *keel* design. The stern rudder, which had been known in the Indian Ocean, Arabian Gulf and Red Sea for many centuries, was now clearly adopted by Mediterranean galleys and cargo ships. Some of the latter also included a highly advanced mix of Mediterranean and northern features of ship design. Such merchant vessels still had to defend themselves, of course, and they also played a major role in naval warfare. Nevertheless, the galleys remained the basic naval striking force.

The average late 13th century Italian fighting galley was about forty-five metres long with a six-metre wide hull drawing one and half metres draft. Above this hull was the broad *telaro* or outrigger, almost eight metres wide, which supported some sixty oars on each side. These rested upon the timber *apostis*. The rowing-chamber where the oarsmen sat was about thirty-seven metres long. Such a galley usually had one mast, about a third of the length of the hull, with a crow's nest; plus a much longer yardarm for its lateen sail. The deck was less than one metre above the water-line, and above this ran the *corsia* which consisted of strong timbers along the ship's entire length to provide longitudinal strength. Sails were stored beneath the *corsia* and a fighting gangway was mounted on top to provide a passageway from one end of the ship to the other.

In battle, a row of *pavise* shields could also be erected along the *apostis*. The crossbowmen aboard sail-powered cargo vessels would similarly be protected by bulwarks, rows of *pavise* shields and by the wooden *fighting castles* on the prow and stern of larger ships in which the marines were normally stationed.

Tactics remained much the same as in earlier centuries. A naval commander might, for example, use coastal features to launch an ambush against passing ships or convoys. The Venetians were described as challenging an enemy to battle by raising a flag which showed a sword with its point uppermost. Naval encounters normally began with long-range archery. Here, of course, powerful and accurate crossbows gave a distinct advantage. The vessels would then normally grapple and their crews would attempt to capture the enemy ship by boarding her.

Galleys tended to fight in line, using small boats for communications, and it was now very rare for them to be lashed together. But this tactic was sometimes used when facing a more numerous opponent. Ships driven by sails alone could play no real role in such tactics, although the larger sail- and oar-powered *tarida* transport galleys were sometimes employed as a reserve force. The details of such Mediterranean naval battles show that grappling irons sometimes had iron chains, which could not easily be cut, while their crews would throw pots filled with soap on to an enemy's decks. This, however, seems to have caused more of a problem for heavily armoured marines than those lightly equipped men who ran barefoot.

The raised *calcar* or beak had long replaced the ram in the bows of a fighting galley. This was essentially a boarding device which a captain would hope to ride up over a rival's *apostis*; thus enabling his own men to jump down into the enemy's weakly defended mid-section. The *calcar* could also be used to smash the enemy's oars but was rarely strong enough to damage the high-sided hull of a merchant ship. Generally speaking, low-lying galleys disliked attacking a tall cargo ship when it was under sail; preferring to catch such vessels becalmed. Under these conditions skilled swimmers or divers could even threaten the cargo ship's hull, if it failed to surrender.

Apart from the increasing importance of crossbows, Mediterranean naval armament remained basically the same as in earlier centuries. The degree of armour expected of naval troops differed according to local traditions; the marines of southern France apparently being among the heaviest armed and thus least agile. Before the changes caused by a greater use of crossbows, all Venetian seamen were expected to have some degree of armour; even if it only consisted of a leather head covering known as a *zupam*, whereas senior members of the crew, such as the mate, had to wear a *panzeram vel lamam de ferro*, probably mail with some plate element. This was later apparently replaced by a *corazzam* or coat-of-plates. Other late 13th century Venetian sources refer to quilted soft-armour, presumably being something like a *gambeson*, and a Balkan

'Venetian fleet defeats that of the Emperor Barbarossa off Punte Salvore', wall-painting by Spinello Aretino in the Palazzo Pubblico, Siena; Italian, 1407–8. The arms and armour in this painting appear old fashioned for the time when it was made. Perhaps the artist, unlike those of earlier generations, was already a product of the Renaissance in being aware of historical differences, since the battle he was illustrating happened many years before he lived. Or it may simply be that lighter forms of arms and armour tended to be used in naval warfare, and this makes them look rather archaic.

type of *clippeos* with iron plates which sounds very like Byzantine-style lamellar armour. Specialised naval weapons included long spears to attack enemy oarsmen, long-hafted *rochet* axes to cut the enemy's rigging, spiked *triboli* to stick in the enemy's decks, and quicklime to throw in his eyes. Yet the crossbow was now of paramount importance; each weapon being supplied with about one hundred *bolts* or arrows, according to Provençal records.

Greek Fire similarly remained a devastating device at sea, though there were now clear references to ships being protected with a *barbotte* consisting of sheets of leather or felt soaked in vinegar. Small stone-throwing engines, *great crossbows* and to a lesser extent *espringals* were still used. These would normally be mounted ahead of the rowing benches on the ship's forecastle; always the most strongly defended part of a medieval warship. Small *mangonels* seem to have been more useful against harbour defences than against other ships, perhaps lacking sufficient accuracy to hit a moving target. Meanwhile *great crossbows* and such devices essentially remained anti-personnel weapons. During the second half of the 14th century, however, several countries started to mount small cannon on their warships.

The Northern Seas

Generally speaking, northern cargo ships were smaller than those of the Mediterranean, while galleys were far fewer and generally less suited to northern conditions. Both the French and English normally used sail-powered *cogs* during their naval raids. The wooden *fighting castles* shown on the sterns and prows of so many high-sided sailing ships in the illustrated sources of this period may have been temporary structures added during wartime. But they are more likely to have been permanent. During the late 13th century the French started to build galleys at Rouen in Normandy, under Genoese technical guidance, whereas the English generally hired their few galleys from Spain or Italy. On the other hand the English did build some oared vessels of their own; these English *balingers* being small vessels with only forty to fifty oars, for use in coastal patrol work.

Both the English and French governments had very few royal ships of their own; those of the English crown being under the authority of the 'clerk of the King's ships' based in the Tower of London. Most fighting ships were hired or commandeered from civilian ship-owners as and when they were needed. These men were, in turn, often also ships' captains and would continue to command their own vessels while in royal service. The acute rivalry between the sailors of East Anglia and those of the *Cinque Ports* along the southern coast was an additional problem for the English authorities. These two groups were, in fact, almost as likely to fight each other as to tackle the French.

During the Hundred Years War the French seized the offensive at sea; attacking English commerce and using sea-borne raids as a way of retaliating against English raiding on land. Such raids normally took the form of attacks upon English sea-ports and those of the English crown's possessions in France. Sometimes they also involved the use of fire-ships. Occasionally, larger forces landed on the open coast, though no real attempts were made to conquer England. For their part, the English concentrated their defences in the coastal town. Meanwhile, the primary role of English warships was to escort the vital convoys which carried troops and supplies from England and the main English-ruled provinces such as Gascony. More rarely, English fleets also attacked French ports. Meanwhile the Scots similarly used seaborne raids as a way of retaliating against English aggression north of the border.

The few available English galleys were generally grouped into small squadrons, and during the second half of the 14th century these, together with other vessels, attempted to control the Channel by maintaining regular patrols. Under 14th century conditions neither side could really 'command the sea', in the modern sense. Yet they did try to 'keep the sea', in the terminology of the time. In other words they attempted to maintain a naval presence in the hope of deterring the enemy from launching too many raids. Encounters between large rival fleets were very rare and almost always accidental. In fact, throughout the 14th century English military commanders were neither comfortable in, nor particularly knowledgeable about, naval warfare. English naval power, such as it was, even went into serious decline from the 1370s onwards.

In Scandinavia and the Baltic, naval warfare had remained remarkably traditional, almost in the old Viking mould, into the early 14th century. But from then on German, or more specifically Hanseatic League, ships and tactics increasingly influenced the naval practices of Denmark, Sweden and even Norway. The eastern Baltic coastline was by now completely under the control of the Germanic Crusading Military Orders, Denmark or Sweden. As a result the indigenous Baltic and Finnish peoples of the area lost any real independent maritime heritage.

Northern ships had rarely attempted to use stone-throwing artillery or any form of larger weapons, even during the 13th century, weaponry largely remaining personal. *Trebuchets* were mentioned very occasionally, but even here it is unclear whether they were for use at sea, or were simply being transported aboard ship. *Great crossbows* were mentioned slightly more often as were, from the early 14th century, *espringals*. The earliest reference to marine cannon in the northern seas may date from 1338, when the French fleet had a few. As yet, however, the English made no use of these new weapons at sea.

River Warfare

The remarkably few references to river warfare in the 14th century seems to suggest that it had virtually died out in western Europe. Nevertheless, rivers remained essential arteries of communication and logistical support. This was particularly true of the Danube which flowed right across the centre of the huge medieval Kingdom of Hungary, and of the various great rivers which reached the Baltic through the Baltic states.

V
BIOGRAPHIES

BIOGRAPHIES

Throughout the Middle Ages political leaders tended to be military leaders as well. As a result, early medieval military leaders were in many cases also rulers. In later centuries, however, there was an increasing tendency for kings and other rulers to delegate military authority to professional soldiers, or at least to members of an aristocracy specialising in such matters. Nevertheless, this was more apparent in the economically and politically advanced parts of Europe than elsewhere. In general it would be fair to say that the simpler the organisation of any given state, the more likely it was to find its leader at the head of its armies.

The following list of personalities is not intended to be a catalogue of great military commanders. Instead, it is a broad selection of military personalities taken from both the higher leadership and the middle if not lower ranks. As such it is designed to shed as broad a light as possible on medieval military command structures, and to a lesser extent on attitudes towards warfare in various countries during various centuries. Inevitably, when dealing with a period such as the Middle Ages, there is an emphasis on those individuals who caught the attention of chroniclers. These in turn tended to come from literate societies. Then there are the simple accidents of history which enabled some biographies to survive whereas information about other, perhaps more important, more interesting or more deserving personalities has largely been lost.

Alfred the Great (King of Wessex, 871–99)

During the early part of his reign Alfred kept English resistance to the Norse-Danish conquest alive when it seemed that no Anglo-Saxon army could defeat the Viking invaders. His famous escape into the marshes of Somerset, and his subsequent rallying of Anglo-Saxon forces, became part of English national legend. The subsequent wars included several serious setbacks; yet Alfred eventually penned the Danes north of a line from London to Chester. He was also largely responsible for beginning the process whereby these Vikings were converted to Christianity.

The latter part of Alfred's reign was largely devoted to codifying Anglo-Saxon law and restoring the high level of scholarship for which England had been famous before the Norse-Viking invasions. Alfred's life was, in fact, later interpreted as an early example of the supposedly typical English experience of glorious victory snatched from the jaws of catastrophic defeat. Nevertheless, he remained king of Wessex rather than a really 'national' Anglo-Saxon or English monarch. He is, however, credited with establishing a highly mobile semi-professional army, as well as the nucleus of an English navy. King Alfred was also quoted as having said that: 'A king's raw materials and instruments of rule are a well-peopled land, and he must have men of prayer, men of war and men of work.'

Attila the Hun (Ruler of the Hun Empire, c.445–53)

As ruler of the Huns, Attila continued the expansion which had been going on for several years. His warriors also overran much of the western half of the Roman Empire. Attila was given the title *basileus* by the Roman Emperor, though he was not the first so-called 'barbarian' to have such a rank. He also had many Germans among his immediate supporters and may have been about to convert to the Arian form of Christianity, which was widespread among various Germanic peoples, when he died suddenly in 453. He was clearly not regarded as a 'divine ruler' by his own Hunnish tribes, but was honoured and buried in the normal Central Asian Turco–Mongol manner. His sprawling empire then almost immediately fragmented.

Bertrand du Guesclin (Constable of France, 1370–80)

Bertrand came from a relatively minor Breton aristocratic family, the Seigneurs of Broon. He was an excellent warrior whose skill was recognised during the earlier stages of the Hundred Years War, when deeds of *knightly prowess* were more obvious than was carefully thought-out strategy. His military ability soon led to his rapid promotion at a time when the French were suffering a series of major defeats at the hands of English invaders. He was captured by the English for the first time at Auray, but was ransomed. He was made *Captain* of Pontorson in 1358, being appointed the French king's lieutenant in the strategic province of Anjou in 1363, and finally became *Constable* of France in 1370.

Bertrand du Guesclin's strategy, supported by King Charles V of France, was to wear down the English invaders but to avoid major battles which the enemy had proved all too capable of winning. Some of his most successful operations were carried out by ruthless professional *routiers* who fought the English in both France and Spain. He was captured again by the English in Spain and was sold to King Edward III of England for £1,483 6s. 4d. This substantial sum clearly indicated his military value. According to the chronicler Froissart, Du Guesclin was well aware of his own value, telling his English captor: 'They are saying in the kingdom of France and elsewhere too, that you are so afraid of me that you dare not let me go.' Bertrand du Guesclin was eventually ransomed, but died of sickness during his siege of Anglo–Gascon-held Châteauneuf-de-Randon in 1380. He was buried in the Royal Church of St Denis, next to the tomb which King Charles V of France had prepared for himself. In fact, the king died later that same year.

Boleslaw I Chobry (King of Poland, 992–1025)

Boleslaw I expanded the frontiers of the principality of Greater Poland as far as the Baltic and was crowned by the German Emperor in the year 1000; thus becoming the first recognised king of Poland. Nevertheless, his wars to the south and west brought Boleslaw into conflict with the German Empire. Consequently Polish expansion ceased in this direction. Expansion to the east similarly brought him into conflict with Prince Yaroslav I of Kiev, whom he defeated; subsequently putting his own son-in-law on the

Russian throne. To the north Boleslaw's armies forced the pagan Prussians to submit, at least temporarily, to Christian baptism in about 1018. During Boleslaw I's reign Poland seemed to be entering the medieval western European world with the establishment of an ecclesiastical hierarchy, a basically feudal administration and the building of several largely wooden castles. But Boleslaw also quarrelled with the Church; even having bishop Stanislas of Cracow assassinated. This bishop was later recognised as a Polish national saint. Boleslaw died in exile and within a few decades Poland had distanced itself, once again, from western Europe; largely as a result of continuing German aggression.

Brian Bórumha (High King of Ireland, 1005–14)
Brian began his career as ruler of the small Irish kingdom of Dal Cais, but took over the kingdom of Munster on the death of his brother. Brian soon came into conflict with the High King of Ireland, Malachy II, and in 997 forced Malachy to recognise him as the dominant king over southern Ireland. In 1002 Brian Bórumha deposed the High King; this being a major constitutional upheaval in medieval Irish history. By 1005 he had become powerful enough to claim primacy over all the other kings of Ireland, but made many enemies in doing so. These enemies included the king of Leinster who then formed an alliance with the Norse-Viking king of Dublin against Brian.

The wars of Brian's reign were extremely savage, with the Irish killing all captives fit for war, enslaving the rest and sometimes ritually raping Norse women. He is chiefly remembered for his struggle against the Norse-Irish which culminated in the great battle of Clontarf in 1014. Here the aged Irish ruler remained in the rear, protected by his guards, but directing the battle and praying for victory. The rout of the Norse-Vikings was complete but confused; one band of Vikings from the Isle of Man killing Brian Bórumha at a moment when the battle seemed to be over. The fragile unity which he had imposed on Ireland collapsed soon after his death.

Catwallaun m Cadfan (King of Gwynedd, c.630–3)
Catwallaun was ruler of the most powerful Celtic principality in north Wales; his kingdom possibly also including the Isle of Man. He revived its military reputation following a defeat by the Anglo-Saxons at Chester in about 614. His most important campaigns were against the superficially Christian Anglo-Saxon kingdom of Northumbria, which had conquered both the Isle of Man and Anglesey. Northumbria then appears to have claimed a vague lordship over the whole of Britain. In 633, in alliance with the pagan Anglo-Saxon king Penda of Mercia, Catwallaun invaded northern England and won a decisive victory at the battle of Hatfield Chase. For a year he ruled over both the Celtic British and those Anglo-Saxons living between the river Thames and the Firth of Forth in what would later become Scotland. But he was not widely seen as a liberator by the local Celtic communities, many of whom had grown used to decades of Anglo-Saxon rule. Catwallaun was defeated and killed near Hadrian's Wall, after which Gwynedd's brief domination of northern Britain collapsed.

The wars between the Celtic British-Welsh in the west and Germanic Anglo-Saxons in the east were no longer a strictly religious struggle between Christians and pagans, as Christianity was now spreading rapidly among the Anglo-Saxons. Catwallaun was also prepared to make alliances with pagans against Christians. His wars were 'national' in the sense of being partly an effort to preserve the Celtic regions of Britain from Anglo-Saxon control, and partly an effort to make Gwynedd dominant. After his death this Welsh power centre in north Wales reverted to a passive role. Catwallaun was recalled by the chroniclers as being: 'a barbarian crueller than a pagan' and as 'exterminating the whole English race within the boundaries of Britain'. He was, nevertheless, the only Celtic-British ruler to destroy as opposed to temporarily defeating an Anglo-Saxon dynasty; namely that of the Kingdom of Northumbria.

Charles Martel (Mayor of the Palace of Austrasia, 719–35)
Charles was the illegitimate son of Pepin who inherited his father's position as *Mayor of the Palace* after a five-year civil war within the Frankish Merovingian state. This left Charles as the effective ruler of all the Franks; the Merovingian kings themselves now being little more than figureheads. His defeat of a Muslim raiding party from Spain in 732 entered European mythology as marking the high-water mark of Muslim-Arab expansion in the west. Charles earned his nickname of Martel (The Hammer) as a result of this battle. He also subdued the Germanic kingdom of Burgundy, the pagan Frisians in north-western Holland and Germany, and the Bordeaux area of south-western France. These campaigns were probably more important than his defeat of a minor Muslim-Arab raiding force, since they laid the foundations of a powerful Frankish empire that would be consolidated and expanded by his grandson, Charlemagne.

Edward the Black Prince (Prince of Aquitaine, 1362–76)
Edward of Woodstock, the son of King Edward III of England, was the most famous English soldier of the 14th century. He was also a ruthless commander who 'won his spurs' under the father's gaze at the battle of Crécy, and then went on to win his own most notable victory at Poitiers. He came to be known as the Black Prince for reasons that are still unclear. He certainly seems to have enjoyed warfare, in addition to being a natural leader.

The contemporary patriotic verses of Laurence Minot described him as 'the most valiant prince of this world throughout its compass that ever was since the days of Julius Caesar and Arthur'. Under the command of Edward the Black Prince and his father King Edward III, England earned a military reputation which it had not possessed before. As the French chronicler Jean le Bel wrote: 'Nobody thought much of the English, nobody spoke of their prowess or courage ... Now, in the time of the noble Edward, who has often put them to the test, they are the finest and most daring warriors known to man.' This was also the time when England developed a sense of national patriotism; itself a new phenomenon in Europe.

Gedymin (Grand Duke of Lithuania, 1316–41)

Under Gedymin's rule, pagan Lithuania began to conquer a vast state in eastern Europe. This began as a defensive war against the Crusading Teutonic Knights and their allies. Before Gedymin's reign, the Teutonic Knights had been making deep raids into Lithuanian territory, but Gedymin replied with a series of devastating counter-attacks in 1322–3 which are said to have killed or captured an estimated 20,000 Christians. He also cultivated the friendship of the Teutonic Order's other Crusading and commercial rivals. The Russian principality of Polotsk had fallen to Lithuania by 1305 and Gedymin's brother was now ruling as prince of the Russian state of Pskov. Prussian refugees from the oppression of the Teutonic Knights fired Lithuanian resistance; but it was the annexation of Russian territory which provided sufficient wealth to carry on Lithuania's struggle.

Gedymin built the strongest army in the area; the core of which consisted of pagan Lithuanian or Prussian tribesmen, though the bulk of the population of the growing empire were, in fact, Christian Slavs. Meanwhile the Russian principalities of Novgorod and Tver used Lithuanian support against the rising power of similarly Russian Muscovy. Gedymin also founded the Jagellonian dynasty which soon brought Lithuania into a political union with the kingdom of Poland; thus creating the second largest state in Europe. He sometimes allowed Christian missionaries as well as merchants and soldiers into Lithuania, but himself remained a convinced pagan. The really massive Lithuanian expansion southwards began under Gedymin's successor, Algirdas.

George of Antioch (Admiral of Sicily, c.1123–52)

George was the greatest naval commander in the Norman Kingdom of Sicily, and the first to be given the Arabic title of *Amīr al-Baḥr* (Commander of the Sea) in 1132. This term entered European languages in various versions of the word *admiral*. George of Antioch was also made Chief Minister of the Norman Kingdom of Sicily and southern Italy. He was a Greek from northern Syria, whose parents migrated to Tunisia where George and his father took service with the Muslim ruler Tamīm Ibn al-Mu'izz. George quarrelled with Tamīm's successor in 1108, disguised himself as a simple sailor and fled aboard a Sicilian ship to Palermo in Norman-ruled Sicily. There he rose through the ranks of a complex naval administration; showing himself to be not only a good organiser and being able to speak several languages, but also a fine seaman with personal knowledge of the North African coast.

George initially won recognition as deputy to the first Siculo–Norman *admiral* Christodulus, and eventually replaced him as 'Commander of the Sea'. He then commanded the only Norman victory in the otherwise disastrous Tunisian expedition of 1123. Most of his naval victories were against the Normans' Christian enemies around southern Italy, though he did temporarily occupy the Libyan and Tunisian coasts in 1148. He also led piratical raids against the Byzantines; including one which brought back skilled silk workers to establish that industry in Sicily. George of Antioch founded the Church of S. Maria del Ammiraglio, now known as La Martorana, in Palermo. This still contains a mosaic portrait of the admiral who died in 1152 or 1153.

Harald Hardradi (King of Norway, 1047–66)

Harald Sigurdsson, known as Hardradi (the Ruthless) was half-brother to St Olaf, King of Norway, and survived the battle in which that saint was killed. He then served as a mercenary in the Byzantine Emperor's *Varangian Guard*. He returned to Norway in 1047, very rich and with a Russian wife; becoming king that same year.

Most of his reign was occupied in a fruitless war with Denmark, and he was unable to take up the Norwegian claim to the throne of England until 1066. He then led a fleet across the North Sea to Shetland and the Orkney Islands, before sailing down the eastern coast of Britain and up the river Humber to capture York; the second city of Anglo-Saxon England. His subsequent defeat and death at the battle of Stamford Bridge may have been overshadowed by the battle of Hastings later that same year, but it did bring to an end two centuries of close political and military relationship between England and Scandinavia. Hardradi is said to have been killed by an arrow in the throat at Stamford Bridge, having taken off his armour to fight *berserk* in traditional Viking manner; perhaps having realised that he was involved in a now hopeless battle.

Sir John Hawkwood (English Captain-General of *condottieri* in Italy, 1364–94)

A professional soldier from Essex, John Hawkwood may have fought at the battles of Crécy and Poitiers against the French during the early part of the Hundred Years War. By 1359 he was in command of a force of 'free-lances', in other words mercenaries, in southern France. During a profitless lull in the struggle between England and France, he took his band of soldiers to Italy where they were first employed by the Marquis of Monferrato. This ready-made army included large numbers of the by now famous English longbow infantry; as well as heavily armoured cavalry and other troops. It adopted the name of 'The White Company' and, under Hawkwood's command, became one of the most effective and sought after mercenary *condottieri* forces in 14th century Italy.

Sir John Hawkwood's military career was so successful that King Richard II of England asked the Republic of Florence to return his body for burial. The Florentines replied in a manner that showed their respect for the English soldier, saying: '... although we hold that it reflected glory upon us and our people, to keep the ashes and bones of the late brave soldier Sir John Haukkodue, who, as commander of our army, fought most gloriously for us ... we freely grant permission that his remains shall return to his native land.' He was eventually buried in the parish church of Sible Hedingham, where he was born, though sadly the tomb has since disappeared.

Henry the Lion (Duke of Saxony, 1142–95)

Henry, Duke of Saxony and later also of Bavaria, spent a large part of his life fighting, first to obtain control of his father's duchies; then to keep them after having on several occasions quarrelled with the German emperors, and on others having prompted a rebellion among his own Saxon feudal lords. Henry the Lion was head of the Guelph family and at times the most powerful nobleman in Germany. When not struggling to retain his own duchies, he concentrated on expansion against Slav tribes to the north and east; even leading an unsuccessful Crusade against the heathen Slavs in 1147. He also achieved a dominant influence in the tangled politics of neighbouring but Christian Denmark.

During various periods of exile he lived in England and Normandy. Towards the end of his life the once warlike duke devoted his life to art and literature. He is also sometimes credited with founding two of the greatest cultural and trading cities of Germany: Munich in the south in 1157 and Lübeck in the far north in 1159.

Krum (Khān of Bulgaria, c.802–14)

Krum was chief of the Pannonian Bulgars who had thrown off Avar domination after the latter were defeated by Charlemagne. He was later proclaimed Khān of the fast expanding Bulgarian Empire. Krum was described as an aggressive and determined war leader; and he certainly proved to be a major thorn in the side of the Byzantine Empire. Nevertheless, his invasions of Byzantine territory resulted in a counter-offensive which burned his palace at Pliska. Krum then retreated with his army into the bleak Balkan mountains where they succeeded in wiping out a pursuing Byzantine force in 811. The Emperor Nicephorus I was killed in this battle; his skull then being made into a goblet which Krum is said to have used during drinking bouts with his leading military men.

Krum returned to the offensive, seizing Byzantine towns and adopting his enemy's policy of sending their inhabitants back to enlarge the population of his own capital, Pliska. There these Greek captives probably contributed to the gradual civilising and Christianisation of the fearsome Turkic Bulgars. Krum himself survived a Byzantine assassination attempt which apparently encouraged him to make further devastating attacks upon the Byzantine capital, Constantinople. He won several further victories before he died from a cerebral haemorrhage during his second siege of Constantinople in 814.

Louis I the Great (King of Hungary, 1342–82)

Louis was a member of the Franco-Neapolitan Angevin dynasty which ruled Hungary in the later Middle Ages. He fought most of his neighbours, both Orthodox and Catholic Christians, as well as pagans. Nevertheless, he supported the Papacy against Venice in Italy. Louis I of Hungary came to be seen as a noble champion of the Catholic Church and as a role model for other Crusaders, despite being involved in wars against Catholic Poland after becoming titular ruler of Poland in 1370. His conquest of Dalmatia in 1381 made Hungary a Mediterranean power, but his campaigns also weakened Orthodox Serbia which was already being menaced by the Ottoman Turks.

In Crusading terms Louis I's reign was not a success, and his title 'The Great' reflected grandiose military schemes which were not always practical. This period of Hungarian history has been described as glorious rather than profitable; Louis himself being a splendid warrior but an inefficient king.

Matilda (Countess of Tuscany, 1052–1115)

Matilda was descended from a family that had been given domination over a large part of north-central Italy in reward for their loyal services to the German Saxon Emperors. But Matilda herself was a dedicated supporter of the Papacy in its struggle against the German Emperors during the late 11th and early 12th centuries. Not only did she use her two politically motivated marriages to further this cause, but she also refused to allow these marriages to interfere with her own colourful personal life. In addition, she devoted the growing wealth and increasingly effective armed forces under her control to the service of Pope Gregory VII, with whom she was said to be on terms of considerable intimacy. These Tuscan armies were, in fact, the main or at least the most consistent military forces available to the Papal cause.

Othon de Grandson (Lord of the Channel Islands, 1277–94 and 1298–1328)

Othon was a professional soldier from the feudal aristocracy of Savoy, in what is now western Switzerland. He took part in the final defence of Crusader-held Acre against the Mamlūks in 1291, then travelled back through various parts of the Middle East. On the way he appears to have made copious notes concerning those areas which he considered suitable as bases for future Crusades to regain the Holy Land. He was, in fact, one of the European military advisers who helped King Hayton of Armenia to reorganise the defences of Cilicia. Later he served King Edward I of England during the Scottish wars.

He also proved himself a competent administrator and local military leader in various English-ruled areas such as Wales, Gascony and the Channel Islands. As a skilled and experienced negotiator, he was sent on many delicate embassies to France, Savoy and Rome. He was similarly nominated as one of 76 high-ranking hostages to guarantee the terms of the Treaty of Canfran, between English Gascony and the neighbouring Spanish Kingdom of Aragon; this being a normal task for a senior member of the 13th century military aristocracy.

Robert I Bruce (King of Scotland, 1306–29)
As the son of the Earl of Carrick, Robert Bruce had at first wavered between loyalty to the English crown and to the Scottish independence party, before deciding on the latter. He then led Scottish resistance to English domination and was crowned King of Scotland in 1306, in defiance of King Edward I of England who claimed suzerainty over the Scots. Robert was defeated by the English at Methven and forced to hide, traditionally on Rathlin Island. He returned to the struggle in 1307 and consolidated his power during the reign of the weak English king Edward II. He then went on to win his greatest victory at the battle of Bannockburn in 1314. This was a carefully planned defensive battle in which he used the traditional Scottish *schilton*, densely packed formations of spearmen, which had been so vulnerable to archery in the past. His victory continues to puzzle military historians who tend to ascribe it to English mistakes; particularly as the English soon proved so effective against the French.

The Bruce family was of Norman origin and Robert was a lowland feudal lord in the Anglo-Norman tradition. Yet he recognised the value of the warrior traditions of the Scottish Highlands. He was also a vigorous commander who seized the opportunity offered by Bannockburn to put further pressure on the English by carrying out raids south of the border. He also used Scotland's ability to stir up trouble in Ireland as a way of diverting English attention. Politically, his successes ensured that Scotland remained independent for several more centuries. He wanted his heart to be buried in Palestine, but its bearer, Sir James Douglas, was killed in Spain, and it was returned for burial in Melrose Abbey.

Stefan Dušan (King of Serbia, 1331–55)
Stefan was sub-king of the Zeta area while his father was King of Serbia. He first won his military reputation against the Bulgarians at the battle of Velbužd in 1330. He was then made king after the Serbian nobility overthrew his father, Stefan Uroš III, because he was considered too peaceable. Dušan tried to maintain good relations with Hungary in the north, while following the traditional Serbian policy of southward expansion at the expense of Bulgaria, the Albanians and the Byzantine Empire. Here he succeeded because there was virtually no resistance from the existing Byzantine military aristocracy who largely welcomed a strong new ruler. He became the most famous and powerful ruler of medieval Serbia and was the first to address a Byzantine Emperor as an equal. He eventually adopted the title of Tsar, and proclaimed himself 'Emperor of the Serbs and Greeks'. He seems to have regarded Serbia as a natural successor to the fast crumbling Byzan-

tine Empire and as a more effective bulwark against the advancing Ottoman Turks. He was still in his prime when he died, and his hastily built, heterogeneous Empire crumbled almost immediately.

Theodoric the Great (King of the Ostrogoths, 471–526)
Theodoric was the son of an Ostrogothic chieftain but was educated in the eastern Roman capital of Constantinople. He led his people from eastern Europe to Bulgaria and then, in 489, having been urged to move on by the Roman Emperor Zeno, to Italy. In fact, Zeno asked him to reconquer Italy on behalf of the Roman Empire. Theodoric killed Odoacer, the 'sub-Roman' ruler of Italy, in 493. As a result he became effectively the independent ruler of the peninsula, though he continued to recognise theoretical Roman imperial supremacy.

In addition to being an extraordinarily capable leader, who kept his migrating Germanic people together during their long and difficult travels, Theodoric proved an effective ruler of Italy. He is generally seen as the greatest of the post-Roman 'barbarian' kings. He encouraged toleration between the various Christian sects, imposed Roman Law on his own Germanic tribesmen, and worked for co-operation between Ostrogoths and Roman Italians. He also surrounded himself with scholars and encouraged a series of dynastic marriages designed to link the rival Germanic 'barbarian states' of the Ostrogoths, Visigoths, Burgundians, Vandals and Franks. But no other barbarian king succeeded in following his policy of continuing the traditions of imperial Rome under a Germanic veneer.

William Duke of Normandy (King of England, 1066–87)
William became Duke of Normandy in 1035, but did not achieve real authority until seven years later. He annexed Maine in 1063, and in 1066 successfully invaded Anglo-Saxon England. During the early part of his military career he had avoided decisive battles, which were notoriously unpredictable. Hastings, in 1066, was, in fact, his first such encounter. Nevertheless, he always remained a very cautious commander, preferring to rely on methodical sieges, blockades and considerable effort to subvert the enemy. He could, however, be extremely ferocious and even barbarous in order to frighten an enemy into surrender.

William was noted for his close supervision of even the most prolonged campaigns, for retaining personal control of events, and for his preoccupation with protecting supply lines. This was normal in 11th century western European warfare, but William was particularly good at it. At the same time he was an imaginative leader who employed the latest military ideas, particularly in the use of castles, to help his relatively small military forces control the large, newly conquered, Kingdom of England. On the other hand, he never allowed these castles to become effective centres of Norman rebellion against his own authority.

William Marshal the Elder (Regent of England, 1215–19) William Marshal was one of those men chosen by King Richard I to look after the Kingdom of England while he himself was away Crusading. He was also selected by the great lords of England to be *Baillie* of the kingdom after the death of King John, during the childhood of King Henry III. In addition to being a practical soldier and an adviser to kings on military matters, he was also famous for his skill at *tournaments*. He was successful both militarily and politically during this very difficult period; being described by colleagues a few years before his death in 1219 as having 'proved himself in time of need as gold is tried in the furnace'. His own loyalty to the young King Henry III was summed up by a quotation recorded in the somewhat adulatory *History of William the Marshal* which was written shortly after his death: 'By God's sword, if all abandoned the king do you know what I would do? I would carry him on my shoulders step by step, from island to island, from country to country, and I would not fail him not even if it meant begging my bread.'

His military career suggests that large-scale strategy was more sophisticated than battlefield tactics in late 13th century western European warfare. It also showed that armies of this period fought to win and for the common good of their own side; not merely for the individual glory of their aristocratic leaders. William Marshal the Elder was made Earl of Pembroke and acquired hugely extensive lands in Ireland.

VI
SOURCES

SOURCES

An enormous number of books and articles include useful information about medieval warfare. Those listed below have been included because they are essential works dealing specifically with this subject, or with some aspect of it, or because they include important information not found elsewhere.

Any such bibliography is bound to be incomplete or lopsided since it reflects the author's own studies and the availability of these sources. Many of the works in this list contain information dealing with several facets of medieval warfare. They have, therefore, been placed either in the most relevant section or, if they cover several periods, in the chronologically earliest section. Most translated original sources have been excluded, although there are some exceptions where the published texts also incorporate secondary information or interpretations. The main reason for this exclusion is that such original sources are so numerous and will be found in the most appropriate of the secondary sources. Unpublished material, such as academic theses, has also been omitted, despite the fact that it often includes some most important new information. Similarly, only works in western European languages, or those with substantial summaries in those languages, are listed.

General Works

Bartlett, R. 'Technique Militaire et Pouvoir Politique, 900–1300', in *Annales, Economies, Sociétés, Civilisations*, XL/5, 1986, pp. 1135–59

Beeler, J. *Warfare in Feudal Europe, 730–1200*, Ithaca, 1971

Bennett, M. 'The Means and Limitations of Military Power in the Middle Ages', in *The Sandhurst Journal*, I, 1990, pp. 1–19

Contamine, P. *War in the Middle Ages*, trans. M. Jones, Oxford, 1984

Devries, K. *Medieval Military Technology*, Ontario, 1992

Haleçki, O. *Borderlands of Western Civilisation*, New York, 1952

Hamilton Thompson, A. 'The Art of War to 1400', in *Cambridge Medieval History*, Cambridge, 1980, vol. VI, pp. 785–98

Jones, A. *The Art of War in the Western World*, London, 1988

Lemerle, P. 'Les invasions et migrations dans le Balkans', in *Revue Historique*, CCXI, 1954, pp. 265–309

Lot, F. *L'Art Militaire et les armées au Moyen Age*, Paris, 1946

McNeill, W. H. *The Pursuit of Power: Technology, Armed Force and Society since AD 1000*, Chicago, 1982

Norman, A. V. B. *The Medieval Soldier*, London, 1971

Oman, C. *A History of the Art of War in the Middle Ages*, London, 1924, reprint London, 1991

Sprömberg, H. 'Die Feudale Kriegskunst', in *Beiträge zur belgisch-niederländischen Geschichte*, Berlin, 1959, pp. 30–55

Verbruggen, J. F. *The Art of War in Western Europe during the Middle Ages*, Oxford, 1977

'Barbarian' Invasions and 'Barbarian' States

Alcock, L. *Arthur's Britain*, London, 1971

Austin, N. J. E. *Ammianus on Warfare: An Investigation into Ammanius' Military Knowledge*, Brussels,1979

Baatz, D. 'Die Römische Jagdarmbrust', in *Archäologisches Korrespondenzblatt*, XXI, 1991, pp. 283–90

Bachrach, B. S. *Merovingian Military Organisation, 481–751*, Minneapolis, 1972

– 'Charles Martel, Mounted Shock Combat, the Stirrup and Feudalism', in *Studies in Medieval and Renaissance History*, VII, 1970, pp. 49–75

– 'The Alans in Gaul', in *Traditio*, XXIII, 1967, pp. 476–89

Barrière-Flavy, C. 'Le costume et l'armament du Wisigoth aux Vème et VIème siècles', in *Revue des Pyrénées*, XIV, 1902, pp. 125–43

Behmer, E. *Das zweischneidige Schwert der Germanischen Völker-wanderungszeit*, Stockholm, 1939

Berger, P. *The Archaeology of the Notitia Dignitatum*, London, 1981

Berresford Ellis, P. *Saxon and Celt: The Struggle for the Supremacy of Britain AD 410–937*, London, 1993

Brown, T. S. *Gentlemen and Officers: Imperial Administration and Aristocratic Power in Byzantine Italy AD 554–800*, Rome, 1984

Browning, R. *Byzantium and Bulgaria: A comparative study across the early medieval frontier*, London, 1975

Clark, G. 'Beowulf's Armour', in *Journal of English Literary History*, XXXII, 1965, pp. 409–41

Clover, F. M. *The Late Roman West and the Vandals*, London, 1993

Collingwood, W. G. 'Arthur's Battles', in *Antiquity*, III, 1929

Collins, R. *Early Medieval Spain; Unity in Diversity, 400–1000*, London, 1983

Coulston, J. C. 'Roman, Parthian and Sassanid Tactical Developments', in P. Freeman and D. Kennedy, eds., *The Defence of the Roman and Byzantine East (Proceedings of the colloquium held at the University of Sheffield in April 1986)*, BAR International Series no. 297, Oxford, 1986, pp. 59–75

Darko, E. 'La Tactique Touranienne', in *Byzantion*, X, 1935, pp. 443–69; XII, 1937, pp. 119–47

Dickinson, T., and Härke, H. 'Early Saxon Shields', in *Archaeologia*, CX, 1992

Dumville, D. N. *Britons and Anglo-Saxons in the Early Middle Ages*, London, 1992

Eadie, J. W. 'The Development of Roman Mailed Cavalry', in *Journal of Roman Studies*, LVII, 1967

Evison, V. *The Fifth-Century Invasions south of the Thames*, London, 1965

Fauber, L. H. *Narses, Hammers of the Goths*, London, 1990

Ferrill, A. *The Fall of the Roman Empire: The Military Explanation*, London, 1986

Fett, P. 'Arms in Norway between AD 400 and 600', in *Bergens Museums Arbok*, 1938

Goffart, W. 'The Date and Purpose of Vegetius' De Re Militari', in *Traditio*, XXXIII, 1977, pp. 65–100

Goubert, O. *Byzance avant l'Islam, vol. II/2. Byzance et l'Oc-*

cident: 'Rome, Byzance et Carthage', Paris, 1965

Grant, M. *The Fall of the Roman Empire – a reappraisal*, Annenberg, 1976

Grosse, R. 'Die Rangordnung der römischen Armee des 4–6 Jahrhunderts', in *Klio*, XV, 1918, pp. 122–61

Härke, H. 'Anglo-Saxon laminated shields at Petersfinger – a myth', in *Medieval Archaeology*, XXV, 1981, pp. 141–4

Harmatta, J. 'The Dissolution of the Hun Empire: Hun Society in the Age of Attila', in *Acta Archaeologica Scientiarum Hungaricae*, II, 1952

Hawkes, S. C. 'Soldiers and Settlers in Britain, fourth to fifth centuries', in *Medieval Archaeology*, V, 1961, pp. 1–70

Jackson, K. *The Gododdin*, Edinburgh, 1969

Jones, A. H. M. *The Later Roman Empire, AD 284–602*, Oxford, 1964

Lindner, R. P. 'Nomadism, Horses and Huns', in *Past and Present*, XCII, 1981, pp. 3–19

Maenchen-Helfen, O. 'The Legends of the Origins of the Huns', in *Byzantion*, XVII, 1944–5, pp. 244–51

– 'Huns and Hsiung-Nu', in *Byzantion*, XVII, 1944-5, pp. 222–43

– *The World of the Huns*, London, 1973.

Menghin, W. *Das Schwert im Frühen Mittelalter*, Stuttgart, 1983

Morris, J. *The Age of Arthur*, London, 1977

Oakeshott, E. *Dark Age Warrior*, London, 1974

Russell, J. C. 'Arthur and the Romano-Celtic Frontier', in *Modern Philology*, XLVIII, 1950–1.

Sánchez-Albornoz, C. 'La Caballería Visigoda', in *Wirtschaft und Kultur, Festschrift zum 70 Geburtstag von Alfons Dopsch*, Leipzig, 1938

– 'El Ejercito Visigodo', in *Cuadernos de Historia de España*, XLIII–XLIV, 1967, pp. 5–73

Setton, K. M. 'The Bulgars in the Balkans and the Occupation of Corinth in the Seventh Century', in *Speculum*, XXV, 1950, pp. 502–43

Stratos, A. N. *Byzantium in the Seventh Century (vol. I. 602-34)*, trans. M. Ogilvie-Grant, Amsterdam, 1968

Teall, J. L. 'The Barbarians in Justinian's Armies', in *Speculum*, XI, 1965, pp. 294–322

Thompson, E. A. *The Goths in Spain*, Oxford, 1969

Todd, M. *Everyday Life of the Barbarians: Goths, Franks and Vandals*, London, 1972

Tomlin, R. 'The Late Roman Empire AD 200–450,' in P. Conolly, ed., *Greece and Rome at War*, London, 1981, pp. 249–61

Tóth, Z. *Attila's Schwert*, Budapest, 1930

Werner, J. *Beiträge zur Archäologie des Attila-Reiches*, Munich, 1956

Wood, M. *In Search of the Dark Ages*, London, 1981

Early Medieval Europe

Abels, R. P. 'Bookland and Fyrd Service in Late Anglo-Saxon England', in *Anglo-Norman Studies*, VII, 1985, pp. 1–25

– *Lordship and Military Obligation in Anglo-Saxon England*, London, 1988

Ager, B. 'A Pattern Welded Sword from Acklam Wold, North Yorkshire', in *Yorkshire Archaeological Journal*, LX, 1988, pp.13–23

Allen Brown, R. *The Normans and the Norman Conquest*, London, 1969

– *The Origins of English Feudalism*, London, 1973

Almedingen, E. M. *Charlemagne, a study*, London, 1968

Ament, H. 'Merovingische Schwertgurtel von Typ Weihmörting', in *Germania*, LII, 1974, pp. 153–61

Arwidsson, G. 'A New Scandinavian form of helmet from the Vendel-time', in *Acta Archaeologica (Copenhagen)*, V, 1934

– 'Armour of the Vendel Period', in *Acta Archaeologica (Copenhagen)*, X, 1939, pp. 31–59

Auer, L. *Die Schlact bei Mailberg am 12 Mai 1082*, Vienna, 1976

Bachrach, B. S. 'Angevin Campaign Forces in the reign of Fulk Nera, Count of the Angevins, 987–1040', in *Francia*, XVI/1, 1989, pp. 67–84

– 'Some Observations on the Military Administration of the Norman Conquest', in *Anglo-Norman Studies*, VIII, 1985, pp. 1–26

– 'The Feigned Retreat at Hastings', in *Medieval Studies*, XXXIII, 1971, pp. 344–7

Bannerman, J. 'The Dal Riata and Northern Ireland in the sixth and seventh centuries', in J. Carney and D. Greene, eds., *Celtic Studies: Essays in Memory of Angus Matheson, 1912–1962*, London, 1968, pp. 1–11

– *Studies in the History of Dalriada*, Edinburgh, 1974

Barlow, F. *Edward the Confessor*, London, 1970

– *William Rufus*, London, 1983

Barrow, G. W. S. *The Kingdom of the Scots*, London, 1973

Bates, D. *Normandy before 1066*, London, 1982

Baudot, M. 'Localisation et datation de la première victoire remportée par Charles Martel contre les Musulmans', in *Mémoires et documents publiés par la Société de l'Ecole des Chartres*, XII, 1955, pp. 93–105

Beeler, J. 'The Composition of Anglo-Norman Armies', in *Speculum*, XL, 1965, pp. 398–414

Biddle, M., and Kjølbye-Biddle, B. 'The Repton Stone', in *Anglo-Saxon England*, XIV, 1985, pp. 233–92

Bradbury, J. 'Battles in England and Normandy, 1066–1154', in *Battle Conference on Anglo-Norman Studies, Proceedings*, VI, 1983, pp. 1–12

Brooks, N. 'The development of military obligations in eighth- and ninth-century England', in P. Clemoes and K. Hughes, eds., *England before the Conquest: studies in primary sources presented to Dorothy Whitelock*, Cambridge, 1971, pp. 69–84

– 'Arms, Status and Warfare in Late Saxon England', in D. Hill, ed., *England before the Conquest*, Oxford, 1978

– 'Weapons and Armour', in D. Scragg, ed., *The Battle of Maldon, AD 991*, Oxford, 1991, pp. 208–19

Brown, S. 'Military Service and Monetary Reward in the Eleventh and Twelfth centuries', in *History*, CCXL, 1989, pp. 20–38

Bruce-Mitford, R., and Luscombe, M. R. 'The Benty-

Grange Helmet', in R. Bruce-Mitford, ed., *Aspects of Anglo-Saxon Archaeology*, London, 1974

Bulanda, E. *Bogen und Pfeil bei den Völkern des Altertums*, Vienna, 1913

Cahen, C. *Le Régime Féodal de l'Italie Normande*, Paris, 1940

Carter, J. M. 'The Feigned Flight at Hastings Re-considered', in *The Anglo-Norman Anonymous*, VI, 1988

Cattier, F. 'La Guerre privée dans le comté de Hainaut', in *Annales de la Faculté de philosophie de Bruxelles*, I, 1889–90

D'Haenens, A. 'Les incursions hongroises dans l'espace belge', in *Cahiers de Civilisations médiévale*, IV, 1961, pp. 423–40

– 'Les invasions normands dans l'Empire Franc du IXe siècle: Pour une rénovation de la problematique,' in *I Normanni et la loro espansione in Europa nell'alto Medioevo. Settimane di Studi del Centro Italiani di Studi sull'alto Medioevo*, Spoleto, 1969, pp. 233–89

Davies, W. *Wales in the Early Middle Ages*, Leicester, 1982

De Paor, M. and De Paor, L. *Early Christian Ireland*, London, 1958

Dienes, I. *The Hungarians Cross the Carpathians*, Budapest, 1972

Douglas, D. C. *The Norman Achievement 1050–1100*, Berkeley, 1969

Drew, K. F. 'The Carolingian Military Frontier in Italy', in *Traditio*, XX, 1964

Duby, G. *The Early Growth of the European Economy. Warriors and Peasants from the Seventh to the Twelfth Century*, London, 1974

Duncan, A. A. M. 'The Battle of Carham, 1018', in *The Scottish Historical Review*, LV, 1976, pp. 1–28

Ellis-Davidson, H. R. *The Sword in Anglo-Saxon England: Its Archaeology and Literature*, Oxford, 1962

Erdmann, C. 'Die Burgenordnung Heinrichs I', in *Deutsches Archiv für Erforschung des Mitteltalters*, VI, 1943, pp. 59–101

Fabian, G. 'The Hungarian Composite', in *Journal of the Society of Archer-Antiquaries*, XIII, 1970

Fasoli, G. *Le incursioni ungare in Europa nel secolo X*, Florence, 1945

Felletti, B. M. 'Recostruzione di uno scudo longobardo de Castel Trosinò', in *Pontificia Accademia romano di Archeologia, Rendiconti*, XXXIV, 1961–2, pp. 191–205

Fitz-Clarence, C. 'Mémoire sur l'emploi des mercenaires mahométans dans les armées chrétiennes', in *Journal Asiatique*, XI, 1827

Fleming, R. 'Monastic Land and England's Defence in the Viking Age', in *The English Historical Review*, C, 1985, pp. 247–65

Foote, P., and Wilson, D. M. *The Viking Achievement*, London, 1970

Friesinger, H. 'Waffenkunde des 9 und 10 Jahrhunderts aus Niederösterreich', in *Archaeologia austriaci*, LII, 1972, pp. 43–64

Fuiano, M. 'La Battaglia did Civitate (1053)', in *Archivio Storico Pugliese*, XI, 1949

Ganshof, F. L. 'Etude sur les ministeriales en Flandre et en Lotharingie', in *Mémoires de l'Académie Royale Belgiques, Classe des Lettres*, 2 ser., XX, 1926

– 'L'armée sous les Carolingiens', in *Ordinamenti Militari in Occidente nell'alto Medioevo. Settimane di Studi del Centro Italiani di Studi sull'alto Medioevo*, XV, Spoleto, 1968

Gasparini, F. 'Le armi dei Langobardi', in *Diana Armi*, IV/2, 1991

George, R. H. 'The Contribution of Flanders to the Conquest of England', in *Revue Belge de Philologie*, 1926

Gessler, E. A. 'Der Kalotten-Helm von Chamosen', in *Zeitschrift für Historische Waffen und Kostümkunde*, III, 1930, pp. 121–7

– *Die Trutzwaffen der Karolingerzeit vom VIII bis zur XI Jahrhunderts*, Basle, 1908

Gilbert, J. M. 'Crossbows on Pictish Stones', in *Proceedings of the Society of Antiquaries of Scotland*, 1975–6, pp. 316–17

Gillingham, J. 'William the Bastard at War', in M. Strickland, ed., *Anglo-Norman Warfare*, Woodbridge, 1992, pp. 143–60

Glover, R. 'English Warfare in 1066', in *The English Historical Review*, LXVII, 1952, pp.1–8

Godfrey, J. 'The Defeated Anglo-Saxons Take Service with the Eastern Emperor', in *Proceedings of the Battle Conference on Anglo-Norman Studies*, I, 1978, pp. 63–74

Hawkes, S. C. ed. *Weapons and Warfare in Anglo-Saxon England*, Oxford, 1989

Hejdova, D. 'Der Sogenannte St Wenzels-Helm', in *Zeitschrift für Historische Waffen und Kostümkunde*, 1966, pp. 95–110, and 1967, pp. 28–54

Hollister, C. W. 'The Five-Hide Unit and the Old English Military Obligation', in *Speculum*, XXXVI, 1961, pp. 61–74

– *Anglo-Saxon Military Institutions on the Eve of the Norman Conquest*, Oxford, 1962

– *The Military Organisation of Norman England*, Oxford, 1965

Hooper, N. 'The Housecarls in England in the Eleventh Century', in *Anglo-Norman Studies*, VIII, 1984–5, pp. 161–76

Hüpper-Dröge, D. *Schild und Speer. Waffen und ihre Bezeichnungen im frühen Mittelalter*, Berne, 1983

John, E. 'War and Society in the Tenth Century: The Maldon Campaign', in *Transactions of the Royal Historical Society*, 5 ser., XXVII, 1977, pp. 173–95

Johrendt, J. *Milites und Militia im 11 Jahrhundert. Untersuchung zur Frühgeschichte der Rittertums in Frankreich und Deutschland*, Nuremberg, 1971

Kosztolnyik, Z. J. *Five Eleventh Century Hungarian Kings: Their Policies and their Relations with Rome*, New York, 1981

Lebecq, S. 'Francs contre Frisons (VIe–VIIIe siècles)', in *CIe Congrés National des Sociétées Savants, Lille 1976, Section de philolgie et de l'histoire jusqu' à 1610, La Guerre et la paix*, Paris, 1978

Lederer, E. *La structure de la société hongroise du début du moyen-âge*, Budapest, 1960

Lewis, A.R. 'La féodalité dans le Toulousain et la France

méridionale (850–1050)', *Annales du Midi*, LXXVI, 1964, pp. 247–59

– *The Development of Southern French and Catalan Society, 718–1050*, Austin, 1965

Leyser, K. 'Henry I and the beginnings of the Saxon Empire', in *The English Historical Review*, LXXXIII, 1968, pp. 1–32

– 'The Battle of the Lech, 955. A Study in Tenth-Century Warfare', in *History*, L, 1965, pp. 1–25

– *Medieval Germany and its Neighbours, 900–1250*, London, 1982

Lund, N. 'The Armies of Swein Forkbeard and Cnut, Leding or Lid', in *Anglo-Saxon England*, XV, 1986, pp. 105–18

Macartney, C. A. *The Magyars in the Ninth Century*, Cambridge, 1930

Manley, J. 'The Archer and the Army in the Late Saxon Period', in *Anglo-Saxon Studies in Archaeology and History*, IV, 1985, pp. 223–35

Mitchinson, R. *A History of Scotland*, London, 1970

Mor, C. G. 'La difesa militare delle Capitanata ed i confine della regionale al principio del secolo XI', in *Papers of the British School at Rome*, XXIV, 1956, pp. 29–36

Musset, L. 'Problèmes militaires du Monde Scandinave (VIIe–XIIe siècles)', in *Ordinamenti Militari in Occidente nell-Alto Medioevo: Settimane di Studio del Centro Italiano di Studi sull'Alto Medioevo*, XV, Spoleto, 1968, pp. 229–91

Nelson, J. L. 'Ninth century Knighthood: The Evidence of Nithard', in C. Harper-Bill, ed., *Studies in Medieval History presented to R. Allen Brown*, Woodbridge, 1989, pp. 255–66

Newman, W. M. *Le Domaine Royal sous les Premiers Capétiens (987–1180)*, Paris, 1937

Nordman, C. A. 'Nordiske Ornamentik in Finlands Järna–alder', in *Nordisk Kultur*, XXVII, 1931

– 'Vapnen in Nordens Forntid', in *Nordisk Kultur*, XII/B, 1943, pp. 59–61

Odegaard, C. *Vassi and Fideles in the Carolingian Empire*, Cambridge Mass., 1945

Partner, P. *The Lands of St Peter*, London, 1972

Peirce, I. 'Arms, Armour and Warfare in the Eleventh Century', in *Anglo-Norman Studies*, X, 1987, pp. 237–58

Petersen, J. *De Norske Vikingesvaerd*, Oslo, 1919

Powicke, M. *Military Obligation in Medieval England*, Oxford, 1962

Priedel, H. 'Die karolingischen Schwerter bei den Westslaven', in *Gandert Festschrift*, Berlin, 1959, pp. 128–42

Rasi, P. *Exercitus italicus e Milizie cittadine nell'alto medioevo*, Padua, 1937

Reynolds, S. 'Eadric Silvaticus and the English Resistance', in *Bulletin of the Institute for Historical Research*, LIV, 1981, pp. 102–5

Ritchie, G., and Ritchie, A. *Scotland, archaeology and early history*, London, 1981

Round, J. H. 'Military Tenure before the Conquest', in *The English Historical Review*, XII, 1897, pp. 492–4

Sander, E. 'Die heeresorganisation Heinrich I', in *Historische Jahrbuch*, LIX, 1939, pp. 1–26

Sawyer, P. H. 'Conquest and Colonisation: Scandinavians in the Danelaw and Normandy', in H. Bekker-Nielsen, ed., *Proceedings of the Eighth Viking Congress*, Odense, 1981, pp. 123–31

– *The Age of the Vikings*, London, 1962

Scragg, D. ed. *The Battle of Maldon, AD 991*, Oxford, 1991

Sebestyen, K. 'L'Arc et la flèche des Hongrois', in *Nouvelle Revue de Hongrie*, LI, 1934

Sergheraert, G. *Syméon le Grand (893–927)*, Paris, 1960

Sinor, D. 'The Outlines of Hungarian Prehistory', in *Journal of World History*, IV, 1958, pp. 513–40

Stanford, S. C. *The Archaeology of the Welsh Marches*, London, 1980

Steuer, H. 'Zur Bewaffnung und Sozialstruktur der Merovingerzeit. Ein Beitrag zur Forschungsmethode', in *Nachrichten aus Niedersachsens Urgeschichte*, XXXVII, 1968, pp. 18–87

Székely, G. 'Le rôle de l'élément magyar et slave dans la formation de l'Etat hongrois', in *L'Europe au IXe–XIe siècles*, Warsaw, 1968, pp. 225–40.

Tabuteau, E. Z. 'Definitions of Feudal Military Obligation in Eleventh Century Normandy', in M. S. Arnold, ed., *On the Laws and Customs of England: Essays in Honour of Samuel E. Thorne*, Chapel Hill, 1981, pp. 18–59

Tackenberg, K. 'Uber die Schutzwaffen der Karolingerziet', in *Frühmittelalterliche Studien. Jahrbuch des Instituts für Frühmittelalterforschung der Universität Münster*, III, 1969, pp. 277–88

Tweddle, D. *The Anglian Helmet from Coppergate*, York, 1992

Van Luyn, P. 'Les Milites dans la France du XIe siècle', in *Le Moyen Age*, LXXVII, 1971, pp. 5–51

Verbruggen, J. F. 'L'armée et la stratégie de Charlemagne', in *Karl der Grosse, vol. I: Personlichkeit und Geschichte*, Dusseldorf, 1965, pp. 420–36

– 'L'art militaire dans l'empire Carolingien (714–1000)', in *Revue Belge d'Histoire Militaire*, XXIII, 1979–80, pp. 289–310, 393–412

Von Mangold-Gaudlitz, H. 'Die Reiterei in dem germanischen und frankischen Heeren bis zum Ausgand der deutschen Karolinger', in *Arbeiten zur deutschen Rechts- und Verfassungsgeschichte*, IV, 1922

Werner, J. 'Ein langobardischer Schild von Ischlan der Alz', in *Bayerischer Vorgeschichteblatter*, XVIII-XIX, 1951–2

Werner, K. F. 'Heeresorganisation und Kriegsführung im deutschen Königreich des 10 und 11 Jahrhunderts', in *Ordinamenti Militari in Occidenti nel'Alto Medioevo. Settimane di Studio del Centro Italiano di Studi sull'Alto Medioevo*, XV/2, Spoleto, 1968, pp. 791–843

Whitelock, D. ed. *The Norman Conquest, its Setting and Impact*, London, 1966

Wickham, C. *Early Medieval Italy, Central Power and Local Society 400–1000*, London, 1981

Zeki Velidi, A. 'Die Schwerter der Germanen nach Arabischen Berichten des 9–11 Jahrhunderts', in *Zeitschrift für Deutschen Morgenländischen Gesellschaft*, XC, 1926, pp. 19–37

The High Middle Ages

Audouin, E. *Essai sur l'Armée Royale au Temps de Philippe Auguste*, Paris, 1913

Barlow, F. *The Feudal Kingdom of England, 1042–1216*, London, 1961

Beamish, T. *Battle Royal: A New Account of Simon de Montfort's Struggle against King Henry III*, London, 1978

Beeler, J. *Warfare in England 1066–1189*, Ithaca, 1966

Bennett, M.'Wace and Warfare', in M. Strickland, ed., *Anglo-Norman Warfare*, Woodbridge, 1992, pp. 230–50

Bisson, T. N. *Medieval France and her Pyrenean Neighbours*, London, 1989

Bloch, M. 'Un problème d'histoire comparée: la ministérialité en France et en Allemagne', in *Revue historiques de droit*, 1928

Borst, A. 'Knighthood in the High Middle Ages: Ideal and Reality', in F. L. Cheyette, ed., *Lordship and Community in Medieval Europe: Selected Readings*, New York, 1968, pp. 180–91

Boussard, J. 'Les Mercenaires au XIIIe siècle', in *Bibliothèque de l'Ecole de Chartres*, CVI, 1945–6, pp. 189–224

Bresc, H. *Politique et société en Sicile, XIIe–XVe siècles*, London, 1991

Caldwell, D. H. *Scottish Weapons and Fortifications 1100–1800*, Edinburgh, 1980

Cardini, F., and Salvini, E. *Montaperti 1260, Guerra, società ed errori*, Sienna, 1984

Cardini, F., and Tangheroni, M., eds., *Guerra e Guerrieri nella Toscana Medievale*, Florence, 1990

Carpenter, D. 'Was there a crisis of the knightly class in the thirteenth century? The Oxfordshire evidence', in *The English Historical Review*, XCV, 1980, pp. 721–52

Champeval, J. B. 'Le rôle du ban et arrière-ban du haut Auvergne', in *L'Auvergne historique, litteraire et artistique, Varia 1909–1912*, Riom, 1913

Chew, H. M. *The English Ecclesiastic Tenants-in-Chief and Knight Service*, Oxford, 1932

Christiansen, E. *The Northern Crusades: The Baltic and Catholic Frontier 1100–1525*, London, 1980

Curtis, E. *Roger of Sicily*, London, 1912

Delbrück, H. *La Tactique au XIIIe siècle*, Paris, 1886

Denholm-Young, N. 'Feudal Society in the Thirteenth Century: The Knights', in *Collected Papers on Medieval Subjects*, Oxford, 1946, pp. 56–7

Dieterich, J. R. *Die Taktik in den Lombardenhkriegen der Staufer*, Marburg, 1892

Dieulafoy, M. M. 'La Bataille du Muret', in *Mémoires de l'Académie des Inscriptions et Belles Lettres*, XXXV/2, 1901, pp. 95–134

Douglas, D. C. *The Norman Fate 1100–1154*, London, 1976

Duby, G. *27 Juillet 1214, Le dimanche de Bouvines*, Paris, 1973
— *France in the Middle Ages*, Oxford, 1991

Ducellier, A. *L'Albanie entre Byzance et Venise (Xe–XVe siècles)*, London, 1987

Edwards, J. G. 'Henry II and the Fight at Coleshill: some further reflections', in *The Welsh Historical Review*, III/3, 1967, pp. 251–63

Flori, J.'Qu'est-ce qu'un bacheler? Etude historique du vocabulaire dans les chansons de geste du XIIe siècle', in *Romania*, 1975, pp. 289–314

Frame, R. 'War and Peace in the Medieval Lordship of Ireland', in J. Lydon, ed., *The English in Medieval Ireland*, Dublin, 1984, pp.118–41

Gaier, C. 'Analysis of Military Forces in the Principality of Liège and the County of Looz from the Twelfth to the Fifteenth Century', in *Studies in Medieval and Renaissance History*, II, 1965, pp. 205–61

Geraud, H. 'Les routiers au XIIème siècle', in *Bibliothèque de l'Ecole de Chartres*, III, 1841–2, pp. 125–47
– 'Mercadier. Les routiers XIIIème siècle', in *Bibliothèque de l'Ecole de Chartres*, III, 1841–2, pp. 417–43

Gillingham, J. 'Richard I and the Science of War in the Middle Ages', in J. Gillingham and H.C. Holt, eds., *War and Government in the Middle Ages: Essays in Honour of J. O. Prestwich*, Cambridge, 1984, pp. 78–91
– 'War and Chivalry in the History of William the Marshal', in M. Strickland, ed., *Anglo-Norman Warfare*, Woodbridge, 1992, pp. 251–63

Giraldus Cambrensis. *The Itinerary through Wales and the Description of Wales*, trans. W. Llewelyn Williams, London, 1908

Gohlke, W. 'Das Geschützwesen des Altertums und das Mittelalters', in *Zeitschrift für Historisches Waffen und Kostümkunde*, V–VI, 1909–14

Grundmann, H. 'Rotten und Brabanzonen. Söldner-Heere im 12. Jahrhundert', in *Deutsches Archiv für Erforschung des Mittelalters*, V, 1941–2, pp. 419–92

Harvey, S. 'The Knight and the Knight's Fee in England', in *Past and Present*, XLIX, 1970, pp. 3–43

Hollister, C.W. 'The Annual Term of Military Service in Medieval England', in *Medievalia et Humanistica*, XIII, 1960, pp. 40–7
– 'The Campaign of 1102 against Robert of Bellême', in C. Harper-Bill, ed., *Studies in Medieval History presented to R. Allen Brown*, Woodbridge, 1989, pp. 193–202

Housley, N. J. *The Italian Crusades: The Papal Angevin Alliance and the Crusades against Christian Lay Powers, 1254–1343*, Oxford, 1982

Kimball, E. G. 'Serjeantry Tenure in Medieval England', in *Yale Historical Publications, Miscellany*, XXX, 1936

Legge, D. M. '"Osbercs doublez", The Description of Armour in Twelfth Century Chansons de Geste', in *Société Ronçesvals. Proceedings of the Fifth International Conference*, Oxford, 1970, pp. 132–42

Leicht, P. S. 'Gasindi a vassalli', in *Rendiconti della reale Accademia nazionale dei Lincei, Scienze morali*, 6 ser., III, 1927

Loud, G. A. 'How "Norman" was the Norman Conquest of Southern Italy?', in *Nottingham Medieval Studies*, XXV, 1981, pp. 13–34

Luchaire, A. *Les Communes Françaises à l'époque des Capétiens Directs*, Paris, 1890

Lyon, B. 'The Money Fief under the English Kings', in *The English Historical Review*, LXVI, 1951, pp. 161–93

Menager, L-R. *Hommes et Institutions de l'Italie Normande*, London, 1981

Menant, F. 'Les écuyers ("scutiferi") vassaux paysans d'Italie du Nord au XIIe siècle', in *Structures féodales et féodalisme dans l'Occident méditerranéen (X–XII siècles): Colloques internationaux du Centre National de la Recherche Scientifique*, no. 588, Paris, 1980, pp. 285–97

Mens, A. 'De Brabanciones of bloeddorstige en plunderzieke avonturiers (XII–XIIIe eeuw)', in *Miscellanea historica in honorem Alberti de Meyer*, Bruxelles, 1946, pp. 558–70

Nicolle, D. C. 'The Cappella Palatina Ceiling and the Muslim Military Heritage of Norman Sicily', in *Gladius*, XVI, 1983, pp. 45–145

– 'The Monreale Capitals and the Military Equipment of Later Norman Sicily', in *Gladius*, XV, 1980, pp. 87–103

Nielsen, K. S. 'Riddertidens vaben i Danmark (Arms and Armour in Denmark in the Age of Chivalry)', in *Vaabenhistyoriske Aarboger*, XXX, 1984

Orpen, G. H. *Ireland under the Normans*, London, 1911–12

Otway-Ruthven, J. 'Knight Service in Ireland', in *Journal of the Royal Society of Antiquaries of Ireland*, LXXXIX, 1959, pp. 1–15

Owens, H. 'Warfare in Pre-Edwardian Wales', in *Transactions of the Anglesey Antiquarian Society*, 1940, pp. 32–45

Packard, S. R. 'The Norman Communes under Richard and John, 1189–1204', in *Anniversary Essays in Medieval History by Students of Charles Homer Haskins*, Boston, 1929, pp. 231–53

Paoli, C. *La battaglia di Montaperti*, Siena, 1869

Paterson, L. 'The Concept of Knighthood in the Twelfth-Century Occitan Lyric', in P. S. Noble and L. Paterson, eds., *Chrétien de Troyes and the Troubadours: Essays in Memory of the late Leslie Topsfield*, Cambridge, 1984, pp. 112–32

Peal, A. 'Olivier de Termes and the Occitan Nobility in the thirteenth century', in *Reading Medieval Studies,* XII, 1986, pp. 109–30

Powicke, F. M. 'Distraint of Knighthood and Military Obligation under Henry III', in *Speculum*, XXV, 1950, pp. 457–70

– 'The General Obligation of Cavalry Service under Edward I', in *Speculum*, XXVIII, 1953, pp. 814–33

Prestwich, J. O. 'The Military Household of the Norman Kings', in M. Strickland, ed., *Anglo-Norman Warfare*, Woodbridge, 1992, pp. 92–127

Pribakovic, D., and Popvic, M. 'Archaeological finds of Weapons along the locality of the Town of Ras Fortifications', in *Vesnik Vojnog Muzej*, XXI–XXII, 1976, pp. 45–7

Salvemini, G. *I balestrieri del Commune di Firenze*, Bari, 1905

Scalini, M. 'Protezione e segno di distinzione: l'equippaggiamento difensivo del Duecento', in *Il Sabato di San Barnaba*, Milan, 1989

Schlight, J. *Monarchs and Mercenaries: A Reappraisal of the Importance of Knight Service of Norman and Angevin England*, Bridgeport, Conn., 1968

Schwietering, J. 'Zur Geschichte von Speer und Schwert im 12 Jahrhundert', in F. Ohly and M. Wehrli, eds., *Philologische Schriften*, Munich, 1969, pp. 59–117

Siebel, G. *Harnisch und Helm in der epischen Dichtungen des 12 Jahrhunderts bis zu Hartemann's "Erek"*, Hamburg, 1968

Simms, K. 'Warfare in the Medieval Gaelic Lordships', in *The Irish Sword*, XII, 1976, pp. 98–108

Sinor, D. *History of Hungary*, London, 1959

Strickland, M. 'Securing the North: Invasion and the Strategy of Defence in Twelfth-Century Anglo-Scottish Warfare', in M. Strickland, ed., *Anglo-Norman Warfare*, Woodbridge, 1992, pp. 208–29

Suppe, F. *Military Institutions on the Welsh Marches: Shropshire, 1066–1300*, Woodbridge, 1994

Urban, W. *The Baltic Crusade*, De Kalb, 1975

– *The Samogitian Crusade*, Chicago, 1989

Vayra, P. 'Cavalieri lombardi in Piedmonto nelle guerre del 1229–1230', in *Archivio storico Lombardo*, X, 1883, pp. 413–22

Verbruggen, J. F. 'La Tactique Militaire des Armées de Chevaliers', in *Revue du Nord*, XXIX, 1947, pp. 161–80

Waley, D. P. 'The Army of the Florentine Republic from the Twelfth to the Fourteenth century', in N. Rubinstein, ed., *Florentine Studies*, London, 1968, pp. 70–108

Wathelet-Willem, J. 'L'Epée dans les plus anciennes chansons de geste, Etude de vocabulaire', in *Mélanges offerts à R. Crozet*, Poitiers, 1966, vol. I, pp. 435–49

Wolff, R. L. 'The "Second Bulgarian Empire". Its Origins and History to 1204', in *Speculum*, XXIV, 1949, pp.167–206

Late Medieval Europe

Allmand, C. T. *The Hundred Years War, England and France at War c.1300–c.1450*, Cambridge, 1988

Arondel, M. *Rome et le Moyen Age jusqu' en 1338*, Paris, 1964

Balard, M. 'Les formes militaires de la colonisation génoise', in *Castrum*, III, 1988, pp. 67–78

Balon, J. 'L'organisation militaire des Namurois au XIVe siècle', in *Annales de la Société archéologique de Namur*, XL., 1932, pp. 1–86

Barber, R. *Edward Prince of Wales and Aquitaine*, London, 1982

– *The Life and Campaigns of the Black Prince*, London, 1986

Barlozetti, U., and Giuliani, M. 'La Prassi Guerresca in Toscana', in L. G. Boccia and M. Scalini, eds., *Guerre e assoldati in Toscana, 1260–1364*, Florence, 1982, pp. 51–67

Bartlett, C., and Embleton, G. 'The English Archer, c.1300–1500', in *Military Illustrated, Past and Present*, I, June-July 1986, pp.10–17; II, August-September 1986, pp. 14–21

Bautier, R-H. 'Soudoyers d'Outremer à Plaisance, leur origine Géographique et le Mécanisme de leurs emprunts (1293–1330)', in *La Guerre et la Paix, Frontières et violences au Moyen Age (Actes du 101e Congrès National des Sociétés Savants: Lille 1976: Section de philologie et d'histoire jusqu'à 1610)*, Paris, 1978, pp. 95–129

Bleuler, G. 'Die Vouge, eine Stangenwaffe des spätern Mittelalters', in *Anzeiger für Schweiz. Altertumskunde*, ns. III, 1901, pp. 179–82

Boccia, L. G., and Scalini, M. eds. *Guerre e assoldati in Toscana, 1260–1364*, Florence, 1983, pp. 51–67

– 'HIC IACET MILES: Immagini guerriere da sepulcri toscani del Due e Trecento', in L. G. Boccia and M. Scalini, eds., *Guerre e assoldati in Toscana, 1260–1364*, Florence, 1982, pp. 81–103

– *I Guerrieri di Avio*, Milan, 1991

Boulton, D'A. J. D. *Knights of the Crown: The Monarchical Orders of Knighthood in Later Medieval Europe 1325–1520*, Woodbridge, 1992

Bowsky, W. M. 'City and Contado. Military Relationships and Communal Bonds in Fourteenth Century Siena', in A. Molho and J. A. Tedeschi, eds., *Renaissance Studies in Honor of Hans Baron*, De Kalb, 1971, pp. 75–98

Burne, A. *The Agincourt War: A Military History of the Latter Part of the Hundred Years War from 1369–1453*, Westport, 1980

– *The Crécy War: A Military History of the Hundred Years War from 1337 to the Peace of Bretigny 1360*, Westport, 1976

Caggese, R. *Roberto d'Angio e i suoi tempi*, Florence, 1922–30

Canestrini, G. 'Della milizia italiana dal secolo XIII al XVI', in *Archivio Storico Italiano*, XV, 1851

Cardini, F., and Tangheroni, M., eds., *Guerra e Guerrieri nella Toscana Medievale*, Florence, 1990

Carr, A. D. 'Welshmen in the Hundred Years War', in *The Welsh Historical Review*, IV, 1968, pp. 21–46

Chew, H. M. 'Scutage in the Fourteenth Century', in *The English Historical Review*, XXXVIII, 1923, pp. 19–41

Ciampoli, D. *Il Capitano del popolo a Siena nel primo Trecento*, Siena, 1984

Contamine, P. 'Les compagnies d'aventure en France pendant la guerre des Cents ans', in *Mélanges de l'Ecole française de Rome, Moyen–âge*, LXXVII, 1975

– *Guerre, état et société à la fin du moyen–âge. Etudes sur les armées des rois de France 1337–1494*, Paris, 1972

Curry, A., and Hughes, M., eds., *Arms, Armies and Fortification in the Hundred Years War*, Woodbridge, 1994

Del Treppo, M. 'Gli Aspetti organizzativi, economici e sociali di una compagna di ventura', in *Rivista storica Italiana*, LXXXV, 1973, pp. 253–75

Delmaire, B. 'La Guerre en Artois après la bataille de Courtrai (1302–1303)', in *La Guerre et la Paix, frontières et Violences au Moyen Age (Actes du 101e Congrés National des Sociétés Savants: Lille 1976): Section de Philologie et d'Histoire jusqu'à 1610)*, Paris, 1978

Devos, J-C. 'L'organisation de la defence de l'Artois en 1297', in *Bulletin Philologique et Historique (jusqu'en 1715) du Comité des Travaux historiques et scientifiques, années 1955*, Paris, 1957, pp. 47–55

Dieters, F. *Die Englischen Angriffswaffen zur Zeit der Einführung der Feuerwaffan (1300–1350)*, Heidelberg, 1913

Dinic, M. J. 'Spanski najamnici u srpskoj sluzbi (Spanish mercenaries in Serbian Service)', in *Zbornik Radova Visantoloskog Instituta*, VI, 1960, pp. 15–28

Drobna, Z. *Medieval Costume and Weapons (1350–1450)*, London, 1958

Ducellier, A. *La Façade Maritime de l'Albanie au Moyen Age: Durazzo et Valone du XIe au XVe Siècle*, Thessaloniki, 1981

Edwards, J. G. 'The Battle of Maes Madog and the Welsh Campaign of 1294–95', in *The English Historical Review*, XXXIX, 1924, pp.1–12

Ferrer i Mallol, M. T. 'Mercenaris catalans a Ferrara (1307–17)', in *Anuario de Estudios medievales*, II, 1965, pp. 15–27

Fowler, K. A. *The King's Lieutenant. Henry of Grosmont, First Duke of Lancaster 1310–1361*, London, 1969

Fügedi, E. *Kings, Bishops, Nobles and Burghers in Medieval Hungary*, London, 1986

Gessler, E. A. *Die Entwicklung des Geschützwesen in der Schweiz*, Zurich, 1918

Ghyszy, P. 'Uber Ailettes', in *Zeitschrift für Historische Waffen und Kostümkunde*, III/10, 1931

Gravett, C. *German Medieval Armies 1300–1500*, London, 1985

Hayes-McCoy, G. A. 'The Gallóglach Axe', in *Journal of the Galway Archaeological and Historical Society*, XVII, 1937, pp. 101–21

Hewitt, H. J. *The Black Prince's Expedition of 1355–1357*, Manchester, 1958

– *The Organisation of War under Edward III, 1338–62*, Manchester, 1966

Housley, N. J. 'The mercenary companies, the papacy and the crusades, 1356–1378', in *Tradition*, XXXVIII, 1982

Keegan, J. D. P. *The Face of Battle*, London, 1976

Knoll, P. W. *The Rise of the Polish Monarchy: Piast Poland in East Central Europe, 1320–1370*, London, 1972

Krollmann, C. *The Teutonic Order in Prussia*, Elbing, 1938

Lane, F. C. *Venice and History: The Collected Papers of Frederic C. Lane*, Baltimore, 1966

– *Venice, a Maritime Republic*, London, 1973

Lewis, N. B. 'An Early Indenture of Military Service, 27 July 1287', in *Bulletin of the Institute of Historical Research*, XIII, 1935, pp. 85–9

– 'The English Forces in Flanders, August-November 1297', in R.W. Hunt, ed., *Studies in Medieval History presented to F.M. Powicke*, Oxford, 1948, pp. 310–78

– 'The Recruitment and Organisation of a Contract Army, May to November 1337', in *Bulletin of the Institute of Historical Research*, XXXVII, 1964, pp.1–19

Lydon, J. F. 'An Irish Army in Scotland, 1296', in *The Irish Sword*, V, 1962, pp. 184–9

– 'Irish Levies in the Scottish Wars, 1296–1302', in *The Irish Sword*, V, 1962, pp. 207–17

— 'The Hobelar: an Irish contribution to Medieval warfare', in *The Irish Sword*, II, 1954, pp. 12–16

Lyon, B. *From Fief to Indenture*, Cambridge Mass., 1957

March, U. 'Die holsteinische Heeresorganization im Mittelalter, in *Zeitschrift der Gesellschaft für Schleswig-holsteinische Geschichte*, XCIX, 1974, pp. 95–139

Martin, P. 'Quelques aspects de l'art de la guerre en Alsace au XIVe siècle', in *Revue d'Alsace*, LXXXVIII, 1948, pp. 108–23

McGuffie, T. H. 'The Longbow as a Decisive Weapon', in *History Today*, V, 1955, pp. 737–41

Michael, N. *Armies of Medieval Burgundy, 1364–1477*, London, 1983

Miller, E. *War in the North. The Anglo-Scottish Wars of the Middle Ages*, Hull, 1960

Minieri Riccio, C. 'Memorie della guerra di Sicilia negli anni 1282, 1283, 1284 tratte da'registri angioini dell'Archivio di Stato di Napoli', in *Archivio storico per la provincie napolitane*, I, 1876, pp. 85–105, 285–315, 499–530

Moor, C. 'Knights of Edward I', in *Publications of the Harleian Society*, LXXX–LXXXIV, 1929–32

Nicholson, R. *Edward III and the Scots. The Formative Years of a Military Career*, Oxford, 1965

Oerter, H. L. 'Campaldino, 1289', in *Speculum*, XXXIII, 1968, pp. 429–50

Olteanu, C. 'L'Organisation de l'armée dans les Pays Roumains', in Al. Gh. Savu, ed., *Pages de l'histoire de l'armée Roumaine*, Bucharest, 1976, pp. 53–9

Pálóczi Horváth, A. *Pechenegs, Cumans, Iasians: Steppe Peoples in Medieval Hungary*, Budapest, 1989

Pamlényi, E., ed., *A History of Hungary*, London, 1975

Petrovic, D. *Dubrovacko Oruzje u XIV veku (Weapons of Dubrovnik in the 14th century)*, Belgrade, 1976

Pieri, P. 'I Saraceni di Lucera nella Storia militare medievale', in *Archivio Storico Pugliese*, VI, 1954, pp. 94–101

– 'Milizie e capitani di ventura in Italia nel Medio Evo', in *Atti del Reale Accademia Peloritana di Messina*, XL, 1937–8

Pollo, S., and Puto, A. *The History of Albania from its origins to the present day*, London, 1981

Praga, G. 'L'organizzazione militare della Dalmazia nel Quattrocento', in *Archivio Storico per la Dalmazia*, CXIX, 1936, pp. 463–77

Pratt, D. 'Wrexham Militia in the 14th century', in *Transactions of the Denbighshire Historical Society*, 1963

Prestwich, M. *The Three Edwards: War and State in England 1272–1377*, London, 1981

Prince, A. E. 'The Strength of English Armies in the Reign of Edward III', in *The English Historical Review*, CLXXXVII, July 1931, pp. 353–71

Ricotti, E. *Storia delle compagnie di ventura in Italia*, Rome, 1965

Sambin, P. 'La guerra del 1372–73 tra Venezia e Padova', in *Archivio Veneto*, 5 ser., XXXVI–XXXIX, 1946–7, pp. 1–76

Sherborne, J. *War, Politics and Culture in Fourteenth Century England*, London, 1994

Skrivanic, G. A. 'Armour and Weapons in Medieval Serbia, Bosnia and Dubrovnik', in *Posedna Izdanja*, CCXCIII, 1957

Soulis, G. C. *The Serbs and Byzantium during the reign of Tsar Stephen Dusan*, Washington, 1984

Southwick, L. 'The Armour depicted on the Hastings brass compared with that on contemporary Monuments', in *Transactions of the Monumental Brass Society*, XIV, 1988, pp. 173–96

Spinei, V. *Moldavia in the 11th–14th Centuries*, Bucharest, 1986

Stefanescu, S. 'Considerations sur l'histoire militaire roumaine aux IIIe–XVIe Siècles', in Al. Gh. Savu, ed., *Pages de l'histoire de l'armée Roumaine*, Bucharest, 1976, pp. 36–52

Stoicescu, N. 'La levée en masse en Valachie et Moldavie (XIVe–XVIe siècles)', in Al. Gh. Savu, ed., *Pages de l'histoire de l'armée Roumaine*, Bucharest, 1976, pp. 60–72

Strayer, J. R. *The Reign of Philip the Fair*, Princeton, 1980

Subrenat, J. *Etudes sur Gaydon: Chanson de Geste du XIIIe siècle*, Marseilles, 1974

Sumption, J. *The Albigensian Crusade*, London, 1978

Thiriet, F. *La Romanie Vénétienne au Moyen Age*, Paris, 1955

Trease, G. *The Condottieri: Soldiers of Fortune*, London, 1970

Urban, W. 'The Organisation and Defence of the Livonian Frontier in the Thirteenth Century', in *Speculum*, XLVIII, 1973, pp. 523–32

Verbruggen, J. F. 'De Goedendag', in *Militaria Belgica*, III, 1977, pp. 65–70

Waley, D. P. 'Condotte and Condottieri in the Thirteenth Century', in *Proceedings of the British Academy*, LXI, 1975, pp. 337–71

– 'Papal Armies in the Thirteenth Century', in *The English Historical Review*, CCLXXXII, 1957, pp. 1–30

Woods, C. T. *The French Apanages of the Capetian Monarchy 1224–1328*, Cambridge, Mass., 1966

Fortification and Siege Warfare

Allen Brown, R. 'The Norman Conquest and the genesis of English Castles', in *Château Gaillard*, III, 1966

– *English Castles*, London, 1954

Anderson, W. *Castles of Europe from Charlemagne to the Renaissance*, London, 1970

Anghel, G. 'Les premiers donjons de pierres de Transylvanie', in *Château Gaillard*, VIII, 1977, pp. 7–20

Bertholet, M. 'Histoire des machines de guerre et des arts méchaniques au Moyen Age', in *Annales de Chimie et de Physique*, 7 ser., XIX, 1900, pp. 289–420

– 'Pour l'histoire de l'artillerie et des arts méchaniques vers la fin du Moyen Age', in *Annales de Chimie et de Physique*, 6 ser., XXIV, 1891, pp. 433–521

Bloch, M. 'Les inventions médiévales', in *Annales d'histoire économique*, 1935

Bradbury, J. 'Greek Fire in the West', in *History Today*, XXIX, 1979, pp. 326–31, 344

– *The Medieval Siege*, Woodbridge, 1992

Brown, R. C. Observations on the Berkhamstead Bow', in *Journal of the Society of Archer-Antiquaries*, X, 1967, pp. 12–17

Cathcart-King, D. J. 'The Trebuchet and other siege engines', in *Château Gaillard*, IX–X, 1982, pp. 457–69

Davidson, B. K. 'Early Earthwork Castles: A New Model', in *Château Gaillard*, III, 1966

De Boüard, M. 'Les petites enceintes circulaires d'origine médiévale en Normandie', in *Château Gaillard*, I, 1964

Eales, R. 'Royal Power and Castles in Norman England', in C. Harper-Bill and R. Harvey, eds., *The Ideals and Practice of Medieval Knighthood, vol. 3. Papers from the Fourth Straw-*

berry Hill Conference, 1988, Woodbridge, 1990, pp. 49–78

Finó, J-F. 'Le feu et ses usages militaires,', in *Gladius*, 1970, pp. 15–30

– 'Machines de jet médiévales', in *Gladius*, X, 1972, pp. 25–43

_ 'Origines et puissance des machines à balancier médiévales', in *Société des antiquités nationales*, nos XI, 1972

Fixot, M. 'Les fortifications de terre et la naissance de la féodalité dans le Cinglais', in *Château Gaillard*, III, 1966

Fournier, G. *Le Château dans la France médiévale: essai de sociologie monumentale*, Paris, 1978

Freeman, A. Z. 'Wall-Breakers and River-Bridgers. Military Engineers in the Scottish Wars of Edward I', in *Journal of British Studies*, X, 1976, pp. 1–16

Fügedi, E. *Castles and Society in Medieval Hungary, 1000–1437*, Budapest, 1986

Gerö, L. *Castles in Hungary*, Budapest, 1969

Gillmor, C. M. 'The Introduction of the Traction Trebuchet into the Latin West', in *Viator*, XII, 1981, pp.1–8

– 'The Logistics of Fortified Bridge Building on the Seine under Charles the Bald', in *Anglo-Norman Studies*, XI, 1988, pp. 87–106

Gravett, C. *Medieval Siege Warfare*, London, 1990

Guicciardini, P. 'Castelli e rocche della Toscana', in *Emporium*, XX, 1917

Hansen, P.V., and Rayce, B. 'Reconstructing a Medieval Trebuchet', in *Military Illustrated Past and Present*, XXVII, August 1990, pp. 9–11, 14–16

– 'The Witch with Ropes for Hair', in *Military Illustrated Past and Present*, XLIV, April 1992, pp. 15–18

Harrison, R. M. 'The Long Walls in Thrace', in *Archaeologia Aeliana*, 4 ser., XLVII, 1963

Harvey, J. *English Medieval Architects*, London, 1954

Heliot, P. 'L'âge du château de Carcassonne', in *Annales du Midi*, LXXVIII, 1966, pp. 7–21

Higham, R., and Barker, P, *Timber Castles*, London, 1992

Hill, D. R. 'Trebuchets', in *Viator*, IV, 1973, pp. 99–114

Hughes, Q. 'Medieval firepower', in *Fortress*, VIII, 1991, pp. 31–43

Jarousseau, G. 'Le guet, l'arrière-guet et la garde en Poitou pendant la guerre du Cent Ans', in *Bulletin de la Société des Antiquaires de l'Ouest*, 1965, pp. 159–202

Jones, M. 'The Defences of Medieval Brittany', in *Archaeological Journal*, CXXXVIII, 1981, pp. 146–204

Jones, P.N., and Renn., D. 'The Military effectiveness of Arrow-Loops: Some experiments at White Castle', in *Château Gaillard*, IX–X, 1982, pp. 445–56

Lawrence, A. W. 'Early Medieval Fortifications near Rome', in *Papers of the British School at Rome*, XXXII, 1964, pp. 89–122

Marsden, E. W. *Greek and Roman Artillery: Technical Treatises*, Oxford, 1971

Mesqui, J. 'A propos de la fortification du pont. Pons castri et castrum pontis', in *Château Gaillard*, XI, 1983, pp. 219–32

– *Provins. La Fortification d'une Ville au Moyen Age*, Paris, 1979

Mot, G. J. 'L'arsenal et le parc de matériel à la cité de Carcassonne en 1298', in *Annales du Midi*, LXVIII, 1956, pp. 409–18

Noyé, G. 'Le château de Scribla et les fortifications normandes du bessin de Crati', in *Societa potere e populo nel'età de Ruggero II (III Giornate normanno-suevi, Bari 1977)*, Rome, 1979

Patrick, J. M. *Artillery and Warfare during the Thirteenth and Fourteenth Centuries, Utah State Univ. Press Monographs VIII/3*, Logan, 1961

Piper, O. *Burgen Kunde*. Munich, 1912; repr. Augsburg, 1993

Ralegh Radford, C. A. 'The Late Pre-Conquest Boroughs and their defences', in *Medieval Archaeology*, XIV, 1970, pp. 83–103

Rashev, R. 'Pliska – The First Capital of Bulgaria', in *Ancient Bulgaria (Symposium, Univ. of Nottingham 1981)*, ed. A.G. Poulter, Nottingham, 1983

Redi, F. 'L'arsenale medievale di Pisa', in E. Concina, ed., *Arsenali e città nel'Occidenti europeo*, Rome, 1987

Renn, D. F. 'A bowstave from Berkhamsted Castle', in *Hertfordshire Archaeology*, St Albans, 1971, pp. 72–4

Ritter, R. *Châteaux, Donjons et Places Fortes: L'architecture militaire française*, Paris, 1953

– *L'architecture militaire du Moyen Age*, Paris, 1974

Salch, C. L. *L'Atlas des Châteaux Forts en France*, Strasbourg, 1980

Sander, E. 'Der Belagerungskrieg im Mittelalter', in *Historische Zeitschrift*, CLXV, 1941, pp. 99–110

Taylor, A. 'Master Bertram: Ingeniator Regis', in C. Harper-Bill, ed., *Studies in Medieval History Presented to R. Allen Brown*, Woodbridge, 1989, pp. 289–304

– *Studies in Castles and Castle-Building*, London, 1986

– *The Welsh Castles of Edward I*, London, 1986.

Turner, H. L. *Town Defences in England and Wales*, London, 1971

Tuulse, A. *Castles of the Western World*, London, 1958

Von Petrikovits, H. 'Fortification in the north-west Roman Empire from the third to the fifth centuries AD', in *Journal of Roman Studies*, LXI, 1971, pp. 178–218

Wilson, D. M. *Civil and Military Engineering in Viking Age Scandinavia*, London, 1978

Yver, J. 'Les châteaux-forts en Normandie', in B*ulletin de la Société Antiquaires de Normandie*, LIII, 1955–6, pp. 28–115

Laws of War and Prisoners

Byock, J. *Feud in Icelandic Saga*, Los Angeles, 1983

Cowdrey, H. E. J. 'The Peace and Truce of God in the eleventh century', in *Past and Present*, XLVI, 1970, pp. 42–67

Cross, J. E. 'The Ethic of War in Old English', in P. Clemoes, ed., *England Before the Conquest*, Cambridge, 1971, pp. 269–82

Duby, G. *Hommes et Structures du Moyen Age: Recueil d'articles*, Paris, 1973

Edwards, J. 'Hostages and Ransomers', in *Medieval World*, VIII, January-February 1993, pp. 17–21

Fehr, H. 'Das Waffenrecht der Bauern im Mittelalter', *Zeitschrift der Savigny-Stiftung für Rectsgeschichte (Germ. Abbt.)*, XXXV, 1914, pp. 111–211 and XXXVIII, 1917, pp. 1–114

Göller, K. H. 'War and Peace in the Middle English Romances and Chaucer', in B. P. McGuire, ed., *War and Peace in the Middle Ages*, Copenhagen, 1987, pp. 118–45

Hanawalt, B. A. 'Violent Death in Fourteenth and Early Fifteenth century England', in *Comparative Studies in Sociology and History*, XVIII, 1976, pp. 297–320

Hay, D. 'Booty in Border Warfare', in *Transactions of the Dumfriesshire and Galloway Natural History and Antiquarian Society*, XXI, 1954, pp. 145–66

– 'The Division of the Spoils of War in Fourteenth Century England', in *Transactions of the Royal Historical Society*, IV, 1954, pp. 91–109

Hildesheimer, E. *L'activité militaire des clercs à l'époque franque*, Paris, 1936

Holdsworth, C. J. 'Ideas and Reality: Some Attempts to Control and Defuse War in the Twelfth Century', in *Studies in Church History*, XX, 1983, pp. 59–79

Jäger, G. *Aspekte des Krieges und der Chevalerie im XIV Jahrhundert in Frankreich. Untersuchungen zu Jean Froissarts Chroniques*, Bern, 1981

Kaeuper, R. W. War, *Justice and Public Order: England and France in the Later Middle Ages*, Oxford, 1988.

Keen, M. H. 'Chivalry, nobility and the Man-at-Arms', in C. T. Allmand, ed., *War, Literature and Politics in the Late Middle Ages. Essays in Honour of G. W. Coopland*, Liverpool, 1976

– *Nobles, Knights and Men at Arms in the Middle Ages*, London, 1994

– *The Laws of War in the Late Middle Ages*, London, 1965

Leclerq, J. 'St Bernard's Attitude towards War', in J. R. Sommerfeldt, ed., *Studies in Medieval Cistercian History*, vol. II, Kalamazoo, 1976

Morris, W. A. *The Medieval English Sheriff*, Manchester, 1927

Painter, S. *French Chivalry: Chivalric Ideas and Practices in Medieval France*, Baltimore, 1940

Reuter, T., ed., *Warriors and Churchmen in the High Middle Ages: Essays Presented to Karl Leyser*, London, 1992

Russell, F. H. *The Just War in the Middle Ages*, Cambridge, 1975

Strickland, M. 'Slaughter, Slavery or Ransom? The Impact of the Conquest on the Conduct of Warfare', in C. Hicks, ed., *Medieval England IV: Proceedings of the 1990 Harlaxton Symposium on Eleventh Century England*, Stamford, 1992, pp. 41–59

Military Theory and Training

Anglo, S. 'Jousting: the earliest treatises', in *Livrustkammeren*, XIX, 1991–2, pp. 3–23

Barber, R., and Barker, J. *Tournaments: Jousts, Chivalry and Pageants in the Middle Ages*, Woodbridge, 1989

Barker, J. *The Tournament in England 1100–1400*, London, 1987.

Bennett, M. 'La Règle du Temple as a military manual, or how to deliver a cavalry charge,' in C. Harper-Bill, et al., ed, *Studies in Medieval History presented to R. Allen Brown*, Woodbridge, 1989. pp. 7–19.

Bowlus, C. R. 'Krieg und Kirche in den Südost–Grenzgrafschaften', in H. Dopsch, ed., *Salzburg und die Slawenmission*, Salzburg, 1986, pp. 71–91

Bradbury, J. *The Medieval Archer*, Woodbridge, 1985

Cirlot, J. E. 'La Evolucion de la lanza en Occidente', in *Gladius*, VI, 1967

Dini, V. *Dell Antico usa della Balestra in Gubbio, San Sepulchro, Masso Marittima nella Repubblica di San Marino*, Arezzo, 1961

Flori, J. 'Encore l'usage de la lance. La Technique du combat chevaleresque vers l'an 1100' in *Cahiers de Civilisations médiévale*, XXXI, 1988, pp. 213–40

Funck-Brentano. *Féodalité et Chevalerie*, Paris, 1946

Gaier, C. 'La cavalerie lourde en Europe occidentale du XIIe au XIVe siècle: un problème de mentalité', in *Revue internationale d'Histoire militaire*, 1971, pp. 385–96

Ganshof, F. L. 'A propos de la cavalerie dans les armées de Charlemagne', in *Comptes Rendus de l'Académie des Inscriptions et Belles-Lettres*, 1952, pp. 531–7

Gillingham, J. *Richard Coeur de Lion: Kingship, Chivalry and War in the Twelfth Century*, London, 1994

Gravett, C. *Knights at Tournament*, London, 1988

Greely, J. N., and Cotton, R. C., trans. and eds., *Roots of Strategy, Book II*, Pennsylvania, 1987

Hatt, J. J. 'Le champ de bataille de Oberhausen (357–1262)', in *Bulletin de la Faculté des lettres de Strasbourg*, XLII, 1964, pp. 427–30

Hatto, A. T. 'Archery and Chivalry: A Noble Prejudice', in *The Modern Language Review*, XXV, 1940, pp. 40–54

Herde, P. 'Die Schlacht bei Tagliacozzo. Eine historisch-topographische Studie', *Zeitschrift fürbayerische Landesgeschichte*, XXV, 1962, pp. 679–744

Jean de Meun, ed., U. Robert, *L'Art de Chevalerie*, Paris, 1897

Legge, M. D. 'The Lord Edward's Vegatius', in *Scriptorium*, VII, 1953, pp. 262–5

Mackensie, W. M. *The Battle of Bannockburn: a study in Medieval Warfare*, Glasgow, 1913

Petrovic, D. 'Les premiers nouvelles sur l'exercise des tirs de l'arc à l'arbalète à Raguse au Moyen Age', in *Vesnik Vojni Muzej*, XVII, 1971, pp. 58–9

Pieri, P. 'Federigo II di Suevia e la guerra del suo tempo', in *Archivio Storico Pugliese*, XIII, 1960, pp. 114–31

Ross, D. J. A. 'l'Originalité de Turoldus: le maniement de la lance', in *Cahiers de Civilisations Médiévale*, VI, 1963, pp. 127–38

Sandoz, E. 'Tourneys in Arthurian Tradition', in *Speculum*, XX, 1945, pp. 389–432.

Vogel, F. C. W. ed., 'L'Education d'Alexandre', in *Bartsh Chrestomathie*, Leipzig, 1875

Webster, K. G. T. 'The Twelfth Century Tournament', in *Kittredge Anniversary Papers*, Cambridge, Mass., 1913, pp. 227–34

Morale and Motivation

Allmand, C. T. ed., *War, Literature and Politics in the Late Middle Ages*, Liverpool, 1976

Ashcroft, J. 'Konrad's "Rolandslied", Henry the Lion, and the Northern Crusade', in *Forum for Modern Language Studies*, XX, 1980, pp. 184–208

Barber, R. *The Knight and Chivalry*, London, 1982

Barnie, J. E. *War in Medieval Society, Social Values and the Hundred Years War, 1337–99*, London, 1974

Bergsagel, J. 'War and Music in the Middle Ages', in B. P. McGuire, ed., *War and Peace in the Middle Ages*, Copenhagen, 1987, pp. 282–98

Bliese, J. R. E. 'Aeldred of Rievaulx's Rhetoric and Morale at the Battle of the Standard, 1138', in *Albion*, XX, 1988
– 'Rhetoric and Morale: A Study of Battle Orations in the Central Middle Ages', in *Journal of Medieval History*, XV, 1989, pp. 201–26

Bromwich, R. 'Celtic Dynastic Themes and the Breton Lays', in *Etudes Celtiques*, IX, 1960–1, pp. 439–74

Duby, G. 'Guerre et société dans l'Europe féodale: la morale des guerriers', in V. Branca, ed., *Concetto, Storia, Miti e Imagini del Medio Evo. Atti del XIV Corso Internazionale d'alta cultura*, Florence, 1973, pp. 449–59

Falk, J. *Etude sociale sur les chansons de geste*, Nyköping, 1879

Flori, J. 'Chevalerie et liturgie, Remise des armes et vocabulaire "chevaleresque" dans les sources liturgiques du IXe à XIVe siècle', in *Le Moyen Age*, LXXXIV, 1978, pp. 247–78

Harper-Bill, C. 'The Piety of the Anglo-Norman Knightly Class', in *Anglo-Norman Studies*, 1979, pp. 63–77

Jackson, W. H. ed., *Knighthood in Medieval Literature*, Woodbridge, 1981

Kiff, J. 'Images of War: Illustrations of Warfare in Early Eleventh Century England', in *Anglo-Norman Studies*, VII, 1985, pp. 177–94

Lejeune, R., and Stiennon, J. *The Legend of Roland in the Middle Ages*, London, 1971

Lloyd-Jones, J. 'The Court Poets of the Welsh Princes', in *Proceedings of the British Academy*, XXXIV, 1948

Loomis, R. S. *Arthurian Literature in the Middle Ages*, Oxford, 1959·

Lot, F. 'La langue de commandement dans les armées romaines et le cri de guerre français au moyen âge', in *Mélanges dédiés à la mémoire de Félix Grat*, Paris, 1946

Mason, E. 'The Hero's Invincible Weapon: an Aspect of Angevin Propaganda', in C. Harper-Bill and R. Harvey, eds., *The Ideals and Practice of Medieval Knighthood. Papers from the Fourth Strawberry Hill Conference, 1988*, Woodbridge, 1990, pp. 121–38

Matonis, A. T. E. 'Traditions of Panegyric in Welsh Poetry; the Heroic and the Chivalric', in *Speculum*, LIII, 1978, pp. 667–87

Rousset, P. 'Note sur la situation du chevalier à l'époque romane', in *Literature, Histoire, Linguistique, Recueil d'études offerts à Bernard Gagnebin*, Lausanne, 1973, pp. 189–200

Woolf, R. 'The Ideal of Men Dying with their Lords in the "Germania" and the "Battle of Maldon"', in *Anglo-Saxon England*, V, 1976, pp. 69–81

Horses, Harness and Land Transport

Bachrach, B. S. 'Animals and Warfare in Medieval Europe', in *L'uomo di fronte al monde animale nell'alto medioevo: Settimane di studio del Centro italiano di studi sull'alto medioevo*, XXX/1/i, Spoleto, pp. 707–64

Bulliet, R. W. *The Camel and the Wheel*, Cambridge, Mass., 1975

Chomel, V. 'Chevaux de bataille et roncin en Dauphiné au XIVe siècle', in *Cahiers d'Histoire*, VII, 1962, pp. 5–23

Clapham, J. H. 'The Horsing of the Danes', in *English Historical Review*, XXV, 1910, pp. 287–93

Davis, R. H. C. *The Medieval Warhorse*, London, 1989

Drugmand, P. 'Les éperons à pointe, de leur origine au 14e siècle', in *Militaria Belgica*, 1988

Flade, J. E., Tylinek, E., and Samková, Z. *The Compleat Horse*, London and New York, 1987

Goodall, D. M. *A History of Horse Breeding*, London, 1977

Hilton, R. H. 'Technical Determinism: The Stirrup and the Plough', in *Past and Present*, XXIV, 1963

Hyland, A. *The Medieval Warhorse from Byzantium to the Crusades*, London, 1994

Jankovich, M. *They Rode into Europe: The Fruitful Exchange in the Arts of Horsemanship between East and West*, tr. A. Dent, London, 1971

Lefebvre des Noëttes. *L'Attelage, le cheval de selle à travers des âges*, Paris, 1931

Megnin, P. *Histoire du Harnachement et de la ferrure du cheval*, Vincennes, 1904

Seaby, W. A., and Woodfield, P. 'Viking Stirrups from England and their Background', in *Medieval Archaeology*, XXIV, 1980, pp. 87–122

Trew, C. G. *The Accoutrements of the Riding Horse*, London, 1951

Naval Warfare, Water Transport and Combined Operations

Abulafia, D. S. H. *Commerce and Conquest in the Mediterranean*, Aldershot, 1993

Amari, M. 'Su i fuochi da guerra usati nel Mediterraneo nel'XI e XII secoli', in *Atti della Reale Academia dei Lincei*, Rome, 1876

Bachrach, B. S. 'Some Observations on William the Conqueror's Horse Transports', in *Technology and Culture*, XXV, 1985, pp. 505–31

Balard, M. *La Mer Noire et la Romanie Génoise (XIIIe–XVe siècles)*, London, 1989

Bennett, M. 'Norman Naval Activity in the Mediterranean c.1060–1108', in *Anglo-Norman Studies*, XV, 1993, pp. 41–58

Brooks, F. W. 'Naval Armament in the Thirteenth Century', in *The Marine's Mirror*, XIV, 1928, pp. 115–31
– *The English Naval Forces 1199–1272*, Manchester, 1932

Burley, S. J.''The Victualling of Calais 1347–65', in *Bulletin of the Institute of Historical Research*, XXXI, 1958, pp. 49–57

Byrne, E. H. *Genoese Shipping in the Twelfth and Thirteenth Centuries*, Cambridge, Mass., 1930

Christides, V. 'Some Remarks on the Mediterranean and Red Sea Ships in Ancient and Medieval Times II: Merchant-Passenger *vs.* Combat Ships,', in *Tropsis*, II, 1987, pp. 87–99

Cohn, W. *Die Geschichte der normannisch-sicilischen Flotte unter der Regieruing Rogers I. und Rogers II*, Breslau, 1910

Dotson, J. E. 'Merchant and naval influences on galley design at Venice and Genoa in the fourteenth century', in C. L. Symonds, ed., *New aspects of naval history: selected papers presented at the fourth naval history symposium*, Annapolis, 1979, pp. 20–32

Dove, C. E. 'The First British Navy', in *Antiquity*, XLV, 1971, pp. 15–20

Finke, H. 'Die Seeschlacht am Kap Orlando (1299 Juli 4)', in *Historische Zeitschrift*, CXXXIV, 1926, pp. 257–66

Gillmor, C. M. 'Naval Logistics and the Cross Channel Operation', in *Anglo-Norman Studies*, VII, 1984, pp. 105–31

Graindor, M. 'Le débarquement de Guillaume en 1066; un coup de maître de la marine normande', in *Archaeologia*, XXX, 1969

Halphen, L. 'La conquête de la Méditerranée par les Européens au XIe et au XII siècles', in *Melanges d'histoire offerts à Henri Pirenne*, Bruxelles, 1926, vol. I, pp. 175–80

Haywood, J. *Dark Age Naval Power: Frankish and Anglo-Saxon Naval Activity from the Origins to AD 850*, London, 1991

Hooper, N. 'Some Observations on the Navy in Late Anglo-Saxon England', in C. Harper-Bill, ed., *Studies in Medieval History presented to R. Allen Brown*, Woodbridge, 1989, pp. 203–13

Jamison, E. *Admiral Eugenius of Sicily*, London, 1957

Katele, I. B. 'Piracy and the Venetian State: The Dilemma of Maritime Defence in the Fourteenth Century', in *Speculum*, LXIII, 1988, pp. 865–89

Kosiary, E. *Woyny na Baltyku X–XIX (Warfare in the Baltic)*, Gdansk, 1978

Kreutz, B. M. 'Ships, shipping and the implications of change in the early medieval Mediterranean', in *Viator*, VII, 1976, pp. 79–109

Lane, F. C. 'The Crossbow in the Nautical Revolution of the Middle Ages', in D. Herlihy, R.S. Lopez, and V. Slessarev, eds., *Economy, Society and Government in Medieval Italy: Essays in Memory of Robert L. Reynolds*, Kent, Ohio, 1969, pp. 161–71

Laporte, J. 'Les opérations navales en Manche et Mer du Nord pendant l'année 1066', in *Annales de Normandie*, XVII, 1967, pp. 3–42

Lewis, A. R. *Medieval naval and maritime history, AD 300–1500*, Bloomington, 1983

– *Naval Power and Trade in the Mediterranean, AD 500–1100*, Princeton, 1951

– *The Sea and Medieval Civilisations, Collected Studies*, London, 1978

Meier-Welcker, H. 'Das Militärwesen Kaiser Friedrichs II. Landes Verteidigung, Heer und Flotte im sizilischen "Modellstaat"', in *Revue internationale d'Histoire Militaire*, 1975, pp. 9–48

Mollat, M. 'Essai d'orientation pour l'étude de la guerre de course et la piraterie (XIIIe–XVe siècles)', in *Anuario de estudios medievales*, X, 1980, pp. 743–9

Mott, L.V. 'Medieval Ship Graffito in the Palau Reial Major at Barcelona,' *The Mariner's Mirror*, 1990, pp. 13–21.

Pascu, S., ed., *Colloquio Romeno-Italiano "I Genovesi nel Mar Nero durante i secoli XIII e XIV" (Bucharest 27–28 Marzo 1975)*, Bucharest, 1977

Pryor, J. H. *Geography, technology and war: studies in the maritime history of the Mediterranean 649–1571*, Cambridge, 1988

– 'The galleys of Charles I of Anjou, King of Sicily, 1264–84', in *Studies in Medieval and Renaissance History*, XIV, 1993, pp. 34–103

– 'The Naval Battles of Roger of Lauria', in *Journal of Medieval History*, IX, 1983, pp. 179–216

– 'Transportation of Horses by Sea during the era of the Crusades: Eighth Century to AD 1285 (part 1. to *c.*1225)', *The Mariner's Mirror*, LXVIII, 1982, pp. 9–27

Robbert, L. B. 'A Venetian Naval Expedition of 1224', in D. Herlihy, R. S. Lopez, and V. Slessarev, eds., *Economy, Society and Government in Medieval Italy: Essays in Memory of Robert L. Reynolds*, Kent, Ohio, 1969, pp. 141–51

Rodgers, W. L. *Naval Warfare under Oars*, Annapolis, 1967

Templeman, G. 'Two French Attempts to Invade England during the Hundred Years War', in *Studies in French Language, Literature and History presented to R. L. G. Ritchie*, Cambridge, 1949, pp. 225–38

Unger, R. W. 'Warships and cargo ships in medieval Europe', in *Technology and Culture*, XXII, 1981, pp. 233–52

– *The Ship in the Mediterranean Economy, 600–1600*, London, 1980

Flags and Heraldry

Adam, P. 'Les enseignes militaires au Moyen Age et leur influence sur l'héraldique', in *Ve Congrès international des sciences généalogiques et héraldiques*, Stockholm, 1961, pp. 167–94

Adelson, H. L. 'The Holy Lance and the Hereditary German Monarchy', in *Art Bulletin*, XLVIII/2, 1966

Braibant, C. *Les Blasons et les Sceaux*, Paris, 1950

Grigg, R. 'Inconsistency and lassitude: the shield emblems of the Notitia Dignitatum', in *Journal of Roman Studies*, LXXIII, 1983, pp. 132–42

Harmatta, J. 'The Golden Bow of the Huns', in *Acta Archaeologica Scientiarum Hungaricae*, I, 1951, pp. 107–49

Leaf, W., and Purcell, S. *Heraldic Symbols: Islamic Insignia and Western Heraldry*, London, 1986

Lillich, M. 'Early Heraldry: How to Crack the Code', in *Gesta*, XXXIII, 1991, pp. 41–7

– 'Gothic Heraldry and Name Punning', in *Journal of Medieval History*, XII, 1986, pp. 239–51

Prinet, M. 'De l'origine orientale des armoires européennes', in *Archives Héraldiques Suisses*, II, 1912, pp. 53–8

Scott-Giles, C. W. *Boutell's Heraldry*, London, 1954

Solovjev, A. 'Les emblèmes héraldiques du Byzance et les Slaves', in *Seminarium Kondakovianum*, VII, 1935, pp. 119–64

Arms, Armour and the Weapons Trade

Adams, A. *The history of the Worshipful Company of Blacksmiths: from early times until the year 1647*, London, 1937

Alm, J. 'Europeiska armborst: En översickt', in *Vaaben-historisk Aarboger*, V, 1947, pp. 107–255

Anstee, J. W., and Biek, L. 'A Study in Pattern Welding', in *Medieval Archaeology*, V, 1961, pp. 71–93

Aroldi, A. M. *Armi e Armature Italiane, fina al XVIII secolo*, Milan, 1961

Arvidsson, G. 'Armour of the Vendel Period', in *Acta Archaeologica (Copenhagen)*, X, 1939, pp. 31–59

Barron, E. J. 'Notes on the history of the Armourers and Brasiers Company', in *Transactions, London Middlesex Archaeological Society*, II, 1911–13, pp. 300–19

Bishop, M. C., and Coulston, J. C. N. *Roman Military Equipment*, London, 1993

Blair, C. *European and American Arms, c.1100–1850*, London, 1962

– *European Armour*, London, 1958

Blomquist, R. 'Medeltida Svard, Dolkar och Slidor funna i Lund', in *Kulturen*, 1938, pp.134–69

Boccia, L. G., and Blair, C., eds., *Dizionari terminologici. Armi difensive dal Medioevo all'Età Moderna*, Florence, 1982

Boccia, L. G., and Coelho, E. T. 'L'armamento di cuoio e ferro nel trecento Italiano', in *L'Illustrazione italiani*, I/2, 1972, pp. 24–7

– 'L'armamento in Toscana dal Millecento al Trecento', in *Civiltà delle Art Minori in Toscana; Atti del I Conegni, Arezzo 11-15 Maggio 1971*, Florence, 1973

Boeheim, W. *Handbuch der Waffenkunde*, Leipzig, 1890

Borg, A. 'Gisarmes and Great Axes', in *Journal of the Arms and Armour Society*, VIII, 1974–6, pp. 337–42

Bruce-Mitford, R. 'The Sutton-Hoo Helmet Reconstruction and the Design of the Royal Harness and Sword-Belt', in *Journal of the Arms and Armour Society*, X, 1982, pp. 217–74

Burgess, E. M. 'Further Research into the Construction of Mail Garments', in *Antiquaries Journal*, XXXIII, 1953, pp. 193–202

– 'The Mail-Maker's Technique', in *Antiquaries Journal*, XXXIII, 1953, pp. 48–55

Buttin, F. *Du Costume Militaire au Moyen Age et Pendant la Renaissance*, Barcelona, 1971

Camerani-Marri, G. *Statuti delle Arti dei Corazzai, dei chiavaioli, ferraioli e calderai e dei fabbri di Firenze (1321–1344)*, Florence, 1960

– *Statuti delle Arti dei Correggiai, Tavolacciai e Scudai, de vaiai e pellicciai di Firenze (1338–1386)*, Florence, 1960

Cederlöf, O. 'The Sutton Hoo Ship-Burial and the Armour of the Vendel Period', in *Journal of the Arms and Armour Society*, I, 1955, pp. 153–64

Cowgill, J., M. de Neergaard, N. Griffiths, et al. *Medieval Finds from Excavations in London 1: Knives and Scabbards*, London, 1987

Davidson, H. R. E. *The Sword in Anglo-Saxon England*, Oxford, 1962

De Hoffmeyer, A. B. 'From Medieval Sword to Renaissance Rapier', in R. Held, ed., *Art, Arms and Armour*, Chiasso, 1979

Denkstein, V. 'Pavises of the Bohemian Type, II, The Origin and Development of Pavises in pre-Hussite Europe', in *Sborník Národního Muzea y Praze (Acta Musei Nationalis Prague)*, ser. A-Historia XVIII, 1964, pp. 149–94

Dillon, H. 'An armourer's bill, temp. Edward III', in *The Antiquary*, XX, July-December 1890

Dondi, G. 'Del Roncone del Pennato e del cosidetto Scorpione: loro origini,', in *Armi Antiche*, 1976, pp. 11–48

Eaves, I. 'The Warwich Shaffron', *Journal of the Arms and Armour Society*, XII, 1987, pp. 217–22

Ellehauge, M. *Certain Phases in the Origin and Development of the Glaive*, Copenhagen, 1945

– *The Spear traced through its post-Roman Development*, Copenhagen, 1948

Enlart, C. 'Les Armes d'haste de l'homme à pied', in *Gazette des Armes*, IV, 1976, pp. 31–41

Finó, J-F. 'Notes sur la production du fer et la fabrication des armes en France au Moyen-Age', in *Gladius*, III, 1963–4, pp. 47–66

ffoulkes, C. *The Armourer and his Craft*, London, 1912

Fossati, F. 'Per il commercia delle armature e i missaglia,' in *Archivio Storico Lombardo*, LIX, 1932, pp. 279–97

Fowler, G. H. 'Munitions in 1224', in *Publications of the Bedfordshire Historical Record Society*, V, 1920, pp. 117–32

France-Lanord, A. 'La fabrication des epées damascées aux époques mérovingienne et carolingienne', in *Le Pays Gaumais*, Virton, 1949

– 'La fabrication des epées mérovingiennes et carolingiennes', in *Revue de Metallurgie*, XLIX, 1952, pp. 411–22

Gaier, C. 'L'évolution et l'usage de l'armament personnel défensif au Pays de Liège du XIIe au XIVe siècle', in *Zeitschrift für Historisches Waffen-und Kostümkunde*, IV, 1962, pp. 65–86

– 'Le Problème de l'industrie Armurière Liégeoise au Moyen Age', in *Chronique Archéologique du Pays de Liège*, LIII, 1962, pp. 22–75

– *Les Armes*, Turnhout, 1979

Gamber, O. 'Orientalische Einflüsse auf die mittelalterliche Bewaffnung Europas', in *Kwartalnik historii Kulturu materialnej*, XXI, 1973, pp. 273–9

– 'Wikingerbewaffnung und spätrömische Waffen Tradition', in *I Normanni e la loro espansione in Europa nell'alto Medioevo. Settimane di Studi del Centro Italiani di Studi sull'alto Medioevo*, Spoleto, 1969, pp. 767–82

Girton, T. *The mark of the sword; a narrative history of the Cutlers Company 1189–1975*, London, 1975

Grancsay, S. V. *Arms and Armor: Essays by Stephen V. Grancsay from the Metropolitan Museum of Art Bulletin 1920–1964*, New York, 1986

Halpin, A. 'Irish Medieval Swords *c.*1170–1600', in *Proceedings of the Royal Irish Academy*, LXXXVI, 1986, pp. 183–230

Harbison, P. 'Native Irish Arms and Armour in Medieval Gaelic Literature, 1170–1600', in *The Irish Sword*, XII, 1976, pp. 173–99, 270–84

Harmuth, E. *Die Armbrust: Ein Handbuch*, Graz, 1986

James, S. 'Evidence from Dura Europos for the Origins of Late Roman Helmets', in *Syria*, LXIII, 1986, pp. 107–34

Jones, P. N. 'The metallography and relative effectiveness of arrowheads and armour during the Middle Ages', in *Materials Characterisation*, XXIX, 1992, pp. 111–17

Keller, M. L. *The Anglo-Saxon Weapon Names treated Archaeologically and Etimologically*, Heidelberg, 1906

Kelly, F. M. 'A Knight's Armour of the Early XIV Century: being the inventory of Raoul de Nesle', in *Burlington Magazine*, XXIV/4, March 1905, pp. 457–69

Knudson, C. A. 'La brogne', in *Mélanges offerts à Rita Lejeune*, Gembloux, 1969, vol. II, pp. 1625–36

Laking, G. F. *A Record of European Armour and Arms through Seven Centuries*, 5 vols., London, 1920–2

Larson, H. M. 'The Armour Business in the Middle Ages', in *Business History Review*, XIV, 1940, pp. 49–64

Lombard, M. *Les Métaux dans l'ancien Monde du Ve au XIe siècle*, Paris, 1974

Macgregòr, A. 'Two antler crossbow nuts and some notes on the early development of the crossbow', in *Proceedings of the Society of Antiquaries of Scotland*, 1975–6, pp. 317, 321

Mann, J. *An Outline of Arms and Armour in England*, London, 1960

– *The Funeral Achievements of Edward, The Black Prince*, London, 1950

Martin, P. 'Wehr-, Waffen-, und Harnischpflichte der Strassburger Zünfte im 14 Jahrhundert', in *Zeitschrift für Historische Waffen und Kostümkunde*, 1975, pp. 102–8

– *Armes et armures de Charlemagne à Louis XIV*, Paris, 1967

– *Armour and Weapons*, London, 1968

Maryon, H. 'Pattern-welding and the Damascening of Sword Blades', in *Studies in Conservation*, V, 1966, pp. 25–35, 52–60

Müller, H., and Kunter, F. *Europaische Helme*, Berlin, 1984

– *Europäische Hieb-und Stichwaffen aus der Sammlung des Museums für Deutsch Geschichte*, Berlin, 1981

– *Historische Waffen*, Berlin, 1957

Nadolski, A. 'Ancient Polish Arms and Armour', in *Journal of the Arms and Armour Society*, IV, 1962, pp. 29–39

– *Studia nad uzbrojeniem Polskim w X, XI, XII w*, Lodz, 1954

Nicolle, D. C. '*The Arms and Armour of the Crusading Era 1050–1350*. 2 vols., New York, 1988

Oakeshott, E. *A Knight and his Armour*, London, 1961

– *A Knight and his Weapons*, London, 1964

– *European Arms and Armour*, London, 1980

– *Records of the Medieval Sword*, Woodbridge, 1991

– *The Archaeology of Weapons*, London, 1960

– *The Sword in the Age of Chivalry*, London, 1964

– 'Some Medieval Sword-Pommels: An Essay in Analysis', in *Journal of the British Archaeological Association*, XIV, 1951, pp. 47–62

Origo, I. *The Merchant of Prato*, repr. London, 1963

Pancoast, H. S. 'The Origins of the Longbow', in *Publications of the Modern Language Society of America*, XLIV, 1929, pp. 217–28

Panseri, C. 'Ricerche metallografiche sopra una spade de guerra del XIIo secolo', in *Associazione italiana di metallurgia, Documenti e contributi*, Milan, 1957, pp. 7–40

Paszkiewicz, M. 'Polish War-Hammers: Czekan, Nadziak, Obuck', in *Journal of the Arms and Armour Society*, VIII, 1975, pp. 225–8

Paterson, W. F. *A Guide to the Crossbow*, ed., A.G. Credland, London, 1990

Payne-Gallwey, R. *Crossbow*, London, 1903

Peirce, I. 'The Development of the Medieval Sword, *c.*850–1300', in C. Harper-Bill, ed., *The Ideals and Practice of Medieval Knighthood. Papers from the third Strawberry Hill Conference*, Woodbridge, 1988

– 'The Knight, his Arms and Armour in the Eleventh and Twelfth Centuries', in C. Harper-Bill and R. Harvey eds., *The Ideals and Practice of Medieval Knighthood (Papers from the first and second Strawberry Hill Conferences)*, Bury St Edmunds, 1986, pp. 152–64

– 'The Knight, his arms and armour *c.*1150–1250', in *Anglo-Norman Studies*, XV, 1993, pp. 251–74

Pfaffenbichler, M. *Medieval Craftsmen: Armourers*, London, 1992

Post, P. *Kriegs-, Turnier-und Jagdwaffen vom früher Mittelalter bis zum Dreissig-jahrigen Krieg*, Berlin, 1929

Puricelli-Guerra, A. 'The Glaive and the Bill', in R. Held, ed., *Art, Arms and Armour: An International Anthology*, Chiasso, 1979, pp. 2–11

Rausing, G. *The Bow, some notes on its origins and development*, Lund, 1967

Rossi, F. *Medieval Arms and Armour*, Leicester, 1990

Royer, P-R. 'Introduction à l'étude des armes à inscriptions profanes du Musées de l'Armée', in *Revue de la Société des Amis du Musée de l'Armée*, LXXXIV, 1980, pp. 5–13

Ruttkay, A. 'Waffen und Reiterausrüstung des 9, bis zur ersten hälfte des 14, Jahrhunderts in der Slowakei', in *Slovenska Archeologia*, XXIII, 1975, pp. 191–216

Rynne, E. 'A Classification of pre-Viking Irish iron swords', in *Studies in Early Ireland: Essays in Honour of M. V. Duignan*, ed. B. G. Scott, Belfast, 1982, pp. 93–7

– 'The Impact of the Vikings on Irish Weapons,' in *Atti del VI Congresso Internazionale delle Scienze Preistoriche – Protostoriche – Roma 1962*, Rome, 1966, pp. 181–5

Sachse, M. 'Damaszen Stahl,' *Deutsches Waffen Journal*, 1981.

Scalini, M. 'Note sulla formazione dell'armatura di piastra in Italia, 1380–1420', in *Zeitschrift für Historische Waffen und Kostümkunde*, 1981

Schreiner, P. 'Zur Ausrüstung des Kriegers in Byzanz, im

Kiewer Russland und in Nordeuropa nach bildlichen und literarischen Quellen', in *Acta Universitatis Upsaliensis, Figura*, n.s., XIX, 1981, pp. 215–36

Scott, J. G. An 11th Century War Axe in Dumfries Museum', in *The Transactions of the Dumfriesshire and Galloway Natural History and Antiquarian Society*, XLIII, 1966, pp. 117–20

– 'Two 14th century helms found in Scotland', in *Journal of the Arms and Armour Society*, IV, 1962–4, pp. 68–71

Seitz, H. 'La Storta – the Falchion', in *Armi Antiche*, 1963, pp. 3–14

Temesváry, F. *Arms and Armour*, Budapest, 1983

Thordeman, B. *Armour from the Battle of Visby*, 2 vols., Uppsala, 1939

Troso, M. *Le Armi in Asta delle Fanterie Europeen (1000–1500)*, Novara, 1988

Tylecote, R. F. 'The Medieval Smith and his Methods', in D. W. Crossley, ed., *Medieval Industry*, London, 1981, pp. 42–50

Von Hefner-Alteneck, J. H. *Waffen: Ein Beitrag zur Historischen Waffenkunde*, repr. Graz, 1969

Wagner, E. *Hieb-und Stichwaffen*, Prague, 1966

Wagner, E., Drobná, and Durdík, J. *Medieval Costume, Armour and Weapons (1350–1450)*, London, 1958

Waterer, J. W. *Leather and the Warrior*, Northampton, 1981

Watkin, J. R. 'A Medieval Buckler from Hull', in *Journal of the Arms and Armour Society*, XI, 1985, pp. 320–39

Zijlstra-Zweens, H. M. *Of his array telle I no lenger tale: Aspects of costume, arms and armour in Western Europe 1200–1400*, Amsterdam, 1988

Firearms

Baxter, D. R. *Superimposed Load Firearms, 1360–1860*, Hong Kong, 1966

Blackmore, H. L. 'The Boxted Bombard', in *Archaeologia*, LXVII/1, 1987, pp. 86–96

Carman, W. Y. *A History of Firearms from the Earliest Times to 1914*, London, 1955

Credland, A. 'The Blowpipe in Europe and the East', in *Journal of the Arms and Armour Society*, X, 1981, pp. 119–47

Foley, V., and Perry, K. 'In Defence of LIBER IGNEUM: Arab Alchemy, Roger Bacon and the Introduction of Gunpowder into the West', in *Journal for the History of Arabic Science*, III, 1979, pp. 200–18

Forestié, F. 'Hughes de Cardaillac et la poudre à canon', in *Bulletin archéologique de la Société archéologique du Tarn-et-Garonne*, XXIX, 1901, pp. 93–132, 185–222, 297–312

Gaibi, A. 'Un raro cimelio piemontese del trecento', in *Armi Antiche*, 1965

– *Le Armi da Fuoco Portatili Italiane*, Milan, 1962

Gaier, C. 'Qui a inventé la poudre?', in *Musée d'Armes*, LXXII, 1992, pp. 15–20

– *Four Centuries of Liège gun making*, London, 1976

Norman, A.V. B. 'Notes on some early representations of guns and on Ribaudekins', in *Journal of the Arms and Armour Society*, VIII, 1974–6, pp. 234–42

Partington, J. R. *A History of Greek Fire and Gunpowder*, Cambridge, 1960

Pasquali-Lasagni, A. 'Note di storia dell'artigliera nel secoli XIV–XV', in *Archivio della Reale Deputazione Romana di Studia Patria*, LX, 1937, pp. 149–89

Petrovic. 'Fire-arms in the Balkans on the eve of and after the Ottoman Conquests of the fourteenth and fifteenth centuries', in V. J. Parry and M. E. Yapp, eds., *War, Technology and Society in the Middle East*, London, 1975, pp.164–94

Rothert, H. 'Wann und wo 1st die Pulverwaffe erfunden?' in *Blätter für deutsche Landesgeschichte*, LXXXIX, 1952, pp. 84–6

Schubert, H. 'The First cast-iron cannon made in England', in *The Journal of the Iron and Steel Institute*, CXLVI, 1942, pp. 131–40

Smith, R. D., and Brown, R. R. *Bombards: Mons Meg and her sisters*, London, 1989

Tout, T. F. Firearms in England in the Fourteenth Century, *The English Historical Review*, XXVI, 1911, pp. 666–702

Wilinbachow, W. 'Note on the History of the Initial Period of the Use of Firearms in Slavonic Countries', in *Kwartalnik Historii Techniki*, VIII, 1963, pp. 215–35

Miscellaneous

Ashtor, E. *Histoire des Prix et des salaires dans l'orient médiéval*, Paris, 1969

Bak, J. M.'The Price of War and Peace in Late Medieval Hungary', in R. P. McGuire, ed., *War and Peace in the Middle Ages*, Copenhagen, 1987, pp. 161–78

Mitchell, P. D. 'Leprosy and the Case of King Baldwin IV of Jerusalem', in *International Journal of Leprosy*, LXI, 1993, pp. 283–91

Pivano, S. 'Lineamenti storici e guiridici della cavalleria medioevale', in *Memorie della reale Accademia delle scienze di Torino (Scienza Morali)*, ser. II/LV, 1905

Prestwich, J. O. 'War and Finance in the Anglo-Norman State', in *Transactions of the Royal Historical Society*, 5 ser. IV, 1954, pp. 19–43

Prestwich, M. 'Victualling Estimates for the English Garrisons in Scotland during the Early Fourteenth Century', in *The English Historical Review*, LXXXII, 1967, pp. 536–43

– *War, Politics and Finance under Edward I*, London, 1972

Prince, A. E. 'The Payment of Army Wages in Edward III's Reign', in *Speculum*, XIX, 1944, pp. 137–60

Puddu, R. 'Istituzioni militari, società e stato fra Medioevo e Rinascimento', in *Rivista Storico Italiana*, LXXXVII, 1975, pp. 749–69

Schlesinger, W. 'Lord and Follower in Germanic Institutional History', in F. L. Cheyette, ed., *Lordship and Community in Medieval Europe: Selected Readings*, New York, 1968, pp. 64–99

Sennhause, A. *Hauptmann und Führung im Schweizer Krieg des Mittelalters*, Bern, 1965

Steuer, H. 'Helm und Ringschwert: Prunkbewaffnung und Rangabzeichen germanischer Krieger', in *Studien zur*

Sachsenforschung, VI, 1987, pp. 189–236

Stotten, P. 'Wandlungen und Gebrauchs der Kriegswaffen im Mittelalter', in L. Von Wiese, ed., *Die Entwicklung der Kriegswaffer und ihre Zusammenhang mit der Sozialordnung,* Cologne, 1953, pp. 118–33

Wolff, P. *Regards sur le Midi médiévale,* Toulouse, 1978

VII
MISCELLANEA

MISCELLANEA

THE LAWS OF WAR

Medieval people were just as concerned about the morality and legal basis of warfare as were those of later centuries. This was particularly true of religious leaders and lawyers, who put considerable time and effort into establishing a satisfactory framework for this least attractive of human activities. As early as the late 4th century Saint Ambrose of Milan tried to differentiate between internal war between Christians and external warfare in defence of Christendom. A generation later Saint Augustine of Hippo maintained that only rulers and officials acting in the line of duty could kill without giving way to hatred and other sinful passions. He also accepted the concept that the punishment of wrongdoers or enemies was an 'act of love' by a just ruler; this being based on an acceptance of the fact that perfect peace was impossible in a sinful world. Throughout the Middle Ages this form of 'radical pessimism' dominated attitudes to warfare and there was a general acceptance that justice and peace must almost inevitably be imposed through governmental violence. It was also widely believed that the sin of waging unjust war rested on leaders rather than their followers, and that war itself could be a remedy for sin rather than being inherently sinful. Justice in war was to be found in the original motivation to violence, in efforts to avoid excessive violence, and in keeping one's word – even to enemies.

The Mausoleum of Theodoric the Goth in Ravenna; Italian, early 6th century. Theodoric's mausoleum is classical or late Roman in the details of its design, yet rather 'barbarian' in spirit. This is particularly seen in the roof which is made from a single huge piece of stone, shipped or brought by some form of wagon from the Istrian peninsula on the other side of the Adriatic. Theodoric the Goth himself, of course, was a product of two cultures; the decayed but still highly respected world of Rome and the vigorous but still crude world of the Germanic invaders.

Below: Château Gaillard, built by King Richard I Coeur de Lion in 1198. Richard of England's 'pretty castle' overlooking the river Seine in Normandy was one of the strongest in northern France, and was intended as a launching-pad for campaigns up the river towards Paris and the heart of the French king's domain. Nevertheless, it fell with relative ease to King Philip II Augustus of France in 1204, largely because even such a strong fortress could not endure a prolonged blockade with a small garrison and inadequate supplies.

Right: The Black Prince's arms, armour and clothing which hung above his tomb in Canterbury Cathedral, to serve as his funeral achievements. In 1954 the very dilapidated originals were replaced by exact modern replicas made in the Tower of London. Funerary objects such as these ensured that several unique pieces of arms, armour and even clothing survived from the late medieval period. The cap of estate and large crest on the left are both made of moulded leather and canvas, the lion's fur being indicated with additional plaster-coated pieces of leather. Both would have been worn over the iron great helm on the right. The jupon or coat is padded with wool and thickly embroidered with gold thread. Again, it would again have been worn over armour. The shield was of light wood, covered with several layers of canvas, plates, paper and leather, with thickly embossed heraldic leopards and fleurs-de-lis of moulded leather nailed to the front. The gauntlets are made of gilded latten, a medieval version of brass, while only the leather covering of the scabbard remains, its inner wooden elements having crumbled away.

In reality the medieval Christian Church had few moral problems with warfare and frequently took part itself. Nevertheless, various kinds of spiritual punishments were still often imposed on soldiers involved in the violence of war. For example they might be denied communion for a certain time. The imposition of fasting or other forms of penance was recorded even as late as the 11th century. More surprisingly, perhaps, the ancient pagan Germanic idea that victory in battle was proved by one side retaining control of the battlefield for three consecutive days survived in some form until the 15th century.

Christian concepts of the Just War drew heavily upon earlier Roman Law, while the Christian ideas of Holy War, which could already be seen in Carolingian times, were strongly influenced by the Muslim concept of *jihād* or spiritual struggle. Later, however, they came to be seen as a punitive response to injuries supposedly inflicted upon Christ or the Christian community. During the 12th century the lawyer Gratian of Bologna was the first to make a clear distinction between Just War and Holy War; the former being to protect the state, the latter to protect the Church.

Whereas canon or religious law provided the moral framework for such aggressive campaigns as the Crusades of the 12th century, the civilian lawyers of the same period contributed to the development of 'rules of War' in an internal Christian political context. Thus they attempted to clarify who could wage war, and upon whom. Concern with Just and Unjust War eventually led to 14th century lawyers defining four kinds of Just Warfare, and three kinds of Unjust Warfare. The former could be between Christians, where one side stood condemned for having previously inflicted an injury upon the other. Taking part in such Just War was permitted by God. Holy War was to further 'God's Intentions' in this world; and here one side stood totally in the right, the other – usually pagans, Muslims or heretics – being totally in the wrong. Taking part in this was a religious duty.

Ironically, perhaps, the three prerequisites for Just War all showed strongly the influence of Muslim legal thinking. These being recognised as due authority, just cause and good intentions. In practical reality, of course, the ruling princes of Europe managed to couch their warlike declarations in terms that enabled both sides to claim just cause.

Although the Middle Ages are sometimes seen as a singularly warlike period of European history, they were also characterised by widespread efforts to control or limit warfare. Governments, of course, tried to ensure that they alone could authorise the use of violence. By the later 10th century the power of rulers had declined in many areas, while that of local military aristocracies increased. The result often lead to widespread anarchy and 'private warfare'. This, in turn, prompted movements such as the *Peace of God* which first emerged in the very disturbed conditions of southern France in the 10th and 11th centuries. It was led by the Church, but also supported by the higher aristocracy who similarly had an interest in stability, if not in a restoration of royal authority. Where the *Peace of God* was imposed, the military classes were obliged to swear oaths stating that they would accept the conditions of the *Peace of God*.

The common people, of course, benefited even more from such peace movements; particularly when the Church, often supported by local militias, excommunicated the most troublesome of a region's military class and had their weapons as well as their horses confiscated. The *Peace of God* movement really only tried to suppress small-scale local violence, and to exempt various non-military groups from involvement in such petty warfare.

The more ambitious *Truce of God* movements which arose in the 11th century attempted to limit the times and places where 'private war' was permitted. They also tried to contain such violence within set rules. Further peace movements in the 12th century imposed new forms of oath; not merely to refrain from taking part in unacceptable activity, but to serve in a peace force or contribute the peace tax which was in turn used to pay for such peace forces.

Some rulers were in a position to insist on their own peace movements. The powerful dukes of Normandy, for example, added the originally Scandinavian idea of prohibiting damage to agricultural tools to the rules of their own Norman peace movement. They also banned 'private war' between Wednesday evenings and Monday mornings, and forbade attacks on anyone on his way to or from the

'David and Goliath' in a carved relief; southern French, c.1145. The inside of Goliath's shield is an accurate portrayal of those used at the time, but his scale armour is probably what the sculptor imagined oriental lamellar armour looked like. As such it is a typical example of the kind of mixture of fact and fantasy seen in a great deal of medieval art. (Church of St Gilles at St Gilles du Gard)

duke's court, or injuring pilgrims or merchants, or burning houses or mills. In southern France the powerful Crusader Military Order of the Templars took a leading role as peace-keepers, often being paid through taxes contributed by the local peasantry. Nevertheless, the main peace-keepers still appear to have been the local counts, senior bishops and papal representatives.

Medieval soldiers had their own accepted ways of waging war, other ways being regarded as unacceptable. In fact, the atrocities and sacrilege of medieval warfare were probably exaggerated by clerical chroniclers for their own reasons. Those most closely involved in war, such as the military aristocracy, had their own concept of Good War and Bad War. The former was characterised by restraint and honourable behaviour; the latter by cruelty and inhumanity. Only the rulers, it seemed, willingly accepted the modern concept of 'total war' as a way of demonstrating power and majesty, as well as being a way of terrorising their rivals into submission.

It was clear, however, that the military élite of nobles and *knights* tended to be much more cruel to their social inferiors than to their fellow *knights*, both in battle and while devastating enemy territory. On the other hand, the presence of such 'lower orders' among their own followers could act as a restraint; particularly if these men had kinsfolk among the potential victims. Even so, the increasingly important role played by infantry in 13th and 14th century western European warfare led to considerably greater savagery. Yet this was not usually undertaken by such infantry, but tended to be inflicted upon them by a *knightly* class which rightly knew that its own military and politically dominant position was under growing threat from foot soldiers of non-noble origins.

The question of who was permitted to carry weapons was another one which exercised the minds of rulers, churchmen and lawyers alike. In general, the population of medieval western Europe was far more heavily armed than those of Byzantium or the Muslim world. Even the higher clergy had become involved in warfare by the 10th century and there appear to have been no restrictions on the 'lower orders' carrying weapons before the mid-12th century. Later still, travelling merchants not only continued to carry swords to defend themselves, but were fully capable of using them. By the early 13th century, however, it appears that efforts were being made, at least in some regions, to deny the non-noble or non-military classes permission to bear arms. Laws promulgated by the Emperor Frederick II in southern Italy in 1231 specified very precisely who and who could not carry weapons. Those permitted to do so naturally included *knights*, the sons of *knights*, merchants while travelling on business, and servants of the crown. Even the commanders of fortified places and *sergeants* were, however, forbidden to do so when outside their own garrison areas. Meanwhile foreigners were entirely banned from carrying weapons; even being forbidden to carry a small knife when inside towns or villages.

Each class of society had its own recognised code of conduct; none more so than the military aristocracy with its concept of *chivalry*. This *chivalry* really had its origins in the Church's efforts to promote the idea of the Christian *miles* or *knight* in the 10th century. He, it was hoped, would be a warrior who served the interests of the Church and, as far as possible, live according to Christian principles. In return, the Church now offered the fighting man a recognised role in Christian society. At the same time a clear distinction continued to be drawn between such a *chivalrous knight* whose sword was, theoretically at least, in the service of Christendom, and the professional soldier who fought solely for a livelihood, and who thus remained damned in the eyes of the Church.

Eventually the originally separate moral value systems of the 'noble' and the 'warrior' fused to become that of the '*Christian knight*'. Even during the 12th century, however, these two differing codes, the *mos majorum* of the nobility and the *mos militum* of the *knights*, remained to some extent separate. That of the higher nobility emphasised learning, justice and generosity as well as military skill, while that of the *knights* focused almost entirely upon reckless courage. Meanwhile, the ancient Roman ideal of man-to-man close combat, despising archery, continued to dominate the *knightly* ethos. Such a value system was, in fact, probably reinforced by the fact that archery normally meant being shot at by social inferiors from a relatively safe distance.

In its fully developed form the code of Christian *chivalry* idealised an impracticable abstinence from killing, in addition to an almost as unattainable avoidance of looting, respect for fellow *knights*, mercy to the weak and the loyalty of comrades to one another which cemented all military societies. At the same time, a desire for personal glory and reputation based upon the old pagan Germanic warrior ethos remained central to the *knightly* code. This now crystallised into the concept of the *preudome* or man of *prowess*; emphasising those military skills without which a warrior was of no use to his comrades.

Such a self-imposed code of conduct only worked where fighting men believed in it. In reality warfare, even in the 12th and 13th centuries when the *chivalric* ideal was at its strongest, included at least as many cases of savagery, mutilation and long imprisonment as it did acts of *chivalrous* generosity. Similarly, while Christian *chivalry* may have dominated *knightly* attitudes in France and some of its neighbours, it would be very misleading to think that it was universal throughout Christian western Europe. In fact, it seems to have meant little to the largely non-noble urban militias who gradually rose to prominence from the 12th to 14th centuries. Other older codes also survived elsewhere. In 13th century Italy, for example, much of even the *knightly* class fought according to the ancient rules of *vendetta*; using assassination, ambush and slaughter in a way thought shocking by some of their northern contemporaries.

Other things, however, remained largely consistent. The breaking of oaths was generally frowned upon, and a man was normally expected to fight on behalf of his legitimate lord, even when the latter was acting wrongfully. Not until the later 13th and 14th centuries did it start to be regarded as wrong, for example, to defend a lesser lord's castle against one's lawful king. But at the same time the gradual collapse of the *chivalric* ideal during the 14th century undoubtedly worried both moralists and military thinkers very deeply.

VICTORS AND VANQUISHED

The Distribution of Booty

Generally speaking, the earlier the historical period, the more important was booty. In some areas warfare was, in fact, one of the most significant means by which precious metals and valuable artefacts were exchanged. This could involve complex but generally accepted arrangements. For example, among the pre-Christian Germanic tribes a division of spoils after victory in battle was done within a roped-off area with the army gathered around to serve as witnesses that everything was carried out fairly. Warfare had to remain profitable in basically non-commercial economies such as those of the early medieval Germanic, Norse and Celtic peoples. Here ancient rules for the sharing of plunder survived little changed by Christian or, in southern Europe, Muslim legal influence. Booty basically paid the cost of war; defeat often spelling economic as well as political disaster for a ruler. Among the earliest surviving such rules are those of the Celtic Welsh king Hywal Dda. They date from the 10th century, but might reflect longer established practice. Here the king received a third; the rest being divided between the soldiers. The leader of the king's war-band actually got a double-share, in addition to a further third of the king's third.

Battlefield booty remained a vital source of income even for an 11th century *knight*, helping him to maintain his increasingly expensive war-gear and horses. Money, precious metals, cattle, other property, arms, armour and prisoners formed the basic booty of Anglo-Scottish border warfare well into the 13th century. Here, highly specialised laws were drawn up to deal with such things as loot and the exchanging or ransoming of prisoners. In fact, such laws still had much in common with those of the earlier medieval centuries. On the English side of the border, prisoners normally went to the lord; horses and military equipment to his men. Booty was even more important to the much poorer Scots, since most of their troops were virtually unpaid. Scotland was also so lacking in metals that anything of iron tended to be taken by Scots raiders.

Even in the highly developed money economy of 13th century Italy, some mercenary contracts stipulated that hired troops retain their booty which would otherwise, apparently, have gone to their employer. Little had changed by the 14th century when the drying up of bat-

tlefield booty and ransoms could cause English knights to object vociferously to any temporary outbreak of peace during the Hundred Years War with France. The English troops' lust for loot was such that special regulations had been introduced to stop men brawling over their prisoners. Not surprisingly, the king kept the most important captured castles, land and enemy personnel. The *contracts* and sub-contracts of the *indenture* system dealt with most of the rest. Usually the senior party took one-third, an ordinary soldier paying a third of his own 'winnings' to his officer, and so on up the chain of command. In naval warfare, perhaps because it was even more expensive, the king normally took half of anything won by a royal ship while the rest was divided between captain and crew; a naval commander normally ending up with one-tenth of the total booty.

Prisoners, Enslavement and the Treatment of Non-Combatants

Although the basic principles governing the division of spoils remained largely unchanged throughout the Middle Ages, the treatment of prisoners changed radically under Christian influence. Yet this did not mean that slaughter, mutilation and enslavement ceased altogether.

In early Christian times, the pagan Germanic tradition of killing all prisoners, including women and children, or of keeping only those of pre-puberty age as slaves, gradually died out. Nevertheless, widespread and indiscriminate massacres as well as enslavement continued to characterise warfare in early medieval western Europe. The influence of the Church only gradually imposed some restraint, while the impact of Roman Law remained minimal. Even in religious terms it was the vengeful principles of the Old Testament rather than the forgiving one of the New Testament which dominated military attitudes throughout the medieval period. This was particularly true when wars involved religion. For example, Charlemagne terrorised his Avar foes by widespread massacres and eventually slaughtered the entire population of the Avar capital.

The Huns' reputation for 'enslaving' captives was, however, not strictly justified. For a start, nomadic society had little use for slaves and as a result those supposedly 'enslaved' by the Huns were actually sold back to their families as soon as possible. Elsewhere in Europe, the enslavement of defeated enemies soon died out, though it did continue where captured pagans or Muslims were concerned. Nevertheless, to some extent the enslavement of fellow Christians persisted in certain fringe areas; most notably in Ireland as late as the 12th century. On the other hand most European naval raids across the 8th and 9th century Mediterranean were specifically intended to seize Muslim slaves. The enslavement of Muslims continued throughout the Middle Ages and was sometimes used as a cover for even less acceptable behaviour. In the mid-13th century, for example, the Pope discovered that some Italian merchant ships were transporting captive Greek, Bul-

garian, Ruthenian and Vlach Christians into slavery, while pretending that these victims were actually Muslim prisoners of war from the Crusader States.

The mutilation of prisoners similarly continued for several centuries; one 9th century Bulgarian ruler slitting the noses of his Byzantine prisoners before sending them home. The Byzantine Emperor replied to this by blinding the great majority of his Bulgarian captives; leaving a handful of one-eyed men to lead the victims back to Bulgaria. Once again such mutilation persisted longer in fringe areas like Ireland than elsewhere, though even in 12th century southern France there were references to captured *sergeants* and militia-men having a hand or foot cut off, while captive *knights* had their ears or noses slit.

'Saint Benedict frees a prisoner', in a manuscript from Monte Cassino; Italo-Norman, c.1070. The freeing of prisoners formed part of the early chivalric ideal of knighthood, and was seen as one aspect of the true knight's concern for the weak and oppressed. The way in which the Saint, shown here dressed as a knight 'off duty', carries his shield on a guige around his neck is also interesting, as is the detailed representation of his early form of war saddle. It has a high cantle and raised pommel; this still being very similar to the Middle Eastern forms of saddle upon which the European war-saddle was based. Only the rider's straight leg indicates a newly developing western European riding technique. (MS. Lat. 1202, f.2r, Biblioteca Apostolica Vaticana, Rome; photograph, Biblioteca Vaticana)

The first real evidence of changing attitudes towards the victims of war was seen in late 10th century France where, for example, punishment for rebellion against the crown was sometimes inflicted only upon the leader and not upon his men. They, in turn, could be pardoned on the grounds that they were simply being loyal to their *feudal* lord. From then on many, though by no means all, examples of the barbarous treatment of prisoners stemmed from a ruler's attempt to terrorise his enemies into submission. By the 12th century even this was regarded as both dishonourable and a waste of potentially valuable ransoms. For example, Christian western Europe began adopting the Islamic practice of offering generous surrender terms to the garrisons of fortified places, while also threatening that if such places were stormed their defenders lost all rights to generous treatment. Even so, surren-

Left: Muslim prisoners in chains', carved column-base; southern French, 12th century. The way in which fellow-Christian and non-Christian prisoners of war were treated differed considerably. From the 11th to 14th centuries Muslims were invariably enslaved, or were simply slaughtered out of hand. (Old Cathedral, Oloron Sainte Marie)

Opposite page: 'Crusaders throwing Turkish heads into Nicea', in the Histoire d'Outremer, from Paris; French, 1229. Throwing dead animals, corpses and assorted garbage into an enemy fortification was a means of spreading disease. Throwing the heads of dead enemy soldiers was, however, a way of undermining enemy morale through terrorism. Here a very early form of counterweight trebuchet is being used for this purpose; the counterweight apparently consisting of a large piece of timber rather than a container of earth, sand or rocks. (MS. Fr. 2630, f.22v, Bibliothèque Nationale, Paris; photograph Bibliothèque Nationale)

der terms could still be very harsh, ranging from exile to the loss of property and the public humiliation of leading prisoners.

With the rise of the *chivalric* code in the 12th and 13th centuries there seems to have been an increasing difference in the ways in which prisoners of various social ranks were treated. The *knightly* class preferred to take fellow *knights* prisoner rather than to kill them; both to win a ransom, to avoid a blood-feud between families, and as a consequence of their strong sense of class-comradeship. By the 13th century *chivalric* conventions even inhibited the victor from asking too high a ransom; so as not to financially embarrass his captive. Nevertheless, enormous sums could still be demanded for high-ranking prisoners.

In complete contrast to such gentlemanly behaviour, the aristocratic military élite often acted with appalling brutality towards the common soldiery of non-noble birth. In return, the latter could act with similar savagery towards enemy *knights*. By the 14th century it seems to have been normal to slaughter those common soldiers not worth a ransom; particularly as their bodies could then be despoiled for such few valuables they might possess. All wounded and dying non-ransomable enemy tended to suffer the same fate.

INTELLIGENCE AND ESPIONAGE

Techniques of information gathering and espionage never reached the same sophistication in medieval western Europe as they did in the neighbouring civilisations of Byzantium and Islam. In fact, there seem to have been few if any organised systems for such purposes until near the end of the period under consideration.

Embassies had played a vital role, both as sources of information and as a means of planting information, in relations between the Roman and Sassanian Persian Empires. Such skills almost certainly did not die out after the fall of Rome, but it does seem that they played a far less important role than previously. Until the 10th century, the sending of a recognisable embassy was probably also largely limited to the more advanced centres of medieval European civilisation such as the Carolingian Empire, the small but sophisticated states of Italy, the kingdom of France and the Ottonian Empire centred upon Germany. By the late 13th and 14th centuries, however, the development of paid professional bureaucracies enabled centralised government to maintain fully fledged intelligence-gathering establishments.

One of the best documented, and perhaps also one of the most effective, was that of 14th century England. The serious threat of French naval raids clearly prompted the need for advance warnings. It was the government's responsibility both to gather and to co-ordinate such information. It was also the government's task to carry out counter-espionage in English ports and those under English control within France. In fact, the English crown's French possessions were a major source of military and naval intelligence; this coming from spies and informers. The French, of course, were doing the same, while both countries recognised the important information-gathering role of official messengers shuttling between the English and French royal courts. Such men were not really spies, of course.

The real spies in English pay were mostly Frenchmen and other foreigners, rather than Englishmen. Merchants were also paid to serve as spies, since they travelled far more than most other people. Other agents played a major role as *provocateurs*; spreading false information and rumours to confuse the enemy. By the late 14th century a very expensive, but also quite effective, English spy network was operating out of English-held Calais. So much so that spy-scares and acts of sudden violence against foreigners were frequent in France. They also flared up in England, though apparently more rarely.

In addition to these sorts of activities, the French and Scots engaged in economic sabotage by trying to flood the kingdom of England with inferior bullion coinage. This threat became a serious matter for the English government in the 13th century and became a major preoccupation in the 14th century. Fear of spies, agents and saboteurs led to a close watch being kept on all foreigners in England; particularly clergymen and, above all, members of the preaching orders of friars. The feeling stirred up against foreign friars was, in fact, reflected in the popular literature and folk-tales of the time. Various laws were passed to deal with these problems; King Edward III issuing a decree which stated that inn-keepers must search foreign guests and make official reports on them and their activities. High-ranking foreign visitors, and sometimes lesser people as well, would be interrogated by the Royal Council of the kingdom.

Those spies who were captured were imprisoned and also interrogated; though there is perhaps surprisingly little evidence that they were harshly punished if found guilty. Punishments appear to have been quite lenient and many such spies seem to have been pardoned; perhaps under an accepted code of practice which ensured that captured English spies were similarly well treated. Leniency towards spies was also a feature of medieval Islamic, and perhaps also Byzantine, practice. In fact the idea that spies should almost inevitably be executed was a more barbaric modern concept.

Evidence for the skilful use of bribery within an enemy's ranks is found much earlier than that for governmental intelligence-gathering organisations. Several successful commanders such as Duke William the Conqueror of Normandy were famous for their ability to foment treachery inside enemy garrisons. Three centuries later the towns of war-torn southern France, and probably those of most other parts of western Europe as well, each had its small localised intelligence system. The town governor or council would send out its own *espias*, spies, and *messatges*, messengers, to gather information and communicate secretly with their allies farther afield. By the late 14th century the Burgundians had earned a singular reputation for their effective use of propaganda and gold, since the Duchy of Burgundy was already one of the richest parts of Europe. Using such unorthodox, and indeed unchivalric weapons, they often undermined enemy morale. This included forged letters to sow dissension, and pretended pilgrims acting as spies and spreading false information.

TRAINING

The idea that the medieval fighting man was merely an individual seeking personal glory or loot with little or no sense of co-operation with his comrades is nonsense. Medieval military training clearly involved individual skills, operating as a unit in support of colleagues, and co-operation between such units. Naturally, however, sophisticated forms of unit training and co-operation were more characteristic of culturally and politically advanced regions, and also of later centuries. The great majority of detailed surviving evidence similarly deals with cavalry rather than infantry; for the obvious reason that cavalry formed a dominant élite within most western European armies throughout the greater part of the Middle Ages.

It is generally agreed that the parade and training skills of the late Roman army had declined by the early 5th century. On the other hand, several of those Germanic peoples who carved out their kingdoms in what had been the western half of the Roman Empire, still based their own training on that of their Roman predecessors. This was particularly apparent when it came to cavalry. The Ostrogoths and Visigoths were both said to have engaged in cav- alry training 'games', while such exercises were similarly re-introduced by the Franks who had little or no tradition of horsemanship themselves. This process was, in fact, seen under both Charlemagne and his successors. Never- theless, it probably only applied to a palace-based military élite; other men learning their military skills through hunting and direct experience of battle. Nevertheless, children were described as playing with toy weapons in the courtyards of noble households.

Learning to endure hard living and, above all, learning to ride were recognised as essential skills for the military élite; it being said that if a boy had not been trained as a horseman before the age of puberty he was only fit for the Church. Other military training involved the use of swords, spears, javelins and archery.

The *quintaine*, or something like it, had been known since Roman times. It consisted of a wooden post with a revolving arm having a target-shield at one end and a bag of sand at the other. This was for individual cavalry train- ing with a spear. On the other hand, most information concerning Carolingian military training involved unit exercises with spears or javelins; just like those of the later Roman armies. Indeed these military exercises were some- times described as 'pagan games' during the 9th century. They clearly emphasised unit cohesion and manoeuvring by groups, rather than merely individual combat skills. As such they had more in common with cavalry training in medieval Byzantine and Islamic societies, than with later medieval western European *tournaments*.

In fact, these *cursores* or *causa exercitii* exercises are high- ly likely to have been more or less directly influenced by the Muslim and Byzantine worlds, than by a distant Roman heritage. For example, a large force of horsemen would charge at another then wheel aside; slinging their shields over their backs to protect themselves as they retreated. The opposing force would then do the same; each side repeating the manoeuvre a number of times.

In contrast to such cavalry training, a completely differ- ent tradition of infantry training evolved in early medieval Scandinavia. The huge fortified bases such as Trelleborg in Denmark may, in fact, have been training centres as much as they were barracks. The Viking *worod* was just such a form of psychological, as well as skill training, which involved considerably more than the giving and par- rying of blows with sword and shield. Here a fully trained swordsman would strike at the foreheads of young trainees; presumably without actually striking them unless they were helmeted. Those who flinched were expelled as unsuitable military material.

More is known in detail about military training in the later medieval centuries. The exercises involved similarly changed; largely as a result of the adoption of the *couched* lance by cavalry and the crossbow by infantry. From the 11th century onwards the training of a young member of the aristocratic or *knightly* military élite really started at the age of twelve, and thereafter it took up most of an indi-

vidual's time. Boys were trained in age peer-groups, learn- ing to look after horses as well as to ride. In addition they were taught the use of a variety of weapons, as well as indulging in wrestling and weight lifting to make them- selves stronger. These young trainees also learned how to plunder an enemy and, by hunting animals, how to use terrain, available cover, to scout and select lines of advance.

Learning to ride in a close-packed *conrois* group of horsemen similarly encouraged a strong sense of group identity or team spirit, in addition to mutual loyalty. These were, of course, essential in the conditions of medieval warfare. Initial training of this kind was normal- ly completed by the age of twenty-two, but this did not mean that a young *squire* or *arminger* was now automati- cally *dubbed* a *knight*. During the 12th century *dubbing* cer- emonies tended to involve an entire group and they were often associated with preparations for a major military campaign. The groups who trained and were sometimes *dubbed* together generally seem to have remained togeth- er as *bachelors* or young warriors who had yet to win or inherit estates of their own. At least this appears to have been the case for several years. On the other hand, young newly qualified members of the military élite might also be encouraged to travel to other courts; even in different countries, in order to serve a variety of lords and thus gain wider experience.

By the 13th century the education of aspiring *knights* also included several other less obviously military skills. From the age of five a boy served his elders, was given reli- gious instruction and helped look after the horses. At seven he was taken away from the company of women and became a *page* while at the same time learning to ride, hunt and use small weapons. At twelve he might leave his father's house for a greater lord's castle where, at the age of fourteen, he could be put in charge of the hunting dogs. At twenty he might become responsible for other aspects of the lord's hunting establishment. A little later the young man could reach the rank of *squire* and begin to travel so as to broaden his experience of the world. But whether he subsequently became a full *knight* depended on luck, wealth, good connections and a variety of other circumstances.

Tournaments as a form of *knightly* entertainment as well as a means of cavalry training, first appeared in 11th century France. This early *hastiludia* or 'lance play' still involved units rather than individuals; squads of five to ten horse- men charging one another with *couched* lances and then fighting in the rough and tumble of a 'friendly' though still highly dangerous *mêlée*. The purpose of such an early form of *tournament* exercise was, like the older exercises of the Roman and Carolingian periods, still to emphasise team- work. By the 12th century such *mêlées* could involve entire *conrois* cavalry squadrons, sometimes even with supporting infantry, in what were in effect mock battles.

Individual *jousting* by two horsemen may have originat- ed as an unofficial pastime before the proper *hastiludia* began. It was less dangerous and perhaps more interesting for onlookers, and had clearly evolved into a form of spectator sport by the late 12th and 13th centuries. Nevertheless, such *jousting* was dangerous and many men were killed or seriously injured, since an opponent's neck, just above his shield, was the primary target for the other man's *couched* lance. Each lance-armed man cantered rather than galloped down one side of a separating fence called a *bohorde*; the participants passed each other on their left sides, shield to shield. Not until the 13th century do blunted weapons seem to have been introduced.

The *tournament* came to England with the Normans, though efforts were subsequently made in the mid-12th century to ban them. Perhaps this was because they sometimes led to disturbances and could encourage family feuds since casualties remained remarkably high. The *tournament* also reached Hungary in the late 12th century; Poland and Sweden in the mid-14th century. It had already reached Italy, perhaps from Germany, in the mid-12th century. There it was enthusiastically adopted despite the fact that the *chivalric* culture and code which the *tournament* reflected never, itself, really took root in Italy. A different form of jousting 'in the Catalan style', which probably reflected the North African light cavalry tactics *à la jinete* which were coming to characterise Spanish warfare, was also adopted in Sicily during the 14th century. Polo, which had originated in India many centuries earlier, similarly reached western Europe from the Muslim world and Byzantium in the 13th century. It was, in fact, known in France as *chicane*, a term which stemmed from polo's Turco-Persian name of *chaugān*.

Infantry training was not taken as seriously in medieval western Europe as it was in the Muslim and Byzantine regions. With few exceptions, it consisted of little more than individual weapons training; above all in archery. There is some evidence for occasional military reviews of the infantry élite of the late Anglo-Saxon army being held in the 11th century. A century later, there is a very rare reference to Anglo-Norman infantry being trained to withstand a cavalry charge. Meanwhile, the remarkable effectiveness of northern Italian militia infantry at about the same period presupposes some degree of co-operative training. Warlike 'games' also formed part of various festivities in 12th century Venice. These involved infantry *mêlées* between the eastern and western *sestieri* quarters of the city, often fighting with quarterstaves on the many wooden bridges of the city. This would probably have involved some of the same skills as would be needed during naval boarding actions. Sword and buckler fighting remained a popular spectator sport, particularly in urban areas, well into the 14th century. At a more élite level, a certain Del Serpente of Milan had written a book *On the Art of Fencing* in 1295; perhaps the first such work on the gentlemanly duel to appear in Europe.

Archery was altogether more serious, or at least more businesslike, with 13th century militia crossbowmen training themselves in return for tax exemptions. They also took part in regular competitions for substantial prizes. The same sort of official competitions for both hand-bow archers and crossbowmen were organised on Holy Days and Sundays by the city councils of Dalmatia, Italy and various parts of the Holy Roman Empire. In at least some of these competitions the shooters stood in a wooden booth, their targets being circular butts; perhaps similar to those known as *bersauts* in 13th century France. Training with the longbow was organised in a similar manner in England where the normal target range was 220 yards (200 metres).

While ordinary soldiers received a greater or lesser amount of military training, aristocratic military leaders gained their skill almost entirely through practical experience, usually in the company of elder members of their own family. Nevertheless, ancient classical works on military theory were known, and were copied by scholars for various rulers. Knowledge of the ancient Greek Aelian seems to have been virtually unknown outside Byzantium, the Muslim world and perhaps southern Italy. But the late Roman tactician and theorist Vegetius was widely respected.

Whether any of Vegetius' ideas were put into practice remains a matter of debate, however. The encyclopaedist Hrabanus Maurus wrote an updated extract of Vegetatius for the Carolingian Emperor Lothar II in the 9th century, but most other medieval versions of this book made little real effort to interpret it in the light of current conditions. One partial exception was Jean de Meun's *L'Art de Chevalerie* written in 1284; this being a very free updating of the late Roman *De Re Militari*.

A sudden outburst of new military writing in the 14th century almost certainly resulted from, and to some extent also reflected, the increasing use of professional mercenary armies. These new works included both practical and theoretical treatises for upper and middle ranking leaders, though not apparently for those lower down the military hierarchy. The latter, of course, were still largely illiterate and so purely practical books of military instructions, such as those being written in 14th century Egypt and Syria, would have found very little readership.

THE SINEWS OF WAR

Taxation and Pay

Taxation, as an aspect of medieval economic and social history, is a huge subject in its own right, and it can only be touched upon very superficially here. It also differed according to period, place and culture. Furthermore, the greatest impact that taxation had upon military organisation came with the increasing use of paid mercenary troops in the 13th and 14th centuries. Prior to that, military taxes tended to be for specific and rather restricted purposes; such as those to pay for Crusading expeditions or the special *tallage* imposed in 12th and 13th century France for the repair and building of fortifications.

'Roland slays Faragut', relief carving; northern Italian, c.1138. Some poetic licence must be allowed for this representation of the Christian hero Roland virtually cutting the villain Faragut in half, through his shield and mail hauberk, with a single mighty sword-blow. Nevertheless, archaeological and other evidence shows that medieval weapons could inflict the most appalling injuries. (Façade of the Church of San Zeno, Verona)

In a more highly developed money economy, like that of 13th century Florence, all the citizens might be taxed before a particular campaign; only the *knights* being exempted because they provided their own very expensive arms, armour and horses. The money thus raised was used to hire mercenaries. In other places, such as France, the crown's demands for money could be camouflaged as enforced 'loans' from the higher aristocracy; loans which were not repaid. The *indenture* system of military recruitment was expensive for both France and England, though the huge cost of the Hundred Years War imposed particular burdens upon France where it consequently led to great increases in taxation.

Direct military pay, rather than feudal rewards in cash instead of land, presupposed the existence of professional or at least temporarily mercenary troops. It also required sufficiently developed money economies to pay such soldiers. During the last decades of the Roman Empire in western Europe, the men were still largely paid in cash. In some instances they were even given additional sums of money to purchase their own clothing. This again indicated that a highly developed payment system was not necessarily synonymous with a comparably highly structured system of military uniforms.

Paid mercenaries continued to exist, to a small extent, throughout much of the early medieval period, but it is not until the 13th century that sufficient evidence survives to shed a useful light on payment structures. In France, by the early 13th century, mercenary *knights* were being paid twice as much as mounted *sergeants*; mounted crossbowmen slightly more than these mounted *sergeants*; infantry crossbowmen and skilled miners much less while other infantry received less again. Some of these sums seem small, but in reality military service was relatively well paid.

A member of even an ordinary infantry levy still got paid twice or three times the amount he would obtain as an ordinary labourer or farm-hand in peace-time. Marines serving aboard some 13th century merchant ships, interestingly enough, were given very little money and food since they were also expected to supplement this income by doing some small-scale trading on their own behalf. Other evidence shows that sailors aboard most 14th cen- tury Mediterranean warships got only a third of the pay of a crossbow-armed marine. On land such crossbowmen would be paid rather more than the shield-bearing *pavesari* with who they served as a team.

The pay of professional military leaders was, of course, considerably higher. Even so the commander of a castle in the service of the Italian city of Pisa might only get three times that of his men; the commander of an important

Venetian fortified town receiving three times that of the man in charge of a small Venetian castle during the 14th century.

Feeding an Army

Relatively little study has been made of the feeding of war-horses in medieval western Europe, at least when compared to the same question in Asiatic and Islamic armies.

'The Israelites subdue the Moabites', in the Maciejowski Bible; French, c.1250. Unlike the great majority of later European artists, at least until Goya in the early 19th century, medieval artists were prepared to show the horrors of war in all their brutality. To some extent they, like their knightly patrons, even seemed to glorify in the savagery of close-combat between heavily armed men. (M. 638, f.12r, The Pierpont Morgan Library, New York)

Nevertheless, it is clear that armies that relied on stall-fed mounts faced very different problems from those, usually of recent nomadic origin, whose horses depended upon available grazing. The Avars of late 6th century central and south-eastern Europe were, for example, regarded as vulnerable to attack in winter because that was when their large herds of grazing war-horses were in poorest condition.

Again, feeding the men in a medieval western European army posed different problems. The reputation of western soldiers for dirt and drunkenness was justified enough; nevertheless, the widespread emphasis on wine did have a good reason. It was simply that the quality of available drinking water was so low, and sanitation so lacking, that without wine most medieval Europe armies would have collapsed as a result of disease, even faster than they so often did. Islamic armies could exist without wine, not merely because alcohol was forbidden to Muslims, but also because their standards of hygiene were hugely superior. The English armies operating in early 13th century Wales, for example, depended on a remarkably sophisticated commissariat and supply network which not only brought food from England, but shipped in large volumes of wine from the English-ruled provinces of Anjou and Gascony in France; this arriving via Bristol. The commissariats of medieval armies were far more effective than popularly imagined, being capable of sustaining large isolated garrisons such as that of English-held Calais in the 14th century, all of whose supplies of wood, wine and weaponry had to come from England by sea.

MEDICAL SERVICES

Medical services were far less developed in medieval western Europe than in some neighbouring civilisations such as Byzantium and, above all, the Muslim world. The superiority of the latter was even reflected in 12th and 13th century French *chansons de geste*. Here the Saracens were frequently portrayed, not only as having greater concern for their wounded but also possessing greater skill in treating battle injuries. For most of the medieval period there were, in fact, virtually no surgeons or doctors in most western armies. Instead unskilled priests tended the wounded and inevitably remained better qualified to offer the last rites than to save a man's life. Priests performed this function in Charlemagne's army and were still doing so even in

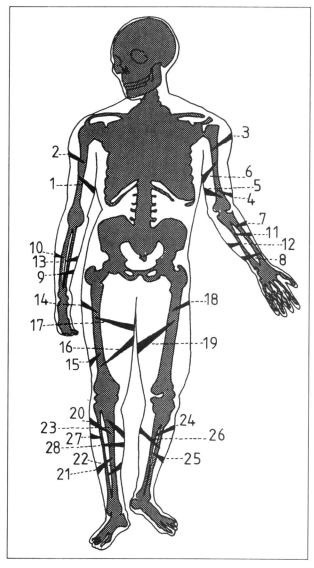

Left: Analysis of wounds to the limb-bones of skeletons excavated from mass graves of the battle of Visby, 1361; with percentages of the total injuries to limb-bones (after Ingelmark)

1–6. *Cuts to the humerus – 6.71% of total*
1. *Ventral cut on the humerus*
2. *Dorsal cut on the humerus*
3. *Lateral cut on the humerus from above*
4. *Lateral cut on the humerus from below*
5. *Medial cut on the humerus from above*
6. *Medial cut on the humerus from below*

7–10. *Cuts to the radius – 3.35% of the total*
7. *Lateral cut on the radius*
8. *Medial cut on the radius*
9. *Ventral cut on the radius*
10. *Dorsal cut on the radius*

11–13. *Cuts to the ulna – 4.88% of the total*
11. *Lateral cut on the ulna*
12. *Medial cut on the ulna*
13. *Ventral cut on the ulna*

14–19. *Cuts to the femur – 12.2% of the total*
14. *Lateral cut on the femur from above*
15. *Lateral cut on the femur from below*
16. *Medial cut on the femur from above*
17. *Medial cut on the femur from below*
18. *Ventral cut on the femur*
19. *Dorsal cut on the femur*

20–26. *Cuts to the tibia – 56.4% of the total*
20. *Lateral cut on the tibia from above*
21. *Lateral cut on the tibia from below*
22. *Medial cut on the tibia from above*
23. *Medial cut on the tibia from below*
24. *Ventral cut on the tibia from above*
25. *Ventral cut on the tibia from below*
26. *Dorsal cut on the tibia*

27–28. *Cuts to the fibula – 16.46% of the total*
27. *Lateral cut on the fibula*
28. *Medial cut on the fibula*

detailed study of these skeletons was made in the 1930s. But even this could only shed light on wounds which struck bone, not those which killed through injuries to soft tissue alone. Nevertheless this study indicated that most bone-damaging injuries were inflicted with sword or axe which involved 456 skeletons, and arrows or spears which involved 126 skeletons. Damage by crushing weapons, however, was hard to distinguish from the effects of centuries of pressure from the surrounding earth upon the cadavers. A much larger number of skeletons, however, showed no bone injuries; clearly indicating death by flesh wounds alone. Finally the degree of damage inflicted in some cases showed the appalling power of medieval weapons upon the body of a victim.

MORALE

Religion

Religion, rather than ethnic origin or political allegiance, was the primary form of individual identity throughout the Middle Ages. Yet religion did not always play as important a role as might have been expected in motivating men to war, nor in maintaining their morale during battle.

12th century Italy, perhaps the most civilised part of western Europe outside Islamic Spain. They would take up their positions in and around a city militia's *carroccio* banner cart where, however, the most sophisticated and rich urban armies may also have had a handful of more skilled surgeons. The images of primitive western military medicine provided by Arabic chronicles of the Crusades is terrifying, though even here the European's use of burnt lead or lead oxide as an antiseptic for superficial wounds was recognised as being quite effective.

The kinds of injuries inflicted in medieval warfare were essentially the same as those recorded in documents from other parts of the world. The mass graves at Visby, on the Swedish island of Gotland, contained the dead of a battle which took place in 1361. A remarkably

'Saint Michael', in a manuscript from Mont St Michel; Norman-French, 980–1000. Several Christian figures were adopted as patrons by the professional military élite of medieval western Christendom. In addition to canonised martyrs who had, in fact, been soldiers in the pagan Roman army, others were reinterpreted in a medieval military mould. These included the archangel Saint Michael, who was regarded as Captain of the Heavenly Host. (MS. 50, Bibliothèque Municipale, Avranches)

'Saint George', lead pilgrim-badge from the river Seine; French, late 13th–early 14th centuries. Pilgrimage formed a central part of medieval western Christianity, and knights, being members of the social and military élite, were better placed to undertake such travels than most other people. Badges appear to have been purchased almost as souvenirs of the journey, and as proof of having reached their destination. It is not known where this lead badge was made, since Saint George was the patron of many religious shrines; but it could even have come from Lydda in Palestine where he was believed to have been buried. (Musée de la Cité, Rouen)

Even so, religious beliefs fundamentally influenced attitudes to warfare and to death in combat.

This, perhaps, was even more true of non-Christian groups in the early medieval period. The nomadic Alans, for example, are said to have had no respect for age, at least where men were concerned, as a man was expected to die in battle. Religion similarly played a totemic role, its symbols being used to protect weapons and thus, by extension, those who wielded them. The feather-like decorations on Hun swords may have been connected with the protective powers of the mythical Varanga bird, an incarnation of Verethraghna, the God of Victory in Persian Zoroastrian mythology. The so-called *Life-Stones* attached to the hilts or scabbards of pre-Christian Germanic swords, which are also mentioned in Norse sagas, are understood to have had the same function. So, of course, had the crosses, abbreviated Biblical quotations and other religious symbols on later Christian weaponry. The blessing of swords was similarly originally done to protect the weapons from the devil or evil eye, rather than being connected with any knightly *dubbing* ceremonies.

Christianity played a vital role in maintaining the morale of Charlemagne's armies when fighting pagan or Muslim foes. Yet even this was a rather temporary phenomenon connected with the Carolingian dynasty's attempts to harness the Church for its own political and cultural ambitions. Under Charlemagne himself priests sang Gradual Psalms for the fallen and gave the Last Rites to the dying, while the Church provided a moral framework and a system of discipline.

By the 9th and 10th centuries, however, the wars between Christians and Muslims in Italy and southern France were clearly not seen as religious struggles or early forms of Crusade; except perhaps by the Church hierarchy in Rome. Muslim troops were, in fact, invited in as allies in local quarrels. Meanwhile, many Christians became Muslim, and vice versa. Religion also played a very minor part in the internal warfare of Christian Ireland before the Norse-Viking invasions. Here the primary military motivation was clearly an individual desire for a warlike reputation, for loyalty or for vengeance; just as had been the case in pre-Christian times. Even though several late Anglo-Saxon rulers had special swords made for their own coronations, these weapons were still more closely associated with inherited 'family luck' and blood-ties, images of manhood, or that state of crazed uncaring

'Saint James of Compostella', statue showing the scallop shells associated with pilgrimage to Santiago di Compostella in north-western Spain; French, 13th century. The Saint has a bag or scrip hanging from the shoulder belt; this also being characteristic of medieval travellers and pilgrims. The sword, carried as a symbol of the endless war against the Muslims in the Iberian peninsula, has its buckled sword-belt wrapped around the scabbard. (Carving on the west front of Amiens Cathedral)

courage known as 'battle fury'. They were also closely connected with various funeral rites. All of these had their roots in the pagan Germanic past rather than in Christianity. They also persisted in a quasi-Christian form into the ethic of later medieval *chivalry*.

From the 11th to 13th centuries, the Church played a far more important role in warfare, stimulating many conflicts while at the same time attempting to channel the warlike energies of the military élite into directions which suited its own interests. For example, the first records of the Pope giving religious *indulgences* to soldiers who fell fighting his enemies came from mid-11th century Italy. At about the same time the Church also became involved in ceremonies connected with the *dubbing* of knights, and thereafter Christianity encouraged the concept of *chivalry* as part of its own efforts to control the *knightly* class.

By the 12th century it was widely believed that, as was said, 'the hermit in his cell, the monk in his cloister, and the *knight* in his lord's chamber' all served in the wider Christian struggle against evil. *Knighthood* now took on a quasi-religious aspect, particularly under the influence of the Crusades and the Crusading Military Orders. Saint Maurice came to be regarded as the patron saint of *knights*, while the warlike Norman military élite venerated the sword-wielding archangels Saints Michael and Gabriel who were seen as leaders of heaven's angelic guard. Other peoples adopted different warrior saints. Christian martyrs who had originally been Roman soldiers proved particularly popular. Saint George was adopted as the dragon-slaying patron of several countries, including England, while Saint Demetrius was popular in the Balkans. Archers and the crossbow 'shooting guilds' or clubs which sprang up across the German Empire in the 13th century took Saints Sebastian and Mauritius as their religious patrons.

The potential clash between duty to a secular lord who was involved in an 'evil enterprise', and the instructions of the Church, was recognised as early as the 12th century; opinion generally coming down in favour of a *knight* remaining loyal to his lord while still attempting to do what was right 'as much as possible'. As yet the complications implicit in the concept of *courtly love* hardly applied since women were still all but excluded from the ideals of *knighthood*. *Courtly love*, in which a *knight* or *squire* was duty bound to honour and pursue the fair sex in a stylised yet still very real manner, developed separately under the influence of Arab-Islamic concepts of romantic love; only being integrated into the ideals of *chivalry* during the 13th and 14th centuries.

By the 14th century, however, the role of religion in motivation and morale had already changed considerably. The loyalties of the military élite were increasingly focused upon the secular state, or at least upon a secular leader, rather than the Church. The concept of nationality was growing ever stronger; particularly in England and France where the first real 'national' armies had appeared. These still made great use of sanctified religious banners and large religious services which were conducted before a battle began. But they tended to revere 'national' saints and incarnations of the Virgin Mary as Our Lady of this or that increasingly 'national' shrine. The names of these religious figures were similarly also used in recognised 'national' battle cries. At the same time certain great cathedral churches were adopted as 'national' shrines. On a more local level, *knights* who came through some particularly hazardous fight often donated a piece of armour to their local parish church in gratitude for their survival. Some of the finest and earliest pieces of medieval weaponry that still exist, do so as a direct result of this practice.

Literature and Literacy

Secular literature was among the most important vehicles whereby the ideals of the later medieval military class were passed on from one generation to the next. In pre-literate early medieval societies, such as that of the pagan Germans and Scandinavians, the great *sagas* fulfilled this function; being recited at gatherings of the ruling élite and their military supporters. Much the same was true of the Celtic regions of Ireland and the British Isles where, however, stories rooted in ancient legends were given a superficial Christian gloss. Meanwhile other epics, such as the Arthurian Cycle and various Welsh tales of the great struggle against Anglo-Saxon invaders, continued to reflect the ideals of a heroic past. These military and social attitudes, emphasising personal glory rather than the *chivalric* ideals of mercy and protection of the weak or poor, persisted until the 14th century when Welsh literature was finally drawn into the mainstream of European culture.

By then the military epics of western Europe had long been dominated by the originally French style of *chanson de geste*, or Song of Deeds. Though still reflecting many earlier warrior ideals, these *chansons de geste* were the primary vehicle through which the ideals of *chivalry* spread across western Europe. They first appeared in Latin in 11th century France; though they were very soon being written and sung in the vernacular tongues of both northern and southern France. Such *chansons de geste* were sometimes apparently even chanted by *cantators* or singers who rode ahead of an army into battle. The greatest period of flowering for this distinctive form of medieval secular literature was the 12th and early 13th centuries.

One of the earliest *chansons de geste* was the *Song of Roland* which has been described as an epic celebration of the newly adopted *couched* lance technique of warfare. Through these *chansons de geste* France, above all its capital city of Paris, maintained its position as the centre of *chivalric* culture throughout the 12th and 13th centuries. Other regions, particularly those of France, also produced many fine *chansons de geste*, including the Champagne area in the north-east and English-ruled Gascony in the south-west. A whole cycle of such epics revolved around the First Crusade, while others reflected the changing attitudes seen at the time of later Crusades. It is interesting to note that in most such verse-tales of the wars between Christianity and Islam, the *knightly* class saw their Saracen foes virtually as mirror images of themselves; equally brave, loyal and skilled, similarly motivated but nevertheless doomed simply because they fought for the wrong cause.

Literacy itself was becoming an increasingly important attribute of a properly educated member of the aristocratic military élite; though not as yet of the ordinary *knights*. The ability to read books which 'ornamented his dignity, explained warfare and gave spirit to his youth' was, for example, regarded as proper for a young nobleman in 12th century France or England. Some Latin was also considered desirable.

Carved wooden misericord, possibly showing 'Sir Gawaine and the Green Knight' from the Tales of King Arthur and the Round Table; English, mid-14th century. The knight's bascinet helmet appears to have an almost flat klappvisier in a rather German fashion, rather than the more common hounskull visor. Compared to Italian and even German illustrations of knights, those from England and France rarely have daggers at their belts. The knight's horse, however, is fully covered by a cloth caparison. (Gloucester Cathedral)

French *chansons de geste* retained their popularity throughout most of the 13th century in France and England while similar literature was avidly read in the German Empire. But attitudes were already changing in Italy where *chivalric* culture and its associated *chansons de geste* had never been taken quite so seriously as they were north of the Alps. Here in Italy the older generation may, in fact, have encouraged the younger *knightly* class to follow the ideals of the *chansons de geste* as a way of keeping a notably turbulent section of society busy with military training and tournaments. As a result various *knightly* associations, such as the Fellowship of the Lion, the Fellowship of the Eagle and the Fellowship of the Round Table, sprang up across 13th century Italy. Even so, such activities always seem to have been rather 'tongue in cheek' compared to similar pastimes in France, Germany and even England, or, indeed, in the more truly *chivalric* parts of southern Italy.

Further changes in attitudes were reflected in the secular literature of the 14th century. Traditional war-oriented, rather than *courtly love*-oriented, *chansons de geste* maintained their popularity in fringe areas such as the north of England. Here, for example, one surviving Arthurian epic still shows strong Celtic literary influence. In France itself, which had been the birthplace of the *chansons de geste*, a resurgence of the *chivalric* ethos was fostered by the royal court instead of the Church. In many areas, notably England and of course Italy, mid and later 14th century military romances were being written for ordinary people as well as for the military élite. These reflected very different social attitudes. One Arthurian romance of Sir Percyvelle de Galles, for example, was written in the English Midlands and reads almost like a burlesque mockery of *knightly* ideals. Several similar attitudes can also be found in Chaucer's *Canterbury Tales.*

Music

Military music was far less developed in medieval western Europe than, for example, in the Byzantine Empire or the Muslim countries. None the less, several Roman and early Germanic traditions survived into the early Middle Ages. Merovingian armies, for example, still used trumpets for signalling. These instruments appear to have become more important under the Carolingians, when they were recorded as being used to maintain morale in battle and help troops re-assemble after a defeat. The Normans similarly used trumpets and horns for battlefield control in the 11th and early 12th centuries. The same was true of early Crusader armies but they, however, soon started copying the Muslim Arabs' and Turks' much more advanced musical traditions; both for military and merely entertainment purposes.

Middle Eastern musical traditions also had a profound impact on western music as a whole; particularly that of the aristocratic élite, court life and *courtly love*. Several new musical instruments were introduced, most notably the Arab *ūd* which became the European lute, mandolin and guitar. The increasing importance of military drums similarly almost certainly reflected Islamic musical influence via the Crusades, Sicily and Spain. Several retained their originally Arabic names; the large *tabour* coming from the *ṭablah* and the small *naker* coming from the *naqqārah*.

Indigenous European instruments continued to be used, of course, particularly in warfare. Some were specif-

ically associated with certain regions, one example being the huge war-horns used by several 14th century local Swiss armies. These were probably much like the alpenhorns which are still played for the benefit of tourists in Switzerland, Austria and southern Germany. In the 14th century, however, such great war-horns would have boomed across the Alpine valleys to terrify an enemy; perhaps accompanied by the fifes, drums and bagpipes played by professional musicians who were paid by the commander of such an army.

'Soldier playing a viol', in the Atlantic Bible; southern French, late 11th century. Music played a very important role in the life of the aristocratic élite of medieval Europe, including the knightly class. Here a soldier plays an early form of bowed instrument, widely used by those itinerant troubadours whose poems and songs carried the ideals and fashions of chivalry from one end of Europe to the other. (MS. Edili 126-6, f.124v, Biblioteca Laurenziana, Florence)

'The Emperor and the commander of his guards', in an Exultet Roll; southern Italian, early 12th century. The costume and weaponry of the figures on this piece of medieval sheet music are strongly influenced by Byzantine fashions which would, however, have been widespread in the Norman kingdom of southern Italy. The writing and musical notation appear upside down because these Exultet Rolls were fed over the front of a preacher's or singer's lectern as he read through them; the picture itself being designed to be seen by the congregation in front of him. (Codex 724.B1.13, pic.17, Biblioteca Casanatense, Rome; photograph, Nadia Murgioni)

Quando tancredus usurpanta sibi regni corona

isti sut filii tancredi

Triumphus Spurii Regis

'Triumphal entry of King Tancred', in the Chronicle of Peter of Eboli; Sicilian, late 12th-early 13th centuries. Although the style of drawing is typical of Christian southern Italy, and the subject is a Christian king, Tancred himself is preceded by officials wearing tall Byzantine-style hats. Next comes a man carrying the king's sword and another carrying a rather miniaturised parasol, a symbol of rulership copied by the Siculo-Norman kings from the Muslim Caliphs of Egypt. The musicians and spearmen in the next rows are all clearly turbaned Muslims from the Norman army's élite Sicilian troops. Even the archers and crossbowmen in the lowest row wear tall pointed hats of a kind rarely seen anywhere else in western Europe. They too are likely to have included Sicilian Muslims and Greeks. (Cod. 120 II, f.102, Burgerbibliothek Berne)

'The Sienese army at the battle of Sinalunga 1363', wall-painting by Lippo Vanni; Italian, c.1370. While a cavalry battle rages just out of this picture, to the right, the Sienese infantry march forward with a few mounted officers. These troops include crossbowmen protected by the spear-armed pavesari with their large pavise shields or mantlets. Ahead of them is an unarmed military band; each man playing a fife and beating a drum. (Palazzo Pubblico, Siena)

LONG-DISTANCE COMMUNICATIONS

Once again, far less detailed study has been made of government organised long-distance or high-speed communications in medieval western Europe than in certain rival civilisations. Even so, it still seems clear that, until the 13th or 14th centuries, these did not reach the same standard of sophistication as was seen in the east, and probably never did so until long after the Middle Ages were over.

One of the earliest references to smoke signals or beacons concerned the Magyars in the 10th century who may have used these to help regroup their forces. The Magyar Hungarians, of course, had been in close military and cultural contact with both Byzantium and Muslim Persia. Fire and smoke beacons may also have been used by the Anglo-Saxons in northern England in 1066, and were clearly used by the Norse inhabitants of the Orkney Islands seventy years later. Both cases could reflect Norse-Viking influence. Here again, the fact that the Vikings had been in such close contact with more advanced eastern Mediterranean cultures may be significant.

Much more detailed information about English beacon warning systems survives from the 14th century. During this period a system that was almost certainly already in existence was greatly improved in the face of the threat from French naval raids. For the first time such beacons also indicated muster points for local defence forces. This 14th century warning and information system consisted of chains of beacons; each guarded, and when necessary ignited, by two teams of six men. One took up its position at the beacon in daytime, the other at night. The primary function of the beacon, however, remained to warn of enemy landings, identify the locations of such landings and raise both local defences and the associated forces from inland shires.

The erection and maintenance of the beacons was the responsibility of local sheriffs or constables. Light cavalry

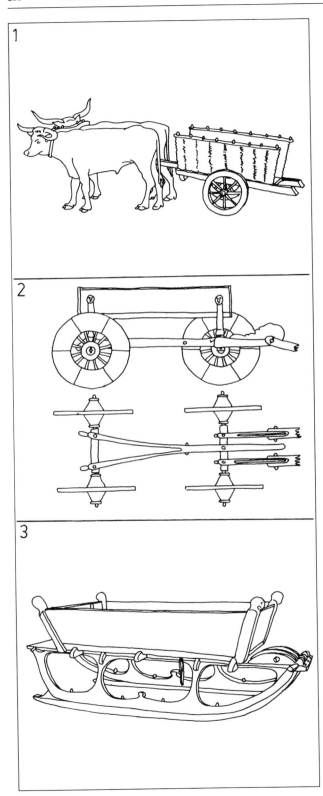

Land transport
1. Bullock cart, 12th century (after Quennell)
2. Simplified side view and plan of a wagon found in the Oseberg ship burial; Norway,
early 9th century (after Foote and Wilson)
3. Simplified drawing of the sledge found in the Oseberg ship burial; Norway, early 9th century

hobelars served as messengers between beacons and as scouts. Meanwhile those teams serving the beacons also had horns, bells and other signalling devices for use in bad weather. The earliest 14th century beacons appear to have consisted of small circular stone structures, each containing a stack of wood. The few surviving examples are less than a metre high, just over two metres in their internal diameter, with flues in their walls to improve the burning of the wood-stack. Pitch was also used to ensure that the wood was easy to light. Later in the 14th century iron cages, fire-boxes or *cressets* came into use, these being raised high on poles and reached by ladders.

Other systems of long-distance communication were used in different circumstances. The Channel Islands, for example, became a vital link in seaborne communications between England and English-ruled Gascony following the loss of Normandy and Anjou to the French in the 13th century. Post-horse systems were never quite as highly developed in western Europe as they were in the medieval Middle East. Nevertheless, a typical example was the one which enabled the English 'Captain of Calais' to communicate with London via Dover. Here, in 1372, various people along the main road between Dover and London were obliged to supply official messengers with fresh horses at what were described as 'reasonable prices'. In comparable Middle Eastern government-run postal systems, the way-stations were actually owned by the government, staffed by government employees and maintained fresh mounts always ready for use by an official messenger.

TRANSPORT

Land Transport

The horse was the most important, but not the only, transport animal in medieval Europe. Nevertheless, there is still widespread misunderstanding about medieval horses; particularly those used in warfare. For a start, a horse needs weight to pull weight, but not necessarily to carry weight where strength is what counts. In other words, a war-horse needed strength to carry a fully armoured cavalryman but it did not necessarily need to be very large. The idea that *knights* rode animals anything like cart-horses is also completely wrong.

Until the late Middle Ages almost all horses outside Spain, and some other areas where the finest animals had already been interbred with the 'hot blooded' Arabian horse, were what would now be considered 'cold blooded' beasts. As such, they were relatively heavy-boned, slow and unresponsive; the nearest comparable existing modern

The fortified Pont Valentré at Cahors; French, 1308. There were probably many fortified bridges in most parts of France, but only a few survive. The Pont Valentré is, perhaps, the most famous. It is defended by two tall towers, one near each end of the bridge. The town lies behind the photographer. This magnificent bridge would have stood, not only as part of the town's fortifications, but also as a symbol of its strength and prosperity.

horse breed being the animal now known as a Cob. There is strong evidence that some Roman horse-breeding centres survived the fall of the western Empire. For example, one of the 7th century Merovingian Frankish kingdom's main breeding estates was south of Auxerre, in the same area as an earlier Roman colony of Sarmatian cavalry. They, of course, had been the best horsemen in the late Roman Empire.

The finest *destriers* or war-horses soon included Arabian blood; this being acquired via various Andalusian or Spanish breeds. As a result *destriers* were far more expensive than any other animals. The large Anatolian and Iranian 'Nisaean' breed of horse may also have been brought back to Europe via the Crusades. In parts of France, even an ordinary horse was worth five times as much as a bull, itself a valuable farming animal, and a war-horse could be four

times the value of an ordinary riding-horse; a really fine *destrier* being worth no less than seven or more ordinary horses.

Pack animals were just as important to a medieval army, and were used in very great numbers. The old Roman road systems of western Europe had probably started to decay even before the Roman Empire itself collapsed. It then certainly fell to pieces under the subsequent Germanic 'barbarian' dynasties. Yet this was not necessarily a symptom of economic or political decline. The carefully surfaced roads of the Roman Empire had been built for wheeled transport. But the introduction of mule trains was in many ways more efficient than the old Roman wagons and had no need of extremely expensive paved stone roads. In fact many new bridges were also added. Even the Roman road system of southern Italy had virtually disap-

peared by the 11th and 12th centuries. Meanwhile, the Roman bridges, which the new trains of pack-animals did still need, were often maintained in excellent repair throughout the Middle Ages.

Two-humped Bactrian camels had been used by the Huns during the nomadic phase of their history as they migrated across the steppe grasslands north of the Black Sea. This animal then seems to have been abandoned as unsuitable once the Huns reached central and western Europe. Camels of the single-humped dromedary or Arabian type were, however, used in Merovingian southern Gaul; having probably been introduced via Spain. Other, more widespread, beasts of burden included the ubiquitous mule, the ordinary pack-horse and the *bardot* or offspring of a horse and she-ass. This name itself stemmed from the Arabic term *birdhawn* meaning a low-bred draught or pack-horse.

Wagons continued to be used in almost all parts of Europe for both civilian and military purposes. The Carolingian Empire even obliged certain regions to provide a specific number of covered wagons for the army. In late 12th century France the king's own élite troops reported-

Pack-horse in the 'Story of the Knight Milo', relief carving; northern Italian, c.1200. Pack-horses and other pack-animals were the most important means of transporting goods and carrying military equipment in medieval Europe. Here the traveller's lazy dog – part of whose head has been broken off – rides on the pack-horse which also carries two substantial panniers. The traveller himself has a large rectangular water-bottle, probably of leather, around his neck. (Façade of the Cathedral of San Donnino, Fidenza)

ly had one cart for every forty or fifty infantry *sergeants*; the *knights* and other cavalry having pack-horses to carry their equipment. Fifty years later other French sources mention seven two-horse carts being needed to transport thirty-five crossbows and 20,000 crossbow bolts. In early 14th century central Italy, mules, as well as such carts, were used to carry both the weapons of the élite crossbowmen and the large shields of the *pavesari* with whom the crossbowmen worked as a team. Much larger wagons remained characteristic of the wide grasslands of eastern Europe; such carts having long been used by the nomadic peoples of

'Sol', or the sun, crossing the sky in a 'chariot' depicted as a two-wheeled cart, in a wall-painting; northern Italian, late 13th century. Despite representing allegorical figures, these two carts are probably realistic enough in their simple and crude style of draw-ing. Both are of the light two-wheeled type and are pulled by the collar or shoulder harness which was developed during the Middle Ages. (Rocca Borromeo Castle, Angera)

these steppe regions. By the 14th century long trains of these massive wagons were being used by merchants and armies alike, as well as by the nomads themselves.

Charlemagne's army had special leather-covered water-proofed carts called *basternae* with which to cross rivers where no bridges were available. Several of the more sophisticated armies of medieval Europe also had highly developed engineering systems which enabled them to cross obstacles such as rivers. The Huns of the 5th century are similarly said to have carried bridging equipment with them on campaign. The rapidity with which the Mus-lim Sicilian engineers serving in the Norman armies of 12th century southern Italy could erect wooden bridges was widely recognised. Even the Anglo-Norman forces of 12th century England included engineers who could clear the road ahead of an advancing army.

River Transport

Rivers played a vital role in military transport as well as in trade throughout much of medieval Europe. Most of the vessels involved were, of course, ordinary river boats and barges, though the 5th century Huns were said to have used dugout canoes, while the late 9th century Magyars made use of coracles. In the early 7th century Merovin-gian Frankish armies relied on river transport perhaps more than most later military forces; their transport craft being called *scarfa*. This tradition was, however, further developed by the Carolingians and may have continued to some extent into later centuries. The early 13th century militia of Toulouse, for example, ferried several large siege engines up-river in barges during the Albigensian Crusade. Other evidence suggests that it was quite normal to transport such heavy equipment by river and by sea

whenever feasible. The English clearly did so during their early 13th century campaigns in Wales.

COMBINED OPERATIONS

Combined operations were central to medieval naval warfare. In fact, it could almost be said that galley warfare existed merely to support combined operations. The latter basically consisted of establishing bridgeheads in enemy territory, raiding enemy ports and coastal regions, and supporting armies already operating in coastal areas. One of the primary functions of defensive naval forces was, correspondingly, to try to hinder such support being delivered to invading armies.

Raiding

Among the most serious of the new military threats faced by the Roman Empire in the 4th century was that of coastal raiding by Germanic tribesmen around the shores of the North Sea. These raiders also extended their activities into the Channel and even down the Atlantic coast of Gaul. In addition the unconquered Celtic peoples of what are now Scotland and Ireland outflanked the fixed Roman defences of Hadrian's Wall to attack northern and western coasts of Britain. The Romans responded in various ways; one of which was the establishment of coastal military zones which included fortified harbours for naval units as well as coastal fortifications which were used as bases for mobile cavalry and infantry forces. The most famous of these was the Saxon Shore in south-eastern Britain. Over subsequent centuries various other peoples continued the Saxons', Picts' and Scots' tradition of naval raiding, the most notable, of course, being the Norse-Vikings. Their victims were, by and large, even less successful than the Romans had been in defending their coasts. More often than not the Vikings were eventually defeated far inland; rarely on the coasts and hardly ever at sea.

Meanwhile the Mediterranean Sea passed from being a largely peaceful Roman 'lake' to become one of the main arenas of conflict between the Christian and Muslim worlds. As a result, combined operations as well as other aspects of naval warfare became highly developed in the Mediterranean region. Here it was soon common for even small squadrons of warships directly to attack the fortifications of enemy-held harbours. Larger ships, including seemingly fragile galleys, used the great spars and yardarms of their massive lateen sails as rams against coastal sea-walls and towers. On other occasions, they were described as having tall wooden towers erected above their decks, to enable their crews to shoot down upon defending troops. Most remarkable of all, perhaps, were the descriptions of 'flying bridges' which were suspended like drawbridges from their *fighting-tops* and *fighting castles*, ready to drop on to the opposing towers as the ships came ashore. One mid-13th century reference to a Genoese 'round ship' or merchant sailing vessel, stated that its main spare or *penne* could be converted to a stone-throwing *mangonel*.

Horse Transports

The most significant advance in the technology of combined operations came with the development of an effective long-distance horse transport capability. The greatest single problem had always been the provision of sufficient drinking water for the animals during a voyage. Stability and protection for the horses was probably achieved by cradling them in canvas slings, as was done in later centuries. The Byzantines and Muslim Arabs inherited the Romans' capabilities in this field; the Muslims then greatly improving on available technology by the 9th and 10th centuries. The Arabs may have been able to do this primarily because they could draw upon the even longer-distance maritime technologies of the Indian Ocean.

The Venetians clearly had acquired similar capabilities by the 10th century; a specialised horse-transport known as a *chelandrion* being recorded as early as 931. This was an oared galley, though presumably of broader and perhaps altogether bulkier proportions than the ordinary fighting galley. By the mid-13th century the French and Genoese terms *chelandre* and *salandria* could refer to both oared transport ships or sailing transports. By then, however, the originally Arabic word *tarida* seems to have been universally used for specifically oared horse-transports; particularly those capable of landing men and animals directly on to a beach rather like modern landing craft. Such *taridas* had one or two doors in the stern; the doors themselves perhaps also serving as loading ramps.

Mid-11th century southern Italian transports could carry about twenty horses each; slightly more than the Byzantines had been capable of in the 8th century. But these were probably ordinary merchant vessels rather than specialised military horse-transports. By the 12th century,

Opposite page, top: A palfrey or riding horse rather than a destrier or war-horse, on a carved capital; southern French, 13th century. The low cantle and pommel on this saddle shows that the animal is for everyday riding rather than for use in battle. Note that the stirrup also has an almost rounded outline; perhaps showing North African or Middle Eastern influence, unless such lighter stirrups were, in fact, still used when riding a palfrey. (South-eastern corner of the cloisters of the church of St Trophime, Arles)

Opposite page, bottom: Illustrated page from the Album of Villard de Honnecourt; French, mid-13th century. Apart from such details as the mail chausses which only cover the front of the rider's head, and the perhaps padded cloth coif worn beneath the mail coif, this superb little drawing also illustrates two interesting aspects of horse harness. They are the sturdy triangular stirrups and the clearly curb form of horse-bit with a strengthening crossbar beneath the animal's mouth. (MS. Fr. 19.093, Bibliothèque Nationale, Paris; photograph, Bibliothèque Nationale).

Left: The castle of Bilhorod-Dnistrovsky in Ukraine, also known as Aq Kirmān in Turkish and Cetatea Alba in Romanian; all of which mean 'White Castle'. It was built in the 13th century as an outpost of the Genoese trading empire, then strengthened by the Genoese, Moldavians and later the Ottoman Turks from the 14th to 17th centuries. There are a number of Genoese colonial fortresses and even small galley-harbours around the Black Sea, but the fortress at Bilhorod-Dnistrovsky appears to be the biggest and perhaps the best preserved. The fortified town originally had thirty-five towers, two outer and three inner gates. (Photograph, Archaeological Museum, Odessa)

larger ships, including those able to carry many horses but not designed to land them directly on to a beach, were known as *huissiers*. These loaded and unloaded their cargoes, including the horses, though doors in the sides of the hull. The *huissier* could also be very large; one Venetian example of 1172 being a three-masted ship capable of carrying almost 1,500 people in an emergency.

Horse transporting capabilities were much more primitive in the northern seas. For example the Scandinavian Viking raiders rarely put horses aboard their ships during the early Middle Ages, perhaps not normally doing so until the Normans of northern France brought this idea back from the Mediterranean in the mid-11th century. A full century later the Danes finally changed their combined operations tactics from the old infantry dominated Norse-Viking pattern to the newer Norman strategy. Despite the fact that Danish ships could still only carry a handful of horses, this new capability steadily gave then a strategic advantage over their Baltic Slav rivals whose ships, though similar in basic design, remained smaller and were thus virtually unable to transport horses in any numbers.

Coastal Landings

Once the Mediterranean horse-transporting capability had been established in the early Middle Ages, it became possible to land quite substantial armies of both infantry and cavalry on an enemy's shore. This gave the invading force a considerable strategic advantage and enabled them to keep the defenders guessing. A relatively small military force might, in fact, be able to establish an effective bridgehead which could then be strengthened while the defenders struggled to concentrate their own troops in the threatened area.

Attempts by defending fleets to maintain standing patrols out at sea, to counter such dangers, rarely proved successful. Even when defending troops were available at the right place and right time, they were even more rarely capable of stopping a beach-landing from taking place. Early in the 12th century, for example, a powerful Siculo-Norman fleet of about three hundred ships carrying a thousand horses, plus their riders and large numbers of infantry, attacked Mahdia in Tunisia. Five hundred armoured cavalrymen were described as storming the beach directly from their ships. A few years later an Anglo-French writer described a comparable operation where the infantry archers disembarked first, to secure the beach, followed immediately by the *knights* who landed and promptly formed up in their *conrois* squadrons.

In 1174 another great Siculo-Norman fleet attacked Alexandria in Egypt. It included thirty-six *taridas*; the fleet as a whole carrying 1,500 cavalry, though perhaps not all were in the beach-landing *taridas*. Other vessels carried siege equipment, perhaps the infantry and probably other

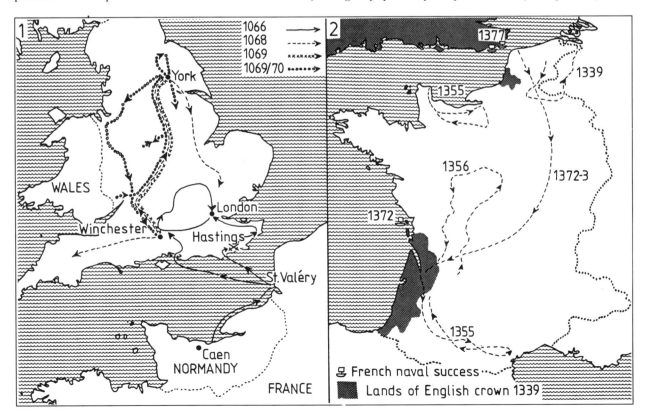

Opposite page:
1. The Norman invasion and conquest of England, 1066–70. The initial invasion was one of the most successful combined-operations of the Middle Ages. It was followed up by reinforcements and several years of campaigning across much of the country. The majority of these latter operations consisted of ravaging rebel or unsubdued territory
2. English chevauchées or ravaging campaigns across France during the early decades of the Hundred Years War. These became increasingly ambitious and lengthy, though often of decreasing effectiveness. Meanwhile the French retaliated at sea and

by raiding the English coast
***Above:** 'Animals disembarking from Noah's Ark', on a carved capital; Siculo-Norman, mid-12th century. While Noah releases a dove at the prow of the ship, the animals start to disembark down a ramp at the other. This was probably still the normal way of transporting animals in the smaller type of Mediterranean ship. Unfortunately, detailed illustrations of those ships that had doors or ramps built into their hulls do not seem to exist for another century or more, though written records prove that such vessels clearly were built by the 12th century. (Cloisters of Cefalu Cathedral)*

horses. Only the oared *taridas* would have been capable of manoeuvring stern-first on to the beach, however. The deeper-hulled sail-powered *uissiers* or *huissiers* must have been obliged to transfer their passengers, horses and cargoes into small boats which then rowed ashore.

FLAGS AND HERALDRY

Banners, Totems and Symbols

Various forms of Roman military insignia, or at least some of the terminology associated with such insignia, survived the fall of the western half of the Roman Empire. Perhaps the most obvious example was the use of a spear to indicate rank or the possession of power. This continued in Byzantium and the early Islamic Middle East, but was also seen in some of the post-Roman Germanic 'barbarian' kingdoms of western Europe. Whether the early Anglo-Saxon use of a flag or standard called a *thuf* actually indicated something like the earlier Latin *tufa*, or was merely an example of residual terminology, is unknown. Slightly more is known about pre-Christian standards in Viking Age Scandinavia, however; many of these apparently being

Left: The campanile or bell-tower of the Cathedral at Koper in Slovenia; probably Venetian, late 12th century, but strengthened and heightened in the 15th century. It was also used as a lighthouse, observation post against Adriatic pirates and even as a final tower of refuge. Such tall campaniles virtually became symbols of Venetian colonial rule around the Adriatic and Aegean.

Opposite page: Episode in the 'Roman de Tristan et Iseult', wall-painting; French, mid-14th century. This kind of chivalric illustration portrays knightly combat in its idealised form, not what it had become by the middle of the 14th century; consequently those taking part appear to be armed for the tournament, not for warfare. The great emphasis given to their coats of arms similarly reflects the central role that such heraldry played in later medieval concepts of chivalry. (Templar Chapel of St Floret Castle, St Floret)

triangular polished bronze objects. The strange symbols seen on many Pictish carved stones from early medieval Scotland are even less understood. Nevertheless, it has been suggested that they could be family or tribal ownership marks; and as such could be regarded as an early form of heraldry.

The primary function of standards, flags and banners remained essentially unchanged throughout the Middle Ages. They served, above all, as rallying points in case of difficulty, and to indicate the direction of an attack. These functions were so important that a standard-bearer was forbidden to strike a blow in battle; most certainly not with the banner itself. A standard-bearer might also be given special clothing; as when the charter of the Church-ruled city of Liège in 1196 specified that the bishop's standard-bearer wear white and ride a white horse with a white *caparison*. Whereas lesser banners would be used for command and control, the death of an army's main standard-bearer, or the fall of his flag, could similarly signal the defeat of the army as a whole.

Early medieval banners rarely had any Christian religious associations, though the banners of several remaining pagan peoples do often seem to have been linked to one or other pagan deity. Military banners had originally been seen as symbols of the Roman Empire's oppression of Christianity, but this gradually changed as the Church itself altered its own attitude towards warfare. In fact the Pope himself is said to have presented a banner to Charlemagne, though a more widespread adoption of Holy Banners or flags blessed by the Church did not appear until the 10th century. This itself may have been yet another example of Muslim influence, since religious banners had played a major role in Islamic armies since the time of the Prophet Muhammad. One of the earliest Christian Holy Banners was decorated with a picture of Saint Michael and was carried by the German Emperor's élite cavalry corps at the battle of the Lech in 955.

Thereafter the use of religiously blessed flags increased, particularly in the 11th and 12th centuries. The Pope's own small army is recorded as having such a banner by

1053. Others were sent by the Pope to his allies or to those campaigning against heretics, pagans and Muslims. The favourite motif on these flags probably consisted of crosses on a gold background.

By the 12th century the distinction between secular and religious banners was becoming blurred. Perhaps the earliest of all European national flags, the *Dannebrog* of Denmark with its white cross on a red ground, originated during an early 13th century Crusade against pagan Estonians. It is, in fact, said to have fallen from the heavens at a moment of military crisis. Various forms and colours of Christian cross were later adopted as recognised national identification marks by various countries; the English perhaps in the early 14th century, the French in the mid-14th century, and the Scots in about 1385. At the other end of the scale the *vexilla* banners of Italian urban infantry militia units were often closely associated with the local or parish church of a particular unit. Local churches also became depositories for local flags, as well as captured enemy banners and, in later centuries, regimental standards. This concept again seems to have gone back to 10th century Islamic influence; probably entering Christendom via Muslim Spain.

Origins and Development of Western Heraldry

The development of a true heraldic system in western Europe started in the 11th and 12th centuries. It brought together three forms of symbolism; colour, geometric pattern and pictorial or mythological motifs.

The colour element may yet again have reflected Islamic influence; probably via the Iberian peninsula in the 10th and 11th centuries, rather than the Crusades of the 12th century. *Azure*, the heraldic term for blue, came from the Arabic *azraq*, while *gules* for red came from the Persian *gil* meaning a red dye for the hair or *gul* meaning a rose. The earliest heraldic lance *gonfanons* of 11th century France were normally of a single colour, while by the early 12th century it seems that men of a single unit often painted their shields, lances and even helmets one colour; perhaps also having lance pennons of the same. Colours remained the most important way of showing family or political connections throughout the 12th century; these being passed on from one generation to the next, long before patterns or motifs were inherited. For example, blue and gold were used by many families linked to the French ruling dynasty before such family connections were indicated by the use of the fleurs-de-lis.

The legends which sought to explain the distant origins of several of the earliest motifs in western heraldry again reflected ancient battles with the Muslims of Spain or the early Crusades to the Holy Land. This seems to have been particularly true of those consisting of geometric patterns, rather than heraldic beasts. *Checky*, for example, was recognised at the oldest of all heraldic patterns; its name coming from the Arab word for *shaṭranj*, meaning both chess and the chessboard pattern used as a shield or banner device in Muslim Spain. The first recognised family

blazon or coat of arms in France was that of the Count of Toulouse. It consisted of the Greek 'Cross of Constantine' and traditionally reflected the count's loyalty to the Byzantine Emperor during the First Crusade. Even the fleurs-de-lis, which became the symbol of the French monarchy, had long been used as a symbol of the Virgin Mary in Byzantium as well as being a popular decorative motif in early Islamic art. Its first recorded connection with the French crown dates from 1147, though the multiple gold fleurs-de-lis on a blue ground was not apparently used as a generally recognised French royal shield motif before the early 13th century.

The most common 'beasts' in western heraldry were the lion and the eagle. The leopard, which was essentially a variation on the basic heraldic lion, may have been adopted by the Count of Anjou as early as 1127. Thereafter it became the leopard of England after the Angevin-Plantagenet dynasty inherited the English crown. The lions of the German imperial family were clearly established by the early 13th century, but would later be replaced by an eagle with the rise of a new German ruling dynasty.

By the mid-11th century individual members of the military élite clearly had different, though still personal rather than inherited, motifs painted on their shields. Since there was as yet no broadly recognised heraldic 'language', warriors who wished to meet and fight in a battle or *tournament* often had to agree beforehand what colour horses and what pattern of shield decoration they would be using. Some of these earlier shield motifs survived into the 12th century. Thereafter they gradually changed into what became, in effect, individual badges, and were inherited as family devices.

Such a process was probably stimulated by the growing passion for *tournaments* on the part of the *knightly* class. Clearly the widely held view that true heraldry specifically resulted from the adoption of the face-covering *great helm* is inaccurate; as distinctive motifs on shields and personal seals appeared before the *great helm* itself. Thereafter, members of the aristocracy started adding such motifs to their helmets, saddles, horse-covering *caparisons* and eventually also their clothing, as well as to their shields and flags. The word *connaissances* now came to have a specifically heraldic meaning, while a lord's *knightly* followers also began using part or all of their leader's heraldic device as their own identification mark. This itself could lead to problems when, for example, two rulers laid claim

to one region. On such occasions both rival rulers might give the territory in question to one of their own followers. As a result, the latter sometimes met in battle, both wearing the heraldic device of the disputed area. There were even references to men rallying beneath one of the enemy's banners and thus being taken prisoner; a common enough phenomenon in 13th century France and England.

The language of heraldry was not universal, however, even within western Europe. In Italy, as in the Iberian peninsula, closer contact with the Muslim world led to the widespread adoption of *cartouches*, or written inscriptions, as part of a *coat of arms*. This was also seen in Byzantium from the 10th to 13th centuries and, for some as yet unknown reason, in 14th century Wales.

The Spread and Uses of Heraldry

The idea of dividing a shield motif and adding other symbols to indicate a family alliance through marriage or common descent appeared in the mid-13th century. During the 13th and 14th centuries non-aristocratic and even non-military associations also began making use of heraldic motifs. These included urban communes, craft guilds and the clergy. Communal heraldry often drew upon that of the local feudal lords, and the idea of adding some aspect of a ruler's or suzerain's *coat of arms* to one's own as a mark of political allegiance became particularly popular in Italy. Here, however, there was far less attempt to control the language of heraldry than was seen in France, Germany or England.

It was almost inevitable that the size of a banner should reflect the importance of its owner; though this only became regularised in the 13th century. Various terms were used for banners of differing sizes in different countries. Large rectangular *banniers* may, for example, have been linked to provinces or regions in Germany before this practice was accepted throughout France; yet by the late 12th century such a *bannier* was normally regarded as a suitable flag for the leader of a large military contingent. The smaller triangular *pennon*, nailed to the shaft of a lance, was largely used as an individual flag. In 13th century Italy larger forms of banner were called *gonfaloni*; the

Left: Relief carving, probably of one of the 'Virtues' with a heraldic shield; French, c.1230. The figure's helmet of a segmented spangenhelm type and his surcoat is either thickly padded or worn over a form of quilted soft armour, as seen at the shoulders. (West front of Amiens Cathedral)

Opposite page: 'Seal of John de Montfort', French, 1248. The De Montfort family coat of arms is prominently displayed on the horseman's shield and the caparison of his horse. The animal also has an early form of chamfron to protect its head; the caparison probably also being lined with mail or at least thickly quilted. (Douët d'Arcq. no. D 713, Archives Nationales, Paris)

small individual unit flags being *vessilli* or, in Latin, *vexilla*. The local cantonal armies of 14th century German-speaking northern and eastern Switzerland also had large banners. These were carried by a senior or respected *venner*, who also kept the banner in his own home. In battle the main cantonal banner was surrounded by the lesser *fähnlein* flags of guilds and smaller communities.

Other Insignia

In addition to flags and banners of various shapes and sizes, other forms of recognition device were used in various parts of Europe at various times. During the first half of the 12th century, before the general use of heraldic coats of arms, for example, armies sometimes clearly wore something by which they could be identified. But more often than not the precise identity of such marks remains a mystery. They could have included pieces of coloured cloth or even plants. By the late 13th century, however, even the humble infantry in sophisticated forces such as that of the French king could be ordered to sew pieces of specifically shaped and coloured cloth to their clothes as 'rallying signs'.

The old windsock form of banner may have re-appeared in imperial Germany during the early 13th century; or perhaps this idea had somehow survived since late Roman or early Germanic times. Or its re-appearance may have reflected more recent influence from the steppe nomadic peoples of eastern Europe, or indeed from the Muslim armies of the Middle East. All of these used such windsock banners. The medieval imperial German silk dragon or windsock was mounted in a cart drawn by four horses; rather like the better-known *carroccios* of Italy. Such *carroccio* carts may themselves have originally been copied from eastern nomads, though the written evidence suggests that they were first used by 11th century Italian urban militia forces. A Hungarian army of the mid-12th century did, however, have such a banner-wagon pulled by four yoke of oxen.

The use of a parasol as a very senior form of insignia clearly stemmed from the Middle East; specifically from the *miẓalla* of the Faṭimid Caliphs of Egypt. The Norman rulers of Sicily and southern Italy used this device, as did the Doges of Venice whose parasol was of cloth-of-gold. Nevertheless it remained extremely rare.

Below: Stained glass window, showing, from left to right: Gilbert de Clare, William Lord Zouch de Mortimer, Richard de Clare Earl of Gloucester, Gilbert de Clare Earl of Gloucester; English, c.1344. Each bears his coat of arms on his surcoat, and each has a typical mid-14th century bascinet. Two figures also have scale or plate-covered gorgeretes protecting their necks. (Abbey of Tewkesbury)

UNIFORMS: THEIR DECLINE AND RISE

The modern concept of a fully uniformed army clearly could not be applied to medieval European forces. It may be slightly misleading even for the preceding Roman period, when the degree of 'uniformity' within the imperial Roman army may well have been exaggerated. Nevertheless, certain aspects of late Roman military costume, which could be regarded as 'uniforms', do appear to have survived the fall of the western Empire itself. The wearing of red cloaks by military leaders in some parts of early medieval southern Europe is likely to have been a continuation of the red military tunics worn by late Roman army officers. There is some small evidence to suggest that other aspects of Roman military dress such as the *chlamys* with its panels of differing colours and sizes, perhaps to indicate rank or status, remained in use not only in the Byzantine Empire but in some of the Germanic successor states for a short while. The same may have been true of those gold or jewelled neck *torques* for élite members of an early medieval ruler's guard which are shown in many pictorial sources.

Even in the early 7th century soldiers descended from traditional Roman military families, in some parts of the kingdoms of Burgundy and of Merovingian France, are said to have worn Roman military costume – or at least costume that was regarded as Roman by their contemporaries. Old forms of traditional official costume were also said to have been worn on suitable occasions in 8th century Papal Rome.

A completely different tradition of 'uniform' costume, or of theoretical sumptuary laws, survived in 7th and 8th century Celtic Ireland. Here each class was permitted a certain range of colours: yellow, black or white for ordinary subjects; grey-brown or red for the nobility; purple and blue for kings alone. Slaves could wear only a single colour, free subjects two, the learned class six, a king seven. These, however, were not uniforms in any real sense of the word.

Perhaps the earliest true uniforms since Roman times were the white tunics worn as a means of recognition by élite Carolingian troops at the battle of Andernack in 876. Apart from this notable exception, the next move in the direction of 'uniform' costume as a means of recognising friend from foe, was the adoption of the cross motif during the early Crusades. Nothing further appears to have been attempted until the 13th century. Certain guild-based militias, particularly those of the rich Flemish cities, then began wearing costume cut from the same coloured cloth. During the late 13th century this practice began to be adopted more widely; three hundred troops from Tournai all being dressed in white tunics and hats when they took part in a siege of Lille. The same colour was still worn by Tournai militias more than fifty years later. At about the same time the surviving financial accounts of Rodez in southern France mention the uniform surcoats which were issued to the town's *sergeants*, along with their

'A donor figure from the Beaumont family', stained glass window; French, 1230–5. This is one of a series of such armoured knights, each prominently showing his family's coat of arms. Here it is displayed on his shield and on the horse's caparison. The knights are also sometimes thought to represent participants in the disastrous Fifth Crusade to Egypt. This figure is particularly interesting because he wears an early form of flat-topped great helm with a fixed face-mask visor which does not cover the sides and rear of the head. (Chartres Cathedral)

weapons. The concept of unit uniforms was also taken up in mid-14th century England, where a levy from northern Wales was put into distinctive clothes. On this occasion, however, it may have been a disciplinary measure; resulting from the fact that these northern Welshmen were regarded as the most turbulent and unruly section of the English army.

THE MEDIEVAL ARMS INDUSTRY

Mining, Materials and Techniques

Compared with many other parts of the medieval world, Europe was rich in sources of iron, the most important being the Tyrol, Styria, the Moselle-Meuse area, the Rhine valley, Champagne, the eastern Pyrenees and Norway. Even so, the economic decline of the early medieval period meant that iron remained in short supply. As a result, old or damaged weapons were usually recycled. Broken swords, for example, were often cut down for use as daggers. Western Europe also had the great advantage that most of its primary sources of iron-ore were also in thickly forested regions. Where iron mines were not close to abundant sources of timber for fuel, as in Norman Sicily, the government tried to keep very strict control over both mining and the limited available forests.

Wood, and to a lesser extent water, were essential for medieval metal production; some 150 cubic metres of charcoal being needed to obtain a mere ten kilograms of malleable iron. Such huge demands for timber led to deforestation in some regions by the 14th century and could have accounted for a gradual turn towards coal as a source of power. This, however, led to different problems, as in 1306 when the governor of Arles banned use of coal in forges because it caused a greater phosphorus and sulphur content of iron which, as a consequence, was weaker than iron smelted using charcoal.

There is virtually no evidence to suggest that the late Roman armies enjoyed any technological superiority over their foes. In fact, the bulk of late Roman arms and armour was of simple, often mass-produced, and even rather inferior quality. This was particularly apparent in the production of iron helmets, none of which were of one-piece construction. Earlier one-piece helmets had, of course, been made of bronze which was worked at a much lower temperature than iron. Nor is there much evidence for any reduction in metallurgical skills following the fall of the western Roman Empire, despite the obvious economic and even cultural decline during this period. The idea that the abandonment of large pieces of iron plate armour from the 5th to 13th centuries reflected an inability to make such objects is clearly wrong, as the required technology was still demonstrated in the form of early medieval helmets. In fact, there was, if anything, an increase in armourers' skills during these centuries; most notably in the appearance of true one-piece iron helmets.

The earliest known European specimen dates from the 9th or 10th century, but this was probably imported from

'Murder of Saint Thomas à Becket', wall-painting; southern Italian, late 12th century. Since the men who killed the Saint were English knights, there is no reason why the artist should have attempted to portray them in alien or 'oriental' armour. The peculiar pattern of small circles covering the hauberk of the leading figure is also unclear. Various theories have been put forward, including the possibility that it represented a cloth-covered jazerain form of hauberk. It is also interesting in only having one mitten for the right hand, the sword-hand. At least one such single mitten form of armour was called a panceriam in an Italian document from about a generation later. (Church of San Giovanni e Paolo, Spoleto)

the Middle East or Central Asia where similar one-piece helmets had been known since at least the early 8th century. The broader history of metallurgy would suggest that the necessary technology actually originated in the Far East and spread westwards via the Muslim world. Western European armourers were, however, clearly capable of making such objects by the 11th and 12th centuries. Hence the skills required for the production of iron plate armour were there over a century before they were actually called upon.

The 12th and 13th centuries similarly saw a very important change in the intellectual climate of Europe. For the first time the educated élite of scholars started to take a positive attitude towards science and technology; more so than had been seen in the early Christian centuries and, in practical terms, more so than had even been the case in ancient Greek or Roman civilisation. This was clearly a result of contact with Islamic civilisation, and of European translations of Arabic works of scientific scholarship becoming more widely available. From the 12th century onwards western Europe became what has been called a 'mechanism-minded world' in which new technologies could be assimilated with relative ease. The mechanical arts were no longer seen as a hindrance to man's spiritual destiny, but potentially as a help.

This view of craft and technology was based on the rational Arabic version of the ancient Greek Aristotelian classification of knowledge and theoretical science; not on the original Aristotelian system itself. It led to some remarkably modern opinions in early 12th century Europe where, at a time when Crusades against non-Christians seemed to dominate the attitudes of the élite, Hugh of St Victor even advocated trade as way of bringing peoples together in peace; including Muslims and heathens.

During the Middle Ages several different methods were, in fact, used to produce iron arms and armour with differing degrees of hardness, from flexible to brittle but sharp. Most of these had been available to late Roman armourers, but had not necessarily been used to any great extent. It may even have been the case that late Roman armour tended to be of non-hardened iron so that it absorbed the shock of a blow; hardening being reserved for blades or at least their cutting edges.

The technique of case-hardening, for example, was known in the classical world but was not highly developed until the 10th or 11th century. Here, the outer surface of an object such as a sword-blade was hardened by repeated heating and sudden cooling; the latter usually being achieved by the blade being 'quenched' in cold water. Another more elaborate technique was that of the *damascene* blade. This may have been known as early as the 4th century BC, though it remained exceptionally rare for many centuries. To produce a *damascene* blade a 'cake' or ingot of high carbon, or mixed high and low carbon, steel was progressively elongated by hammering. The technique also enabled a sword-smith to concentrate the hardest metal along the cutting edge while leaving the centre of the blade relatively soft and flexible. As a result the blade could be bent, but was virtually impossible to break. It also had the characteristic surface pattern of a true *damascene* blade. The density of this so-called 'watering' was caused by the differing crystallisation processes in higher and lower carbon steel. Its density similarly indicated the quality of the weapon, as well as being highly decorative.

Pattern welding is sometimes known as 'false damascene' which suggests, incorrectly, that a *pattern welded* weapon was somehow inferior. The technique first appeared in Germany in the 3rd century and resulted from strips of hard and soft iron being twisted together, then repeatedly heated and beaten flat. This was not true welding, as the available European technology could not yet achieve sufficient heat for such welding. *Pattern welding* had, however, been used for swords in the late Roman period. It continued to be used for most weapons during the early

Vulcan forging armour', in the Eneide of Heinrich von Veldeke manuscript; German, late 12th–early 13th centuries. The ancient Greek pagan god hammers an early form of great helm into shape, while beneath his forge lies a crumpled mail hauberk and what may represent the lining of a coif. (MS. germ. fol. 282, f.39v, Staatsbibliothek zu Berlin)

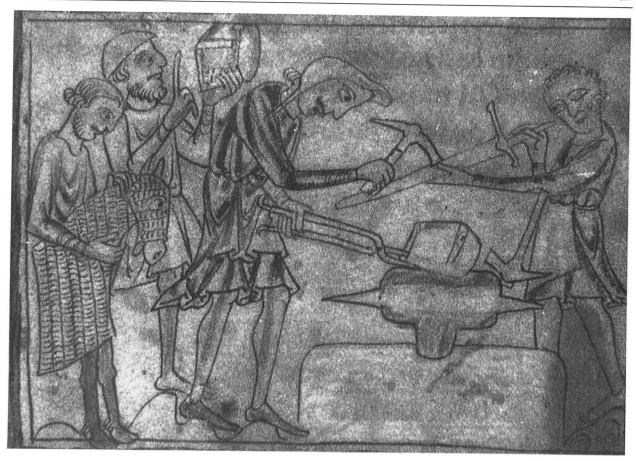

Armourers at work in the Roman de Toute Chevalerie; English, mid-13th century. Illustrating the shaping of a great helm appears to have been a medieval artist's favourite way of showing armourers. Here, however, another man on the right checks the alignment of the quillons on a sword-blade

which still lacks its grip and pommel. On the left, other craftsmen are checking the shape of a great helm and apparently fitting the front half of a horse armour to half a model horse! (MS. 0.9.34, Trinity College Library, Cambridge; photograph, Master and Fellows of Trinity College)

medieval centuries, but only seems to have been seen in small knives by the 10th to 12th centuries.

By the 9th century the famous sword-blades of the Rhineland, which were exported throughout most of Europe, were no longer made by folding or twisting strips of hard and soft iron. Instead their smiths used a system of piling or laminating such strips; a technique which probably demanded higher temperatures. This in turn was replaced by the 'single bar' structure of 11th to 15th century western European blades made from a single strip of higher and more consistent quality steel. Since sufficient-

ly high temperatures were now possible, true welding also came into use, particularly when adding narrow strips of hard steel to simple wrought iron knives or daggers; thus providing their cutting edges.

Cast iron required yet another form of advanced metallurgical technology. It was first seen in 2nd century BC China, where it had been made possible by the development of pumping devices which forced air through a furnace and thus achieved much higher temperatures. Cast iron appears to have been unknown in the Roman Empire. By the 5th century such a technique enabled Chinese smiths to produce steel by mixing cast and wrought iron together, the result being almost as good at directly smelted decarburised steel. The technology reached the Middle East by the 11th century, but it does not seem to have arrived in western Europe until the late 15th century.

Nevertheless, some steel was being made in Europe by the 10th century; in tiny quantities and perhaps almost by accident. The fact that it is associated with the Scandinavian Vikings leaves open the possibility of Middle Eastern Islamic or Byzantine technological influence. But high carbon steel remained extremely difficult to make. Production was largely confined to Scandinavia,

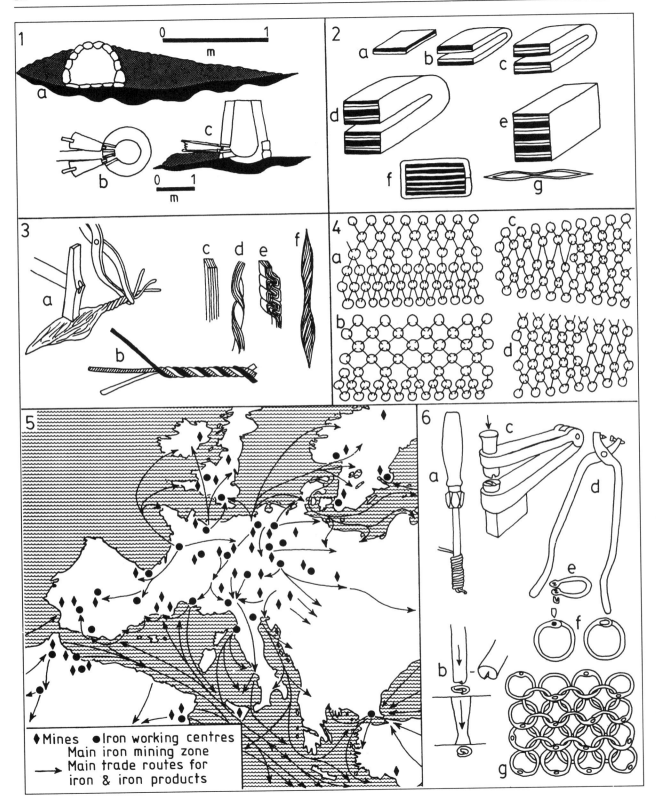

It has been suggested that the widespread replacement of plate armour by mail armour during the later Roman and early medieval centuries was partly because mail was simpler and cheaper to make. It was certainly manufactured in great quantities. The mail-maker's craft became even more mechanised after the development of water-powered wire-drawing machines in the mid-14th century; perhaps leading to a reduction in relative costs and a further increase in volume production. Mail itself, however, remained essentially a standard and largely unchanging form of protection. There was, for example, no such thing as the 'banded mail' described in many earlier books on arms and armour. Variations in construction were minor; the mail of medieval western Europe almost invariably consisting of alternating punched or welded links and riveted links, each being connected to four others.

Not all armour was of iron. Nor, in fact, were all weapons. Copper continued to be used in some very backward areas such as Finland and may even have been used for decorative parade helmets in 11th or 12th century France, though this remains dubious. The decoration of arms and armour was usually done by adding silver, gold, brass or other alloys as inlaid patterns or inscriptions, but many other materials were used for armour, particularly in periods of experimentation such as the 13th century. These included whalebone, horn, leather, *cuir-bouilli* or hardened leather, and latten, an alloy of copper, zinc, lead and tin.

Since large numbers of western European, particularly German, sword blades were exported in great numbers without any form of hilt being attached, the latter were generally added locally. In medieval Poland hilts were often of horn, while in Scandinavia and parts of the Baltic they were sometimes of bronze. It is interesting to note that these exported sword blades had a very long *tang* which could be cut to whatever length the hilt-maker required. The fashion for using whalebone, particularly for arm-defences, seems to have been characteristic of France, Germany and Holland during the late 13th and 14th centuries; such protections being held together with a covering of strong canvas.

Various forms of leather, however, were much more important and widespread. The first semi-rigid pieces of western European body armour were probably of leather rather than of iron; perhaps being of vegetable tanned cattle hide, *cuir-bouilli*, buff leather, or rawhide. A leather *quiret* or body protection for a tournament in 1278 took sixteen unspecified animal skins. Another *cuirie* body armour of buff leather was described as being lined with *carda*, coarse linen.

Cuir bouilli was not, as is often thought, 'boiled' leather; since boiling would simply make it softer. Instead, the leather was soaked in melted wax, then hardened and shaped by heating and drying in a mould. Deer-skin leather was apparently considered best. Some English armourers who made leather body-armour from sheep-skin were, in fact, the subject of official complaints in

parts of Russia and the Iberian peninsula, until the late Middle Ages. Even so, it was relatively widespread by the 14th century. Recent chemical analysis of several pieces of later medieval plate armour shows that, contrary to what had been expected, none of them consisted of cold-beaten iron. Instead, they were of mild steel which had been 'worked' or beaten at a temperature of about 500 degrees centigrade; a quite sophisticated technology for the period.

The habit of *proofing* the higher quality and more expensive pieces of armour seems to have revived at about the period of the mid-14th century. It involved shooting at the armour in question with crossbow bolts, some of which themselves had specially tempered steel heads by the year 1401.

'Arrest of Jesus', carved capital; southern French, late 13th century. Like so many common soldiers in the art of the 13th century, one of these men has a mail coif but no other visible armour beneath his surcoat. He is also armed with a large flanged mace. This weapon was of Middle

Eastern origin but became widely popular, particularly in France, by the mid-13th century. (Cloisters of the church of St Trophime, Arles)

'Effigy of Jean d'Alluye' from the Abbey of Clarté-Dieu in Touraine, showing what is believed to be a Middle Eastern or Spanish-Muslim form of light sword; French, mid-13th century. This sword, and above all its hilt and even the way its scabbard is attached to the belt, is so unlike other

western European swords of the mid-13th century that a more exotic origin has been suggested. Perhaps Jean d'Alluye brought it back from some campaign overseas, and was so proud of the weapon that he wanted it included in his funeral effigy. (Cloisters Museum, New York)

1327. The effectiveness and lightness of *cuir bouilli* armour was such that it remained in use throughout most of the 14th century; not only in hot countries such as Italy but even in England.

Wood was another vital material, most obviously for the shafts of spears or axes. The late Romans reportedly preferred ash or hazel for this purpose. Some early medieval shields seem to have been of a layered, almost plywood, construction with an inner layer of oak and an outer of alder. A surviving 11th century German text indicates that a form of cheese-paste was used as the glue. The thicker shields of 13th century England, and probably elsewhere,

were made of willow and poplar. England also imported hard fine-grained boxwood from Bordeaux for use in making dagger-handles; as well as yew for longbows which came from many countries, most notably Italy. Italy itself imported cornel or dogwood from northern Anatolia for the making of crossbows.

Arms Manufacture

The late Roman *fabricae* or state-run armaments factories have been the subject of many studies. This was clearly a mass-production system; forty-four such *fabricae* being listed in the early 5th century *Notitia Dignitatum*, while archaeological evidence suggests that smaller unlisted *fabricae* were attached to many provincial Roman military units.

Some of these do seem to have survived the fall of the western Roman Empire, at least for a while. It similarly seems possible that several Italian cities, such as Pisa and Lucca, retained their arms industries from Roman times well into the medieval period. The same may also be true of Liège, some Flemish centres and Soissons in central France. On the other hand, most of the armourers of the Merovingian and even early Carolingian centuries were migratory smiths, operating small mobile forges as they moved around the country. The same seems to have been the case in 5th and 6th century Celtic Britain where weapons smiths travelled from petty state to petty state, offering their services to local rulers who in turn treated them as honoured guests.

Several parts of western Europe had, however, risen to prominence as centres of arms production by the 11th century. Over the next four hundred years a few of these outstripped all others in terms of volume production, the quality of their arms and armour, and as centres of fashion or new ideas. The most important of all were in southern Germany, the Rhineland of western Germany, and Lombardy in northern Italy. Other regions continued to manufacture arms and armour, of course, though largely for local consumption. These minor centres of production could clearly be rather old fashioned; as was the case with Holland in comparison with Flanders.

The importance of weapons smiths is clearly indicated by the early appearance of separate armourers' guilds; some of the first being recorded in 13th century Italy. In Venice, for example, the smiths were now divided into ordinary smiths and specialised sword-makers. The latter were, in turn, closely associated with scabbard, belt and armour makers. Even before the appearance of separate guilds, the craftsmen themselves were undoubtedly highly specialised and skilled. For example, the crossbow makers of early 13th century Paris were already divided into those making the weapons and those making the bolts. These armourers were similarly highly paid; Parisian helmet makers reportedly earning more than an ordinary *knight*. Most would have been local men, though a certain Richard the Saracen worked as an armourer in early 13th century Paris, and a Peter the Saracen was working for King John of England in 1205. At a less specialised level, the women of a 13th century French castle were described not only as making clothes for their fighting men, but also sewing the cloth parts of armour and fine-leather elements such as helmet-linings. Even the wife of a rich Italian arms merchant was still 'sewing helmets' in the late 14th century. Artists were similarly drawn in, being paid handsome sums for decorating the surface of tournament armour and harness.

Ordinary mass-produced items, not surprisingly, tended to be made where the basic materials were most easily available. For example, although crossbow bolts were made in many 13th century English cities, the largest centre of production was the castle of St Briavel in the Forest of Dean where iron, charcoal and wood were all abundant. Similarly, ropes for siege engines were manufactured in Bristol which, as one of the country's main ship-building centres, already made ropes in large quantities. Meanwhile soft-armours of quilted cloth were made by the Guild of Tailors and Linen Armourers in London.

Countries with less developed economies tended to fall back on more primitive systems; 12th century Poland, Bohemia and Hungary imposing a form of tax on certain villages to be paid in simple arms and armour, while other communities were expected to raise horses. The Balkans were different again. By the 14th century this region included highly sophisticated mercantile cities like Dubrovnik, where resident armourers formed a well paid industrial élite, whereas in inland rural areas much weaponry appears to have been made locally. The skills involved could still be highly sophisticated. For example, the making of composite bows was so complicated and lengthy that it had to be learned from childhood.

Whereas the crude workmanship and simple design of much late Roman weaponry pointed to mass production by low-skilled craftsmen, modern experiments indicate that it took about 128 heatings and 43 hours of work to make a normal early medieval form of *pattern-welded* blade. This increased to almost 75 hours if the making of a hilt, scabbard and belt were included. The finest decorated sword could take at least 200 hours; approximately one month's work. Forging the blade alone needed from 500 to 750 kilograms of charcoal. It probably took as long to make a mail *hauberk* as it did one of the finer forms of sword. Time was also the main ingredient in the making of composite bows, since season and weather both influenced the harvesting of suitable wood as well as the humidity and temperature needed for each stage of construction. In fact, it seems that a single bow took a year to make. Consequently they were made in batches, each stage awaiting suitable conditions for completion.

Simple longbows such as those used by the famous infantry archers of 14th century England were, by comparison, crude and easily made weapons. They were clearly made in huge numbers under the pressure of the Hundred Years War. Records for the year 1359 listed 20,000 bows being made in thirty-five locations, plus 850,000 arrows and 50,000 bowstrings, all for delivery to the kingdom's main arsenal in the Tower of London. Even in the previous century, crossbow bolts were being delivered 50,000 at a time, 500 being packed in each barrel for transport.

The Arms Trade

Arms and armour were distributed in various ways. Even in the late Roman period they could travel great distances, several better quality Roman swords having been found in 5th to 8th century Scandinavian and Baltic grave-sites. Most of the mail found in an early medieval Scandinavian context is also of eastern Mediterranean or Middle Eastern origin; acquired either as booty or trade or being handed down through many generations of inheritance. On the other hand, it appears that some arms-manufacturing centres were already catering for a wider market even in the early 6th century when, for example, Ostrogothic Italy may have exported *spangenhelm* forms of helmet to several surrounding countries. Elsewhere in early medieval western Europe, tribute from subjects to their ruler, and gifts from rulers to their followers, were a more important means of distribution than was trade.

The economic revival which began under the Carolingians may have meant that the relative cost of weaponry went down from the 8th to 11th centuries. Changes in arms and armour itself, or at least in the amount of equipment a member of the military élite was expected to possess, may then have caused it to rise once again from the 12th to 14th centuries. During the 12th century inheritance remained a very important source of weaponry; the English Assize of Arms in 1181 forbidding a man to sell, pawn or even give his weapons to any other person. Battlefield loot also played an important role, perhaps more particularly for those of lower rank.

Nevertheless, new weaponry obviously was purchased, usually by individuals though communes as well as governments were also buying arms and armour in bulk by the 14th century . Evidence from 12th and 13th century Genoa shows that the prices of specific items could fluctuate considerably, though the main differences in price reflected quality. This and other evidence similarly shows that armour was getting very expensive by the mid-13th century; full *knightly* equipment, plus a horse, equalling the average annual revenue of an English *knight's fief.* Perhaps as a result armour was often rented, the full price only being paid if it were lost.

Each part of Europe seems to have had its own recognised distribution centres, some of which were also places of manufacture. Toulouse, Montpellier and Avignon, for example, fulfilled this role for much of southern France in the late 13th century. Here merchants acted as middlemen between the manufacturers, who might be as far away as Italy, Germany or Spain, and the customers. Not surprisingly, governments tried to control such trade, especially in times of war, insisting that neither arms nor strategic materials including timber for ship-building be exported without a government licence.

Nevertheless, arms and armour of western European origin continued to reach remarkably distant lands. In the 11th century German swords were relatively well known in the Balkans. In the 13th and 14th century Italian weaponry poured into the Balkans through the ports of Dubrovnik in Dalmatia and Durrës in Albania. Poland imported swords from the Rhineland and although the Pope tried to ban sales to the pagan peoples of the Baltic, western arms still found their way there; as is shown by their presence in a number of grave-sites. The Baltic Letts, and probably their neighbours, also acquired weaponry

from Russia. The pagan Lapps of the far north exchanged metal goods for Arctic furs, while European knives and spear-blades have even been found in medieval Eskimo sites in the American Arctic; not to mention those far more dubious medieval weapons finds elsewhere in North America. The exportation of European weaponry to Muslims was, of course, forbidden by Papal decree. Nevertheless, it still took place. During the mid-12th century at the height of the Crusades, for example, Genoa seems to have been selling large quantities of arms and armour through the Moroccan port of Ceuta; such items being camouflaged as other forms of trade-goods in the financial records.

The considerable economic expansion enjoyed by western Europe in the 14th century was mirrored in the arms

'Guards at the Holy Sepulchre', carved panel from Strasbourg Cathedral; Franco-German, Rhineland, c.1345. It is rare for an armoured soldier to be shown from the back in such detail as the man on the right. The fact that he is resting his arm on a great helm suggests that this might go over the bascinet which he is already wearing. The man on the left also has a bascinet, here seen with its klappvisier raised. Note also the vambrace, probably made of hardened leather with iron reinforcing strips, and clearly buckled inside the arm, worn by this figure. (Musée de l'Oeuvre Notre Dame, Strasbourg)

trade which appears to have flourished as never before. As a result new ideas and new fashions spread rapidly, while skilled armourers moved to whichever country paid them best. Some new fashions even helped the sale of poor-quality goods, or the resale of battle-damaged ones. The helmet-makers of early 14th century London, for example, were accused of hiding such defects beneath the cloth-covering which was coming into fashion for certain helmets. This incident contributed to the establishment of a separate guild of registered helmet-makers in 1347; this being done so that the trade could be adequately regulated.

The role of Italian arms merchants in the 14th century was clearly very important, though it may also have been exaggerated by the very fact of the survival of the extraordinary and almost complete business records of Francesco di Marco Datini; known as the 'Merchant of Prato'. He, for example, bought arms from northern Italy and Germany, traded in uncut sheet iron for visors and arm-defences, tin studs for shields, got samples for armour and harness from Barcelona to check their quality, hired weaponry to those unable to pay the full price, bought captured equipment from the winning side then sold it second-hand to whomever would buy, and sent agents to buy up weaponry when an outbreak of temporary peace during the Hundred Years War led to a glut on the market.

Merchants like Datini could certainly have been found throughout most of Europe, dealing in Venetian arms in late 14th century Albania as it faced the advancing Ottomans, or providing new German equipment to those German mercenaries serving in Serbian armies, or car-

rying Swedish crossbows to the Teutonic Knights on the other side of the Baltic and perhaps even transporting wagon-loads of weaponry from northern or central Europe across southern Poland and Moldavia to the Black Sea ports. Much of the latter almost certainly ended up in the Islamic armies of Persia and the Middle East.

FIREARMS: THEIR ORIGINS AND DEVELOPMENT

Gunpowder

For many years the origins of gunpowder have been obscured by national prejudice, with several countries claiming its invention or its development as an effective weapon. Although more recent scholarship has shown that gunpowder as an explosive and incendiary material was invented in China, the early development of projectile-shooting guns remains a matter of some debate.

Almost wherever they are found, the earliest references to explosive mixtures that can be identified as primitive forms of gunpowder are closely associated with earlier, highly sophisticated forms of petroleum-based incendiary liquids such as *Greek Fire*. By the High Middle Ages this was a much more advanced chemical mixture than the substance first invented in the eastern Mediterranean several centuries earlier. It had also clearly reached France via the Crusades by the mid-12th century; then reaching England and other parts of northern Europe by the late 12th century. *Greek Fire* also remained in use in western Europe well into the 13th century, while apparently declining in popularity in the Middle East. This was not as yet, however, a really explosive mixture.

True gunpowder needed another vital ingredient; namely saltpetre which may have been discovered and

Vambrace, couter and the lower plate of a rerebrace, arm defences; possibly French or Italian, late 14th century. Although this is only one small part of a larger suit, or 'full set', of armour, it shows *the complicated shapes that later medieval armourers had to forge from the mild steel of which such pieces of armour were usually made. (Private collection)*

added to *Greek Fire* in the Islamic world. The next step, leading to that dry explosive powder now known as gunpowder, was made in China; probably during the early 11th century. The first clear Chinese description of explosive gunpowder dates from 1044 and refers to grenades of various sizes. These had developed further by the early 13th century, when they were joined by a form of gunpowder flame-thrower with a range of more than three metres. This in turn may have led to a small form of bamboo 'gun' that fired one or more small pellets, which was mentioned in 1259. Some kind of gunpowder device does seem to have been used by the Mongols in Hungary in 1241, and here it is worth noting that the Mongol invasion force involved in the invasion of central Europe did include some Chinese soldiers.

The first known Middle Eastern reference to an incendiary material that included saltpetre is found in a book on warfare written in late 12th or early 13th century Iraq. Similarly the *sihām khiṭaʿiyya* or 'Chinese style' fire arrows used by 13th century Muslim armies had an incendiary cartridge attached which probably contained a very early and primitive form of gunpowder. An extremely important Arabic book on incendiary and explosive weapons written in about 1270 in Egypt or Syria not only includes a recipe for gunpowder which modern experiments have shown to be highly effective, but also contained information about fuses and even the hand-held *midfaʿ* or gun. This latter reference could, however, have been a 14th century addition to the manuscript. Nevertheless, there is

Chamber or separate loading-breech of a small cannon; probably German or Scandinavian, late 14th–early 15th centuries. Such items were made of cast iron. The narrowed end would have slotted into the breech of a *small cannon. Several could be loaded, ready to be placed in a gun in rapid succession. This example, however, appears to have burst or otherwise been damaged at its rear end. (Museum of Estonian History, Tallinn)*

still strong evidence to suggest that, though the Chinese invented gunpowder, the Muslim armies of the Middle East were the first to use it to fire bullets of one kind or another.

While there is difficulty in interpreting the exact meaning of Arabic and even Chinese terms relating to explosive mixtures, this is an even greater problem with 13th century European sources. For example, the *Liber Igneum*, or *Book of Fire-weapons*, which was written in the mid-13th century, described both explosive and rocket forms of gunpowder as well as fuses; just as did Arabic manuscripts of the same period. Its early sections were attributed to a certain Mark the Greek and they used Arabic terminology comparable to that seen in sources from various parts of the eastern Mediterranean. This *Liber Igneum* probably played a major role in transmitting eastern gunpowder technology across Europe. Parts of it were, in fact, copied by Albertus Magnus, the teacher of the mid-13th century English scientist, Roger Bacon.

The recipe for gunpowder written down by Bacon himself is, however, surprisingly inferior to that in the *Liber Igneum*, being unable to cause an explosion or even to power a rocket. Nor does Bacon deal with fuses. In fact Bacon's writings are couched in such obscure, almost coded, language that he seems to be trying to hide what he was actually writing about. Perhaps this was for fear of the Church's reaction. Altogether it gives the impression that Roger Bacon was a persecuted transmitter of information from outside Christendom, rather than being an inventor of new ideas himself.

Though the idea that gunpowder was invented in early 14th century Germany is now disproved, the Germans do seem to have been the first to extract the vital ingredient of saltpetre from animal dung, this having previously come from a very few natural outcrops, or from rare types of marine salt deposits. The first clear references to gunpowder in Germany itself date from 1330 and 1331, whereas gunpowder had been used as an explosive by the English against the Scots as early as 1304.

Cannon

Who it was that first made and used metal guns again remains unclear. The first clear Chinese versions are no earlier than those in western Europe; the earliest surviving dateable Chinese cannon coming from the 1370s, while the earliest Middle Eastern versions are still a matter of scholarly argument. On the other hand the *bussen met kruyt* mentioned in the archives of the Flemish city of Ghent in 1313, and again at the siege of Metz in 1324, almost certainly meant 'cannon with powder'. The earliest European picture of a gun is in an English manuscript, again with possible Flemish influence, dating from 1326.

These earliest guns were more normally known as *pots de fer*, 'iron pots', and fired what looked like a large crossbow-bolt with an iron or brass flight. A two-metre-long all-iron 'arrow' of this kind was, in fact, found in Russia. It dates from the late 13th or 14th centuries and is associated with

a Mongol siege, or a Russian defence, of the princely city of Vladimir. Such oversized arrows were, however, soon replaced by stone or metal cannon balls.

The first cannon were clearly quite small, but their success led to experiments with larger weapons. They were also relatively cheap and could be manufactured in quantity for the richer governments of the 14th century; particularly after European metalworkers had learned to smelt and then cast large quantities of metal. Most 14th century guns were, in fact, still made of brass or latten. The cannon-makers not only supplied the barrels, shot, moulds to make shot, *tampions*, carriages and powder; they also hired themselves out as highly paid gunners.

At first the guns appear to have been mounted on a board which could be tipped up or down to range the shot, or simply be bedded in the earth to fire at a pre-set target. *Trunnions* on each side of the barrel, which enabled it to be elevated or lowered easily, were not invented until the 15th century. The limited range of early weapons also meant that various types of wooden screens were erected in front of the guns to protect their crews from enemy crossbowmen while they reloaded. An iron *drivell* or ramrod was used to load the gun; disc-shaped wooden *tampions* separating the powder from the shot and helping to contain the exploding gases. The guns were then fired by placing a metal *touche*, already heated in a brazier of coals, against the *touch-hole*. Despite their obvious limitations, these new gunpowder weapons had an enormous moral effect. This was not only because of their noise and smoke, but because of the horrible wounds they could cause; wounds which smashed flesh and thus almost invariably became fatally septic, unlike the relatively clean cutting wounds of traditional medieval weapons.

From the second quarter of the 14th century guns of various kinds became increasingly common. In Italy, a legal document of 1326 refers to a *maestro delle bombarde*, 'master of the *bombard*'; cannon next being mentioned in various wars of 1331 and 1341. Even the Pope's own army had cannon by 1350. The first references to bronze and iron cannon being manufactured in Germany date from 1346 and 1348. The French may have used cannon during a raid on the English port of Southampton in 1338, and they clearly made greater use of such weapons than did the English during the early part of the Hundred Years War. The English themselves were unusual in using *bombards* against the French in open battle at Crécy in 1346, since such weapons were still normally reserved for siege and counter-siege operations. At Crécy the English may, in fact, have been attempting to frighten the French army's Genoese crossbowmen. The first references to firearms in the Balkans date from 1351, the first in Poland from 1383. In each case the weapons had clearly arrived from western Europe.

European gun terminology was still varied and confusing, though it does seem to have related to specific types of weapon. Whereas the early *bombard* was a short-barrelled but relatively large calibre weapon used in siege warfare,

Bombard, late 14th–early 15th centuries; the most common type of cannon in the 14th century. This example has a cast-iron powder chamber at the back and a barrel that is made either of wrought iron hoops over longitudinal iron splints or has such hoops added for greater strength. (Military Museum, Budapest)

the later 'great guns' were larger forms of *bombard* moved in carts, but not fired from them. By 1386, for example, the fortified English port of Southampton was defended by almost sixty large-bore cannon; the largest having a calibre of more than 50 centimetres.

The *couleuvrine* or 'snake' was a longer barrelled gun which probably originated in 14th century Germany and soon came to be used in open battle. The first real 'field artillery' piece was likely to have been the *ribaudequin*, though even this was first used in sieges. Its name originally referred to the cart on which several small-bore but long-barrelled guns were mounted. These became increasingly widespread from the mid-14th century; being known as *ribaudequins*, *ribaudekins* or *ribaldis*. Efforts to provide massive firepower by constructing multiple *ribaudequins* could go to extraordinary lengths. Antonio della Scala, the ruler of Verona in northern Italy, had a weapon with no less than 144 *ribaudequin* barrels mounted in three tiers, each tier in four sections, to be fired by three gunners. The whole apparatus was almost seven metres high, being on a wagon pulled by four horses. Fortunately, perhaps, it proved too cumbersome to use.

The late 14th century finally saw the development of guns with separate breech-chambers or *thunder boxes*. Several of these could be ready loaded and placed in the gun's breech one after the other to provide a brief burst of rapid fire. The larger type of such breech-loading gun seems to have been known as a *veuglaire* or 'fowler'; the smaller as a *crapaudeaux* or 'toad'.

Handguns

The first apparent mention of a hand-held gun in Europe comes in a description of the defence of the northern Italian town of Forli in 1284. But this is so much earlier than any other reference, that it is likely to have been a later insertion or a misunderstanding. The weapons in question were called *sclopi* or *sclopeti* which were, however, regarded as 'recent German inventions' in the memoirs of a mid-15th century Pope. Perhaps the original author meant *cerbottano* or 'blowpipe', which was widely used as a hunting weapon in the nearby lagoons of north-western Italy.

The first definite hand-held guns were normally known as *couleuvrines à main*; later types being known in England as *handgonnes*. These squat miniature cannon were attached to the ends of long poles which were then held under the arm or on the shoulder; often being fired by a second man. The length of the pole probably resulted from the need to ram unreliable early forms of gunpowder hard into the short barrels of such weapons. Some early hand-guns also had hooks beneath their barrels; these being placed over a wall or parapet to take the shock of recoil.

They all remained very rare before 1360, but thereafter rapidly became cheap and abundant. Such economic factors gave them obvious advantages over the now highly accurate and powerful, but also sophisticated and expensive, crossbows of the late 14th century. By the end of the 14th century, however, several improvements had appeared. For example, it was found that a longer barrel increased muzzle velocity, and did away with the need of a long mounting pole; this being replaced by a shorter stock which also permitted more accurate aiming. Cast-metal bullets similarly became increasingly common in Italy, though stone ones remained the norm in France and England.

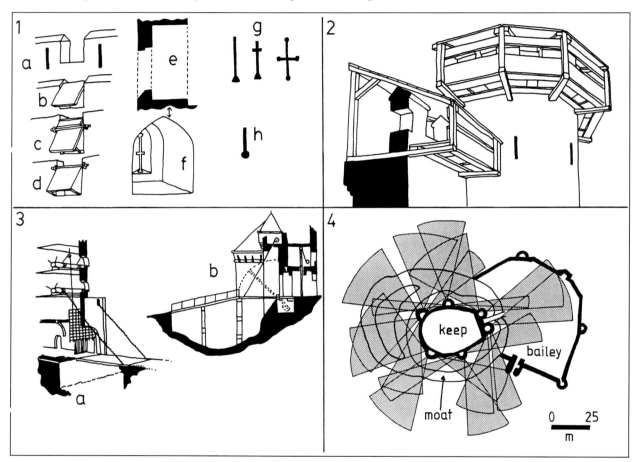

Defensive architecture details

1.a Battlement with simple 'crenellation' consisting of 'crenel', merlon, raised pieces, here pierced by arrow-loops. (after Gravett)

b Hinged wooden shutter added to the crenel as used from the 13th century (after Gravett)

c–d Other forms of shutter. (after Gravett)

e–f Section and internal view of a 13th–14th century embrasure and arrow-loop. (after Gravett)

g External views of arrow-loops from the late 12th to the 14th centuries. (after Gravett)

h Late 14th century loop-hole designed for small or hand-held guns. (after Gravett)

2. Wooden hoarding around a tower and sectional views of a hoarding mounted on top of a wall, 13th century. (after Gravett)

3. Two systems for raising a drawbridge and portcullis:

a Both drawbridge and portcullis are raised by chains pulled by winches in rooms directly one above the other.

b The drawbridge is raised by a winch that has to pull minimum weight as the rear of the bridge forms a counter-weight which descends into a pit as the front of the bridge is raised; meanwhile the portcullis to the rear is still raised by a winch alone.

4. Areas covered by longbow arrows shot from the embrasures of the keep of White Castle, Gwent; late 12th century; according to experiments carried out by Jones and Renn, 1982.

VIII
GLOSSARY

acie: small cavalry formation, England and Germany.

acton: quilted soft armour, 14th century Ireland (see also *aketon*).

adobe: 'dub' or make a knight.

adorator: late Roman palace guardsman.

agrarii milites: early medieval peasant troops in Germany.

ailettes: small pieces of wood or parchment worn on the shoulders for heraldic display, 13th and 14th centuries.

aire, airig: nobility of Celtic Ireland.

aketon: quilted form of soft-armour, from the Arabic word for 'cotton (see also *acton* and *hoqueton*).

amīr al-baḥr: 'Commander of the Sea', Arabic title used in Norman Sicily and southern Italy; the original term behind various European versions of the title *admiral.*

angaria: duty of defending a city or settlement's fortified walls in Italy.

angon: Germanic barbed javelin with long iron socket.

apostis: bulwarks along the *telaro* outrigger of a galley.

arbalesres à tour: windlass-spanned crossbow.

armati: bodyguards of Merovingian Frankish ruling family.

armigeri: possibly a group within the *squires* with more aristocratic origins, 14th century.

arming cap: padded cap or coif worn beneath a metallic helmet.

arming doublet: padded garment worn beneath later medieval plate-armour, to which small pieces of mail could also be laced to protect chinks in the plate-armour.

arrière-ban: general levy in France and the Norman states.

arrière-guet: patrolling town or city streets and checking on the *guet* wall-patrols, France (see also *estialgach* and *reyregach*).

arsenal, arsenale: originally a ship-building yard, subsequently also meaning a military storage depot (from the Arabic term *dār al-ṣināʿah*).

asbergumm: mail hauberk, 13th–14th century Italy.

auctenta: unclear officer rank in late Roman army.

aunlaz: short dagger of English infantry, 14th century.

aventail: mail fringe attached to the edge of a helmet protecting the neck and throat.

azure: heraldic term for blue colour; from the Arabic *azraq.*

bachelor, bacheliers: young knight awaiting inheritance or a fief from his lord.

baculus: symbolic wooden club or mark of office of Norse origin.

badas: urban daytime lookouts posted on neighbouring high points.

bagnbergae: late Roman and early medieval leg protections.

baile: military unit, Celtic Ireland and western Scotland.

bailli: ruler's representative or commander in a castle or fortified place.

bainbergae: leg protections, Carolingian Europe.

baldric: strap or belt to support a scabbard, worn over the shoulder rather than around the waist.

balinger: type of small English galley for coastal patrols.

ballista: late Roman, Romano-Byzantine and early medieval stone-throwing and large frame-mounted arrow-shooting device; also a later medieval crossbow.

ballista de torno: large crossbow probably *spanned* by a windlass.

ballistam ad tornum: large crossbow probably *spanned* by a windlass.

ballistarii: possibly operators of frame-mounted siege-machines in the late Roman army.

ballok dagger: dagger having a grip and guard resembling male sexual organs.

bán: provincial lord or governor, 14th century Hungary.

banderia: paid retainers or private army of a 14th century Hungarian military leader or nobleman.

bandi: military unit, Italy.

bandiera: Italian military unit or company with a trumpeter, fifes or drums.

bandifer: standard-bearer, Italy.

bandiforus: unclear officer rank in late Roman army.

bandwa: military unit or flag, early medieval Germany.

banière: military unit or flag, medieval France.

banieren: military unit or flag, medieval Germany.

bannier: large rectangular military flag.

bannum: general levy of all people with military obligations, early medieval Europe.

barbotte: method of protecting a ship against *Greek Fire*, consisting of sheets of leather or felt soaked in vinegar.

barbuta, barbata: style of *bascinet* helmet which also protected the sides of the face.

bard: horse armour (see also *trapper*).

bardot: pack-animal, offspring of a horse and she-ass (from the Arabic word *birdhawn* meaning an inferior pack-horse).

bascinet: relatively light form of helmet also protecting the rear and sides of the head.

baselard: broad tapering dagger with H-shaped hilt.

basternae: waterproof cart used to cross rivers, Carolingian period.

bastide: small fortified 'new town' along strategic routes or near sensitive frontiers, 13th century France.

bataelgen: army divisions, Germany.

batailles: army divisions, France.

battaglie: army divisions, Italy.

battle: military division, England.

battlements: crenellations along the top of a fortified wall or tower.

beacon: wood-stack either in a stone structure or an iron container used as part of a warning system: smoke by day, fire by night (see also *cresset*).

beffroi: 'belfry', mobile wooden tower used in siege warfare (see also *berfriez*).

belette: 'weasel', probably a low movable wooden shed-like structure which could be moved forward against enemy fortifications.

benefice: land given in return for military service, Europe.

berdona: slender-bladed thrusting dagger (see also *bordon*).

berfriez: mobile wooden tower used in siege warfare (see also *beffroi*).

bergfried: tall fortified tower, either

isolated or within a curtain wall, Germany.

bersaut: archery target, 13th century France.

berserk: 'bare-chested' warrior or fighting-mad hero, Anglo-Saxon England and Scandinavia.

besagews: circular plates to protect elbow and shoulder.

biarchus: junior officer rank in late Roman army.

biffa: trebuchet with an adjustable counterweight, late 13th–14th centuries (see also *boves*).

blazon: heraldic design or coat of arms.

bohorde: fence separating men involved in a *tournament*, particularly when *jousting*.

bolt: short arrow shot from a crossbow (see also *quarrel*).

bombard: most common early form of short-barrelled cannon, 14th century.

bordon: slender-bladed thrusting dagger (see also *berdona*).

bourgeois: citizens of a city, normally considered 'middle class' by modern standards.

boves: form of beam-sling *mangonel*, France and Italy (see also *biffa*).

boyar: tribal nobleman, military commander or senior aristocrat, Bulgaria and the Romanian principalities.

braquier: girdle with straps to support mail *chausses*.

bras de fer: armour for the arms.

brassards: pieces of armour for the arms, late 13th century.

bretache, bretesche: covered wooden hoarding on top of a fortified wall, or a protruding stone or wooden structure around a window partway up a wall.

brigandine: semi-rigid, often decoratively as well as functionally fabric-covered body armour of sometimes very small pieces of iron.

broch: Pictish tower-fort or refuge.

brunia: unspecified form of early medieval European body armour.

bucellarii: late Roman military servants or private guardsman; guards of Romano-Byzantine nobility, commanders or rulers.

büchsenmeister: master gunner, 14th century Germany.

bussen met kruyt: probably very early form of cannon with gunpowder, early 14th century Flanders.

butscarls: probably mercenary naval troops, 11th century Anglo-Saxon England.

buzogány: light cavalry mace of Turkish origin, Hungary.

caable: single-arm torsion-powered stone-throwing *petraria*, northern France, 13th century (see also *calabres, chadabula* and *chaablum*) of northern France.

caballarios: cavalryman in 11th century southern France.

caer: fortified site, Wales.

cain: non-noble military obligation tied to tenancy of a particular piece of land, Scotland.

calabres: single-armed stone-throwing *petraria*, southern France 13th century.

calcar: ship's beak or ram, well above the waterline to assist in boarding enemy vessels.

cambieras: mail protections for the legs (see also *chausses* and *stivaletti*).

campiductor: regimental drill officer in late Roman army.

candidati: Romano-Byzantine guard unit.

cantator: singer who rode ahead of an army into battle, 11th–12th centuries.

cantref: 'one hundred farmsteads', basis of military recruitment in Wales.

caparison: medieval European decorative horse-covering, often including a protective layer.

capitani: senior officers in Italian urban armies.

Capitano del Popolo: commander of militia in Italian city under a 'popular' rather than aristocratic government.

capmalh: mail coif, southern France.

caporale: officer in charge of smallest cavalry formation, 14th century Italy.

cappelus de ferro: 'war hat', helmet with a brim.

captain: middle-ranking military commander, usually appointed by a

government authority.

carroccio: banner-wagon and rallying point, medieval Italy.

cartouche: written inscription as part of a coat of arms.

casa-torre: large fortified house in an Italian city.

cashel: Celtic Irish ring-fort.

castella: small Romano-Byzantine frontier fort.

castellani: officer in command of a citadel or tower, 14th century Italy.

castle guard: form of local feudal military obligation imposed on knights and military élite.

castrae: Roman and early medieval European fortification or castle.

castron: small Romano-Byzantine frontier fort.

cataphract: heavily armoured Romano-Byzantine cavalryman.

ceathramh: smallest military unit, early medieval western Scotland.

centaine: English militia unit, supposedly of a hundred men.

centenae: élite troops of a Merovingian Frankish king.

centenarius: senior officer rank in late Roman army.

ceorl: Anglo-Saxon free man.

cerbottano: 'blowpipe', 13th–14th century Italy; from the early Persian *zivah-dān*, via the Arabic *zabtāna*.

cervellière: close-fitting round helmet, sometimes worn beneath other forms of protection.

cet: large military unit, Celtic Ireland.

chaablum: stone-throwing *petraria*, northern France, 13th century (see also *caable* and *chadabula*).

chadabula: stone-throwing *petraria*, northern France, 13th century (see also *caable* and *chaablum*).

chamfron: piece of horse armour protecting the animal's head (see also *coopertus* and *copita*).

chansons de geste: warlike epic in verse-form, normally in French.

chapel de fer: brimmed helmet or war-hat.

château de bois: wooden siege-castle, usually movable.

chats châteaux: 'cat-castle', movable shed-like structure to protect the entrance to a siege-mine, with an additional wooden castle attached.

chaugān: Persian name for the game

of polo (see also *chicane*).

chausses: mail protections for the legs (see also *cambieras* and *stivaletti*).

checky: chequerboard pattern used in heraldry, from the Arab word *sha ṭranj* meaning both chess and the chessboard pattern.

chelandre: transport ships, 12th–13th century France.

chelandrion: oared galley for transporting horses, with a beach-landing capability, 10th century (see also *chelandre* and *salandria*).

chevauchée: defensive operation within its own area; also a military raid, 14th century France.

chicane: medieval French name for polo.

chivalry: code of behaviour and social attitudes associated with the later medieval knightly military élite.

chlamys: large woollen garment worn by Roman soldiers.

Cinque Ports: 'Five Ports' of southern England which, from the 12th century, provided ships to serve as war-ships in the king's fleet: Hastings, Romney, Hythe, Dover and Sandwich.

cirator: junior officer rank in late Roman army.

cirotechas: probably gauntlets, Serbia.

clibanarius: heavily armoured Romano-Byzantine cavalryman.

clippeos: iron armour of Balkan or Byzantine origin, used at sea, probably lamellar, 13th–14th century Italy.

cnihtas: élite troops in 11th century Anglo-Saxon king's retinue.

coat-of-plates: semi-rigid armour worn over or beneath a mail *hauberk*, consisting of plates of iron or other material fastened to leather or fabric, also known as a *pair of plates* or simply as *plates*.

cog: type of square-rigged northern Europe sailing ship with a stern rudder.

coif: close-fitting head covering which goes beneath the chin; also a mail coif either attached to a *hauberk* or separate.

coirasses: body armour, probably of hardened leather, 13th century southern France.

cols sfrachis: shoulder and neck protection, probably like a *tippet*, southern France.

coltello: short infantry stabbing sword, 14th century Italy (see also *corta spada*).

comes: commanding officer in late Roman army.

comestabilis: officer in command of a Venetian military unit.

comestabilis equester: commanding officer of an overseas Venetian garrison.

comitatus: regular or semi-regular military force attached to a ruler, nobleman or military commander in Romano-Byzantine and Germanic 'barbarian' states.

commission of array: royal officials charged with organising and summoning local militias, 14th century England.

commorth: non-noble military obligation tied to tenancy of a particular piece of land, Wales.

compagna: militia or mercenary unit or company, Italy.

companie: militia unit, France.

condottieri: mercenary troops under contract to a specific employer, later medieval Italy.

conestabilaria: cavalry unit, France, England and Italy.

connaissances: heraldic patterns by which individual knights were recognised.

conroi: cavalry squadron, France.

conroten: cavalry squadron, Germany.

consigliere: 'consul', officer rank in Italian urban militia.

constable: a senior officer in a royal or noble household, normally responsible for military discipline and organisation.

constabularie: militia unit led by a constable, France.

constabularium: theoretical unit of ten men, early 12th century England.

constantble: leader of a militia unit or levy, France.

consul: leader or representative of an urban quarter, social or craft association in an Italian city; also an urban and sometimes military leader in France.

contado: rural area immediately around an Italian city and dependent upon that city.

coopertus: piece of horse armour protecting the animal's head, probably of hardened leather (see also *copita* and *chamfron*).

copita: piece of horse armour protecting the animal's head, probably of hardened leather (see also *chamfron*).

corazza, coraczas: semi-rigid cuirass, usually of hardened leather, 13th–14th century Italy.

corda: short-sword or large dagger, 14th century Dalmatia, possibly derived from the Turco-Persian and Arab *kard* dagger.

corietumm: leather cuirass, 13th century Europe.

cornage: non-noble military obligation tied to tenancy of a particular piece of land, northern England.

corsia: timbers runing along a galley to give it longitudinal strength.

corta spada: short infantry stabbing sword, 14th century Italy (see also *coltello*).

cotteraux: infantry mercenaries of unclear origins, 12th century France.

couched lance: technique whereby the weapon was held tightly beneath a horseman's upper right arm.

couleuvrine: 'snake', longer barrelled cannon of the mid and later 14th century.

couleuvrine à main: early form of hand-held gun or miniature cannon, 14th century France.

courtly love: code of accepted social behaviour in which a *knight* or *squire* was expected to honour and pursue the fair sex, 13th–14th centuries.

coustell: infantry short-sword (see also *couteau, custellarius* and *cultellus*).

couteau: infanty short-sword (see also *coustell, custellerius* and *cultellus*).

couter: cup-shaped piece of armour protecting the elbow joint.

couvertures à cheval: horse armour.

couvertures de plates: rigid or semi-rigid horse armour, 14th century France and England.

cranequin: rack-and-pinnion system of *spanning* a crossbow.

crannog: artificial defensive island in early medieval Scotland and Ireland.

crapaudeaux: 'toad', smaller type of later 14th century breech-loading cannon.

cresset: iron container for a fire-beacon, on pole reached by a ladder.

croc: obscure form of staff-weapon.

cropure, crupper: armour for hindquarters of a horse (see also *crupière*).

crow: long pole with a hooked end, to pull opponents from behind cover in siege warfare.

crupière: armour for hindquarters of a horse (see also *cropure, crupper*).

cultellus: medieval Latin term for a short sword, possibly referring to a *seax* in the early medieval period (see also *coustell, couteau* and *custellarius*).

cuirass, pair of cuirasses: semi-rigid body-armour, usually of hardened leather, 13th–14th centuries (see also *curie*).

cuir-bouilli: hardened leather, soaked in wax then heated and moulded.

cuirs à bras: pieces of hardened leather for the arms, 14th century.

cuman: German name for light cavalry auxiliaries of Kipchaq Turkish origin.

cuneos: small closely packed cavalry formation in late Roman and medieval European armies.

curiales: Roman ruling élite.

curie: semi-rigid *cuirass*, probably of hardened leather (see also *quiret*).

curragh: large skin-covered boat used by early medieval Celtic peoples of western Britain, Scotland and Ireland.

cursores: offensive cavalry troops in Romano–Byantine army; also a form of unit cavalry exercise in Carolingian times.

causa exercitii: cavalry training exercises in Carolingian times (see also *cursores*).

curteni: members of the ruler's court including élite troops, Wallachia.

curtes: fortress, Carolingian Europe.

custellarius: infantry short-sword (see also *couteau, coustell* and *cultellus*).

custodes: officers responsible for guards on gates, walls and towers of an Italian overseas colony.

dague à rouelles: 'rowell dagger', having disc-shaped pommel and guard.

damascene: form of metal-working in which an ingot of high or mixed high and low carbon steel produced a weapon, usually a sword-blade, with a distinctive surface pattern commonly called 'watering'.

damoiseau: armoured cavalryman of lower status than a *knight*, late 13th century England.

dardiers: javelin-armed light infantry, Gascony.

davach: military unit sufficient to crew one ship, early medieval western Scotland.

defensores: defensive cavalry troops in Romano-Byantine army.

demi-greaves: armour for the shins, 14th century.

destrier: war-horse of a medieval *knight* or other member of the military élite.

diarchy: a state divided into two parts, each under a separate government but forming one state.

diener: lightly armed military servants, 14th century Germany.

dienstleute: non-noble 'serf cavalry' in Germany.

distringitori: 'explainers', officer rank in Italian urban militia.

dithmarschen: peasant infantry from northern Germany.

donjon: stone keep, or central or primary tower of a medieval castle.

donzel: young nobleman or low-status member of the military élite, 12th–13th century southern France.

dorobanți: local defence formations, probably to guard mountain passes, Wallachia.

dorodrepanon: possibly cutting spear or staff-weapon in 6th century Romano-Byzantine army.

draconarii: standard-bearer in late Roman army.

dreng: tenant with military obligation associated with holding of land, ex-Viking areas of England.

druzyna: élite troops of a Polish ruler.

dubbing: ceremony whereby a warrior, usually a *squire*, was raised to the rank of *knight*.

ducenarius: senior officer rank in late Roman army.

dull: early medieval Celtic battle array.

dux: Romano-Byzantine frontier governor.

earldorman: king's representative responsible for local militia levy, Anglo-Saxon England.

échelle: cavalry squadron, France.

echielle: military unit, often of élite troops, medieval France.

ecu: cavalry shield, France and Italy.

ecuyer: squire, armoured cavalryman of lower status than a *knight*, 14th century England.

embrasure: hole in a wall or tower, for observation or from which to shoot.

enarmes: straps for the left arm, inside a shield.

equitatore: cavalryman in an overseas Venetian garrison.

escudier: paid military servant or soldier of lowly origin, southern France.

espalier, espaulière: shoulder protection (see also *spaulder*).

espias: spies, southern France 13th–14th centuries.

espringal: medieval European frame-mounted large arrow-shooting machine with two separate arms (see also *spingarda, spingala* and *springolf*).

establida: garrison responsible for defending a wider region, southern France.

estialgach: patrolling walls of a fortified town, southern France (see also *reyregach* and *arrière-guet*).

exarch: semi-autonomous Byzantine provincial governor.

excubitores: Romano-Byzantine guard unit.

exploratores: scouts in late Roman army.

fabricae: state-run armaments factories of the late Roman Empire.

fähnlein: small flags of guilds and small communities, 14th century Switzerland.

falchion: form of heavy straight sword with a single cutting edge, the blade often broadening rather than narrowing towards its tip.

falco, falcione: staff-weapon with a long slightly curved single-edged blade, often with a substantial hook on the back for dragging down horsemen.

Familia Regis: Royal Household including military retinue, France and the Norman states, 11th–14th centuries.

fauld: lower extension of a *cuirass* or *coat-of-plates* covering part of the belly and buttocks.

faus, faussal: probably forms of *faussart* or *falchion*.

faussart: heavy single-edged infantry weapon.

feditori: cavalry forces of Italian city communes, 13th–14th centuries.

feni: military leaders of Celtic Ireland.

fideles: closest military followers of an early medieval Germanic ruler; those owing military obligation in medieval Italy, usually from rural areas.

fief: territorial estate to support a *knight* and his equipment.

fighting castle: wooden structures on the prow and stern of larger sailing ships, where the vessel's defenders were concentrated.

fighting top: strong wooden 'crow's nest' position high on a warship's masts, from which marines could shoot upon enemy crews.

flanchards, flanchières: armour for the front and sides of a horse.

fleurs-de-lis: heraldic pattern in the form of a stylised flower; recognised badge of the French ruling family, late Middle Ages.

foederati: 'allies' of Roman and Romano-Byzantine armies, normally from frontier regions.

folgepflicht: military levy or rural militia, Germany.

franciska: early medieval Frankish throwing axe.

fyrd: local military levy, Anglo-Saxon England.

gach, gag: patrolling the walls of a fortified town, southern France (see also *guet*).

gaesa: obscure form of staff-weapon, possibly like a *gisarme*.

gafluch, gafeluc: small javelin of Welsh origin.

galati: castle, Romanian-speaking regions of Wallachia and Moldavia, from the Arabic term *qal'a* via Turkish.

galee al scaloccio: galley in which several men pulled one large oar.

galee alla sensile: 'galley in simple fashion' in which one man pulled one oar.

galleon: small form of galley, not the same vessel as the galleons of the 16th and 17th centuries.

galloglas axe: long-hafted war-axe used in later medieval Ireland and western Scotland.

galloglass: professional infantry, later medieval Ireland and Scotland.

gambeson: medieval padded or felt garment normally worn beneath armour (see also *wambasia*).

gants de fer: iron gauntlets.

garde: sentry-duty at town gates in daytime, France.

garde de la mer: coastal militia, 14th century England.

gardingi: guards of the Visigothic king.

garniso: garrison responsible for defending a town, southern France.

gasindii: military retinue of a Frankish nobleman in Italy.

gasmouli: Byzantine marines of mixed Greek and western European descent.

gastaldii: military retinue or representives of the king in Lombardic Italy.

gaveloc: small javelin of Welsh origin.

gazerant: form of mail armour construction with integral padded lining and probably cloth covering (see also *jazerenc*).

gens: people or 'race' based upon ancient Greek ideas of inherited ethnic differences.

gens d'armes: 'men-at-arms', armoured cavalry.

gentiles: local forces in various parts of the Romano-Byzantine Empire.

gesithas: military retinue of an early Anglo-Saxon ruler.

ghiazzerina: mail hauberk of *jazerant* construction, Italy.

gisarme: staff-weapon, probably having a curved blade with or without a hook at the back (see also *jusarme* and *guizarme*) .

gladius: short Roman infantry sword.

gleven: cavalry unit usually consisting

of a man-at-arms and his followers, Germany.

goedendag: infantry weapon resembling a long-hafted mace with a cutting or thrusting blade mounted on top, 14th century Flanders.

gonfali: Italian militia companies.

gonfalonieri: standard-bearer, Italy.

gonfanon: middle-sized military banner.

gonuklaria: Romano-Byzantine leg protection.

gorgerete: protection for neck and throat.

gorgerete pizaine: large protection for neck and shoulders.

gorgieri: neck and perhaps shoulder protection, Italy.

grand salle: 'great hall' in a castle or palace, for ceremonial purposes.

great crossbow: large form of crossbow, often on a pedestal or frame.

great helm: helmet fully enclosing wearer's head.

Greek Fire: petroleum-based liquid incendiary weapon.

gregarii: mercenary troops in Norman states.

grèves: greaves.

grithmen: convicted or suspected criminals seeking sanctuary in one of the small territories known as 'royal liberties' in northern England.

gualdana: devastation of enemy territory, Italy.

guérite: 'sentry-box', unclear form of wooden siege structure.

guet: mounting watch on urban ramparts, usually at night, France (see also *gach, gag*).

guette: watch-tower attached to a castle or other fortified place.

guizarme: staff-weapon, probably having a curved blade with or without a hook at the back (see also *jusarme* and *gisarme*).

gules: heraldic word for red colour; from the Persian *gil* meaning a red dye for the hair, or *gul* meaning a rose.

gyula: aristocratic or military rank, second only to that of a royal prince, largely in the Transylvanian provinces of the Kingdom of Hungary.

hadnagy: Magyar tribal duke and military commander.

halberd, halbard: infantry pole-arm normally incorporating an axe-blade, plus a hammer at the back and a thrusting spike on top.

hallenbarten: early form of *halberd,* Germany.

handgonne: hand-held gun, late 14th century England.

harnas de gaumbe: leg-armour.

hastiludia: 'lance play', early form of cavalry training by units of horsemen with lances (see also *mêlée*).

haubergeon: short-sleeved version of a mail *hauberk,* normally used by non-élite troops.

hauberk: mail armour for body and arms.

haubier: mail *hauberk,* 14th century Low Countries.

haubregon: short-sleeved version of a mail *hauberk,* 14th century Low Countries.

heaume: normal term for *great helm* covering the face and later also the sides and back of the head.

heaume à vissere: probably a later form of *great helm* with a movable visor.

herce: 'harrow' formation in which archers fought in close co-operation with dismounted *men-at-arms,* often within a thicket of sharpened wooden stakes, 14th century England.

here: Scandinavian term for an army.

hippo-toxotai: composite spear-and-bow-armed armoured cavalryman of the later Romano-Byzantine army.

hoardings: wooden defensive structures on top of a fortified wall.

hobelar: light cavalryman, originally from Ireland, later also recruited in England.

honved: local defence militia, 15th century Hungary.

hoqueton: cotton-quilted form of soft-armour (see also *acton* and *aketon*).

hospodar: military governor of Moldavia.

housecarl: professional soldier in king's retinue, 11th century Anglo-Saxon England.

huissier: large Mediterranean transport ship, believed to have loading doors in the sides of the hull, 12th–13th centuries (see also *uissier*).

hundred: subdivision of a shire, basis of military organisation in Anglo-Saxon England.

ilarch: infantry squad leader in Romano-Byzantine army.

indenture: system of recruitment in which military leaders were contracted to raise an agreed number of troops.

indulgence: remission of punishment for sin after sacramental absolution and penance; frequently offered by Christian churchmen usually in return for some kind of payment.

inermes: unarmoured horsemen, early medieval Europe.

iqtaᶜ: military estate, Arab-Islamic areas.

ispán: provincial governor and military leader, Hungary (see also *zhupan*).

Italian Grip: fencing technique in which the forefinger of the right hand was wrapped around one quillon of the sword's hilt.

iunaci: infantry, Wallachia (see also *voinici*).

jack: semi-rigid fabric-covered body armour of very small pieces of iron.

jawshan: lamellar cuirass, Islamic regions.

jazerenc, jazerain: padded and lined mail *hauberk,* 12th–13th century Europe, based on the Arab-Islamic *kazāghand* from which the word originated (see also *gazerant* and *kazāghand*).

jeddart axe: characteristic long-hafted war-axe of the Scottish Borders, late Middle Ages.

jihād: Muslim concept of spiritual struggle, also including war against the infidel.

jinete: small horse; also light cavalry tactics of medieval Iberian peninsula.

jobbágy: settled regional militia, Hungary.

jomsvikings: 'brotherhood' of professional soldiers, 11th century Denmark.

jousting: individual combat between lance-armed cavalrymen during a *tournament.*

judeţe: military district, Wallachia.

jund: territorial military organisation, Arab-Islamic areas.

jusarme: staff-weapon, probably having a curved blade with or without a hook at the back (see also *guizarme* and *gisarme*).

juvens, juvenes: younger members of the military aristocracy who had not yet come into their inheritances, northern France and Norman England.

karias, karya: tribal army among Baltic peoples.

kastron: Byzantine fortified town and centre of military administration.

kazāghand: mail hauberk with integral padded lining and decorative fabric covering, Arab-Islamic (see also *jazerenc* and *jazerain*).

keel: type of north European cargo ship.

keiromanika: Romano-Byzantine gauntlets.

keverang: regional military unit or basis of recruitment, early medieval Cornwall.

khatangku dehel: scale-lined fabric or felt coat, Mongol, 13th and 14th centuries.

knechte: knight, 13th–14th century Germany.

knechte der freiheit: 'knights of freedom' in the service of 14th century German cities.

knézat: provincial governor or local ruler, 14th century Romania.

knight: member of the aristocratic military élite, England.

kolariya: neck protection or gorget, Serbia.

laeti: military colonists of late Roman period.

laich: warrior, Celtic Ireland.

lambrequin: helmet decoration of cloth.

lames: pieces of overlapping armour in the *laminated* system of construction, usually in a horizontal manner.

lamieri: cuirass or *coat-of-plates,* Italy.

laminate: system of construction of armour in which narrow but quite long *lames* overlap one another, usually horizontally.

lance: heavy cavalry spear; also basic cavalry unit in 14th century western Europe.

lanciarii: possibly spear-armed infantry in late Roman army.

landrecht: rural levy or militia, Austria.

lantweri: general levy in German-speaking areas.

latrunculi: banditry or raiding, Baltic states.

lavra: Romano-Byzantine monastic retreat, often fortified.

leidang: levy of ships, men and military equipment, Viking Denmark.

leorde: king's army, early medieval Kent.

lettres de retenue: instructions permitting an *indentured* military leader to recruit troops.

liek: small cavalry formation, Germany.

life-stones: small stones, often semi-precious, attached to the hilt or scabbard of pre-Christian Germanic swords for totemic purposes.

limes: Roman military frontier zone.

limitanei: Roman frontier auxiliary troops.

lithsmen: sailors, 11th century Anglo-Saxon England.

lluric: early medieval Celtic mail hauberk; from the Latin *lorikis*.

llys: fortified residence of a Welsh lord or prince.

lociservitor: late Roman officer in a deputy role.

lorikis, lorikion: (Latin, Greek) late Roman and early medieval mail *hauberk*.

mace: short-hafted weapon with an essentially blunt but heavy head, designed to break bones or smash armour.

machicolation: overhanging structure on a fortified wall to enable defenders to shoot down upon the enemy.

magister militum: commander of armies in the late Roman Empire.

magistri militum: senior military commanders in the divided western and eastern halves of the later Roman Empire.

maisnade: lord's military household, southern France.

majordome: Carolingian ruler's military deputy.

man-at-arms: fully armoured cavalryman, 14th century England.

manches de fer: iron armour, probably for the lower arms, as a *vambrace*.

manganikon: Byzantine *mangonel* stone-throwing siege engine.

mangonel: beam-sling stone-throwing siege engine.

mantlet: large shield, or a piece of defensive hoarding used in field fortification.

march: frontier region, England and France.

margrave: frontier or 'Marcher' lord in medieval Germany (see also *marquis*).

marquis: frontier or 'Marcher' lord in medieval Italy (see also *margrave*).

marshal: senior officer in a household responsible for various aspects of military organisation.

martinella: bell with presumed communication function in a *carroccio* banner-wagon, Italy.

masnada, masnata: military retinue in early medieval Europe.

masnadieri: paid armed retainers, 13th century Italy; later meaning ruffians or assassins.

Mayors of the Palace: chief ministers of the Merovingian Frankish state who took control of the state from the powerless later Merovingian kings.

mêlée: disorganised individual combat following the break-up of a cavalry formation; also a form of mock-combat cavalry training involving teams of horsemen (see also *hastiludia*).

mesnie: military retinue, early medieval Europe.

messatges: messengers, southern France 13th–14th centuries.

midfaʿ: early form of small gun, early 14th century Arab Middle East.

milites, miles: professional soldiers in early medieval western Europe, usually cavalry, forerunners of the *knight*.

millenarie: English militia unit, supposedly of one thousand men.

ministeriales: non-noble 'serf cavalry' in Germany; *knights*, often of non-noble origin, serving in a French lord's court.

mizalla: parasol, mark of rulership in the *Faṭimid* Caliphate of Egypt.

mormaer: regional governor and perhaps military commander, Pictish Scotland.

mos majorum: ideal code of conduct of the later medieval nobility.

mos militum: ideal code of conduct of the later medieval *knightly* class.

motte and bailey: type of castle consisting of a tower on a raised earth mound with a wooden stockaded area around the outside.

mourtatoi: ex-Byzantine crossbow troops in Venetian Crete.

mufflers: mail mittens forming an integral part of the sleeves of a *hauberk*.

naker: small drum, often used in warfare; from the Arabic *naqqārah*.

naqqarah: Arabic term for a small drum, often used in warfare (see also *naker*).

numeri: garrison troops, Byzantine Italy.

nut: swivelling element in a crossbow which holds and then releases the bowstring.

oklopa: mail *hauberk*, Serbia.

ocreae: late Roman and early medieval leg protections.

onager: Romano-Byzantine and medieval stone-throwing device.

optimates: cavalry élite of early Byzantine central army, originally of Germanic origins.

optio: quartermaster in late Roman army.

ost: offensive military force operating outside its own immediate region, France.

page: first rank or duty during the training of a young member of the aristocractic military élite in medieval western Europe.

palazzo communale: centre of administration and sometimes of urban defence in an Italian 'republican' city.

pale-axe: long-hafted pole-axe, England.

palfrey: ordinary riding horse, not used in battle.

paličnik: 'mace carrier', court officer or official, 14th century Serbia.

panceriam, pansieri: unclear form of body armour, sometimes with long sleeves, possibly fabric-covered or scale-linen, 13th century Italy, perhaps from the German term *panzer* meaning armour.

panzerati: men-at-arms, armoured cavalry 14th century Germany.

pattern welding: technique of producing a sword-blade or other weapon from strips of hard and soft iron, twisted together then repeatedly heated and beaten.

pauldron: substantial piece of armour for the front of shoulder, late 14th century.

pavesari: 'shield-men', Italian heavy infantry sometimes forming a two-man team with a crossbowman.

pavise: large form of shield or *mantlet*, normally used by infantry.

Peace of God: movement which began in 10th century southern France to limit the effects of localised 'private war'.

pecunia: non-noble military obligation tied to tenancy of a particular piece of land, Isle of Man.

pedites: infantry forces of Italian city commune.

pedyt: early medieval Celtic infantry.

penne: main spar of a medieval Mediterranean ship.

pennon: small, usually triangular, flag nailed to the shaft of a *lance*.

penteula: commander of a prince's *teula*, military following, Celtic Wales.

periknemides: Romano-Byzantine arm defences.

perriere: small stone-throwing engine (see also *petraria* and *pierrie*).

petraria: small stone-throwing engine (see also *perriere* and *pierrie*).

petraria turquesa: early name for an *espringal*.

peytral, payttrure: armour for the front of a horse.

pierrie: small stone-throwing engine (see also *perriere* and *petraria*).

pieve: detachment of rural militia, Italy.

pike: very long infantry spear wielded with both hands.

pikte: *pike*, long-hafted spear.

pilum: earlier Roman javelin.

piratae: sailors trained to fight at sea, Anglo-Norman England.

pisane, pizaine: large stiffened mail- or scale-lined *tippet* covering the throat, shoulders and part of the upper arms and chest.

plates: coat-of-plates; later a *cuirass* of full plate-armour.

plumbata: late Roman lead-weighted javelin.

podesta: governor or military commander of an Italian city or overseas colony.

poitral: breast-strap, part of horse harness to stop a saddle sliding backwards.

pole-arm: weapon normally having a cutting and thrusting blade, used by infantry (see also *staff weapon*).

poleyns: armour for the knees.

poll: extension at the back of a *chamfron* to protect the upper part of a horse's neck.

pons: perhaps separate gauntlets, France.

popoli: ordinary citizens of an Italian city commune.

portcullis: iron grid lowered behind the normally wooden gates of a fortified town or castle, known since Roman times.

posse comitatus: formation in English coastal defence militia.

pot de fer: 'iron pot', early form of cannon, early 14th century France.

pourpoint: quilted and perhaps sometimes scale-lined form of *soft armour*.

praefectus: Roman military rank sometimes given to leader of tribal *foederati*.

praeventores: scouts in late Roman army.

preudome: 'man of prowess', *knightly* ideal of military skill and strength.

primi: general term for late Roman officer.

primicerius: adjutant to a commanding officer in late Roman army.

proofing: testing the quality of a piece of armour by shooting at it.

protostrator: 'commander of troops', Byzantine rank also used in 14th century Italo-Angevin Albania and Epirus.

provocateur: agent spreading false information and rumours to confuse an enemy, 14th century France.

pueri: bodyguards of Merovingian Frankish ruling family.

pykesteve: English form of *pike*.

quarrel: short arrow shot from a crossbow (see also *bolt*).

quintaine: cavalry training target consisting of a wooden post with a revolving arm.

quiret: leather body armour, 13th century.

rabhadhh: alarm system against raiders or cattle rustlers, Celtic Ireland.

rath: stone ring-fort, Celtic Ireland.

reeve: ruler's local representive and sometimes local military leader, England.

renner: men-at-arms, armoured cavalry 14th century Germany.

rerebrace: piece of armour for the upper arm.

reyregach: patrolling walls of a fortified town, southern France (see also *estialgach* and *arrière-guet*).

reysa: high-speed raiding tactics, 13th–14th century Northern Crusades in Lithuania.

ribaudequin, ribaudekin, ribaldi: light form of cannon mounted on a cart, often multi-barrelled; the name originally referring to the cart rather than the gun.

riter: knight, Germany.

rochet: naval axe with exceptionally long handle, used to cut an enemy ship's rigging.

ronco, roncone: obscure form of Italian staff-weapon, perhaps a long-bladed axe or a form of trident.

round ship: medieval merchant ship, so called because it was much broader in the beam than a galley, usually referring to Mediterranean types.

routiers: infantry mercenaries of unclear origins, 12th century France.

Royal Household: see *Familia Regis*.

saba: Romano-Byzantine mail *hauberk*.

sabatons: armour for the feet, 14th century.

sable, sabia: late 14th century sabre, central and eastern Europe.

saga: epic tale, almost always violent, sometimes in verse, about the heroes of the pre-Christian Germanic and Scandinavian worlds.

salandria: transport ship, 13th century Italy.

saraceno: coastal defensive tower, Italy.

sax: Germanic short sword or large dagger (see also *scramasax* and *seax*).

scara: élite palace troops of the Carolingian army.

scarfa: river boat or barge, early 7th century France.

scharen: military unit, sometimes of élite troops, medieval Germany.

schieri: military units, sometimes of élite troops, medieval Italy.

schiltron: all-round defensive infantry formation, Scotland and Wales.

scholae: Romano-Byzantine guard unit.

schynbalds: greaves for the lower legs.

sclopi, sclopetti: hand-held guns, late 14th or 15th century.

scotas: urban night-time scouts who listened for suspicious noises in times of danger.

scramasax: Germanic short sword or large dagger (see also *sax* and *seax*).

scutage: 'shield money' paid in lieu of feudal military service, England

scutiferi: peasants with military obligations tied to their possession of land, Italy.

scutum: general name for shield, Italy.

seax: Germanic short sword or large dagger (see also *sax* and *scramasax*).

secura: battle-axe.

seigneur: feudal landlord or local aristocrat in later medieval France.

seirch: early medieval Germanic term for a mail *hauberk*.

semispatha: 'half-sword', Romano-Byzantine short sword.

semissalis: junior officer rank in late Roman army.

senator: senior officer rank in late Roman army.

seneschal: governor or ruler's representative in a town or city.

seréement: very close-order riding in cavalry *conrois*.

sergeant: professional soldier of non-noble origin, usually infantry.

sergeant à cheval: mounted *sergeant*, non-noble cavalryman.

serk: early medieval Germanic term for a mail *hauberk*.

sesti, sestieri: section or quarter of Italian city, basis for raising militia forces.

setzschild: infantry *mantlet* shield to be rested on the ground, Germany.

sfakiot: warlike inhabitant of southern Crete under Venetian rule.

sgabal: mail neck and shoulder protection, like a *pisane*, 14th century Ireland.

shenkela: possibly a cuirass, Serbia.

sherif: ruler's representative and sometimes local military leader, England.

shire: basic territorial administrative unit in England and much of Scotland.

shtitova: shield, Serbia.

signiferi: standard-bearers in late Roman army.

signori di notti: night patrols maintaining law and order in Venice.

sihām khiṭāʿiyya: 'Chinese' fire arrows used by 13th century Muslim armies, probably explosive.

sirvens: non-noble member of the military élite, southern France.

skjaldborg: 'shield wall' around a leader, Scandinavia.

skraelings: Norse name for Eskimos and North American Indians.

societas militum: 'societies of *knights*', military and political organisations in Italian cities.

societas peditum: 'associations of infantrymen', military and political organisations in Italian cities.

socii: military retinue of late Merovingian nobleman.

soercheli: lower-ranking free military class of Celtic Ireland.

soernemen: ruling élite of Celtic Ireland.

soft armour: armour normally lacking a metallic element, usually padded, quilted or of felt.

soldato: paid soldiers, Italy, usually professional.

spade schiavonesche: 'Slav sword', relatively short slashing weapon of western Balkans, 14th century.

span: action of drawing back the string of a crossbow and attaching it to the *nut*.

spangenhelm: helmet constructed of several segments, normally attached to an iron frame.

spanning hook: single or double iron hook attached to a broad belt, used to *span* or draw back the string of a crossbow.

sparth: long-hafted axe, usually of Scottish or Irish form, 13th and 14th century England.

spatha: long Roman cavalry sword.

spatharii: noble bodyguard of Byzantine and late Visigothic rulers.

spaulder: shoulder protection (see also *espaulière*).

spiculum: late Roman long javelin.

spiess: *pike* with a hook at the back.

spingarda, spingala, springolf: alternative Italian and German names for *espringal.*

splint: piece of armour used in the *splinted* form of construction in which long narrow elements were used; normally to protect the limbs.

squire: member of the military élite either aspiring to the status of a *knight*, or merely having less equipment and thus lower status.

staff-weapon: weapon with long haft or handle, usually of wood, with blades designed for cutting as well as thrusting (see also *pole-arm*).

stafnbúi: 'stem man', élite naval warrior stationed at the prow of a ship; Viking Scandinavia.

stipendiarii: paid troops in the Norman states.

stipendiary knight: *knight* receiving money payment rather than land in return for feudal military obligations.

stivaletti: protections for the legs and feet, probably a form of *chausses*, 13th–14th century Italy.

stocco: thrusting dagger.

stock: rigid piece of wood attached to the flexible bow of a crossbow, on which the arrow rested and to which the trigger mechanism was attached (see also *tiller*); also the wooden element holding the metal barrel of a hand-gun.

stradiotti: light cavalry of the late Byzantine Empire, Balkan states and of Balkan origins in late medieval Italy.

strājeri: frontier troops, Wallachia and Moldavia (see also *stradiotti*).

strutere: destruction or raiding, Baltic states.

superventores: possibly 'rearguard commandos' in late Roman army.

surcoat: fabric garment worn over armour.

szeklers: non-noble military community, usually serving as light cavalry, in later medieval Hungary.

ṭablah: Arabic term for a large drum, often used in warfare (see also *tabour*).

tabolaccium amplum: extra large form of cavalry shield, 13th–14th century Italy.

taboloccium anglum: late 13th and early 14th century Italian large, basically rectangular, shield with 'angled' corners.

tabour: medieval drum often used in war, from the Arabic *ṭablah*.

talevas: especially large form of cavalry shield and infantry mantlet, England and France (see also *tavolaccio*).

tallage: tax imposed for the repair and building of fortifications.

tampion: wooden disc separating the powder from the shot in a gun barrel.

tang: extension to a sword-or knife-blade which passed inside the hilt or grip.

targe, targiam: large form of cavalry shield, including kite-shaped variety.

tarida: large Mediterranean transport galley, usually for horses, of Arab origin.

tavolaccio: especially large form of cavalry shield and infantry mantlet, England and France (see also *talevas*).

telaro: outrigger supporting the oars on a galley.

terra firma: Venetian territory on the Italian mainland.

terre maritime: coastal strip under separate local defence administration, 14th century England.

tesák: single-edged Bohemian dagger, said to resemble a *falchion*.

testières de cheval: piece of horse armour protecting the animal's head (see also *chamfron*).

teula: bodyguard or warband of a medieval Celtic ruler.

thane: landowner with military obligation, medieval northern England and Scotland.

thegn: landowner with military obliga-

tion, Anglo-Saxon England.

theme: Byzantine military province.

thorax: Romano-Byzantine *cuirass*, probably *lamellar*; also a *coat-of-plates*, 14th century Bohemia.

thuf: form of standard or banner used by the Angles, early medieval England, from the late Roman *tufa*.

thunder box: separate breech-chamber used with various types of later 14th century cannon.

tiller: rigid piece of wood attached to the flexible bow of a crossbow, on which the arrow rested and to which the trigger mechanism was attached (see also *stock*).

ţinuturi: military district, Moldavia.

tippet: neck and shoulder protection, normally of mail; large piece of mail protecting the throat, shoulders and part of the upper arms and chest.

tír unga: naval-military unit, medieval western Scotland.

tisućnik: 'leader of one thousand', officer in 14th century Serbian army.

toiseach: army commander, Pictish Scotland.

tongue: name sometimes given to the large arrow-like missile shot from an *espringal*.

toracibus: late Roman and early medieval *cuirass* of scale or lamellar.

torque: neck ornament worn by élite troops or military commanders, late Roman and early medieval period.

torre: tower, especially a single tower within an Italian urban commune.

touche: metal rod heated in a brazier and used to fire a cannon.

tournament: gathering of knights to take part in competitive cavalry exercises of various kinds.

trapper: horse armour (see also *bard*).

trebuchet: counter-weight beam-sling stone-throwing engine.

tref: early medieval Welsh tribe.

triboli: type of spiked *calthrop* thrown on an enemy's deck in naval warfare.

tribunus: commanding officer in late Roman army.

tripantumm: trebuchet with a secondary

movable counterweight, late 13th–14th centuries.

Truce of God: movements which arose in 11th century France in an attempt to limit the time and place in which 'private war' was permitted.

trunnions: large studs on each side of a gun barrel, enabling it to be elevated or lowered within its carriage, from 15th century.

tuatha: tribal army, Celtic Ireland.

tubator: trumpeter in late Roman army.

ūd: Arab and Persian stringed musical instrument, adopted in medieval Europe as the lute.

uissier: large Mediterranean transport ship, believed to have loading doors in the sides of its hull, 12th-13th centuries (see also *huissier*).

valvassores: non-noble cavalry in medieval Italy.

vambrace: piece of armour for the lower arms.

Varangian Guard: élite palace unit of the later Byzantine Empire, recruited from Scandinavian mercenaries and latterly from Anglo-Saxon exiles and adventurers.

vassi dominici: Carolingian élite troops resident near the Imperial Palace.

vassus: warrior in close attendance on an early medieval ruler.

vatlette: lowest status of armoured cavalry 'man-at-arms', 14th century England.

vavasseurs, vavassores, vavassini: non-noble cavalry in France, England and Italy.

venner: standard-bearer in 14th century Switzerland.

ventail, ventele, ventaille: flap of mail attached to a mail *coif* to be laced across the chin or lower part of the face.

verutum: late Roman short javelin.

vessilli: unit of militiamen, Italy.

veuglaire: 'fowler', larger type of breech-loading cannon, later 14th century.

vexillum: military banner of militia unit, Italy.

vicarius: second-in-command of an army in late Roman Empire; also a senior officer in an Italian overseas colony, 14th century.

vicinanze: quarter or section of an Italian city, with its own militia unit.

vidame: officers in early Italian urban armies.

viertelmeister: commander of urban militias, 14th century Germany.

vintaine: English militia unit, supposedly of twenty men.

viteji: cavalry, Wallachia (see also *vitez*).

vitez: knight and other types of élite cavalryman, 14th century Serbia and Bosnia (see also *viteji*).

voinici: infantry, Wallachia (see also *iunaci*).

voivode: provincial governor or local ruler, 14th century Hungary, Serbia and Romania.

volk: Germanic tribe or people of the early Middle Ages.

völkerwanderung: 'wandering of people', the Age of Migrations in the early Middle Ages.

voud: urban militia unit including both cavalry and infantry, 14th century Flanders.

vouge: obscure form of staff-weapon.

voynik: semi-feudal provincial cavalryman, Balkan states (see also *voinici, iunaci* and *wojnuk*).

vrysoun: cloth helmet decoration, late 14th century England.

wagenburg: field fortifications made of wagons or carts.

wambasia: medieval padded or felt garment normally worn beneath armour, England (see also *gambeson*).

wapentake: subdivision of a shire, basis of military organisation in Scandinavian northern England.

warda: professional castle-garrisons, early medieval Germany.

war-hammer: hammer-shaped mace, usually with a spike at the back.

war-scythe: simple form of *pole-arm* weapon with a blade resembling that of a scythe but pointing upwards.

wojnuk: member of the minor military aristocracy, 14th century Serbia.

worod: infantry training with sword and shield, Viking Scandinavia.

wyax: double-bladed axe, England.

zhupan: Balkan and Central European provincial governor or commander (see also *ispán*).

zupam: form of leather head protection used by sailors, Venice 13th–14th centuries.

INDEX

Figures in *italics* indicate captions for illustrations